The Sun-Gods of Ancient Europe

Typeset by Tradespools Ltd, Frome, Somerset
and printed in Great Britain by
Courier International, Tiptree, Essex
Published by B. T. Batsford Ltd
4 Fitzhardinge Street, London W1H 0AH

A CIP catalogue record for this book is
available from the British Library

ISBN 0 7134 5856 9

The
Sun-Gods
of
Ancient Europe

Miranda Green

B. T. Batsford Ltd, London

For Circê

Lo, in the orient when the gracious light
Lifts up his burning head, each under eye
Doth homage to his new-appearing sight,
Serving with looks his sacred majesty;
And having climb'd the steep-up heavenly hill,
Resembling strong youth in his middle age,
Yet mortal looks adore his beauty still,
Attending on his golden pilgrimage;
But when from highmost pitch, with weary car,
Like feeble age he reeleth from the day,
the eyes, 'fore duteous, now converted are
From his low tract, and look another way.

William Shakespeare

Contents

Acknowledgements

The following institutions are thanked for allowing me to publish illustrations in this book: Avignon, Musée Calvet; Cambridge, University Museum of Archaeology & Anthropology; Cardiff, National Museum of Wales; Carlisle, Tullie House Museum; Dublin, Commissioners of Public Works; København, Nationalmuseet; Köln, Römisch-Germanisches Museum; Milton Keynes Archaeology Unit; Nîmes, Musée Archéologique; Saverne, Musée Archéologique; Stuttgart, Württembergisches Landesmuseum; Surrey Archaeological Society; Trier, Rheinisches Landesmuseum; Zürich, Schweizerisches Landesmuseum.

I wish to express my thanks to the following individuals for their help: Eric Aldhouse; Edward Besly; Joanna Bird; Dr Aubrey Burl; Professor John and Mrs Bryony Coles; Professor George Eogan; Professor & Mrs John Ferguson; Nick Griffiths; Paul Jenkins; Shelagh Lewis; Frances Lynch; Dr Jarl Nordbladh; Brian Ramsden; Colin Richardson; Mick Sharp; Professor Derek Simpson; Dr Graham Webster; Bob Williams.
Finally, I should like to thank Stephen for all his encouragement and wise criticism; and Antigone and Oedipus, without whom life would be so dull!

Illustrations

 # *Preface*

The idea of a book about sun-cults in ancient Europe appealed to me not only because I have long cherished a fascination for religion, especially that of the Celtic world, but also because my doctoral thesis consisted of a study of the sun-god in Romano-Celtic Europe. In the course of this research, I came to realize that acknowledgement of the sun as a divine force is demonstrated by images, symbols and structures which form part of the archaeological record from at least as early as the Neolithic. I would not argue the existence of direct continuity in belief-systems and religious practices throughout prehistory, but it is, however, valid to trace the tangible evidence for the veneration of the sun throughout the period in question, since there would appear to have been fundamentally similar thought-processes behind the totality of the evidence.

Graham Webster shares with me a great interest in the religions of the past, and it is to him, as Archaeology Editor for Batsford, and to Peter Kemmis Betty, Managing Director, that I owe the invitation to write this book. John and Bryony Coles introduced me to the rock-art of southern Norway and Sweden on an enjoyable and informative Prehistoric Society tour in May 1988. The Open University provided me with the opportunity both to travel to Scandinavia and also to investigate the Celtic sun-god in Provence, the German Rhineland and Alsace, during the course of my original research.

— 1 —
Prelude

This book has been written in order to explore and to understand the way in which humankind expressed reverence for the sun as a religious force in barbarian (non-Mediterranean) Europe during later prehistory and the Romano-Celtic period. I begin my investigation in the Neolithic, when evidence for a sun-cult first manifests itself in the fourth/third millennia BC, but the main period of my study covers the time from roughly 2000 BC to AD 400. In much of central, eastern and northern Europe during this period, a reverence towards the sun as a divine phenomenon appears to have dominated man's attitude to the supernatural.

1 Interior of the chamber at Bryn Celli Ddu, Anglesey, with the sun shining through; the entrance to the passage grave faces the May Day sunrise. Mick Sharp

The subject of solar religion is often considered with a degree of scepticism, for two reasons. First, there is an understandable reticence on the part of archaeologists towards the religious aspect of the human past. This prejudice is at the same time comprehensible and regrettable, as Ralph Merrifield rightly and persuasively argues in a recent book: 'Ritual and magic were formerly part of everyday life, but by association with fantasy, fiction and occultism they have now acquired an aura of sensationalism that has discouraged investigation'.[1] The avoidance of religious interpretation of the evidence by modern scholars is easy to understand, in that they may fairly pose the question of how, as archaeologists – students of material culture – they can possibly come to grips with the thought-processes of past societies. But Sir Mortimer Wheeler reminds us that excavators dig up not things but people,[2] and thus we should not turn our backs on the quest for understanding what has always been a fundamental part of human consciousness, a recognition of forces beyond mankind's control and outside his comprehension. The second problematical aspect of this book's theme is that the study of solar religion, in particular, provokes perhaps the greatest degree of scepticism among archaeologists. Thus, whether one is dealing with the imagery of megalithic tombs, Bronze Age rock-art or Romano-Celtic sculpture, there seems frequently a perverse desire to interpret symbols which strongly resemble the sun as anything other than solar. I hope to demonstrate that, necessary caution notwithstanding, it is possible to achieve a degree of insight into ancient European religion, and that a judicious and systematic exploration of the evidence will go some way towards an interpretation both of man's attitude to the sun and, also, of his consciousness – as a sentient being – that the world held powerful supernatural entities which needed to be propitiated, appeased, cajoled and invoked. From at least the Neolithic to the Roman period, pagan European communities drew symbols of the sun, built shrines and fashioned images which acknowledged its daily and seasonal behaviour, its essential heat- and light-giving properties, and its multifarious functions and associations.

Throughout the period under scrutiny, the manner in which humans perceived and depicted the sun provides the main clues as to the beliefs they held. We will see that the sun could be envisaged in a number of physical forms – as a plain or radiate circle, a wheel, a spiral, a swastika or an eye; not all of these designs evoke the physical image of the sun. Each of the symbols reflects a different, though related, aspect of the sun's character or function. The use of such motifs is also significant from the Neolithic in that they were associated with the dead, and this is a tradition which we will see recurring throughout prehistory. In the later Neolithic, in addition to the carving of solar motifs on tombstones, graves themselves could be elaborately constructed in order to capture the rays of the sun at particular moments of the day or at specific times of the year.

During the Bronze Age, we begin to see evidence of complex rituals and ceremonies associated with the cult of the sun. Such structures as the stone monument at Stonehenge argue for a sharp awareness of the power and prestige of the sun and an ability on the part of its human worshippers to use its movement in the sky as a calendrical device to assist farmers in the agricultural year. Solar cult-activity was especially strong in northern Europe, where the horse-drawn cart with its solar disc at Trundholm in Denmark suggests a complicated ritual, the concern of which may have been to persuade the sun to return after winter's darkness. Scandinavian rock-art, too, conveys a preoccupation with solar imagery, perhaps associated with fertility; very similar ritual is witnessed in the Camunian rock-art of north Italy. Throughout Europe, miniature bronze sun-symbols in the form of spoked wheels were buried with the dead, reaffirming the sepulchral connections of the sun which are seen in the Neolithic. During the Bronze Age, there is little evidence for sun-gods in anthropomorphic form, though the clay figure at Dupljaja in Yugoslavia may be a candidate. But what is very striking is the close association between solar symbols and images of animals, in particular horses, stags and aquatic birds. It is interesting that beasts appear as recurrent companions of the sun-disc prior to the development of the tradition whereby the sun-gods were perceived and portrayed as humano-divine images.

The Iron Age provides a link between earlier prehistory and the Roman period. The first iron-working phases in Europe see the continuance of the tradition of solar veneration which is first observed in the preceding Bronze Age. From this period onwards, the symbols of the sun are consistently present on armour and jewellery, and as small votive objects and personal talismans. We begin, now, to see a close link between the sun and war: symbols of the sun's power to avert injury were placed on those parts of body-armour where men were at their most vulnerable – the head, chest and genitals. The association between the sun and the dead, foreshadowed in earlier periods, is still present, and solar amulets are sometimes the sole grave-goods in Iron Age cemeteries.

The sun-cult attained its full florescence as a formalized and anthropomorphic religion during the Romano-Celtic phase of western European culture, from about the first century AD. Now, for the first time, it is possible to recognize specific, fully-developed and identifiable sun-gods portrayed in human form and accompanied by solar attributes. The concept of the sun as a supernatural being has now been completely transformed from a simple visual symbol to a divinity in the true sense, an entity to whom people could relate inasmuch as he was perceived as a larger-than-life version of themselves.

Throughout our period, the divine sun is projected as a force with many different roles and concerns. Solar religion manifests itself not simply in acknowledgement of the overt functions of the sun as provider of light and heat, but also in recognition of influences that are more wide-ranging than the elemental force itself. The sun's dualistic character, with its light and dark side, runs as a thread through the different phases of prehistoric and Romano-Celtic Europe. The Bronze Age sun-disc at Trundholm, with its gilded solar 'day' and plain bronze 'night' surfaces displays similar life-death imagery to that presented in the Celtic Jupiter-Giant sculptures where the sky-god pits himself against the monstrous forces of the underworld. The image of the sun-god in Romano-Celtic Europe demonstrates, in its most developed form, the functions of the divine sun that can only be inferred for earlier periods: that the solar powers were rulers of the cosmos, guardians of humans and animals. Most importantly, they presided over the most crucial of human concerns: fertility of human communities, their livestock and crops, death and regeneration in the life hereafter.

The attitude of ancient man towards the sun may perhaps be likened to that of the painter Vincent Van Gogh who was, in his last years, obsessed by the heat, light and colour of the sun: 'His story is . . . the tale of a lonely heart which beat within the walls of a dark prison, longing and suffering without knowing why, until one day it saw the sun, and in the sun recognized the secret of life.'[3]

— 2 —
Birth of a Sun-Cult

A distinctive feature of many of today's great religions is that the objects of worship – the god or gods – are invisible and have to be taken on trust or faith. The same was true, to an extent, in some of the sophisticated cults of the past. But in the barbarian Europe of prehistory, there was a powerful set of belief-systems which were based on the veneration of visible and perceivable natural phenomena. Humans observed their environment – the heavens, the weather and the apparent capriciousness of natural forces – and endowed them with supernatural powers. Of these, perhaps the most dominant was the inexplicable phenomenon of the sun, which mysteriously appeared by day and vanished at night, was warm for half the year and withdrew much of its heat for the other half. The sun-cult in Europe had early beginnings, as we shall see, but it persisted into and beyond prehistory. In historic times, it developed from an animistic to an anthropomorphic cult and, indeed, has survived in some form until the very recent past.

Religion and the natural world

This book is about an aspect of religion, in a part of the western world where pagan belief-systems were never fully formalized into the mythological and hierarchical panthea that characterized the Classical world and the East. So in order to pursue the theme it may be helpful briefly to look at the whole concept of religion, and the animistic element of it to which the sun-cult in Europe really belonged. Man's relationship to nature could be said to be divisible into two categories: first, things which he is able directly to control and second, phenomena which he is powerless to influence.[1] Religion may be defined as a way of explaining the natural forces which form the second group, and belief involves the realization that what is believed in is the result of a suprahuman presence. Religion, then, involves the human reaction to the superhuman or, as James puts it:

> 'The recognition of and the endeavour to establish and maintain beneficial relations with the supra-mundane sacred order manifesting itself in the Universe and controlling its processes and human affairs, whether collective or personal.'[2]

There is a distinction between religion and belief: belief is the realization of superhuman

2 Rock-carving of praying figure and sun-disc from Camonica Valley. Paul Jenkins, after Anati

power which must be propitiated by magic, ritual, votive offerings or sacrifices; religion is the means of establishing and maintaining a good relationship with the supernatural so that it will work for rather than against you. A religious experience will involve reciprocity between humankind and the supra-mundane. The purpose of ritual behaviour, in whatever form, is the union between humans and a supra-normal or divine entity.[3]

Animism, that is the recognition and worship of the spirits perceived to exist in natural phenomena, is said to be the 'minimum definition of religion',[4] by which is meant that it is the simplest, least sophisticated form of belief-system. There is no theology and, in its most basic form, no anthropomorphism. In simple, pre-industrial pagan societies, people knew that they had somehow to propitiate and to harness the forces or agencies they encountered in the world over which they had no secular means of control. The first farmers were especially vulnerable to these forces: crops could fail through blight one year and flourish the next; drought or flood could wreck their lives and cause starvation. There are two related ways of reaching the divine: by repetitive, sympathetic magic and by image-making. In terms of solar belief-systems, an example of sympathetic magic is the fire-festivals, where bonfires were lit at mid-summer to assist the sun as it reached its solstitial apex in its annual journey across the sky. An example of image-making is the simple replicas of the sun which were scrawled as rayed or concentric circles on rocks by Neolithic people at Val Camonica in northern Italy (Fig. 2) to acknowledge the sun's arrival in the morning and its sinking into the underworld at night.[5]

The sun was one natural phenomenon which people needed to be able to control in order to survive and flourish. It could both give and destroy life; it disappeared and had to be wooed so that it would always return. Like rain, man required the sun to be moderate, not extreme; its value as a life-source was praised but its capriciousness feared. We need to delve deeper into the psychology underlying the crucial importance of the sun in the European past; why, from at least 3000 BC people made images of the sun or venerated it in other tangible ways recognizable in the archaeological record.

Sun veneration in the ancient world

The sun and the sky

The veneration of the sun is absolutely comprehensible: first, in a cloudless sky, it is visually very prominent, too bright to look at and very clearly dominating the entire sky during the daytime. The sun is the only star in the Universe that is sufficiently close to us on earth for its spherical shape to be truly discernible.[6] It is the one main light-source for earth and, as

such, is essential to all life. But what is interesting is that it was not in all cultures that the sun was considered as the main source of light. Indeed, it is after all, almost fully daylight before the sun is visible over the horizon, and there is still bright light when the sun disappears behind clouds. So it is reasonable for people to have made a distinction between the sky and light on the one hand and the sun on the other. We have only to look at the Book of Genesis to see that God created the light as one task: 'And God said, let there be light . . . and he called the light Day',[7] and only later created the sun to rule the day and the moon the night: 'And God made two great lights; the greater light to rule the day, and the lesser light to rule the night.'[8]

So there could almost be imagined a kind of rivalry between the sun and the sky as dominant phenomena. There is an important distinction between them, and the sky has separate spheres of influence to which the sun has only peripheral relevance. The sky controls the heavens, clouds, rain and storms, and sky-religions may or may not embrace the sun. But the sun can only shine and produce heat; it has little to do with lightning and rain. The sun, indeed, may in hot dry lands be seen as a threat and could be feared and cursed as an enemy, while the sky was propitiated as an ally. Herodotus speaks of the tribe of the Atarantes of Libya[9] who cursed the sun but invoked the sky for its rain-making properties. Egypt was a special case; though arid, the Nile provided all the water it needed to sustain life and thus the sun was not feared but welcomed as a divine friend. In the Greek world, there was a very specific relationship between the sky-god Zeus and the sun. Zeus, 'the bright one', was originally nothing but the daylight sky, perceived of as an animate being,[10] but many surnames or epithets attached to Zeus' name are solar: on Chios, 'Zeus of the Burning Face' was invoked, and we know of 'Zeus the Scorcher' at Thorikos in Attica.[11]

The sun as a life-giver

In spite of the rivalry of the sky, the sun itself possessed a profound and persistent belief-system in early Europe, flourishing particularly perhaps in a relatively cold, wet, dark climate. We will see later how developed and crucial was the sun-cult in Scandinavia, where winter is long and dark, and spring comes late and reluctantly. In northern Europe, the winter solstice was and is a cause of celebration because it precedes lighter, warmer days.[12] In a phase of the Central and North European Bronze Age, there was a temporary deterioration of the climate, which grew colder and wetter, and this seems to have given rise to a particularly vigorous solar-cult activity which leaves abundant archaeologial traces.[13] For north Europeans, the sun was an important visual beacon of hope, associated always with battle for human existence in a hostile environment. Much of the religious material culture of the Bronze Age in central and northern Europe can be recognized as a magical response to the desire to make the sun appear and warm the earth after night and winter.[14]

The development of agriculture in the Neolithic meant that the new farmers needed to be able to measure time. Activities had to take place regularly day by day, season by season. Thus, people used the sun's movement across the sky as a calendar to measure the length of days and the seasons[15] (but it is interesting that, in early Greek culture, the seasons had an autonomy totally separate from the sun's influence[16]). The Mesolithic hunters and gatherers of earlier phases of the Stone Age could recognize seasonal patterns in the fluctuating food supply as represented in the abundance

3 Exterior of Balnuaran of Clava SW, Scotland; the passage faces the midwinter sunset. Prof. Derek Simpson

of fauna and flora. They would track the movement of the sun and store food for lean times, but it was for the farming year that an approximate calendar was especially crucial,[17] and we will show that it may be possible to see such calendars in the megalithic monuments of the later Neolithic and earlier Bronze Age.

Even more important to the Neolithic farmers of Europe than the calendrical significance of the sun in the sky was its demonstrable powers of fertility. Farmers would have observed that crops grew well only where they received adequate sun and perhaps saw that shaded plants did not flourish.[18] The visual image of the sun helped to promote the fertility association in that its beams, striking, penetrating and fertilizing the earth (indeed like rain), could be seen as analogous to the phallus entering the female.[19] The rise and set of the sun could parallel not only life and death but also the rise and fall of the phallus.[20] A further fertility association lies in colour: the sun is the shade of ripe corn at harvest-time. Certainly in temperate climates the sun was a giver of life,[21] inextricably connected with the ripening of crops; it was not simply seen as symbolic of life, it *was* life, especially in lands and periods where the lack of a written language made complex conceptualization difficult. The coming of the dawn after the 'death' of night and the appearance of the sun epitomized the awakening and the stirring of life itself.

The sun, death and destruction
Many belief-systems incorporate an apparently contradictory polarization or dualism: thus, a god of life often presides also over death; a mother-goddess may frequently be a destroyer. Belief in the supernatural force of the sun also encapsulates dualism, and this is natural for several reasons. First, the sun is perceived to disappear each night: it must go somewhere, and many early peoples envisaged its journeying to the underworld. Certainly, the Neolithic and Early Bronze Age

communities of Camonica Valley appear to have seen a very positive link between the sun and the earth as home of the dead.[22] If one looks for a parallel in non-European religion, the Egyptian sun-deity travelled along an underground river at night, lighting up the underworld as he went.[23] This death symbolism may be present in the association of the sun with burial rites in barbarian Europe. Passage graves like Newgrange, which we will look at presently, show evidence of a connection between sun and death, and Bronze Age cremation-rites may be related to a celestial vision of the afterlife, where the smoke wafted the transformed body and soul to heaven. Other, not unrelated, factors led to a belief in the chthonic power of the sun: the Greek Zeus had such an underworld role in presiding over the germinating corn-seed in the ground, which lay 'dead' in the soil and was then brought to life:[24] both sun and rain resurrected the seed and life came from death. But the sun is sometimes seen as a destroyer; we have seen that in a hot, dry land, the sun can be an enemy.[25] It can scorch and wither life, and we know that some ancient tribes vilified the sun for parching the land.[26] War, conquest and destruction go hand in hand, and the sun may be related to all three: at dawn, the rays of the sun disperse and blot out the stars in an allegory of killing.[27] As a warrior, the sun can despatch solar arrows in the form of rays, to destroy or blind; and Apollo's arrows could carry plague. The war-death role may have had a passive presence in ancient Europe, but in central America, among the Toltecs and Aztecs (of the sixth and thirteenth centuries AD respectively) the warring sun required human sacrifice and human blood to rejuvenate himself after battling with the gods of night.[28] Quite possibly, also, sympathetic magic was reflected in the colour imagery of blood and the setting sun.

Hunting and fire are two further aspects of solar imagery and ritual which relate both to destruction and to beneficent protection. The rays of the sun may be seen as the arrows and javelins of the divine hunter, and this imagery is very widespread. Apollo was a solar hunter, and on the other side of the world the Mayan sun-deity, like Apollo, was not only a hunter but also a patron of the arts.[29] The hunter role of the sun may be associated with zoomorphic images, like the lion with its power and golden, sun-like mane, or the high-flying predator, the eagle, with its sharp eyes, analogous to the sun's penetrating brightness.[30]

According to a version of the Prometheus myth – where the half-god, half-man Titan stole fire on behalf of mankind – Prometheus obtained fire by rising to heaven and lighting a torch from the fiery wheel of the sun.[31] The fire–sun association is completely appropriate in terms of light and heat; a number of European fire-festivals are recorded which make this link (see Chapter Six). We have spoken already of midsummer bonfires, lit to encourage the activity of the sun.[32] One solstice ritual recorded as taking place in many parts of Europe almost until the present day is at the festival commemorating the birth of St John the Baptist. The ritual at Basse Kontz on the Moselle exemplifies the tradition: here, a wheel was set on fire and rolled down the Stromberg Mountain to the river, in magical imitation of the sun's descent from its highest point in midsummer.[33] The idea was that if the wheel rolled unimpeded to the water, the local people would enjoy a lucky year and a good wine harvest. So a link between the fertile benevolence of the sun, the purification of destructive fire and an abundant grape-yield was made.

The sun as ruler

In the East, in Egypt and Babylon, solar deities were associated with kingship[34] since the sun was conceived as ruling and controlling the sky, brighter than moon and stars and dominating the earth. For two reasons the sun could be envisaged as a law-giver and a keeper of justice and order: first, because the sun kept to a regular system of movement across the sky, and secondly, because it was perceived as all-seeing and penetrative.[35] The Babylonian sun-god Shamash, in his great shrine at Sippar, was supreme judge and law-giver, avenger of crime and upholder of virtue.[36] The principle of order may have been important as an inspiration to the builders of Stonehenge, itself an undertaking requiring a high level of organization and which in its Beaker phase was oriented to the rising of the midsummer sun.[37] The sun was widely regarded as controller of the Universe and therefore of mankind. Philarchus[38] stated that when the Greeks sacrificed to the sun they brought no wine to his altars since 'the god who holds together and controls the Universe ought to keep strictly sober'.[39] The Nabataean sun worshippers of Arabia had no such sensitivities but readily poured libations in the solar god's honour.[40]

The role of the sun as controller and keeper of justice is related to its image as a protector and preserver. We will see later that the sun was a healer and guardian against all the evils that can befall mankind, and was constantly fighting for good in the world. In Plato's *Republic*, the sun is presented in the writer's concept of the 'Proportion', as specifically associated with goodness.[41] So even in a society where sun-worship *per se* was not taken too seriously, the sun and the good were still linked.

The sun as an eye

The perception of the sun as an eye is related to its role as an all-seeing judge in the Universe. Like many pre-technological peoples, the early Greeks saw the sun and the moon as the eyes of the animate sky.[42] In Greek and Egyptian mythology, epithets applied to sun-gods demonstrate the power perceived as in their eyes: Pharos of Egypt was struck blind because he could not control the weather – the prerogative of the sky-powers, but he was later given oracular gifts in order that he might do honour to the sun-god of Heliopolis.[43] Again in Egypt, on images of the sun-god, the eye portrayed on a solar disc could represent the head of the divinity.[44] In Egypt, Greece and many other literate cultures of the ancient world, the all-seeing role of the sun gave it an association with the eye. Greek drama is full of allusions to the link between the eye and the sun. Aeschylus, in *Prometheus Bound*, refers to the 'all-seeing circle of the sun'.[45] In *Oedipus Coloneus*,[46] Sophocles writes, 'may the all-seeing sun give thee and thine such a sad old age as mine'. The poet also makes Antigone refer to the 'great eye of the golden day'.[47] In addition to these links, the property of light was recognized as common to both the eye and the sun. Important, too, is the physical resemblance between the rays of the sun and the lashes of the eye. The sun will blind all who look at it directly, so there is an adverse affinity between the sun and the eye, and the latter is recognized as being subordinate to the former. In this connection, there was also perhaps an association between the destructive capacity of the sun and that of the evil eye[48] or the mesmerizing and fatal effect of the eyes of a snake on its prey.[49]

In Chapter Three we will examine in more detail the close link in physical imagery between the eye and the sun. We will see also in Chapter Six that, in an early Celtic context, the eye and the sun came together in a specifically healing role, where the solar force is particularly associated with eye-disease and where clarity of vision is connected with light. This has an interesting parallel in modern Hinduism, where the sun is venerated for its ability both to cure eye-afflictions and to strengthen sight.[50] In the great therapeutic shrines of Celtic Gaul, water, sun, healing and eyes were all closely identified one with the other. Water is again important as a symbol of light and clarity, a purifier like the sun itself. Water reflects the sun's light, as do eyes, and both can

be looked on as the mirrors of the world. The eye is the window of man's soul and water perhaps the window of the earth or of the chthonic regions, both lit by the supernatural force of the sun. Interestingly, again, the link between sun and water is demonstrated in such fire-festivals as that of St John the Baptist mentioned earlier, where the flaming, wheel-like replica of the sun is bowled downhill towards water.[51]

The imagery of the sun

To understand how early man in Europe projected the image of the sun as a venerated force, we should first step back from the particular and briefly examine the concept of image-making, what function images perform and how they are created. The depiction of an object can be seen as the valuation of something and a desire to possess it.[52] This is the magical perception of image-making: somehow, by portrayal of something, it is placed within the grasp of the image-maker or his patrons. Symbols or images are fundamental to humans in society because they present the means of establishing a conception of the natural world which then forms a reference system within groups of human beings. A symbol may be seen as a communication system, a kind of pictorial language, and this is how modernists interpret the primary function of, for example, Bronze Age Scandinavian rock-art.[53] A symbol or image also has the purpose of directing people's attention towards the supernatural, or evoking the supra-mundane; they point to an existence beyond the present, often to an irrational, incomprehensible world.[54] In studying any one kind of image – sun-symbols for instance – we have to remember that all images are, to a greater or lesser extent, the result of convention. The artist, even of a veristic image, is unable accurately to transcribe exactly what he sees. He may only translate his perceptions into terms suitable for the medium.[55] In constructing then looking

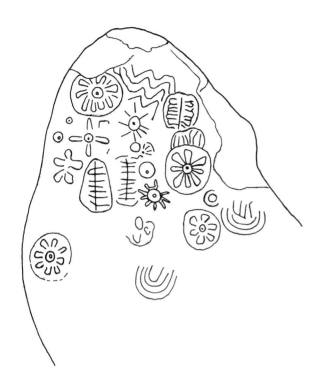

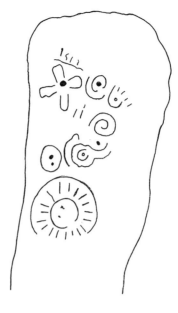

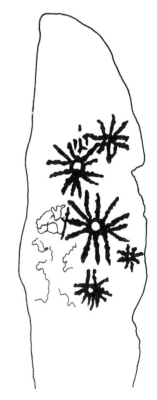

at an image, the artist and the spectator or worshipper go through a number of mental processes: sight, perception, identification, image-making and interpretation/evocation.[56]

But there is more than one type of solar image. At the simplest and most animistic, the sun will be portrayed as it is perceived, perhaps as a simple or rayed circle, maybe with an inner disc. But as religion grows more complicated, the sun may, instead, be seen as a deity rather than as just an elemental force: thus it may be given human or animal form. In societies with a mythology, or a series of legends and stories about perhaps a whole pantheon of gods, new images may be born from those myths. An example of this is Helios-Apollo who travelled in a sun-chariot in the Classical world. In Egypt, by contrast, the sun-god was often conveyed by boat or was winged. The more complex an image, the likelier it is that there are legends and tales about the deity depicted.

4 Carved stones at Loughcrew, Ireland. Height of left-hand stone: 1.4 m (4 ft 9 in.). After Twohig

If we were to ask a child to draw a picture of the sun, the chances are that he or she would draw a circle with diverging rays. This is precisely the manner in which the sun is portrayed in Neolithic imagery.[57] But long before the invention of the spoked wheel in Europe (around 1500 BC), the image of the sun was depicted in the form of a circle with internal lines radiating from a central point to the circumference, precisely like a spoked wheel. Several sun-images may appear in one megalithic tomb-monument, sometimes on the same stone (Fig. 4).[58] Usually these solar symbols are isolated depictions but occasionally they appear as if perceived among other, lesser heavenly bodies. This happens on the Neolithic rock painting at Pala Pinta de Carlão in Portugal, where the sun is associated with points or dots.[59] In the first phase at Camonica Valley, which dates to the later Neolithic, the sun was depicted as a simple disc and only in later phases was projected as a deity.[60] Before the First Dynasty in Egypt at Heliopolis, Re was manifested as the sun in the sky by means of the image of a solar disc.[61] Re was simply the sun personified, in that Re was the name for the sun.[62] With the coming of metal to Europe, the sun could be portrayed more vividly in the form of small solar images of bright gold or bronze which physically resembled the sun in miniature and reflected light.[63] Gold would have been especially favoured as a 'solar' metal since, not only is it sun-coloured, but it is also easy to work and, when pure, does not tarnish or dim with time – a truly divine substance.

In sophisticated, conceptualizing systems of belief, the sun could be presented as an image whose physical attributes were more complex than the simple disc hanging in the sky. During the Bronze Age in barbarian Europe, the sun came to be thought of as a spoked wheel, because the sun both resembled a wheel and rotated like one. This mode of conceptualization leads to one of the main Indo-European images of the sun-god,[64] manifested from Greece and northern Europe to India: that of the sun or sun-deity being carried across the sky in a wheeled vehicle or chariot. In Greece, the worship of Helios was important only on Rhodes; elsewhere such straightforward (though anthropomorphized) animism was perhaps considered somewhat barbaric.[65] But Helios was represented as a solar charioteer; we see him on a red-figure krater, rising from the sea in his quadriga (four-horse chariot).[66] A wheeled vehicle is a suitable medium for the sun's carriage, since it is both a means of conveying the sun-disc across the heavens and it has wheels which themselves can evoke sun-symbolism. Boats could also be employed to transport the solar disc: Re sailed along the Nile in a sun-boat at night,[67] and Helios himself had a boat as well as a horse-drawn carriage on the red-figure vase mentioned above. Indeed, the idea of a solar boat is very widespread in the Bronze Age of temperate and northern Europe, appearing as a motif on metalwork and on Scandinavian rock-art (Chapter Four).

One final point about the conceptualization of the sun as a deity is that in nearly all cultures the sun is perceived as male. This is a natural conception since its dominant, phallic, fertilizing characteristics place it firmly within the orbit of masculine divinities. The Graeco-Roman, Egyptian, Central American and Celtic sun-deities are male; and in Babylon, Shamash of Sippar was presented as a bearded, mature man whose image shows him facing his attribute, a disc with a four-pointed 'star' inside it, beams flickering between the points.[68] But the sun-god is not invariably male: in Japanese Shintoism, which is a form of animism, the sun is a goddess[69] who legendarily hid in a cave when displeased and deprived the world of light. The great British Celtic healer-goddess Sulis of Bath is etymologically a solar deity, though in terms of her imagery she appears in the guise of the Roman Minerva.

In succeeding chapters, we will see that certain animals play a large part in the visual imagery of the sun-cult in Europe. Here, a brief word about the nature of this zoomorphic perception will suffice. In general, animals become a specific part of a god's iconographic repertoire because of particular qualities possessed by that creature. For instance, the swan was a natural associate of sun-gods because of its dazzling white plumage and perhaps also because of its noble bearing and impressive wing-span. The swan is Helios-Apollo's attribute;[70] water-birds and sun-wheels are persistently associated in European Bronze and Iron Age imagery. Indeed, the pan-Indo-European nature of this link is demonstrated by the combined symbolism of the sun and swan in the Indian Veda.[71] Of four-footed mammals, the two dominant sun-creatures are the horse and the stag. Horses drew the vehicle which carried the sun; they are swift and noble beasts and, in later prehistory, were associated with speed, power and prestige. We will see that solar deities and horses were consistently linked in European cult-imagery from the Middle Bronze Age to the Romano-Celtic phase. Stags are less obvious companions of the sun, but there is a recurrent connection which begins very early. One reason may be the perception of a physical resemblance between the rayed sun and antlers. In a Spanish

5 *Antler-sun motif painted on rock from Tajo de las Figuras, Spain.* After Sandars

6 *Sun/antler motif on rock from Laxe de Rotea de Mende, Iberia.* After Briard

7 *Combined antlers and suns at Camonica.* Paul Jenkins, after Anati

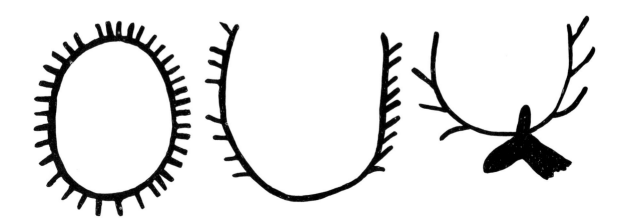

Neolithic rock-shelter at Tajo de las Figuras, a sun-image has 'antlered' rays (Fig. 5);[72] and this is paralleled elsewhere (Fig. 6). Conflated stag-sun imagery recurs in the earlier Bronze Age at Val Camonica in north Italy, where stags have antlers which meet in a solar circle (Fig. 7). A second reason for the stag-sun connection may be concerned with fertility: we have seen how the sun itself was an image of fecundity, with its role in germinating seed. Stags, with their aggression in the rutting season, could also have been endowed with fertility-symbolism. There is also the resemblance between antlers and the trees of the forest: stags shed their antlers in the autumn and grow them in the spring, just as many trees seasonally shed and grow their leaves. A third link between stags and the sun may be because of the hunting role of the sun (p. 19), which may have led to a kind of symbolic symbiosis between the supernatural force and his zoomorphic prey. In Greek mythology, the sun-god Helios is indirectly associated with stags in the *Odyssey*,[73] when Odysseus brings down an enormous stag which lives in the realms of Circê, a daughter of the sun-god and perhaps herself solar. But in Greek myth, the solar deities are more frequently associated with cattle,[74] and Helios has two daughters who tend his herds.[75]

The earliest sun-cults in barbarian Europe

Humankind must have begun to speculate about the nature of the sun early, probably as early as the Middle Palaeolithic and Mesolithic periods.[76] From as early as the Middle Palaeolithic burials, like that of a Mousterian individual at La-Chapelle-aux-Saints (Dordogne), were, maybe deliberately, oriented east-west, to the rising and setting sun,[77] though too much should not be made of this kind of orientation.

In the Neolithic period, art on the stones of burial structures and pots shows images of the sun in full radiance.[78] Indeed, it is worthwhile to look in some detail at this megalithic sun-imagery because it is the earliest unequivocal evidence we have for solar veneration in Europe. Collective burial in tombs constructed artificially was a tradition followed in western Europe from the beginning of the fourth millennium until the end of the third millennium BC. Of the two main types – gallery graves and passage graves – it is the latter that has produced most of the art.[79] The presence of such carvings on funerary monuments does suggest that it was placed there for a religious purpose.[80] It is certainly not present purely for decoration, since it is not of a particularly high artistic standard and, in addition, the art was often carved on an orthostat or lintel before the stone was placed in position and was subsequently invisible. So a religious purpose for the art seems likely. Many ideas have been suggested as to the precise function of this art: it may have acted as secret bonding signs to the people who had been in some manner initiated into an arcane ritual or belief, and Twohig argues,[81] moreover, that the tombs themselves may have provided a bond between members of a social group by reinforcing the status of leaders of such groups and presenting a kind of nucleus or focal point for the whole settlement or cluster of people. Burl[82] would go further, seeing in the art a religious association between the dead buried in the tombs and the symbols carved on the stones, and specifically between the underworld and the sun.

In attempting to establish early sun-cults in Europe, a major concern is images which resemble the sun on the stones of many passage graves, from Ireland to Iberia and from Denmark to Brittany. In current scholarship,[83] there is some scepticism about interpreting circles with or without radiating lines as solar symbols, but they are repetitive images, occurring over a very wide area of Europe, and it is difficult to find a more plausible explanation. The wheel-like symbols cannot *be* wheels since passage grave art appeared some millennia before the spoked wheel came into being in these regions. Moreover, two sites in Iberia – Antelas and Granja de Toniñuelo, Badajoz[84] – contain stones with associated suns and moon-crescents.

It is the passage graves of Ireland, Brittany and Iberia that have produced the most evidence suggestive of solar symbolism. The Irish cemeteries of County Meath, especially Knowth, Dowth and Loughcrew, generally dated to the mid-third millennium BC, have produced numerous stones with carvings of circles, rayed circles and wheel-like designs (Figs. 4, 8).[85] Each tomb apparently had a repertoire and style which was distinctive to itself.[86] But variations on the 'sun-motif', if that is what it is, are common on several passage-grave stones. Dowth has produced radiate and wheel-like sun-signs;[87] at Knowth, there are many suns including the so-called 'sun-dial' stone, which has 18 rays spreading from a central hole, positioned just to the left of the entrance to the tomb.[88] Loughcrew displays a bewildering variety of 'suns', including a distinctive and repeated daisy-like motif.[89] A

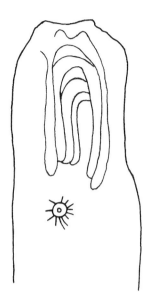

9 The Dolmen de Tachen Paul, Ploemeur, Brittany. Height: c. 1 m (3 ft). After Twohig

standing stone at Sess Kilgreen (Co. Tyrone) is decorated with a combination of radiate and concentric circles.[90] In non-Insular passage-grave art, unequivocal solar motifs are absent, but at the Calderstones, Liverpool, six stones in a circle were decorated with spirals and concentric circles;[91] and the grave at Barclodiad y Gawres on Anglesey was engraved with many different abstract designs including both clockwise and anti-clockwise spirals.[92] I will not, at this stage, go into details of the possible relationship between spirals and solar symbolism, but I will return to the question in Chapter Three.

Some of the Breton and Iberian passage graves have produced art which is suggestive of sun-veneration, though solar motifs were by no means dominant within the complete repertoire of symbols. Of these, the Breton passage-graves date from about 3700–2500 BC.[93] The Morbihan region has most evidence

8 The boundary-stone, Dowth, Ireland. After Coffey

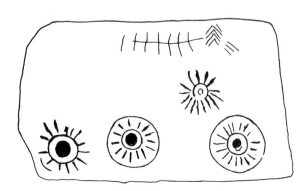

of 'solar' passage-grave art: the Dolmen de Mané Lud is decorated with a rayed sun and a dot-in-circle associated with boat representations[94]. The Dolmen de Tachen Paul was carved with a rayed dot-in-circle[95] (Fig. 9); and the tomb of Petit Mont, Arzon was ornamented with large spoked wheel-like motifs (Fig. 10).[96] The Iberian megalithic tombs are nearly all passage graves, some dated by C14 to around 3000 BC.[97] Here, the radiate suns, wheel-like symbols and concentric circles are a dominant theme. I will mention only a few of the most spectacular examples, such as Granja de Toniñuelo, a dolmen which has produced

11 *Megalith with suns and stag; Carapito, Spain. Height: 2.6 m (8.5 ft). After Twohig*

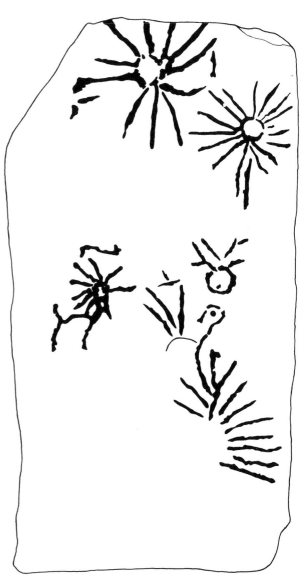

10 *The Dolmen du Petit Mont, Arzon, Brittany. Diameter of wheel-shaped symbol: 50 cm (20 in.). After Péquart and Rouzic*

no less than five sun-motifs,[98] one of which occurs with curious designs which could represent ploughing, and another which has a radiate sun and associated moon-crescent.[99] A stone at Carapito has two large radiate suns and, interestingly, a stag with its head and antlers treated as if it, too, is a sun-motif (Fig. 11).[100] We may recall the earlier discussion where a link between stags and sun-cults was suggested.

It is very difficult to interpret the exact meaning of these sun-like images occurring on passage-grave stones. If we may assume that the signs are symbolic, then either they are purely abstract or they represent something in the natural world. Some of the symbols do appear to be abstract – the lozenges, chevrons and zig-zags, for instance. But others – people and axes to name but two types – are depictions of real objects, and I see no reason not to place the radiate 'suns' and other circle-variants in this latter category. Harbison[101] believes that the Boyne tomb-symbols could represent the gods worshipped and the world and life they created, and this argument seems reasonable. We have already seen a conceptual link between the sun and death or the under-world and, later in the book, we will come across tangible evidence of a strong association between the solar and chthonic forces. The solar motifs engraved in passage graves could have been placed there as a comfort to the dead, as a reminder that rebirth and renewal would take place; we will see presently that there is evidence, apart from the art, for a solar religion associated with megalithic tombs.

There is other Neolithic art which is suggestive of a need to represent the sun. At Val Camonica, the earliest rock-engravings in what must have been a sacred place for at least 2000 years, are later Neolithic, and at this time simple sun-symbols, usually in the dot-in-circle form,[102] were carved in honour of the supernatural power of the sun, sometimes with the depiction of a man praying to the image, offering homage to this life-giving force (Fig. 2). A rock-shelter at Tajo de las Figuras in Iberia produced a painted sun-symbol whose rays are in the form of antlers (Fig. 5).[103] But small objects, too, demonstrate the power of

12 Fragment of copper vessel with stags and suns from Las Carolinas, Iberia. After Maringer

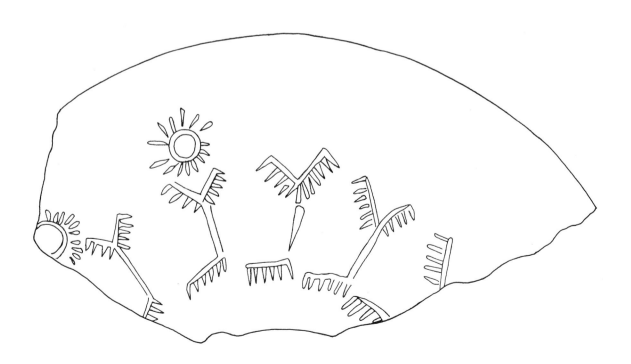

the sun during the Neolithic and very early metal-using phases in Europe: an incised copper vessel fragment from Las Carolinas in Spain again combines stag-sun symbolism (Fig. 12),[104] and at Auriac (Aude) in southern France, a bowl belonging to the Chasséan industry of the early Neolithic has internal decoration in the form of a rayed sun.[105] Italian pots, too, have sun-like motifs: vessels at Serra d'Alto and Leporino, belonging to the third millennium BC, are ornamented with rayed suns.[106] In Chapter Three we will look more closely at the relationship between sun- and eye-imagery, in terms of the physical motifs themselves. But here, it is worth glancing at some small Neolithic objects on which are represented pairs of symbols, looking like sun-bursts, but whose position and double form make them interpretable as eyes. Stone and bone plaques from Iberia are decorated with these eye-suns (Fig. 13); and one example, at Granja de Toniñuelo[107], is from the megalithic burial-chamber which produced true sun-symbols. A similar plaque at Vila Nova de San Pedro in Portugal has simply one isolated rayed sun.[108] A small bone anthropomorphic image at Estramadura in southern Spain has eyes which resemble suns; and these are strongly reminiscent of pots with pairs of eyes at, for example, Los Millares in Iberia[109] and Denmark.[110] The treatment of all these paired eye-motifs is strongly suggestive of a dual ocular-solar symbolism: the sun-like treatment of these eyes seems deliberately to have been to evoke the image of eye and sun as parallel sources of light.

Light, sun and tombs

Neolithic art provides one method of examining how early man may have regarded and venerated the sun, by copying its image and thus attempting to control it by magic. But reverence for the sun could manifest itself in other ways, and the 'solar' art of some passage graves is supported by other evidence for the

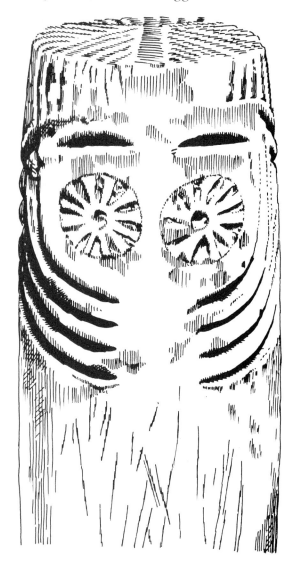

13 Neolithic bone cylinder with eyes or suns; Estramadura, Spain. Height: 19.5 cm (7.7 in.). Paul Jenkins, after Torbrügge

14 Newgrange at the winter solstice, with the sun shining through the 'roof-box'. By permission of the Commissioners of Public Works, Ireland

cognisance taken of the sun by Neolithic tomb-builders. First, there does sometimes appear to have been a genuine connection between orientation and the movements of the sun and moon (Figs. 1, 3, 14–16). This could have been because of a conceptual affinity between the dead and the natural world.[111] Also, it may have been necessary for there to be a light-source for the ritual taking place in some Neolithic tombs, and this may account for orientation towards the rising sun. In a recent study[112] Bradley has put forward a convincing argument for the role played by light and darkness in both Insular and Breton megalithic tombs. He suggests that one feature influencing the design of chamber-plans could have been the desire to create specific areas of light and darkness. In complex graves, one effect was the creation of contrasting zones of dark and light, maybe in acknowledgement of the distinction between the inner and outer worlds: the side-chambers containing human bones would be in shadow, while the entrance and passage would be lit. The positioning of passage grave art may sometimes be significant in this respect: cairn T at Loughcrew had a decorated stone at the rear of its final chamber which was carefully located to be lit by the equinoctial sunrise.[113]

Perhaps the most spectacular example of solar influence in tomb construction is Newgrange in Ireland. The entrance to the passage grave faces south-east, and the tomb itself is so sited that the passage slopes uphill from the edge of the mound to the central chamber. Whatever the reason for the specific construction of Newgrange, the fact is that it was built so that, at the time of the winter solstice (21 December) and for a few days before and after, the rays of the rising sun would penetrate to the end-chamber of the tomb (Fig. 14). The central line of the passage was purposely oriented to a point where, on the shortest day, the sun climbs over the horizon and its rays strike directly through the doorway of the

grave. But it was not simply a question of orientation, since the problem of the uphill gradient of the passage had to be overcome. This was brilliantly achieved by the construction of a 'roof box' in the entrance which channelled the beams of the rising midwinter sun and caused them to strike, as a narrow pencil of light, across the chamber-floor to the end-recess, flooding the tomb with light. This 'roof-box' is situated over a small gap between the first two roofslabs of the passage and forms a small opening above the doorway, which allows the sun's rays to enter horizontally at a

15 Exterior of the Newgrange 'roof-box' at Newgrange. Dr Aubrey Burl

sufficiently high level for them to penetrate the length of the upward-sloping passage. The device enabled the sun to shine briefly into the end-chamber even when the entrance to the tomb was blocked (Fig. 15).[114] There was a similar contrivance far away at the site of Maes Howe on Orkney, where an aperture was left in the entrance, this time to allow the rays of the midwinter setting sun to enter and wash over the dead (Fig. 16).[115]

Was the sun-ritual – if correctly interpreted – at Newgrange and Maes Howe for the living or the dead? Certainly the sun could be perceived to light and warm the dead deep in the tomb and once the entrance was blocked the rays would be for the dead alone. Midwinter, like death itself, was perhaps dreaded; the sun was at its furthest from earth, at its least powerful, and the days were cold and short. Maybe the capture and concentration of the sun's rays through the roof-box magically strengthened the sun for spring and, in parallel, caused the dead to awaken after the winter-like sleep of death. There is a suggestion, too, that the grave may not only have served a funerary function but could also have been carefully planned as a calendrical device in order to mark the winter solstice, so that farmers could calculate forward from the shortest day to the time to begin sowing the spring crop.[116] We

16 Light from the midwinter sunset penetrating down the passage at Maes Howe, Orkney. Mick Sharp

will meet the concept of the solar calendar in Chapter Four when we examine the role of Stonehenge in the earlier Bronze Age, when the axis of the stone monument was oriented towards the rising of the midsummer sun.

The earliest henges and stone circles

The greatest and most famous of the British stone circles is Stonehenge, which we will look at in Chapter Four since its importance for us lies in the earlier Bronze Age phases. But the earliest circles are perhaps as early as the mid-fourth millennium BC, and it is often claimed that these circles have a religious association with the sun. Indeed, it is frequently pointed out[117] that the first Neolithic monument at Stonehenge itself occupied a significant position in that its latitude is where the directions of the midsummer rising sun and the mid-summer rising moon at its extreme southerly standstill position are at right-angles. So it could be argued that the position of this early monument was carefully chosen with an all-round horizon in mind. Woodhenge, too, in the later Neolithic apparently altered its earlier alignment and became an ellipse, oriented towards the midsummer sunrise;[118] and several early circles were deliberately elliptical, arguably so that they were aligned on a solar or lunar event.[119] If there is significance in these orientations, we have to be cautious on two counts. Arguing for complicated astronomical/observational functions for stone circles begs the question as to whether, for calendrical purposes, Neolithic farmers needed to work out more about the sky than they could actually see.[120] The other matter on which reticence is required concerns the imputation of a religious significance for monuments which are oriented towards the sun. Certainly, without any external evidence, it is unwise to assume sun-worship since, as Atkinson observes,[121] many of our churches are aligned with equal precision on the rising of the sun at the equinoxes, and there may be as little relationship between the orientation of certain prehistoric monuments and the sun as an object of veneration.

Conclusion

This chapter has covered two issues: the first part, in introducing the concept of sun veneration and symbolism, has necessarily ranged widely over space and time. In a sense, what has been attempted is an examination of what beliefs could be evoked by the acknowledgement of the sun as a supernatural and as a divine entity. Animism, wherever it occurs in the world, follows and has followed similar basic principles of perception, image-making and worship by means of magic. What is especially interesting is the different kinds of emotion which the divine sun could provoke: it was a beneficent, fertile and healing life-force, giving light and life to the world; it may be a warrior-protector, a hunter or a destroyer; it may float in a boat, fly or be driven across the sky in a horse-drawn carriage. Indeed, we may witness the transformation of the sun-image itself from that of a focus of worship to that of an anthropomorphic divinity, with a mythology and hierarchical identity. The second part of the chapter looked at the sun-cult in Europe from its beginnings. In the Neolithic, the sun's image was confined to its physical appearance: conceptualization had not yet taken place, and the image was captured on the walls of tombs, on pots and on other objects so that the solar disc itself could be reverenced. But even in this early period, the sun was beginning to assume the complicated dualistic role, as guardian of the living and the dead, which was to become such a distinctive feature of the cult until the end of the pagan era in barbarian Europe.

— 3 —
The Image of the Sun

What do we perceive when we look at the sun? In its full radiance, we can no more than glance at it and look away before our eyes are damaged: even a glance can temporarily blind us or fill our retinas solely with the sun's image. First and foremost it is a circle, a blazing orb of light, with beams or rays emanating from the sphere itself. Unlike the moon, its circular shape does not change, except when eclipsed; its rays may disappear at sunset or when the sun is glimpsed from behind thin cloud, but the essential circularity remains until the sun sinks below the horizon. So man's perception of the sun is dominated by its circularity.

When we look at the way that mankind in ancient Europe depicted the image of the sun, we see immediately that this obvious circularity dominated his perception. But what is more interesting is that man did not simply look at the sun and copy what he saw to the best of his ability. He went further and interpreted and superimposed new images of the sun which were not based entirely on his visual perception.

This chapter is concerned solely with the way that man in barbarian Europe captured the solar image as a supernatural entity and depicted it: in rock-art, on pottery, on metalwork. For most of prehistory, the sun was depicted as an inanimate object; it is not until the beginning of history, when the Romans dominated much of Europe, that the sun was

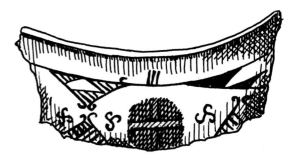

17 Hallstatt pots with solar designs from Bavaria and Poland. Jenkins, after Déchelette

recurrently portrayed as a deity, with solar symbolism an adjunct to his essential anthropomorphism. In understanding how the sun was envisaged as an entity in itself, it is images of the elemental force *per se* that provide the clues.

Our evidence here is drawn from the physical shapes fashioned by people to portray the sun. This in itself poses problems. In the first place, in dealing with non-literate societies, it is not a simple matter to distinguish symbol from ornament. How do we know if a rayed circle painted on a pot is the symbol of the sun, honoured as a supernatural being, or simply a pleasing design? Megaw mentions the difficulty of interpreting the meaning of 'symbols' for an Iron Age Celt. Where repeated and common motifs such as triskeles occur, these could be aesthetically pleasing, non-religious designs, semi-symbolic charms; but others 'may have a significance as profound as a crucifix has for a Christian'.[1] A related problem concerns the need to be careful not to interpret every disc or spiral as solar, unless there is independent evidence for this argument.[2] Prehistoric European art is full of ring-and-dot decoration: this *can* be a method of depicting the sun, but it need not be, and most certainly is not in very many instances. There are particular problems in judgement where functional objects are ornamented in what is an apparently solar manner. We are on surer ground when dealing with, say, rock-art, which is generally considered to have some symbolic function concerned with ritual and religion[3] and is often, like Palaeolithic cave-art,[4] seen as a kind of pictorial language, a semiological system for disseminating coded messages. But even where Bronze Age rock-art is concerned, we have to be careful to look at the whole gamut of the art and not take what appears to be solar symbolism out of its context.

The fundamental nature of solar symbolism and imagery is attested by its widespread distribution in ancient Europe. During the Bronze Age, the first phase of metal-using, the brightness of both gold and new bronze made these metals appropriate for depicting images of the sun. The toothed or denticulate rims of some miniature wheels, both in barbarian Europe and the Greek world, imitated the rays of the sun.[5] Schutz would see the rattles associated with sun-symbols in Bronze Age Europe as instruments to summon the sun-god (Fig. 53),[6] likening this to the sounding of discs associated with the cult of the sky-god Zeus at Olympia. A great deal of our evidence for European sun-symbolism comes from Bronze Age metalwork. Here, it is the repetition of the sun-like imagery which serves to convince us that there was a genuine tradition of solar veneration. But in Bronze Age prehistory it is the rock-art of Scandinavia and north Italy which shows the strongest and most interesting physical evidence for solar imagery. We will look presently at the different types of sun-motif, but one or two features should be mentioned in this introductory context. Whilst images of the sun are common in this symbolic art, only a few display unequivocal evidence for sun-worship as such. An example is the scene on the Engelstrup rock in Denmark where a disc is placed between a man and a woman who raise their arms to it in reverence.[7] At Mont Bego in the Alpes Maritimes, an extraordinary representation seems to display the sun underground, escaping from earth, beginning to throw its rays, and in full glow at its zenith.[8] The rock-art of Scandinavia, in particular that of the Bohuslän region on the Swedish side of Oslo Fjord, is unique not only in its portrayal of various kinds of sun-image but also in depicting what appears to be a merger between man and the physical manifestation of the sun. Sometimes human figures are represented with the central parts of their bodies replaced by sun-discs – in the form of either concentric circles or spoked wheels.[9] We will discuss these images more fully in Chapter Four; I mention them here because they are variations on physical aspects of sun-images occurring within the context of Bronze Age Europe.

The image of the circle

The rayed circle

It is natural that the images which are closest to the sun as perceived by the human eye are those based on the phenomenon of the circle. Most obvious perhaps is the rayed circle and variations on this, representing the sun at full effulgence. The sun's beams are seen to radiate everywhere, to penetrate every corner of the sky and earth, and to fertilize the ground with their heat and light. The rays are the mediators between the fiery circle of the orb itself and the human and animal world. Heat is felt by means of these rays, and they are perceived as being the means by which light travels from sky to land. The sun as a radiate being is an image common to most ancient societies. The Roman Sol and Greek Helios are depicted with radiate heads, as is Asakku, the Sumerian solar demon.[10] The Babylonian god Shamash is represented on a ninth-century BC relief as a humano-divine being accompanied by a four-pointed star-like image inside a disc, with wavy beams flickering between the points of the star;[11] we know that this is a sun-image because it is accompanied by an inscription which reads 'the image of the sun, the Great Lord who dwells in the temple . . .'.[12]

In Neolithic and Bronze Age Europe, we generally have only the image of the rayed sun itself, without an anthropomorphic depiction. But it occurs with sufficient regularity to make it believable as a true solar symbol. In the Neolithic, the sun is usually displayed fully radiate.[13] Deep in a cave at Baudinard on the left bank of the Verdon Gorge (Var), which produced late Neolithic and Early Bronze Age material, have been found schematic rock-paintings which may date to the same period, including sun-images, generally with 8 or 16 rays.[14] The symbols consist only of lines radiating out from a single point, rather than a circle surrounded by rays. Passage graves in Ireland and Brittany (Chapter Two) have produced a number of rayed circles (Figs. 4, 8–10), sometimes enclosed within an outer circle, sometimes the main disc having a central dot or point.[15] If these motifs, when found in Neolithic caves or graves, do represent the sun, then the idea may have been magically to bring the sun into the dark places where it normally cannot penetrate and, in the case of tombs, to light the way for the dead.

Rayed circles are common in Bronze Age metalwork, pottery and rock-art (Fig. 17). Late Bronze Age pots at Queroy à Chazelles in the Charente region have depictions of rayed circles, men and horses;[16] Hallstatt bronze bowls, dating to the very end of the Bronze Age, may be decorated with radiate circles or wheel-motifs.[17] A Hallstatt belt-plate from Kaltbrunn in Germany is just one of many instances of metalwork decorated with a combination of horses and rayed suns.[18] A variation is seen again at Kleinklein in Austria where a Hallstatt bucket-lid is ornamented in repoussé with radiate-haired infantry and horsemen whose beasts have radiate manes (Fig. 18);[19] and at the Hallstatt Cemetery itself a sheet-bronze vessel is decorated with rayed sun-motifs, the rays terminating in knobs, as if to combine circularity and radiateness in a different artistic form.[20] Iron Age Villanovan cinerary urns have rayed sun-symbols along with other solar motifs, again perhaps to illuminate the dead in the otherworld;[21] in Iron Age Iberia pots were painted with radiate suns and swastikas, and at Amerejo, a pot was ornamented with two radiate circles flanking a swastika.[22]

European rock-art abounds in symbols of rayed suns: at Le Valais in the Swiss Alps, concentric and rayed circles are associated with depictions of people.[23] Suns with rays are dominant motifs at Val Camonica, especially in the Bronze Age phases (Fig. 19);[24] on one representation the matchstick-figure of a man grows out of one of the sun's rays.[25] Anati has noted pairs of sun-symbols at Camonica, one with external rays and the other with lines turned inward like a spoked wheel, as if to represent the day- and night-time sun;[26] and many of the circular motifs in Scandinavian rock-art have external or internal radii,[27] with perhaps the same meaning.

The motif is still current on Celtic depictions of the Roman phase in western Europe, where their unequivocally religious character is attested by their occurrence on figurines of deities. Rayed circles, wheels (see below, pp. 56–60) and other solar motifs appear in abundance on pipe-clay figurines of a Celtic version of the Roman goddess Venus.[28] Interestingly, there are a few much earlier figures of what can probably be interpreted as divinities associated with rayed motifs, dating from the beginning of the French Bronze Age. A striking example is the 'statue-menhir' of a goddess at Rocher des Doms, Avignon, who has a symbol consisting of seven rays emanating from a central hole carved on her chest, in the rough position of the heart (Fig. 20).[29]

18 Hallstatt bronze bucket-lid from Kleinklein, Austria. Diameter: 35.7 cm (14 in.). Paul Jenkins, after Steyr Exhibition Catalogue (Anon 1980a)

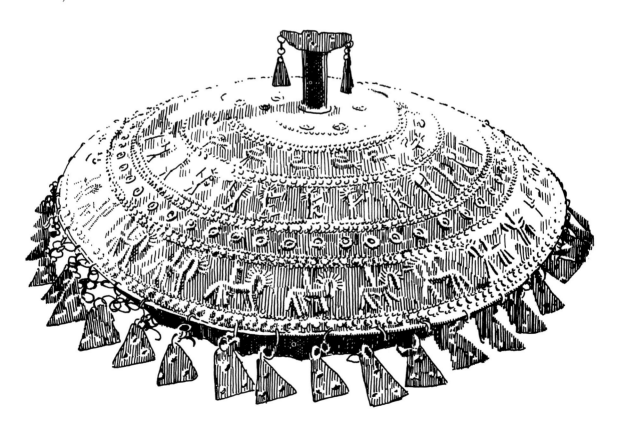

19 The different types of sun-disc represented at Camonica Valley. Miranda Green, after Anati

Flowers

Other symbols were used for the portrayal of the sun, which are visually similar but not identical to the radiate circle. These include flower-motifs and eyes. Both these have, in common with the rayed circle, the features of circularity and radiating lines. There is a strong physical resemblance between some flowers – like sunflowers and daisies – and motifs representing the solar image. In some instances, there may have been a symbolic link as well. Boyne passage grave art at Loughcrew includes a distinctive and prominent petal or daisy-design (Fig. 4)[30] in association with other, more directly solar, symbols of circles

with internal or external rays. We may trace the presence of flower- or rosette-motifs elsewhere and much later in ancient European religious art: some of the solar wheels held by the Celtic sun-god in the Romano-Celtic phase are rose-shaped in appearance;[31] and the Celtic hammer-god Sucellus, known to have solar and celestial associations, was honoured with small bronze figures of the deity ornamented with rosettes and other, more clearly solar, signs of wheel and swastika.[32] Rosette-like flowers occur in association with circle- and wheel-motifs on Romano-Celtic tombstones of the Mediomatrici in Alsace (Chapter Seven);[33] and a clay figurine of a goddess at

Rézé in northern France (Fig. 94) holds three objects which look like hybrid wheel/flower symbols: on the back of the figure is a huge 'sun-burst' and her hair is decorated with solar designs.[34] Unambiguously solar is the eight-petalled rosette near the apex of a triangular plaque at Mauer an der Url in Austria, dedicated to the Syrian sky-god Jupiter Dolichenus. Here the flower-symbol is associated on the plaque with Jupiter's celestial image of the eagle,[35] thus providing a direct link, in a Roman context, between flowers and sky-symbolism. In the Roman world, roses represented a pledge of eternal spring beyond the grave; they were painted on tomb-walls and mentioned in funerary inscriptions.[36] It is easy to see why flowers could reflect renewal and rebirth and when, in addition, the particular flower physically resembles the sun, the link between sun and flower-images is readily comprehended, since the sun itself had a role in fertility and regeneration of life in the seed. This may account for the single flowers found as decoration on, for instance, Cretan and Mycenaean pots;[37] on coins of Knossos dated to 500 BC, there is a motif of a swastika with a central eight-petalled flower, an eight-rayed sun or a crescent moon.[38]

The eye

The eye to menace the wheel of the sun

> Aristophanes *Thesm. 17*

The image of the eye forms a further link with the solar motif for varied reasons. First, the eye can be seen to resemble the sun, with the iris representative of the sun's orb and the lashes its rays, or even the iris itself can look like the sun, with rays or bands of colour radiating out from the central pupil. Secondly, the eye is, of course, intimately bound up with light, like the sun. Ancient Greek thinkers argued that sight was produced by a fire kindled inside the eye, which crossed the external air and met objects which it then saw, rather like light crossing a lantern. The eye, like the sun, may

20 Early Bronze Age statue-menhir from Rocher-des-Doms, Avignon. Height: 26 cm (10 in.). Miranda Green

be seen as a penetrative light seeking out reality and truth.[39] The Greeks thought of the sun and the moon as the eyes of the animate sky,[40] and lightning was conceived of as a flash from an eye, as if it were a piercing glance from a fiery, divine eye.[41]

Eyes are and were regarded as the window of the soul, the expression of personality and the key to the individual's whole being. When the eyes close in sleep, this mirrors death, in the same way that an eclipse of the sun during daylight or its disappearance at night emulates the darkness of death. So the eye and the sun can symbolize both life and death. Just as the sun is seen as central to life, so the eye is recognized as the pivot of human consciousness:

Seeing. We might say that the whole of life lies in that verb – if not ultimately, at least essentially . . . to see or to perish is the very condition laid upon everything that makes up the Universe.[42]

Within the context of the supernatural, the eye is associated with the sun, since the position of the latter in the sky gives it unlimited vision over the world: only a supreme solar god has this power. It is appropriate that human eyes are unable to look at the sun and are thus inferior to the divine celestial eye: a copy or symbol of something is always less powerful than the original. In imagery, just as the head may represent a complete god or individual *pars pro toto*, so the eye may represent further reduction and itself reflect the whole being: the winged eye may symbolize the sun Re in Egypt, the wings an image of speed and perhaps the rapid eye-movements of dreams.[43]

If we examine some of the imagery of ancient Europe, the resemblance between the eye and the sun is very striking, I think deliberately so. On Neolithic pots and bone artefacts in Spain (Fig. 13), exemplified by finds from the Los Millares Cemetery and the site at Estramadura, there are pairs of symbols which are probably to be interpreted as eyes but which, if not paired, would look very like suns, with lash-like rays. Pots from Danish passage graves bear similar motifs.[44] A stone in a megalithic chamber at Granja de Toniñuelo in Iberia has similar paired symbols;[45] and at Montmaurin (Haute-Garonne), a Neolithic or Bronze Age image consists of a cylindrical stone with human features, hair depicted as striations and eyes which look like suns or wheels with rays emanating from a central point and surrounded by an enclosing circle.[46]

It may be that the preponderance of sun-like eye-motifs in, say, Neolithic Iberia, suggests the veneration of the penetrative property of the sun as an all-seeing eye. Certainly, for whatever reason, the eyes are stressed on these early images and, in my view, they may well resemble the sun for positive reasons. Giving an image large eyes may enhance its potency. It may even be that the eyes may work for good or evil according to the actions of the individual who may have venerated such images. There is a link between the powerful, potentially damaging solar eye and the evil eye:[47] the eye of Medusa could work for evil and for good, and the image of the 'gorgoneion' – a stylized symbol of the Medusa's head – gave good luck by cancelling one evil eye with another;[48] if you wear the image of the Gorgon, you make the evil eye to your enemy and are thereby protected yourself.[49] What is interesting about the 'gorgoneion' is that, though it is the eye of the Gorgon that possesses the power, the whole head has become a kind of protective solar motif. A very sun-like Medusa appears on Romano-Celtic tombstones in the Pyrenees: on one the Gorgon is accompanied by two small wheel-symbols,[50] themselves solar motifs. The device of the 'gorgoneion' was worn on the cuirasses of Athene-Minerva and by mortal soldiers[51] in precisely the same manner as apotropaic sun-wheels were worn on Late Bronze Age or Hallstatt shields and breastplates;[52] and this is paralleled on Iron Age stone images of warriors, who may wear the interchangeable motifs of 'gorgoneion' or spiral[53] or solar wheel.[54] Very like a sun-god is the male Gorgon on the great temple-pediment at Bath,[55] with its radiating snake-hair and beard, and belonging to the shrine of the goddess Sulis, whose name is solar.

Circles and spirals

We can move from images of the sun where the radiate character of such motifs dominates the artistic form to other circular patterns which may, at times have solar associations, notably the single or concentric circle and also the spiral. The realm of the circle is where there is most need for caution in the attribution of symbolic meaning. A circle is, after all, a pleasing geometric shape, a natural motif for ornament and, in the case of objects like pots, their own circularity encourages circular decoration. In invoking symbolism for the circle or concentric circle, we need to call upon evidence which is external to the motif itself; we have to look at associated, less equivocal designs, at context or other endorsing features. We have two tasks – one to establish that symbolism is present, the other to connect this symbolism with the veneration of the sun.

It seems clear that, in Neolithic and Bronze Age Europe, the sun may be depicted as a simple or concentric circle.[56] In Egypt, too, the sun was envisaged as a disc.[57] In modern Hindu sun-symbolism, the sun is represented as 12 concentric circles, one for each hour of the day.[58] In European prehistory, circles of different types abound, but running through this palimpsest of decoration is a strain of symbolism which we may, albeit tentatively, associate with the cult of the sun. Sometimes such circular motifs may be merely a tacit acknowledgement of the sun as supernatural force; others may be seen as more positive evidence for solar invocation.

We have already seen that rayed circles are prominent in some of the Irish passage graves. Circles without external rays are common too, and often these are associated with the less ambiguous solar motifs (Fig. 4). At Dowth,[59] a concentric circle is combined with a cluster of rays enclosed by a circle. At Loughcrew, a series of concentric half-circles are suggested as reflective of the rising or setting sun.[60] Burl would see the circles in passage grave art as very possibly solar,[61] but I think we need to distinguish between simple and concentric circles. The sun can be perceived as a circle within a circle, with its central orb and surrounding nimbus of light, when it is too bright to see individual beams. But simple circles could mean other celestial bodies – the full moon or planets, and the Loughcrew semi-concentric circles could even depict rainbows. What we can say, fairly confidently, is that in passage grave art there is clear indication of solar imagery, which gives support to the celestial interpretation of other, less positively identifiable motifs.

Circular designs are ubiquitous on Bronze Age metalwork, and a great deal of reticence is required in attributing specific symbolism to such universal decorative patterns. A feature now is not simply the use of metal but also the employment of gold, which itself has solar connotations on account of its colour, purity and its untarnishable brightness. It would thus be tempting to see the gold-leaf concentric circles below the rim or gunwale of the Bronze Age shale boat-model from Caergwrle in North Wales[62] as sun-motifs. The boat is liberally ornamented with gold-leaf, representative of waves, eyes and oars; but the circles are probably best interpreted as shields rather than suns, similar to those adorning the hundred miniature gold boats found in a cache within a pot beneath a stone at Nors Thy in Jutland.[63] One should perhaps be equally sceptical about the sun associations of the north European Bronze Age gold bowls from such places as Boslunde and Mariesminde, dated to around 1500–1400 BC,[64] which are decorated with concentric circles or wheel-motifs on their bases.[65] Two features of these bowls, however, make me hesitate before dismissing them out of hand. One is that these vessels are frequently fitted with horse-head handles (Fig. 21); we will see presently that the horse and the sun were very closely allied. The other feature is the placing of 11 of these bowls within a sheet-bronze vessel at Mariesminde in Denmark,[66] which itself is lavishly ornamented with the recurrent motif of solar wheel and duck-prowed boat (Fig. 46a) (see Chapter Four).

The earliest Irish 'sun-discs', sheet-gold dress-ornaments dating to the very earliest Bronze Age or Beaker period, are frequently decorated with either cross-in-circle or concentric circle motifs (Fig. 22).[67] These may have nothing to do with a sun-cult, but the later Bronze Age 'sun-discs', which are larger and may be of gold or bronze, are another matter. These are frequently decorated with concentric circles, like that at Lattoon, Co. Cavan.[68] Unequivocally solar is the gilded bronze disc at Trundholm in Denmark (Fig. 45), pulled on a miniature wagon by a bronze horse and decorated with concentric circles and spirals, and to which we will return (see also cover illustration). There is other Scandinavian bronzework, too, which must possess a

22 Early Bronze Age gold 'sun-disc' from Wexford, Ireland. Diameter c. 9.5 cm (3.7 in.). Miranda Green, after Butler and Waterbolk

21 Gold vessel with 'solar' decoration and horse-head handle from Mariesminde, Denmark. Paul Jenkins, after Glob

solar association. The so-called 'sun-drum' from a bog at Balkåkra near Ystad, Scania, for example, consists of a cylinder whose lid is a flat disc decorated with lines and concentric circles; the cylinder itself is supported on ten model wheels (Fig. 23).[69]

Later Bronze Age metalwork belonging to the 'Urnfield' phase of Central European culture, named after the practice at this time of burying the cremated remains of the dead in urns in large flat cemeteries, contains much symbolism that is overtly solar, and here concentric circles play a major role in the motifs. The 'wheel-and-water-bird' solar imagery on many sheet-bronze vessels (Chapter Four) may degenerate into squiggles or Ss and circles:[70] this happens on a *situla* (bucket) at Rivoli in north Italy.[71] Urnfield belts, like that at Uioara de Sus in Romania,[72] are frequently decorated with wheels and concentric circles.

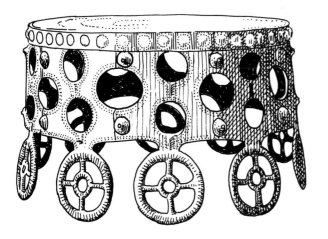

23 *Bronze Age bronze 'sun-drum' from Balkåkra,*
Scania. Diameter of cylinder: c. 40 cm (15.7 in.).
Paul Jenkins, after Glob

24 *Bronze Age gold cone from Etzelsdorf.* Paul
Jenkins, after Menghin and Schauer

We find the same combination on curious cone-shaped gold 'vessels' (Fig. 24), like that at Etzelsdorf in Bavaria, probably dating to the Middle Bronze Age, which is adorned with bands of sun-wheels and circles.[73]

25 Types of sun-symbol depicted on southern Scandinavian rock-art. Paul Jenkins, after Gelling and Davidson

The Bronze Age rock-art of both Scandinavia and north Italy contains images of both unequivocal rayed suns and rayless circles, either simple or concentric (Figs. 19, 25). The 'disc-men' of the Bohuslän region of southern Sweden have bodies in the form of either spoked wheels or concentric circles.[74] But at Begby in Norway, the convention for both wheeled vehicles and suns is the dotted circle; rays and spokes are never depicted.[75]

The introduction of the iron-using phase in various parts of barbarian Europe continued the combination of different kinds of circular symbol on functional objects, which is so characteristic of the Bronze Age. Thus Hallstatt bronze bowls and belts of the seventh and sixth centuries BC may combine concentric circles, wheels or rayed suns;[76] Villanovan cinerary urns in north Italy may be ornamented with wheels, swastikas, concentric circles and true sun-motifs.[77] Concentric circles appear in the position of the sun on Iron Age coins, and on an Armorican gold stater[78] the motif occurs in the middle of a swastika-symbol; we will see shortly that the swastika was an important solar design. The combination of concentric circle and swastika recurs on Romano-Celtic swastika-brooches, which are decorated at the centre and the angle of the arms with concentric circles.[79] Solar and concentric circle symbols recur in association in Romano-Celtic Europe: pipe-clay figurines of native goddesses bear rayed suns, wheels and double circles.[80] A Breton statuette from Bro-en-Fégréac bears wheels, concentric circles and a pattern which could represent a maze.[81]

If, as we have observed, concentric circles appear on objects or on rock-art in association with less equivocal solar signs, we have to ask the question as to whether or not they represent precisely the same phenomenon as, say, a spoked wheel or a radiate sun. With rock-art, we have the problem of contemporaneity: apparently juxtaposed symbols may belong to different phases of art. On Urnfield metal-

work, it can be seen that the concentric circle could be a stylized form of the wheel, with its felloes and hub only depicted. In other instances, it is difficult to be sure. We argued earlier that it is appropriate, in terms of physical resemblance, for the sun to be portrayed as either a radiate sphere or a double circle. Where the two forms occur together, it may be that the circle represents the sun before or after its zenith or even at night, whilst the rayed sun-circle would reflect the full radiance of the solar orb. Alternatively, the dotted circle could represent the speed of a solar wheel, where the spokes are so blurred that they cannot be readily discerned.

Before leaving motifs based on concentric circles, we should look at a phenomenon of imagery which is essentially very similar though not identical, namely the spiral. Spirals are very widespread in Neolithic contexts: in Maltese art they are the dominant motif in many of the megalithic structures,[82] and in passage grave carvings spirals of various forms and directions are persistent motifs.[83] Sometimes, it is possible to see that spirals may at least be *associated* with solar symbols, though they may not themselves share this symbolism. In some British passage grave art spirals and radiate suns appear together.[84] Some scholars see the double spirals in Maltese and Boyne megalithic art as representative of eyes;[85] others believe that the ever-winding spiral may reflect the journey of humankind through life.[86]

Bronze Age gold and bronze 'sun-discs' may be ornamented with circles or spirals.[87] Interestingly, the Trundholm 'sun-chariot' (see cover illustration and Fig. 45) with its great solar disc has one gilded and one bronze face, as if to represent the day and night of the sun; on the gilded surface are concentric circles and on the 'dark' face are spirals.[88] On a Swedish rock-carving at Vestfold, the disc-body of a man is replaced by a spiral;[89] and a very Late Bronze Age axe at Megyaśzo in Hungary is decorated with a wheel and spirals,[90] the latter perhaps to be seen as stylized water-birds, in reflection of the bird-terminalled sun-boat which is so common in later Bronze Age European solar imagery. The Bronze Age clay deity at Dupljaja in Yugoslavia, mounted on a cart or chariot, has a solar wheel-symbol on the base of his vehicle and spiral-decoration on his clothes (Fig. 88).[91] A Late Bronze Age hoard at Petit Villate (Cher) contained a model wheel, a small star-shaped charm and a spiral-amulet.[92]

There are three intrinsic aspects of spirals which we need to consider, irrespective of motifs associated with them. One is the link between spirals and labyrinths, which may look very similar. Pliny[93] recorded that the labyrinth at the temple of Hawara in Egypt was generally held to be sacred to the sun. Diodorus[94] and Pliny both say that the labyrinth at Knossos was built in imitation of the Egyptian one. Labyrinths were probably dance-floors in origin,[95] but it is possible that they could also represent the passage of the sun through the sky. This is supported by the association of the labyrinth with the swastika, a solar motif well-authenticated in later prehistory (see below). Cook notes the Greek vase-painters depicting Theseus with the minotaur portrayed a building decorated with swastikas, and on coins minted at Knossos in the mid-first millennium BC the labyrinth is represented by a swastika.[96] So the associations we have noted between spirals and solar motifs on non-Mediterranean imagery may be genuine. Maze or labyrinth-like designs occur in the southern French Bronze Age rock-art of Mont Bego,[97] and at Camonica Valley, where sun-symbolism was so prevalent in the carvings of local Bronze Age communities, a labyrinth/spiral-image has been depicted with a human face at its centre (Fig. 26).[98] In Celtic Gaul, pipe-clay figurines of goddesses in the Roman period are decorated with sun-signs and associated spirals.[99] A second feature of spirals which

may provide clues to interpretation is the fact that the motif is made up of a long, continuously winding and circular pattern. This unbrokenness of line may be important. Burl's view of spirals on passage grave art as symbols of life's passage through time could be valid; and, if there is a solar association, then the eternity of the sun's journey through day and night could make the spiral an appropriate motif. A third feature is the double-spiral which may, in simplified form, take the shape of an S-motif; and there is some very positive evidence to suggest a solar connection here. A simple S-shape resembles a half-swastika, and an S on its side could, in Romano-Celtic contexts, represent the thunderbolt or lightning-flash of the sky-god: the bronze god at Le Châtelet (Haute-Marne) bears a thunderbolt made up of S-shaped strands, and moreover he carries S-shaped objects on his shoulder (Fig. 68).[100] In early Iron Age Villanovan Italy,

26 Labyrinth/face-image from Camonica Valley. Paul Jenkins, after Anati

cremation-vessels are decorated with radiate suns, concentric circles, birds and Ss;[101] and curious motifs on Hallstatt pottery in Bavaria consist of an S or spiral with an extra stroke, as if to represent a curvilinear triskele.[102] An association between S and sun-motifs occurs in Urnfield metalwork,[103] where the solar boat (Fig. 46) with the prow and stern in the form of a long-necked water-bird, may become stylized and show merely two S-shapes flanking the solar wheel or circle. But it is in Celtic western Europe that S and solar emblem become really closely allied; in the excavations of a Roman villa at Grand-Jailly (Côte d'Or), a miniature sun-wheel had three S-motifs soldered on to it (Fig. 27).[104] A Romano-British pot at Silchester[105] bears ornament in the form of alternating wheels and Ss; and the Romano-Celtic solar wheel-god himself may[106] carry a wheel with curvilinear S-shaped spokes. There is further evidence of this nature to link the S or double-spiral with solar imagery: I

27 *Romano-Celtic wheel-pendant from Grand-Jailly, Côte d'Or, with attached S-symbol and solder for two further motifs, which have been lost. The spokes have been ribbed to catch the light.* Miranda Green, after Déchelette

will mention only one more occurrence – a third-century AD altar to Apollo Belenus ('brilliant Apollo') from Vivarais in Gaul, which bears an S-sign and two swastikas.[107] The connection between the S, swastika and a Celtic god of light seems here to be unassailable.

Linear images associated with the solar cult

The swastika

'Swastika' is a Sanskrit word derived from 'su' (well) and 'asti' (it is). It is also called a crooked or 'gammate' cross, because the shape can be broken down into four gammas joined at the centre. Strictly speaking, the gammate cross is only a true 'swastika' when the arms turn to the right; a left-turning crooked cross is more properly called a 'sauvastika'. In Hindu iconography, the right-armed symbol is that of the male principle, representative of sun, light, life; the left-turning motif reflects the female principle, representative of night and destruction. The swastika is a widespread apotropaic or good-luck symbol, occurring at its earliest in Europe in pre-palatial (Neolithic) Crete[108] and in Asia Minor at Hissarlik in Anatolia, on beads and clay discs dating to around 2000–1500 BC.[109] The motif was recurrent in the Greek world from Minoan and Mycenaean periods to Classical times, often associated on pots with horses, which may also (see below) imply a solar symbolism for the swastika in Greece from the earlier Bronze Age.[110] Swastikas and suns or moons are associated on Cretan coins minted in about 500 BC.[111] A Greek red-figure pot from Apulia in southern Italy associates Apollo or Helios in his sun-chariot with a swastika, placed like a protective sign on his chest,[112] and on other Greek pots the swastika appears as an apotropaic motif on the chest or genitals of warriors (Fig. 29).[113] Attic-Boeotian brooches bear swastikas;[114] at Damascum in Epirus, a silver drachma bearing

28 Romano-Celtic bronze swastika-brooch from Köln. Width: 2.6 cm (1 in.). Miranda Green

the head of Apollo has on the reverse the image of the Delphic tripod between two swastikas.[115]

The swastika is equally prevalent in barbarian Europe: in Iron Age Iberia, pots were painted with radiate suns and swastikas.[116] In the later Bronze Age and Hallstatt phases of Central Europe, the swastika appears on wagons and belt-plates;[117] and the single swastika marked on an Iron Age amphora at Martigues in Provence[118] may imply the presence of a solar sign rather than a decorative pattern. Armorican Iron Age coins bear swastikas, one with its arms ending in horse-heads,[119] precisely similar to a Romano-Celtic brooch at Köln which is in the form of a swastika again with horse-head arms.[120] Both coin and brooch combine the motif of swastika with concentric circle; horse, swastika and circle are once more associated on a Late Iron Age stele

at Robernier (Var),[121] and earlier at Iron Age Este in north Italy (900–800 BC) an incised urn again bears horse and swastika images.[122] But it is during the Romano-Celtic phase in western Europe that the solar association of the swastika becomes really clear. Most important are a group of altars from sacred sites in the French Pyrenees (Figs. 30, 31), which bear either a swastika or a sun-wheel symbol, sometimes both, and some of which are dedicated to Jupiter, a local Celtic version of the Roman sky-god, whom we will see (Chapter Five) was conflated in Celtic lands with the indigenous sun-god. These altars are found only at these high mountain sanctuaries, as at Montmaurin and Le Mont Saçon.[123] Figurines of the Celtic hammer-god Sucellus bear wheels, crosses and swastikas,[124] and we know that there was a close affinity between this deity and the celestial powers of the Celtic supernatural world.

What does the swastika as a symbol represent? It is, I think, a complex image, and one with a close solar link. First and foremost, it would seem to represent rotary movement[125] and, if in close association with the wheel, represents above all the rotating aspect of the

29 Greek pot decorated with warrior wearing solar amulets. Paul Jenkins, after Déchelette

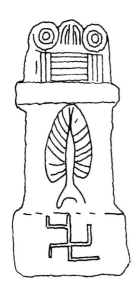

30 Romano-Celtic altar carved with tree and swastika from the Pyrenees. E. R. Aldhouse, after Espérandieu

31 Romano-Celtic altar with wheel and swastika from the Pyrenees. Width: 10 cm (4 in.). Miranda Green

sun (Fig. 28). Whilst a true wheel has spokes and a nave to reflect the circular, beaming sun, the swastika reflects the movement of the orb across the sky. In assessing the presence of the swastika-motif in early Mediterranean civilization, we cannot be sure that the motif is not there simply because of its beauty, but in Romano-Celtic contexts there is an unambiguous association between the swastika and the sun.

It is possible that, in some circumstances, the triskele could possess similar solar connotations to the swastika. The two symbols look quite alike, the swastika having four 'arms' to the triskele's three. In both, the idea of movement is an important part of the visual imagery. Déchelette [126] believed that the triskele could have been derived from the swastika. Bavarian Hallstatt pots are decorated with curious motifs of three curving lines joined at the centre (Fig. 17), resembling a hybrid swastika-triskele;[127] coins of Aspendos in Pamphylia (Turkey), dated to around 500 BC, carry strange images of three whirling human legs (rather like the symbol of the Isle of Man), some with a central wheel or sun-symbol;[128] and a spear from the Brandenburg area of Germany, dating to the period of the barbarian invasions, bears symbols of lunar crescent, swastika and triskele.[129] Megaw points out[130] that many of the so-called decorative motifs in La Tène art may have possessed profound symbolism. Here the triskele is a dominant motif and, whilst there is little intrinsic evidence, it is possible that, originally at least, the three-armed design may have possessed solar significance in addition to the triadic magic so dear to the Celtic soul. Thus the triskeles on the Llyn Cerrig shield-boss[131] may have been devices to protect the bearer from hurt, much as the swastika guarded the warrior on the Greek pots alluded to earlier. The charm may have been the more potent because of the combination of triplistic and solar symbolism. The triskele within a circle on the later second-early first century BC Moel Hiraddug plate [132] combines the three-armed motif with a circle, which may again enhance a solar interpretation. This hybrid design recurs on a sheet-gold 'sun-disc' of fifth-century BC date at Schwarzenbach, Kr St Wendel in Germany, which is decorated with a chain of triskeles or three-armed whirligigs. [133]

The cross

The motif of the cross is at its simplest a sign which is evocative of space and radiation of light. The arms of a cross reach out in four directions; it commands space, and it has quite clear links with the sun in its radiating lines. Two kinds of cross concern us here: the vertical/horizontal equal-armed cross, and the diagonal or St Andrew's cross. Both may embody solar significance, and there is frequently associated evidence to suggest such a symbolism in the pagan world. Indeed, the cross resembles a rimless four-spoked wheel or a hybrid sun-star image (while technically the sun is a star, there is a marked physical difference in our perception of the solar sphere on the one hand and the twinkling, pointed star on the other). One of the reasons for using the term 'sun-disc' for the Early Bronze Age or Beaker dress-ornaments in Britain and Ireland[134] is that they often bear cruciform decoration (Fig. 22). These discs, of Irish gold, are generally unassociated when they occur in Ireland[135] but appear in Beaker contexts in southern Britain such as Mere Down in Wiltshire.[136] 'Sun-discs' are small, sheet-gold decorative objects, with perforations showing that they were originally attached to clothing or perhaps to buttons. They may have no association whatever with solar imagery, but their being made of gold, their circularity and their frequent cruciform designs all contribute to their resemblance to the sun. In addition, discs such as that from Wexford (Fig. 22) have denticulate incised patterns round the circumference, further suggesting a solar image. There could

quite possibly, therefore, have been a good-luck-charm element to their presence which was made the more potent by a visual link with the sun.

Later in the Bronze Age and the beginning of the Iron Age, crosses decorated pottery and metalwork, usually with no evidence for solar, if any, symbolism. But sometimes associated motifs suggest that, in certain distinct instances, this four-armed sign may evoke the space of the firmament or the rays of the sun itself. A Late Bronze Age pot from Queroy à Chazelles (Charente) is ornamented with a frieze below its rim, with sets of 'pin-men', horses, a radiate sun and crosses;[137] and a similar combination of motifs appears on a bronze bucket-cover of Hallstatt Iron Age date from Kleinklein in Austria, with repoussé crosses, wheels and schematized horses (Fig. 18).[138] The horse as a solar associate has been alluded to already and will be fully examined later.

In the later Iron Age and especially during the Romano-Celtic phases, the cross, particularly the St Andrew's cross, comes fully into its own as a celestial symbol. Romano-Celtic swastika-brooches from Gaul and the Rhineland frequently bear diagonal crosses instead of concentric circles at the central junction of the four arms[139] (Fig. 28). Significant, too, may be the presence of the X on an image of the Celtic equestrian solar god at Scarpone (Moselle).[140] Finally, the Gaulish hammer-god Sucellus, who possessed a solar aspect to his cult,[141] was often invoked with bronze images of a Jupiter-like being bearing a hammer and pot and with sun-wheels, swastikas, circles or diagonal crosses on his body (Fig. 32).[142]

Before we leave the symbolism of the cross, we should allude briefly to the very specific link between the sun and the cross which occurred in a Roman context at the interface of paganism and Christianity. Constantine, like his immediate imperial predecessors, worshipped the Unconquered Sun. In AD 312, as he marched to the Milvian Bridge to fight

Maxentius for the Empire, Constantine had a vision of a cross superimposed on the sun, and he heard the words 'Triumph in this'. He promptly adopted this double motif for the shields of his soldiers and won his victory. But it should be recalled that, even after Constantine's 'conversion' to Christianity, he retained his old allegiance to the sun, and the cult only gradually merged with that of Christ. In AD 321, the seventh day of the week was pronounced a day of rest because it was Sunday.[143]

Hands

There are some motifs which appear, more indirectly, to have been visually linked with solar symbolism. One of these is the hand-sign, where the human hand is depicted with spread, star-like fingers. By far the most important evidence here is that of the rock-art of Scandinavia and north Italy. On the Danish island of Bornholm are carvings of outstretched hand-prints, the fingers pointing, like the arms of a cross, in four directions.[144] In the Bohuslän region of southern Sweden, and at Val Camonica in northern Italy, appear human images with enormous radiate hands like rayed suns (Fig. 33), and on occasions spread-hand symbols appear on ships in the same manner as sun-wheel motifs.[145] Sometimes on the rock-art the solar association is quite clear: at Djupedal, Svenneby in Sweden, an image of a man with a sun-disc-body, erect phallus and sword has arms ending in great radiating fingers;[146] and at Torsbo, Kville, a man with a sun-wheel body is associated with another male image with spread fingers.[147] Hands and wheel-symbols are associated at Almsted-Gammelgård (Denmark);[148] and at Skivum in Jylland a small stone bears the image of an eight-spoked wheel or sun with a hand-sign attached to a continuation of one of the spokes beyond the wheel's rim.[149] Most curious of all the Scandinavian symbols are the discs whose external circumference is bristling

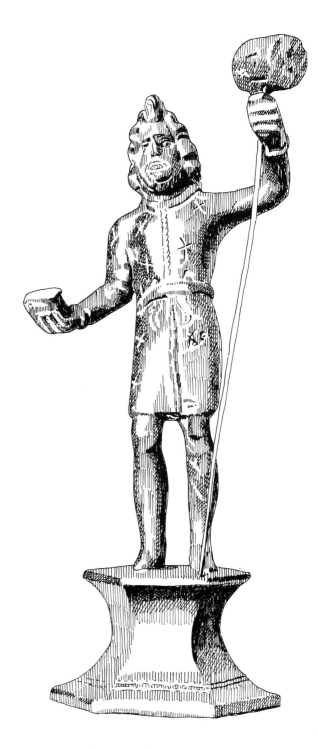

32 Bronze figurine of hammer-god with crosses on body from Prémeaux, Burgundy. Height: 12–15 cm (4.7–6 in.). Paul Jenkins

with three-pronged symbols which could represent stylized hands;[150] and a bronze panel at Wismar in Germany dating to around 1200 BC (therefore making it coeval with much of the rock-art) has a similar hand/disc motif, together with representations of ships, S-designs and wheels,[151] the associated signs lending credence to a solar connection. Certainly, in terms of visual imagery, these discs with 'hands' attached greatly resemble a beaming or flaming solar sphere. Sun-like hands occur on prehistoric imagery apart from the rock-art of Bronze Age Scandinavia and north Italy: a Neolithic rock-painting at Bacinete in Iberia has huge sun-like hands, and a megalithic tombstone at Klein Meinsdorf in Germany is carved with a cross-in-circle, hands and feet.[152]

33 Rock-carvings of men with huge spread hands from Naquane Rock, Camonica Valley. Miranda Green

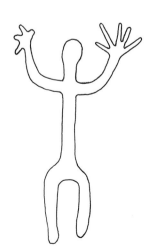

The theme of hand and wheel-sign is repeated on Celtic metalwork of the Iron Age and Romano-Celtic phases in western Europe: miniature bronze hands of the Italian Iron Age are decorated with concentric circles; possibly also Iron Age is a wheel-pendant from Valais in Switzerland bearing five denticulate, hand-like sub-pendants.[153] A small bronze ring belonging to the Iron Age or Romano-Celtic period at Isômes (Haute-Marne) has nine miniature objects hanging from it, including a radiate sun, a lunar crescent and a model hand.[154] Interestingly, the association of hands and light is clearly present at the Romano-Gaulish healing sanctuary at Essarois in Burgundy, which was dedicated to Apollo Vindonnus, whose Celtic surname means 'clear' or 'bright'.[155] At this healing shrine, votive hands formed one of the types of offering to the god.

The link between hands and solar symbolism is appropriate, from a visual point of view. The palm of the hand and the spread fingers resemble the orb and rays of the sun. In addition, the hand may represent other ideas which are apposite to a cult-association. Hands can suggest healing or prayer: the outstretched hands on Scandinavian petroglyphs perhaps imply supplication, perhaps to a sun-god.

The 'barillet' and the axe

There is a close connection between the Celtic hammer-god Sucellus and solar imagery and depictions of this god often carry what seem to be sun-motifs (see above). Sucellus' hammer may have a role as a thunder-weapon and, physically, the god is portrayed as having a strong affinity with the sky-god Jupiter. What is even more interesting is that, on certain images of Sucellus, the divinity carries a very curious attribute instead of the hammer or mallet usually in his possession. This strange implement has been given the name 'barillet' by French scholars, and there is no trans-

34 *Bronze figurine of hammer-god with 'barillet' from Vienne, Isère.* Paul Jenkins, after Boucher

lation in English: it consists of a shaft on top of which is a cylinder or barrel with rays or spokes at the ends of which are tiny barrel-like hammers. A good example of this occurrence is the bronze figurine from Vienne (Isère) (Fig.

34) where, significantly perhaps, the main 'barrel' is decorated with concentric circles.[156] The only stone example known to me is that on a sculpture at Dôle (Jura) where a similar 'barillet' is associated with a bird and a small wheel-symbol.[157] This is a curious hybrid of hammer, barrel and sun-wheel, and the only way it may be understood is by assuming that this compression of symbolism is deliberate. On Burgundian stone monuments the Celtic hammer-god frequently appears with a barrel, perhaps perceived as full of red wine, as a symbol of the fertility of the region and perhaps of resurrection (as an allegory of blood) and renewal. With the 'barillets' we may be seeing conflation of the striking power of the hammer, the well-being motif of the barrel and the potency and supremacy of the sun.

Axes bear no physical resemblance to the image of the sun, but there nonetheless appears to be a link between the symbolism of the axe and the sun from the Bronze Age. The double-axe so beloved of the Minoan period of Bronze Age Crete may have been a symbol of lightning.[158] Certainly oriental Baals, like Dolichenus and Hadad-Zeus, carry double-axes,

and they were storm-deities.[159] Bronze model axes were offered at the great Greek temples of Zeus at Dodona and Olympia at least as early as the tenth century BC.[160] It is also possible that the double-axe reflects regeneration. This idea may be associated with sacrifice and the release of the blood of the slain bull to fertilize the earth; in addition, the physical resemblance between the double-axe and the butterfly, with its apparent death and rebirth, could point to such a symbolism for this weapon.[161] If the double-axe was linked with lightning, then its solar connections may stem from the primitive attribution of the same origins for lightning and the sun.[162] Certainly in Bronze Age Europe both single- and double-axes were associated with solar motifs. Late Bronze Age axes were decorated with swastikas,[163] sun-wheels or the ubiquitous sun/water-bird motif (Figs. 35 and 36).[164] Hallstatt Iron Age axe-models may be associated with horse and circle motifs (Fig. 36),[165] and Romano-Celtic axe-models are often decorated with solar symbols: at the temple-site of Woodeaton (Oxon.), one axe-model is ornamented with a swastika, a second with a ligatured X and a

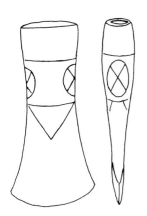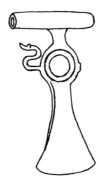

35 *Late Bronze Age axes with wheel- and swastika-decoration from north Italy*. Miranda Green, after Déchelette

36 *Hallstatt axe-models from north Italy (left) and Hallstatt*. Miranda Green, after Déchelette

third with a concentric circle. A recently discovered miniature bronze axe of Romano-British date, from the vicinity of the temple at Thornborough (Bucks.), is marked with three circles (Fig. 38).[166] Perhaps most significant of all is the Romano-Celtic pendant from Balèsmes (Haute-Marne) (Fig. 39),[167] which consists of a sun-wheel, lunar crescent and double-axe. Maybe here sun, moon and lightning or storm-energy are all combined in acknowledgement of the supreme power of the Celtic sky-god.

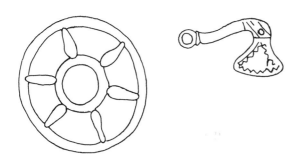

37 Bronze wheel- and axe-models from a child's grave. Dürrnberg, Austria. Miranda Green, after Pauli

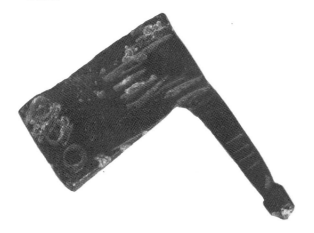

38 Romano-British miniature bronze axe decorated with circles from Thornborough, Bucks. Length of blade: c. 2.5 cm (1 in.). J. M. Cornwall, by permission of Mrs Shelagh Lewis

39 Romano-Celtic wheel-pendant, Balèsmes, Haute-Marne. Paul Jenkins, after Déchelette

Animals and the solar image

It is the rightful province of other chapters in this book to examine the meaning of animal-associates of the sun-cult in prehistoric and Romano-Celtic Europe. However, there is evidence that such a close link exists between solar and zoomorphic symbolism that sun and beast actually merge into a single solar motif. This is most striking in the depiction of stags, especially in rock-art where much was made of the visual connection between stags' pronged antlers and radiate sun-circles. Certainly, for the Bronze Age peoples carving on the rocks of Camonica Valley or southern Sweden, the stag seems to have played an important part in solar ritual (Figs. 7, 40). This may be partly due to the antler/sun connection in visual perception, but it may also be because the stag is virile, potent and aggressive during the rutting season and possesses enviable speed.

Aggression, dominance, fertility and swiftness may equally be qualities ascribed to the sun as a supernatural force.

This visual association between sun and stag begins in the Neolithic: in the Iberian passage grave of Carapito (Fig. 11) is found a stag with its head in the form of a rayed sun associated with two other sun-images.[168] A combination of antlers with a solar symbol recurs on a Neolithic rock-painting at Tajo de las Figuras in Spain (Fig. 5);[169] and stags and suns appear together incised on a copper pot at Las Carolinas (Fig. 12).[170] Bronze Age Iberian rock-art continues this theme: sun and antlers are conflated at Laxe da Rotea de Mende (Fig. 6).[171] But it is in the Bronze Age rock-art of north Italy and Scandinavia that stag and sun appear, from the imagery, to have been closely integrated in a consistent fashion. Stags pull sun-discs, like a horse drawing a cart, in Bohuslän,[172] and suns and stags frequently occur together at Camonica.[173] But even more evocative of the intense association is where antlers and sun are fused to form a solar-deer image. This happens at Kyrkestigen, Svenneby, in southern Sweden where stags are depicted with their antlers meeting in a rayed solar circle.[174] In the same area is the image of a stag in a ship with its antlers again curling together in a sun-symbol,[175] much as genuine solar motifs are associated with ships in this petroglyphic imagery (see Chapter Four). At Massleberg again the motifs of ship and deer are linked in a scene where the stag's antlers sprout a huge sun-motif;[176] and at Södra Ödsmäl, Kville, a man with a solar disc-body is attached to the antlers of one stag, while two other deer with enormous antlers pull a two-wheeled cart.[177] At Camonica in Italy, the conflated imagery is very similar: here the stag may penetrate the circle of the sun (Fig. 40).[178] Conflation between stag- and sun-imagery is strikingly displayed on the rock-art at Cemmo (Fig. 7); here the antlers on a stag's head are in the form of a radiate semi-circle, which exactly

resembles half the circumference of a rayed solar disc. Again, at Paspardo, either incomplete sun-circle or antlers may be depicted. On another image at Cemmo, a complete rayed circle is treated in a similar manner.[179]

40 *Rock-carving of stag and sun-disc from the Camonica Valley*. Paul Jenkins, after Anati

To a lesser extent, similar fusion may be found between celestial symbolism and the bull. This is more understandable in that the horns of a bull naturally evoke the sky-image of the moon's crescent. The bull possessed a persistent association with sky-cults in Greek religion from very early on, the rosette-shape on the foreheads of Minoan bull-statuettes in the early second millennium BC may provide evidence of a link between the bull and solar imagery. In later Graeco-Roman religion, the bull was the constant companion of Zeus-Jupiter.[180] If we return to the prehistory of barbarian Europe, there is occasional evidence of a visual association between the sun and the bull. This occurs on the Bronze Age rock-art of Mont Bego in the Alpes Maritimes, where bulls' heads are depicted with their horns meeting in a circle which may be solar.[181]

Horses, though inextricably bound up with the European sun-cult, are not usually themselves visibly solar. However, the image of the horse which draws the great Bronze Age solar cult-vehicle at Trundholm may evoke its close associations, in that the eyes of the beast have a distinctly 'solar' appearance, with deliberate patterning round the eye-sockets (Fig. 89).[182] Finally, in linking animals with sun-imagery, we should allude to the boar which, in Iron Age and Romano-Celtic contexts, is almost invariably depicted with erect dorsal bristles. On Iron Age coins,[183] boars are often shown associated with sun-symbols; some scholars[184] would see an actual connection between the dorsal spines and the rays of the sun, citing a Germanic myth in which a divine boar journeying to the lower world, shines brilliantly like the travelling sun.

The wheel

The spoked wheel is one of the most widespread and popular images of the sun and is sufficiently distinctive to be treated separately from other circular designs. It can be seen as either a solar circle with inverted rays or a radiate sun with central orb or nave, rays or spokes, and the surrounding nimbus of light, the felloe or wheel-rim. Wheels as sun-motifs are particularly characteristic of the later prehistory of temperate Europe. From the time that vehicles with spoked wheels were driven in central and western parts of Europe – from the beginning of the first millennium BC[185] – the wheels themselves came to be used as solar symbols. In the Classical world, writers made the equation between the wheel and the sun:

Stage-carpenter, when you want to send the wheel spinning aloft, say Hail, thou light of the sun.[186]

Then, in these circumstances, was not to be seen the sun's wheel soaring aloft with generous light.[187]

In Graeco-Roman religious thought, the sun was envisaged as an ever-moving object traversing earth by day and the lower regions at night.[188] The factor of motion as well as physical similarity would make the wheel a natural equation for the image of the sun. The situation is complicated by the image of the chariot of the sun-god, which was common in the Classical world and in other Indo-European cultures. Helios-Apollo is persistently represented, for example on Greek pottery, in a wheeled vehicle drawn by two or four horses, and thus there is a further association between wheels, movement and the sun. Horse and wheel are replicated images on a fragmentary Bronze Age silver band from the island of Syros near Delos, a depiction which Déchelette[189] would see as a prototype for European sun-chariots such as that at Trundholm. The sun as the eye of justice or Nemesis may account for the wheel seen suspended above the heads of Pluto and Persephone on fourth-century BC Greek vases from the area of Apulia in southern Italy.[190] The Roman Fortuna had a wheel of chance, its random spinning and stopping, like a roulette wheel, signifying the mutability of human affairs and the fickleness of Fate. But here also there may be a solar association, in that the very ancient Roman goddess Fors Fortuna had a festival at the time of the summer solstice.[191]

The equation of the sun and the spoked wheel may have come about partly because of the status implied by the latter. Ownership of a light, manoeuvrable, spoked-wheel vehicle drawn by the fleet and prestigious horse may have led to an association between secular and divine power. The factor of movement is characteristic of both wheels and the sun, and the horse would have seemed an appropriate beast to pull the solar chariots of Apollo in Greece and the sun-disc of the anonymous heliolatric deity honoured at Trundholm. The link between wheels and the image of the chariot provides a further possible aspect to the significance of wheels in celestial symbolism, in that it is often believed that the wheel could represent not simply the sun but also the rolling of thunder, caused by the chariot of the sun rumbling across the sky.[192]

One interesting feature of sun-imagery in prehistoric Europe is the occurrence of wheel-like symbols in Neolithic passage grave art (Figs. 4, 8, 10). These *cannot* be spoked wheels *per se* since they appear two millennia prior to the adoption of such objects in western Europe.[193] In later phases of prehistory there may be doubt as to whether sun or wheel is represented, but in Neolithic imagery the motif of a 'spoked wheel' has to imply the symbolism of either an abstract concept or the sun itself. Many of the Boyne and Breton passage graves are decorated with 'spoked wheel' type motifs in addition to the less equivocal radiate sun-images. At the Dolmen du Petit Mont in Brittany, the 'wheel' symbol is large, dominating the stone;[194] and Irish tombs are carved with a multiplicity of varied 'solar' motifs including circles, radiate patterns, sun-like rayed spheres and signs which precisely resemble spoked wheels.[195] The megalithic tombstone at Klein Meinsdorf is decorated with a ring-cross or four-spoked 'wheel' symbol, hands and feet,[196] as if here the deceased is represented in shorthand form together with the protective image of the sun to guide him on the dark path to the afterlife.

The abundant evidence for the sun-cult in Bronze Age Europe manifests itself above all in the symbolism of the wheel. Sometimes a full-size chariot could evoke solar imagery in the way its wheels were decorated: the vehicle at Coulon, Deux-Sèvres possessed wheels

41 Silver Iron Age coin with horse, sun and wheel from Bratislava, Czechoslovakia. Diameter: 2.7 cm (1.1 in.). Paul Jenkins, after Duval

with toothed ornamentation which, when they moved, would suggest a fiery solar effect.[197] The image of the sun shows itself above all in rock-art, sheet metalwork and jewellery, and the same traditions continued from the later Bronze Age Urnfield phase through to the Hallstatt Iron Age (see Chapter Four). Throughout this long period of time, vessels, pendants, armour and miniature wheels, from hoards and graves, all carry the recurrent symbol of the wheel (Figs. 48, 50). The dominance of this motif manifested itself also in the rock-art of Scandinavia and northern Italy.[198] The Celtic Iron Age saw the increased use of the wheel as an amulet, and we begin to see its association with a divinity. Wheel-models were buried with the dead (Fig. 37), being worn as talismans or apotropaic amulets during life. On Celtic coins, the sun

42 Plate from Gundestrup Cauldron, with wheel-god and attendant. Paul Jenkins

was persistently displayed as a true wheel (Figs. 41, 91). The iconography here is complicated since the prototype theme frequently chosen for the reverse of Celtic coins was that of Apollo's solar chariot, derived from coinage of Philip II of Macedon. The image undergoes schematic transformation in the hands of Celtic artists, and often a horse with a single wheel beneath is all that remains of the original Greek design. There is significant evidence here that wheels and sun-motifs are very closely linked: whilst some coins bear the image of a horse with a wheel below and a radiate sun above, on others (Fig. 91) the wheel and sun may change places and it is the wheel which soars aloft in the sky above the horse.[199] On a beautiful silver coin from Bratislava is the image of a horse with a triple phallus or teat – thus taking the depiction into the realms of the supranatural and the sanctity of triplism – with above it a large realistic wheel, with convex spokes, hub

and felloe, in the position of the sun (Fig. 41);[200] and a Thracian silver tetradrachm struck by the tribe of the Deroni displays a superb hybrid star-sun-wheel symbol with central orb, rays like spokes and the felloe as a series of dots which may also reflect the heavenly bodies which accompany the sun in the sky.[201]

Before we leave the Iron Age, we need to glance at the imagery of the Gundestrup Cauldron, for here we have an early glimpse of what may be a solar deity (see also Chapter Four): on one of the plates of the great silver cult-vessel, whose iconography is at least partly Celtic in theme,[202] is a god being offered half a large wheel by an acolyte or devotee (Fig. 42). Other more schematized wheels with petal-shaped or lobate spokes appear on the vessel in company with a female image: here solar symbolism is suggested by the tiny rays which surround the wheel-rims.

The wheel as a celestial symbol is attested

without any doubt by evidence from Romano-Celtic Europe. It is consistently associated with a Celtic version of the Roman sky-god Jupiter on more than 200 stone monuments,[203] where it is often held like a shield by images of sky-horsemen bearing thunderbolts and dedicated to Jupiter (Fig. 98). The Celtic character of these images is demonstrated by their distribution and by the fact that the Roman celestial divinity is neither a horseman nor is he manifested as a sun-god in Graeco-Roman iconography.[204] It is the function of other chapters to discuss the significance of the sun-god in the Celtic world. Here I will pick out a few points which are especially relevant to the solar symbolism of the wheel itself. An altar at Nîmes[205] bears the image of a wheel with slanting external rays or flames, as if a fast-moving, fiery wheel were depicted. One is reminded of the tale of St Vincent, a martyr who, commenting on pagan cults in Aquitania in the fourth century AD, observed a rite involving a flaming sun-wheel being rolled down a hillside,[206] presumably the original festival copied in Christian times for the celebration of the birth of St John the Baptist. Model wheels are common in Romano-Celtic contexts (Figs. 83, 85) and we now have independent evidence that miniature objects of many kinds had a sacred purpose, being repeatedly found in shrines.[207] Indeed a wheel-model found at the Roman *colonia* of Augst in Switzerland bears the fragment of a votive inscription (Fig. 83).[208] Some of these models and the sculptured representations also show features of interest: the rims of some models are toothed and jagged, as if to reflect the sun in movement;[209] others have pointillé decoration on the felloe, which would catch the light when turned.[210] Spokes and felloe may be ribbed or knobbed, again enhancing their solar appearance, and others are decorated with sun-flower-like motifs.[211] Certain of the stone wheels are equally 'solar' in appearance: at Bad Dürkheim in the Rhineland, a Roman quarry-face was carved, probably by indigenous workers, with incised swastikas, horses and wheels, of which some are on stalks, like the ceremonial ones of Bronze Age rock-art (below, Chapter Four) (Fig. 25). One of these wheels has external rays round the felloe.[212]

The amount of realism and non-realism in Romano-Celtic wheel-symbols varies considerably. Many wheel-brooches and some sculptured motifs are more 'sun-like' and less like true wheels. The four-spoked examples must be seen as schematic representations, since a genuine wheel made of wood and iron would need at least six or eight spokes to be viable. But there may be more realism in the Bronze Age four-spoked wheel-images since cast bronze wheels on Bronze Age vehicles could have just four spokes. On some Romano-Celtic stone cult representations, the spokes are depicted as impossibly wide or narrow.[213] Here only the *idea* of a wheel is present. But other cult wheel-images are very faithful to realism: on an altar dedicated to Jupiter and Silvanus at Aigues-Mortes in southern Gaul are two faithful copies of wheels with nave, spokes and felloe and even the shrunk-on iron tyre is carefully replicated.[214] One oddity is the wheel carved on a stone at Bois-de-la-Neuve-Grange (Bas-Rhin) (Fig. 43), whose spokes have curious antler- or branch-like extensions,[215] as if the stag-sun imagery of the Bronze Age rock-art is here repeated. The floreate solar symbolism alluded to earlier in this chapter is present not only on bronze wheel-models but on stone depictions also,[216] as if again there is conflation between the two solar images of wheel and flower.

The fact that many Romano-Celtic and earlier wheel-images are such true copies of functional wheels leads me to argue that in later prehistory and the Roman phase in Europe, the wheel as a cult-symbol has a significance as an image in its own right, as well as being a sun-motif. Great care is sometimes taken to portray a cult-wheel with accuracy.

So it may be that in some instances the wheel is representative of not only the sun but also a solar cart as well, a sun-chariot like that at Trundholm or the vehicle of Apollo-Helios in Classical imagery. The thunder-association of chariot-wheels trundling across the sky may also be valid. Apollo's chariot on a Greek red-figure vase is accompanied by a thunderbolt, and wheel and thunderbolt appear together consistently in Romano-Celtic imagery.[217] If, as some scholars believe,[218] the Gaulish Celts thought that thunderbolts were an emanation of the sun, striking and fertilizing the earth by inducing rain, then the very close affinity between wheel- and thunderbolt-images is entirely appropriate.

43 Romano-Celtic gravestone with sun-wheel/antler/tree decoration from Bois-de-la-Neuve-Grange, Bas-Rhin. Height: 31 cm (12 in.). E. R. Aldhouse, after Espérandieu

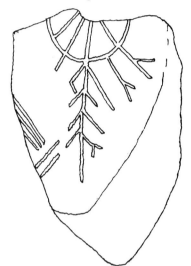

— 4 —
Cult and Ceremonial in Later Prehistory

The widespread adoption of metal-working in barbarian Europe at around the beginning of the second millennium BC coincided with the burgeoning of sun-imagery. Metals themselves were natural media for solar representation: both gold and new polished bronze gleam with a 'solar' brightness, providing an immediate link between the image and its medium. For whatever reason, people living in temperate Europe during the last two millennia BC found it important to invoke the sun: Gimbutas makes this point about the intensity and unequivocal character of Bronze Age symbolism:

> The sun-disc, the concentric circle, the wheel, the cross, the water-bird, the bull-horns, and the clattering pendants represent a gamut of 'celestial' symbolism, which is inseparable from the role of light, motion, and sound in symbolism, the functions of the sky-deities, the idea of the sun as a life-giving force, and the inextinguishability of life.[1]

We know, for instance, that the climate deteriorated during the course of the Bronze Age, becoming colder and wetter. Volcanic eruption in Iceland seems to have been, in part

at least, a causative factor, leading to widespread desertion of farmland found to be no longer viable, with consequential population movement and social dislocation. Perhaps these events, and the obscuring of the sun by dust and cloud, stimulated the propitiation of the sun, resulting from the fear that it would desert the earth and would fail to appear one morning, or provide spring and summer warmth and light one season.[2]

This chapter is concerned with the cult of the sun from the beginning of the Bronze Age until the end of the pre-Roman Iron Age in non-Mediterranean Europe, a period of about 2000 years. This is a long time, and in looking back at the evidence from a twentieth-century viewpoint, it is all too easy to be guilty of rushing, as Sprockhoff puts it, 'through the space and time of prehistory in seven-league boots'.[3] But, having admitted this danger, it is possible nonetheless to advance the counter-argument, equally valid, that religious practices are and were extremely conservative. People are perhaps more reluctant to alter belief-systems than any other part of material or spiritual culture. Neither in the present chapter nor in this book as a whole is a close continuity of cult or belief presented as an argument. But it is proposed that prehistoric communities continuously regarded such natural (or supra-natural) phenomena as the sun as forces to be appeased, invoked and venerated. Sometimes, the evidence for this reverence manifests itself in a consistently and intensely similar manner over more than a thousand years. To take just one example which we will meet later in this chapter, the images of the sun and the water-bird together first appear in the Urnfield period, about 1300 BC, but the two motifs are still sporadically present in the Gaulish Iron Age in the one or two centuries before Christ. The theme is too idiosyncratic to have been re-invented during the thousand-year period, and the implication must be that the motif of sun and water-bird evoked similar symbolism to both Urnfield and Iron Age communities.

Stonehenge: a temple of the Bronze Age

At the end of Chapter Two, we glanced briefly at the question of the solar significance of megalithic stone circles of the Neolithic. But it is during the earlier Bronze Age that the most famous stone circle, Stonehenge, blossomed into the kind of monument – albeit one of con-tinual change – that is such a familiar part of the landscape of Salisbury Plain. Stonehenge has frequently been claimed as a 'solar temple', and it is thus worth scrutinizing the evidence, divorcing it from the wilder realms of spec-ulation and fantasy, and assessing what can really be claimed about the symbolic signif-icance of this monument.

Stonehenge is unique in the world: its active use spanned a period from around the end of the fourth millennium to the end of the second millennium BC. Some 700 years after the origi-nal bank-and-ditch henge was built, a radical reconstruction took place in which about 80 bluestones from Preseli in Dyfed were set up to form two concentric circles, with the en-trance pointing towards the rising sun at its most northerly position at midsummer. At the same time, the original entrance to the earth-work was widened to match the new axis. This construction probably belongs to the Beaker phase. About a hundred years later, a new larger-scale sarsen stone structure was erected, ousting the unfinished bluestone set-tings of the earlier phase. The axis of the lin-telled circle and horseshoe of the new structure again pointed towards the midsummer sun-rise, and this orientation was further enhanced by two large stones set together in the earth-work entrance, of which only one, the so-called 'Slaughter Stone', survives. Next, about 20 of the bluestones from the setting dis-mantled at the end of the first Beaker phase were chosen to be erected in an oval setting on the line of the later bluestone horseshoe, but this was quickly abandoned and the oval set-ting demolished. But the final reconstruction of Stonehenge followed almost immediately: the uprights of the oval setting were re-set in a horseshoe and re-shaped to alternating forms of pillar and obelisk. The remaining unshaped bluestones were now erected in a circle of about 60 stones. In the latest phase, around 1100 BC, the sunrise-oriented Avenue, dating in origin to the very first stone phase of the monument, was extended to the River Avon.[4]

There is no doubt that the axis of the Early Bronze Age bluestone and sarsen settings of circles and horseshoes was deliberately, though roughly, pointed to where an observer standing in the centre of Stonehenge would see the sunrise on the longest day of the year. As Atkinson has commented,[5] a study of British Neolithic and Early Bronze Age stone circles suggests that their builders may have pos-sessed a precise knowledge of the way the directions of the sun's and the moon's rising and setting vary through time. So we may certainly go so far as to admit that there was some kind of solar alignment on the axis of which Stonehenge was built. But it is, I think, dangerous to go much further than this and to postulate exact scientific astronomical observations and the presence of sight-lines which could, for instance, predict eclipses of the sun and moon.[6] The trouble with any attempt to argue anything as detailed and complicated as this is the danger of reading too much into what may be chance. Stonehenge is too ruined for genuine and original sight-lines with the horizon to be recoverable with any certainty. Care, too, has to be taken not to conflate sites or elements of different dates. All that may have concerned ancient observers of the sun was the ability to watch positions of the rising and setting sun on the horizon, an annual circuit with the direction of sunrise and sunset varying from the northernmost limit at midsummer to the southernmost at midwinter. The four obvious positions for any ancient 'astronomer' to mark would have been the extreme limits of the rising and setting sun at the two solstices.[7] A 'sun-watcher' standing at the centre of Stonehenge[8] would thus have been able to calculate the correct time for festivals and ritual, and to advise farmers on the seasonal rhythm of their work.

So was the sun actually venerated at places like Stonehenge, or was it merely a convenient calendrical device? In a sense, this is a spurious question, since sacred and profane or secular activities were never entirely separate in pagan societies. But it would be an unimaginative and prosaic individual who could gaze at Stonehenge and not see, in that massive building with its soaring monoliths, an act of reverence and propitiation to supernatural forces. Observatory or not, Stonehenge may well have been a monument erected to honour the sun.

The sun and Bronze Age gold

Gold is the sun's metal: its shining yellow surface and untarnishable properties form an obvious link with the bright sphere in the sky. Pure gold is incorruptible (except in contact with mercury), easy to work, relatively rare and precious and, to societies who venerated the sun as a high supernatural force, gold would be a natural medium to choose for offerings to the solar power. At about the time that the great Beaker monument at Stonehenge was erected, in the early second millennium BC, the earliest Irish gold ornaments were being made, in the form of thin sheet-gold discs of 1–12 cm ($^1/_2$–5 in.) diameter (Fig. 22).[9] Similar discs have been found in Beaker contexts in southern Britain. At Mere Down in Wiltshire,[10] a small Beaker round barrow was raised over a grave cut into the chalk. Here two bodies were interred, a man and a woman in an attitude of embrace. With them was buried a Beaker assemblage of a copper knife, a slate bracer or archer's wristguard, a bone spatula and two gold 'button-caps' or disc-shaped dress-ornaments bearing cruciform decoration, probably made in the Wicklow mountains. Discs like these are often found in pairs and usually possess one or two central perforations: they were originally glued onto a backing as an ornament for buttons or clothing. The prototypes for the Irish discs were probably north European, but Taylor[11] has pointed to the decorative parallels between the Beaker discs and European racquet-headed pins of the central European Úňetice Culture. It is the decoration which has led to the supposition that these early gold discs may have been linked with a solar cult. Several, like the pair from Mere and another set from County Wexford[12] display a cross-in-circle motif, and others may have radiate lines or concentric circles; the Wexford discs have, in addition, a jagged pattern round the circumference which adds to the sun-like appearance. All this decoration certainly suggests a desire to imitate the image of the sun. All we can say is that such discs, worn on clothes, may have possessed solar talismanic properties in addition to their primary ornamental function.

Later in the Bronze Age, larger gold discs

were made, generally for mounting onto a bronze or other backing.[13] Once again, the discs of Ireland and northern Europe display an affinity indicative of a unity in tradition. The most spectacular of these objects is the gilt bronze disc mounted on the Danish Trundholm 'sun-chariot' (see below); at Tødsø Mors, also in Denmark, a gold disc was buried with a dead person in a wooden coffin.[14] Other similar discs appear, for example, at Moordorf in Germany (Fig. 44),[15] and at Lattoon, Co. Cavan, the latter perhaps made as late as the eighth century BC. These later discs differ from the Beaker ones in being much larger and clearly not meant as dress-ornaments. Indeed, we know from Trundholm that they could be used for a religious purpose. The decoration differs also, in that the early cruciform design gives way to compass-drawn or punched concentric circles. We have already seen in Chapter Three that circles as well as cross-in-circle or wheel-like motifs could represent the solar image.

The Trundholm disc is virtually unique in its association with a horse-drawn carriage (Fig. 45). But during the Bronze Age other gold imagery apparently links the solar motif with horses. There is a group of later Bronze Age north European gold bowls or cups, like those from Boslunde and Mariesminde (Lavindsgaard) in Denmark (Fig. 21),[17] which bear basal decoration in the form of concentric circles, radiate patterns, cruciform or spoked-wheel symbols. One of the gold cups found in the sheet-bronze vessel at Mariesminde is ornamented with an image resembling a five-spoked wheel or rayed sun surrounded by small concentric circles. This find is one of 11 similar handled bowls found as a hoard in a bronze container, itself decorated with the typical Urnfield solar motif of wheel and water-bird.[18] What is particularly significant about these gold vessels is that the 'solar' imagery on the body of the bowls is combined with long sinuous handles terminating in

44 *Bronze Age sun-disc from Moordorf, Germany. Diameter: c. 14.5 cm (5.7 in.).* Paul Jenkins, after Torbrügge

horses' heads. In Chapter Six the consistent association of horse and sun in European symbolism is discussed. If we recall the imagery of Trundholm with its horse-drawn sun-disc, the relationship between the horse and 'solar' symbols on the north European gold bowls may likewise suggest a cult-image of the sun linked to horse, even though here the objects may have a function as drinking-cups over and above their religious symbolism.

The other striking category of gold object which may well have been associated with a solar cult during the Bronze Age is a group of curious gold 'cones' or tall vessels, probably dating to around 1200 BC, decorated with horizontal bands of circles and wheel-shaped motifs (Fig. 24). One of these cones comes from Avanton (Vienne), ornamented with row upon row of circles.[19] The cone at Schifferstadt in Germany once contained aromatic gums[20], suggesting its association with some kind of religious ceremony. The most complete example is a tall, slim cone, 95 cm (37 in.) high, from Etzelsdorf near Nuremberg in

45 The Trundholm sun-chariot, Denmark.
Length: c. 60 cm (24 in.). By permission of the
Nationalmuseet, København

Bavaria.[21] This spectacular object, made of
beaten gold, is decorated with densely clustered rows of circles, triangles and wheel-
motifs. Exposed to the sunlight, the Etzelsdorf
cone would be dazzling to look at, the
repoussé ornament serving to enhance its
brightness: the row of wheel-suns would stand
out among the bands of decoration, and the
whole object, soaring towards the sky, would
have been a suitable offering to the sun, replicating its beams and bearing countless imitations of its image on its surface. It is easy to
imagine these shining gold cones being carried
in processions and dedicated in solar ceremonies, perhaps at particular times of the year
in order to propitiate the sun and to ensure that
it never failed its people. Such objects could
have been used to invoke the sun at the critical times: midwinter, when it was at its
most remote from the earth; spring, when the
presence of the sun was essential for crop-
germination and growth; and midsummer, to
encourage the yellowing corn and secure a
good harvest.

Carriages and cauldrons

In Chapter Three an attempt was made to explain the association of the imagery of the sun and the wheel. The physical resemblance between the two images makes the link an obvious one, and this correlation is strengthened by the property of movement common to them both. During the European Bronze Age, the association between the sun and spoked-wheeled vehicles forms a substantial part of our evidence for solar veneration. The adoption of spoked wheels in temperate Europe by the later second millennium BC[22] coincided with the use of miniature wheels as pendants, perhaps amulets,[23] and the connection between the image of the sun and the wheel was probably established at this time.

The solar wagon

It may have been the visual link between the wheel and the solar image which caused Bronze Age communities to envisage the divine sun as carried in a wheeled vehicle across the sky. In Chapter Six the concept of the solar chariot will be examined, and I have no wish to pre-empt that discussion here. Nevertheless we need to look briefly at some of the evidence since the tradition of the sun-carriage is rooted in part firmly within the cult-imagery of the north European Bronze Age. Sometime between 1400 and 1200 BC a ritual took place at Trundholm in Denmark, which involved the deliberate breakage and burial of a bronze horse-drawn wagon, bearing the image of the sun (Fig. 45). The Trundholm 'sun-chariot' is probably a miniature replica of a larger carriage driven in solar cult-processions and ceremonials, perhaps in an attempt to woo the sun in winter. The solar disc, gilded on one side and decorated with rays, circles and spirals, was mounted vertically on the wheeled platform and pulled by a slender horse.[24] The disc, with one shining and one dull, ungilded surface, is thought to represent the diurnal and nocturnal aspects of the sun. Later in this book (pp. 116–19) we shall see that the sun and the horse enjoyed a close association in ancient European religion. The swift horse was long considered a suitable means of conveying the sun across the sky, either on its back or pulled in a chariot. But one interesting feature of the Trundholm horse has only recently come to light:[25] this is that the animal, which was perhaps cast in central Europe,[26] is wearing a decorative head-harness or chamfrein, in imitation of a real one of leather and bronze. The Trundholm horse is one of the earliest pieces of evidence for the use of the chamfrein, which was a prestige-item of horse-gear; its presence here would appear to acknowledge the high status of this horse and its appropriateness to transport the divine sun across the heavens. Moreover, the specifically solar character of the beast is proved beyond doubt by the radiate decoration of the harness around its eyes (Fig. 89).

A final point about Trundholm concerns the imagery of the sun-disc carried on a horse-drawn wagon, and precisely what is being represented: is the chariot real, in that the sun is actually perceived as travelling in a vehicle, or is the cart present merely to reflect movement, the sun being conceptualized as rolling under its own momentum, like a wheel? The north European image of horse and sun-vehicle was not unique to Trundholm: apart from fragments of a similar carriage-model at Tågeborg in Scania,[27] Scandinavian rock-art presents the image of a two-wheeled wagon carrying the sun and pulled by a horse or deer.[28] Indeed, the gold 'sun'-decorated bowls with horse-head handles may be part of the same image-tradition (Fig. 21). The bronze 'sun-drum' at Balkåkra also in Scania may be another version of the wagon-borne sun.[29] This curious object consists of a cylinder, its top decorated like the sun, supported on ten model wheels. Traces of wear in the holes beneath the rim suggest that it was hung up, perhaps in a shrine to the sun-god, after it had been carried in ceremonial processions (Fig. 23). There is further late pre-historic evidence for a link between the sun, horses and wagons: the wheels of the sixth-century BC bronze-sheathed funerary wagon at Býčiskála in Czechoslovakia[30] had ribbed spokes which would catch the light when it rolled forward, and the sides of the vehicle were decorated with repoussé swastikas, themselves potent solar symbols. The carriage, covered in new bronze and drawn by horses, would surely have made a glittering spectacle, and the sun may well have been invoked here at the funerary rites of the dead person, whose corpse was conveyed to its grave on the wagon.

Vessels and weather-magic

The Urnfield cultural tradition of the later central European Bronze Age included persistent imagery which associated the sun-wheel with the water-bird. Urnfield culture was roughly coincident with the decline of Mycenaean power and lasted from about 1300 to 700 BC.[31] The most distinctive pattern of behaviour, which characterizes the Urnfield tradition for archaeologists, was the rite of cremation in urns in flat cemeteries, a custom which gives rise to the term 'Urnfield'. From the thirteenth century onwards, new sheet bronze-working techniques produced such objects as body-armour and large bronze vessels, prestige drinking-equipment used by the élite and possessing a ritual function.[32] This bronzework was frequently decorated with an idiosyncratic motif of a sun, presented as either a spoked wheel or a concentric circle, flanked or supported by water-birds or sailing in a bird-prowed and -sterned boat (Figs. 46 a and b). This motif gained prominence on both sides of the Alps, adopted by Villanovans living in north Italy and by bronzesmiths of central Europe. By means of the elaborate system of exchange of prestige metal goods, the motif of sun and bird travelled with the sheet-bronze vessels and other objects from central and

46a Urnfield sheet-bronze vessel, decorated with sun and bird-ship, from Mariesminde, Denmark. Height: 37.5 cm (14.8 in.). By permission of the Nationalmuseet, København

46b Interior of Urnfield vessel with sun-wheel and water-bird symbols from Siem, Denmark. By permission of the Nationalmuseet, København

western Europe to Scandinavia. Thus over a wide region containers adorned with this bird-ship-sun image formed part of the secular and religious repertoire of the later Bronze Age.[33] Certain variations may be distinguished within this general homogeneity of symbolism.

Danish *situlae* (buckets) like those at Siem or Mariesminde[34] display true bird-ships carrying realistic wheel-like suns; whilst on some of the Italian vessels the motif has degenerated into a circle flanked by S-shaped squiggles.[35]

There was an association, in terms of cult-function, between the Urnfield bronze vessels decorated with wheel-and-water-bird and a group of curious objects known as *Kesselwagen* or 'vessel-carts'. These belong to the same later Bronze Age phase and consist of cauldrons on wheels (Fig. 47), frequently with the water-bird symbol in the round. Of interest is that there is an Old Testament[36] reference to vessels on wheeled stands which were apparently part of the liturgical apparatus of Solomon's temple. In an Urnfield context, vessels may have carried the cremated remains of a dead individual, and they are often found in rich graves.[37] An example is the *Kesselwagen* at Orăštie in Romania, a cauldron on wheels with bird protomes (the head and neck only) attached to it.[38] Another container, at Acholshausen in Germany, carried on four wheels, has birds 'pulling' it at front and back.[39] There are many variations on the *Kesselwagen* wheel-bird theme: water-birds may sit on the axle or axle-pin of a miniature cart, sometimes with no vessel present; the birds may pull wagon-models or, indeed, form the body of the vehicle itself.[40]

The association between these *Kesselwagen* and the Urnfield *situlae* with repoussé wheel-bird imagery is clear: on both the elements of wheels, birds and container are normally present. The symbolism of wheels and birds is consistent. The bird-ship of the *situlae* may represent similar concepts to the bird-vessel of the *Kesselwagen*. The wheels of the latter may serve a dual function as transport and as solar symbols. It may well be that both the *situlae* and the *Kesselwagen* were used in weather-magic; as symbolic containers to encourage or collect or to drive away rain and propitiate the sun.[41]

47 *Bronze Age cauldron on wheels, Skallerup, Denmark.* Paul Jenkins, after Glob

The vessel-sun-bird image survived the Urnfield phase of central Europe and was still present when iron was first adopted by craftsmen and patrons (around 750–700 BC). The wealthy bronzework associated with cremation graves at the Hallstatt cemetery in Austria has given the cultural term 'Hallstatt' to particular types of object found all over Europe at the commencement of the iron-using phase of prehistory. In Grave 507 at Hallstatt itself, a vessel-stand was decorated in repoussé with wheels and water-birds in horizontal bands (Fig. 48);[42] and at Kleinklein, also in Austria, a bronze bucket-lid bears complex images of sun-wheels, circles and soldiers, cavalry and infantry (Fig. 18).[43] Interestingly, the footsoldiers have spiky, radiate hair and the manes of the horses are similarly treated, as if in imitation of the sun. Sometimes, the sun is represented alone: the cylindrical bucket at Kleinklein is ornamented with wheels picked out in dots,[44] and at Hallstatt a bucket-lid has knob-ended rayed suns as its principal decoration.[45]

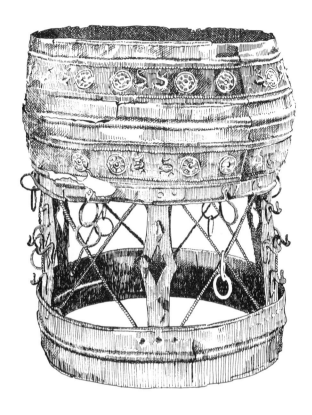

and north Italy. Hallstatt pottery, perhaps in imitation of metal vessels, frequently displays motifs of rayed suns, wheels or swastikas, sometimes in association with horses, people or birds (Fig. 17).[48] One Silesian pot bears a symbol which is an interesting combination of wheel and sun, a cross-in-circle but with external rays.[49] The earliest Iron Age Villanovan culture of Venetia (commencing as early as 900 BC) has produced pots with the ubiquitous dual symbol of sun-wheel and water-bird, evidence of the consistent communication between northern Italy and central Europe.[50]

So containers in the European Bronze and earliest Iron Ages were repeatedly decorated with very specific solar symbols, frequently accompanied by water-birds. We have seen that, on some *situlae*, this imagery takes the form of a bird-ship carrying the sun. So instead of a sun-chariot, we have water-travel, perhaps the conveyance of the sun over the sea at night (see Chapter Six, pp. 115–16). We will see soon that in Scandinavian rock-art, the sun and ships are recurrently associated. Sometimes the water-bird alone represents the connection between sun and water, which is

48 Hallstatt sheet-bronze container decorated in repoussé with wheels and birds. Height: c. 32 cm (12.5 in.). Paul Jenkins, after Torbrügge

Apart from the large sheet-bronze containers, smaller metal and pottery vessels repeat the solar theme during the Hallstatt and later Iron Age: often the water-bird image is present as well. Hallstatt bronze bowls may be ornamented with wheels, rayed or concentric circles.[46] We should mention, too, the unique sixth-century BC gold bowl from Altstetten, Zürich[47], which bears images of deer, suns and crescent moons (Fig. 49). Stags were closely associated with solar cults, and we will later observe the very direct links between the two images seen in the rock-art of Scandinavia

49 Sixth-century BC gold bowl decorated with deer, suns and moons from Altstetten, Zürich. Diameter: 25 cm (10 in.). By permission of the Schweizerisches Landesmuseum, Zürich

already present in the form of the container it-self. It is possible that the two properties of flight and swimming intrinsic to a water-bird give the image the symbolism of linking upper and lower worlds, the elements of air and water. Thus the sun is seen to possess dominion over both and to have power over weather and all aspects of life. The derivation of the sun-water-bird theme is obscure: maybe the tradition owes something to Mediterranean influence, in that the swan belonged to Apollo and this deity possessed a solar function within the Greek pantheon (at least from the fifth century BC and perhaps much earlier). The white swan with its wide wing-span is, in any case, an appropriately 'solar' bird.

Ornaments and talismans

Throughout the first millennium BC and for some centuries before, there is archaeological evidence for the use of solar imagery as a motif both on functional objects and in personal ornaments. I would argue that the symbol of the sun was being employed as a talisman or amulet, to avert the forces of evil and to bring good luck to the wearer or owner of the object decorated with the sun's image.

Armour, weapons and other implements were endowed with solar symbolism from the later Bronze Age to the end of the pre-Roman Iron Age. Urnfield body-armour often bore the familiar motif of the sun-wheel and water-birds: a good example is the bronze greave of the eleventh century BC from Rinyaszentkirály in northern Hungary, decorated with two sun-wheels each flanked by two water-birds (Fig. 50).[51] Hallstatt belts may bear wheels, swastikas, water-birds, horses and stags as motifs,[52] all of which are solar or associated with the sun-cult. At Kaltbrunn in Germany, a sixth-century bronze belt-plate bears repoussé lines of horses and radiate suns.[53] The carvings on the early first-century AD arch at Orange display helmets and cuirasses bearing wheel-

shaped amulets (Fig. 51);[54] and on a Celtic coin at Marseille, a helmeted head is depicted with a similar solar talisman.[55] It is worth noting Sprockhoff's remark: '...the appearance on Celtic helmets of a wheel-motif which, isolated on a flat surface, almost seems like the emblem of a secret society'.[56] Other Celtic sculpture, like that of the warrior from Fox-Amphoux in Provence,[57] shows the recurrent use of the sun-wheel as a talisman against wounding. Offensive weapons, too, may be marked with the efficacious symbol of the sun: a Hallstatt grave yielded an iron dagger with its gilded hilt in the form of two adjacent wheels,[58] and in a La Tène inhumation, also at Hallstatt, an iron and bronze sword-sheath bears motifs of two men confronting each other holding a wheel between them.[59]

50 Urnfield sheet-bronze greave from Rinyaszentkirály, Hungary. Miranda Green, after Gimbutas

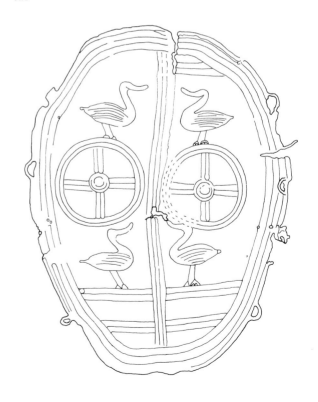

Another La Tène sword, at Allach in Bavaria bears sun- and moon-motifs,[60] and both solar and lunar images are depicted on an Iron Age anthropomorphic-handled dagger at Kastel.[61] Knives found as far apart as Bronze Age Scandinavia and Iron Age Italy bear the symbol of the sun: Scandinavian later Bronze Age knives are frequently decorated with swan-heads and solar wheels; one has a miniature wheel attached to the tip of its blade;[62] another, at Vester Lam in North Jutland, bears the incised image of the sun pulled by a horse,[63] as if in recollection of the solar carriage at Trundholm. A variation on this theme forms the incised decoration on a Danish razor at Laaland, Ketting, where a bird pulls the sun-disc, and part of the implement is itself formed of a stylized bird-head.[64] Far to the south, an Iron Age knife-sheath from Lake Garda near Verona, with a solar design, demonstrates the persistence of this tradition.[65]

Personal jewellery from the Middle Bronze Age to the end of the Iron Age displays the same predilection for imagery based on the sun-wheel, sometimes with the accompanying water-birds. As early as 1500 BC, pins consisting of a long shank and vertically-mounted head in the form of a spoked wheel were worn and buried often in female graves, in pairs (Fig. 52). Their main *floruit* was in the Middle Bronze Age[66] but they occur sporadically into the later Bronze Age and even the Iron Age.[67] The main homeland of these European wheel-pins is the Middle Rhine and Lower Main, but they were widely adopted in France; we should remember also that wheel-pins appear

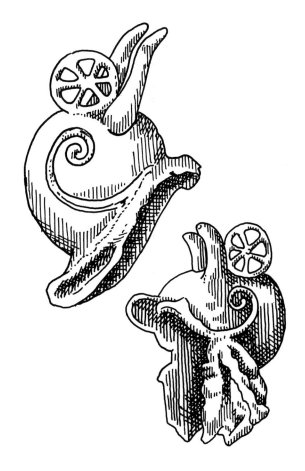

51 Iron Age helmets decorated with solar-wheel amulets carved on Orange arch. Paul Jenkins, after Ross

52 Bronze Age wheel-headed pin from Haguenau Forest. Length: 24 cm (9.78 in.). Miranda Green, after Gaucher

in Greek contexts towards the close of the second millennium BC.[68] Sepulchral finds in Germany and France during the Middle and later Bronze Age are common, as in the grave at Baiersech in south Germany.[69] In the context of graves, one interesting discovery made at the 'hypogée de Saran' (Marne) was that someone in the Bronze Age engraved a wheel-headed pin on the wall of a Late Neolithic Seine-Oise-Marne tomb.[70] It is impossible to be sure that wheel-pins held any solar significance at all, but there is some circumstantial evidence to support such a claim. First, the wealth of sun-symbolism in the European Bronze Age must be borne in mind. In addition, Gimbutas[71] has pointed to Tumulus Culture pins with disc-heads bearing decoration in the form of spirals, circles, swastikas and stars, which may reflect similar traditions. Finally, there is the irrefutable evidence of a ritual concerning some of the wheel-pins, whereby before they were interred with the corpse, the shank of the pin was broken off and the wheel-head alone accompanied the deceased to the underworld: this occurred, for instance, at Mühltal in Germany,[72] and it is possible that the idea behind such an act was the enhancement of the solar symbolism of the pin when its owner died.

During the Urnfield and Hallstatt phases of European prehistory, people wore pendants of which the essential element was the miniature sun-wheel. They hung from belts, as in a hoard at La Loubière (Hautes-Alpes),[73] and in a grave at Cremieu (Isère).[74] Some pendants were complicated, like the Urnfield example from Hungary with two water-birds, five wheel-models, rattles and chains (Fig. 53),[75] and the sun and bird ornament at Rimaszombat in Czechoslovakia.[76] Simpler sun and bird-ship motifs appear on such Late Bronze Age pendants as those from Charroux (Allier) and Ferté Hauterive (Fig. 54),[77] and at the Grünwald cemetery in Germany.[78] Pendants of Hallstatt date exhibit the same imagery:

53 Urnfield bronze pendant with wheels and birds from Hungary. Diameter of wheels: c. 3 cm (1.2 in.). Miranda Green, after Kossack

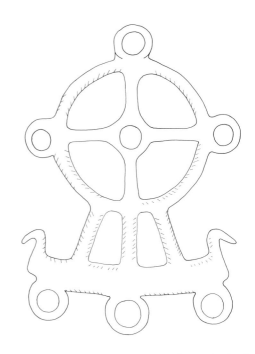

54 Late Bronze Age pendant in form of wheel and bird-ship from Ferté Hauterive, France. Diameter: c. 4 cm (1.5 in.). Miranda Green, after Gaucher

a pectoral ornament from Forêt de Moidons (Jura) was made up of an openwork rectangular band with rings, seven-spoked wheel-suns and with a duck or swan at each end of the rectangle;[79] and an Iron Age pendant at Naix (Meuse) has five miniature four-spoked wheels hanging from it.[80] During the Iron Age pins, brooches and torcs were given solar imagery: Villanovan brooches were decorated with swastikas[81] and, as far apart as Suippes in the Marne region of France and Stradonice in Czechoslovakia, brooches were worn hung with miniature sun-wheels.[82] A swan's neck pin found at Danes Graves in Yorkshire has its ring-head in the form of a coral-inlaid wheel.[83] Bronze torcs (necklets) in the Marne area, at Pogny and Catalauni[84] bear the old Urnfield images of sun and water-birds (Fig. 55); and in a La Tène grave at Nemejiče in Czechoslovakia was buried a miniature wheel-amulet on which perch water-birds (Fig. 56).[85]

55 Iron Age bronze torc with sun and bird decoration from Somme-Taube, Marne. Diameter of torc: 20 cm (7.9 in.). Miranda Green

56 Iron Age chain jewellery decorated with wheels and birds from grave at Nemejiče, Czechoslovakia. Paul Jenkins, after Déchelette

Wheel-models also formed the central image of certain curious Early Iron Age rattles and chains, which may have taken part in solar cult-ceremonial, as attachments to maces or ritual staffs carried by priests: one of these was buried in a grave in the Hallstatt cemetery;[86] another at Libna bei Krsko in Yugoslavia consisted of a wheel with hand-amulets suspended from it, attached by a chain to the head of a mace-like object:[87] we saw earlier (Chapter Three) that the hand as a symbol may have had an affinity with the cult of the sun.

Miniature wheels of metal and clay began to appear in central Europe from about 1500 BC;[88] some at least may have been solar amulets. Pare[89] sees a development of models during the Bronze Age from naturalistic wheel-depictions to a more amuletic design. There is some validity in this, but many Late Bronze Age and Iron Age miniature wheels are very realistic, as if the concepts of genuine wheel and sun-symbol were very closely allied. Bronze models in the Late Bronze Age occur frequently in hoards,[90] or in sepulchral contexts: a woman was buried in the Grünwald cemetery with seven five-spoked wheel-sun models and a four-spoked example with a ring threaded through it.[91] Clay wheel-miniatures, together with human- or bird-images, occur on Urnfield and Hallstatt sites,[92] probably not to be seen as amulets but perhaps rather as votive objects for offering in shrines or tombs.

Whilst Bronze Age wheel-models from hoards or graves are often clearly part of belts or ornamental pendants, in La Tène Iron Age contexts, they may occur in quantities but with no evidence for their use. Thus, their ubiquitous presence at *oppida* all over the Celtic world is enigmatic: they may have been worn, but they were probably votives, offered as tokens of veneration, perhaps to a sun-god who only manifested himself fully during the subsequent Romano-Celtic phase (Chapter Five). *Oppida* in Czechoslovakia, like Třísov[93] and Hradiste[94] have produced realistic models,

but sometimes[95] the rim or felloe may have denticulation, in imitation of solar rays. This happens also at Fully in Switzerland, where a model has its nine spoke-ends jutting beyond the felloe.[96] People living in *oppida* like Manching in Bavaria,[97] Bibracte and Alesia in France[98] wore or dedicated miniature wheel-sun images, and at the Dürrnberg in Austria, a young girl was buried with axe- and wheel-models (Fig. 37),[99] perhaps to light her way and protect her from harm in the otherworld; certainly she had not enjoyed good fortune in this life, in that she died when she was ten years old or younger, and had always been stunted. Many La Tène individuals were buried with solar images: at Basel[100] and Wederath,[101] there were major Iron Age and early Roman cemeteries where often the only grave-goods found accompanying each corpse were single tiny wheel-models. Unequivocally votive are models from temples: at the Late Iron Age and Gallo-Roman site of Lavoye (Meuse) quantities of lead wheelets were found in what was probably a shrine.[102] At Villeneuve-au-Châtelot (Aube), a double-ditched rectangular sanctuary contained Gaulish and Roman money and numerous lead, bronze and silver wheel-models.[103] These temple-finds prove the religious nature of some wheel-representations. For more positive evidence of an association between the wheel, the sun and divine forces, we have to look forward to the less equivocal imagery-traditions of Romano-Celtic Europe (Chapter Five).

The symbolism of rock-art

One of the most evocative groups of evidence for the veneration of the sun in prehistoric Europe is in the great palimpsest of imagery presented by the rock-art of Scandinavia and north Italy. Here solar symbols are just one of a vast range of motifs which were carved on the rock surfaces. The Scandinavian art, found above all in Denmark and on both the Swedish and the Norwegian sides of Oslo Fjord, cannot be dated more closely than between 1500 and 400 BC, but 1000 BC may be used as a central dating-point. Certainly there are links between motifs on the rocks and Bronze Age metalwork designs.[104] The art was not placed at random; flat, sloping rock surfaces were chosen, often crossed with water-channels; the images are frequently clustered, leaving blank spaces, sometimes apparently to avoid the water-runs. The carvings were associated with populated areas of good arable land, sometimes close to the sea, not in inaccessible mountain areas, unlike the north Italian, Camunian petroglyphs. The north European artists probably belonged to farming or cattle-breeding communities, though they would probably themselves have been specialists. There is a spatial relationship between the carvings and graves, and it is probable that large areas of art functioned as religious centres for local groups.[105]

If we are to assess the role played by the sun in rock-art, we need first to examine the status of these images as a whole, in terms of their purpose. It is necessary to consider the petroglyphs within the context of the society they belonged to rather than as an isolated entity. Certainly the art is symbolic; the pictures

57 Bronze Age rock-carving with multiple sun-wheels from Lille Strandbygård, Bornholm. Paul Jenkins, after Glob

do not describe reality but consist of sets of limited, special images. We have to be careful, though, not to equate symbolism with religion in this context. Symbols were and are fundamental to human society, providing a reference system and a means of communication by pictorial language.[106] It may be argued that the art could be symbolic without being religious, but the preferred view is that, like some Palaeolithic cave-art,[107] the messages conveyed by rock-art may be a semiological means of addressing supernatural powers, perhaps in order to increase the efficacy of cult ceremonies.[108] Bahn has suggested that Palaeolithic art depicted spirit-creatures, and that the water running down rocks played a positive role in linking the spirit-world with that of earth.[109] The same may be true of Scandinavian Bronze Age rock-imagery, which chose water-channelled surfaces, but did not encroach on the water-runs themselves. In trying to interpret imagery on rock-art, we have to take care not to link symbols which may be chronologically separate: sometimes images may have been added to a rock surface over centuries, creating a palimpsest which it does not make sense to treat as a related set of motifs. What we have to do, therefore, is to look for repeated image-associations. If, for example, we find ships and suns recurring together on a number of rocks in different localities, it is probably valid to treat these as genuinely linked symbols.

That the sun was frequently depicted in Scandinavian rock-art is not in doubt. But we must not overestimate the importance of the solar image in terms of its veneration: it is only one motif among many. However, the apparent swing towards sun-cults in the European Bronze Age which can be distinguished in metalwork, and which may have come about because of the worsening climate, could account for the repeated presence of the sun in Scandinavian rock-imagery.

One Danish sun-decorated rock has gone down in folklore as having retained its symbolic potency into modern times: the story is that a stone at Venslev, decorated with three pairs of solar signs, was blasted by farmers because it was in the way of fieldworking. But the complete rock flew up into the air and then miraculously came to rest intact and with its pictures upside-down, magically protected by the supernatural powers of its images.[110]

In Scandinavian rock-carvings, the sun is depicted alone or associated with other images. Sometimes it appears as a true wheel, usually with four spokes, and sometimes as a circle, radiate, plain or with a central dot (Fig. 25).[111] Cart-wheels and suns may be portrayed identically,[112] and where two or four wheels are grouped wagons rather than suns may be intended. In any case, the two symbols may be closely allied, as we have seen. The interpretation of circles or 'wheels' alone is equivocal in terms of whether solar images are intended. Görmann[113] would link the wheel-signs on the rock-art with Urnfield bronzes, which are of broadly similar date.

In Denmark, the island of Bornholm has produced a large concentration of wheel-carved stones,[114] several found in or near burial-mounds. The rock at Lille Strandsbygård has no less than 12 wheel-signs[115] and virtually no other motifs (Fig. 57). Often the Danish rocks present the ambiguity of whether suns or wheels are intended, but at Fjerritsler[116] a four-spoked 'wheel' sign has external solar rays; and at Engelstrup a scene is portrayed which may well relate to solar worship: here a man and a woman raise their arms in homage towards a circle between them.[117] The cult-character of the 'sun-discs' is clearer on some of the Oslo Fjord concentrations of rock-art, especially in Östergotland in southern Norway and the Bohuslän region of south Sweden. Some discs in these areas resemble suns, others are more truly wheel-like, but one distinctive feature is that the discs are often depicted carried by people, as at Solberg

58 Bronze Age rock-carvings with suns and ships from Bohuslän. Paul Jenkins, after Gelling and Davidson

in Østfold, where a man holds up a dotted circle in his hand,[118] and some are on stands with one or more legs (Fig. 25).[119] The implication is that these images are imitations of wooden discs, perhaps replicas of the sun carried on ceremonial or ritual occasions.

Repeated associations of 'sun-discs' and other images strengthen the notion that the sun played a significant role in cults represented in Scandinavian rock-imagery. Three groups are particularly distinctive in this regard: the disc associated with ships, with animals and with human figures.

One of the most repeated composite motifs on north European rock-art consists of the ship and the sun-disc (Figs. 58, 59), and the association between these two images on Bronze Age metalwork springs immediately to mind. Wheel-like suns appear above or beneath

ships, or they may be attached to the vessels in some manner (Fig. 60). Above a ship-figure at Massleberg, Bohuslän, is a huge star-like image which cannot be anything but a sun-burst, associated with lur (trumpet) players.[120] A rock at Herrestrup in Denmark is carved with a flotilla of six ships with a large sun hanging above them (Fig. 59),[121] and this relationship is repeated time and again.[122] At Madsebakke on Bornholm, a ship is shown associated with a complicated solar image consisting of a four-spoked wheel surrounded by a ring of dots, as if to represent the sun circled by other heavenly bodies. The sun-disc may be beneath the ship,[124] as if reversing the image on bronze vessels, where the ship carries the sun. Often the solar motif is actually attached to the boat in some manner: the disc may be on a stand or stalk which rises from the hull of the ship,[125] or

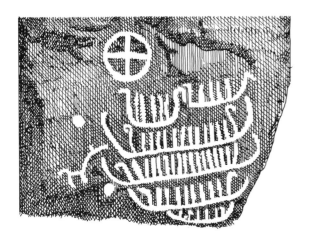

59a Bronze Age rock-carving with ships, sun and horse from Herrestrup, Denmark. Paul Jenkins, after Glob

59b Carving with ship and suns on stands from Egely, Bornholm. Paul Jenkins, after Glob

attached to the gunwale of the vessel.[126] At Bjornstad in southern Norway are three ship-carvings, the largest boat being over 4 m (13 ft) long; this ship has a sun-disc attached to the prow,[127] as if it is being pulled along by the sun's power. Sometimes ship and sun-wheel are linked with animal-imagery. At Massleberg, a ship is associated with a deer from whose antlers springs a huge sun-symbol; and a rock-painting at Allesby, Kville in the same area of Bohuslän displays a composite deer-ship with an antlered head forming the prow and stern.[128] Horse-drawn suns accompany ships at, for example, Kalleby in southern Sweden (Fig. 61)[129] and at Madsebakke on Bornholm.[130]

The ship is the commonest associate of the sun-disc in Scandinavia.[131] At Kalnes, Østfold, in Norway, a carving depicts many ships, suns and animals on a smooth sloping rock face. The ships here are clearly representations of hide-boats, but some may be winter-sledges

60 Bronze Age rock-carving of ship bearing sun on stem from Hornes, Østfold, Norway. Miranda Green

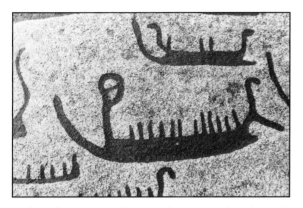

rather than water-borne ships; maybe there is deliberate portrayal of summer and winter travel, perhaps tying in with a fertility ritual, where ships were carried round the fields in spring. Conveyance of the sun forms an important part of prehistoric imagery, whether drawn by horses or carried in boats. The idea behind the symbolism may have been the magical assurance that the sun would reappear in spring and by day, and that the enactment of a cult-drama is displayed in the carvings. Whatever the precise nature of the relationship between sun and ship, it is clear that both played a crucial role in the symbolism. The ship may carry or be carried by the sun, and it is clear that for some, probably fertility, ritual, the presence of both sun and water was necessary. The frequency of ship-pictures must mean that the sea figured largely in people's lives, and it is worth noting that, in the area of Bohuslän, the Bronze Age coastline had many inlets, and the rock-exposures in the associated low-lying land, for instance in the region of Tanum, were used intensively for rock-art. By contrast, in the land-locked Camonica Valley of north Italy (see below) ship-images are absent.

61 Bronze Age rock-carving with ship and horse pulling sun-wheel from Kalleby, Bohuslän. Paul Jenkins, after Glob

Horses and stags and other indeterminate animals are frequent companions of the sun-disc. The animal pulling a wheel-symbol on a pole at Kalleby, Bohuslän (Fig. 61), may be a horse drawing a sun, or a wagon, or both concepts may be conflated.[132] At Madsebakke on Bornholm, a ship carries a horse-drawn disc[133] as if here the sun were transported by both land and sea; and at Lilleborge near Frederikstad in Norway, the ship, horse and sun are again associated.[134] Stags have a complicated relationship with the solar image: the presence of antlers made it natural both for the sun's rays and the antlers sometimes to be merged into a single composite image. Thus at Massleberg[135] a huge sun springs from the antlered head of a stag, and another beast, possibly also a deer, has a four-spoked wheel attached to its nose.[136] At Fossum, Tanum a deer is depicted with enormous sun-like antlers; and there are numerous instances of discs with antler-like motifs projecting from the rim.[137] In a complex scene depicted at Södra Ödsmäl in Bohuslän, a man whose body is in the form of a solar disc is attached to the antlers of a stag.[138] One of the Massleberg rock-panels includes a stag with huge spreading antlers hunted by a disc-bodied man and surrounded by dogs. Composite sun-antler imagery is something we will see repeated at Val Camonica, where deer and sun possessed a strong affinity in the Bronze Age. As with the Camunians, the Scandinavian artists seem to have perceived a visual link between antlers and solar rays and thus the stag is adopted as an appropriate associate of the divine sun. Like the horse, the stag is sufficiently virile and fast to accompany the solar force and to be intimately connected with it. The hunt-scene at Massleberg may display a cult-drama in which the sun is magically ensnared and controlled by its human subordinates.

Perhaps the most curious sun-imagery is that of the 'disc-men', which are characteristic of the rock-art around Oslo Fjord, especially in Swedish Bohuslän (Fig. 62). The images are of male human figures, frequently ithyphallic and bearing weapons, with the central portion of their bodies replaced by a sun-disc,[139] which may either be in the form of a spoked wheel or a concentric circle.[140] Sometimes the head instead may be in the form of a circle or wheel;[141] on a figure at Østfold, south Norway both the head and the body are replaced by wheel-shapes;[142] and at Uppland[143] the disc has human legs as the only anthropomorphic element present.

Two features stand out above all: one is the very frequent ithyphallicism of the figures; the other is their recurrent possession of weapons – spears, swords or long-shafted axes. Indeed the two elements of sexuality and aggression – phallus and weapons – are closely linked, and it is impossible, perhaps deliberately so, to distinguish sword from phallus unless both are present. Often spears and axes are of exaggerated size.[144] Sometimes the two disc-men confront each other, brandishing their weapons.[145] These exchanges may represent ritual combat, perhaps beween winter and summer: this may be true especially if a radiate or spoked-disc man faces a concentric circle-bodied opponent. But these are confrontations of equals, not struggles between strong and weak: it is the combat itself rather than the result which is important. As well as conflict, there is apparently comradeship between disc-men; at Kville, two 'solar' figures seem to be reaching out to each other.[146] The disc-men may be associated with other images which are linked to solar motifs: weapon-bearing men with sun-bodies occur with ships.[147] We have already noted the disc-man with his hunted stag at Massleberg and attached to a set of antlers at Södra Ödsmäl.[148]

So there is a repeated association between disc-men, ships, stags, weapons and potency. All of these motifs may be connected with fertility-ritual: at Finntorp, Tanum a wheel-bodied man appears to copulate with a woman with long hair (Fig. 63),[149] strengthening the association. But it is possible that where disc-men are ithyphallic, this may not always signify fertility: instead the imagery may convey simply the message of 'man' or 'warrior', in a kind of code similar to that seen in the exaggerated calf-muscles of some rock-art men, giving the image of strength for running or fighting.[150] But what do the disc-men actually represent? Some scholars would argue that the 'sun-discs' are no more than representations of shields; but this cannot be so in many examples where both arms are depicted free. Sometimes disc-men hold up large discs on stands,[151] as if to emphasize their solar role. Other images, of discs on stands, which cannot represent humans or gods, have anthropomorphic features added.[152] Maybe the most plausible explanation for these sun/man images is that some represent imaginary figures associated with the cult of the sun, and others may be portrayals of living worshippers bearing the insignia of the solar force (Figs. 62 and 64).[153]

Anthropomorphic individuals without disc-bodies may nonetheless possess other solar features: many male figures have enormous outspread hands[154] which resemble suns or stars. At Skivum in Denmark, a human hand actually forms the continuation of the spokes of a solar wheel-symbol.[155] One image at Litsleby, Tanum has hands like suns or trees, and in the association of tree- and sun-motifs at Solberg, Østfold, in Norway we may be witnessing either a visual connection between branches and rays (as already observed with antlers) or a conceptual relationship between the sun and trees as fertility symbols. Taken as a whole, the disc-men or 'sun-men' exhibit powerful and complicated imagery: they are warriors and sexually potent; they are intimately connected with the sun; their identities as humans merge with that of the solar force. In one sense the imagery displays a personal relationship between man and the sun: the source of heat and light is not here

a remote sphere in the sky but an integral part of life on earth. To demonstrate and foster this close kinship, ceremonies took place where the sun was perceived in human form, or his worshippers could emulate his image in veneration of his omnipotence.

Camonica Valley

The second main region of Europe whose rock-art is significant for its sun-symbolism is Val Camonica near Brescia in north Italy (Fig. 19), The valley's situation is very different from the Scandinavian locations in that it lies in the inaccessible heart of the Italian Alps.

62 Bronze Age rock-art with 'sun-men' from Bohuslän. Paul Jenkins, after Gelling and Davidson

It is one discrete area in difficult, mountainous country, a pass used by animals and an important hunting region for the Camunians. The entire valley was perhaps sacred for three millennia,[156] with many images being superimposed one on the other through time. The earliest rock-carvings are probably Neolithic, and not until the first century BC, just before the Romans occupied the area (16 BC) did the tradition of engraving wane and die out. If one looks at the whole range of images, it is possible to discern that more than three-quarters of them involve the sun or the stag (more than a hundred scenes depict the sun in some form), and certainly during the Bronze Age these two concepts were clearly central to Camunian religion.[157] In the Neolithic, the images on the rocks were simple, the sun appearing as a radiate, plain or 'spoked' disc,[158] perhaps adored by one or two persons (Fig. 2). We have to remember that in the Neolithic and Early Bronze Age, wheel-like discs cannot represent spoked wheels as such, and thus a solar interpretation is all the more likely. In the earlier part of the Bronze Age, sun-images began to be associated with other motifs, like the stag: there are paired suns, with inner and outer rays, as if day and night are represented.

64 *'Sun-man' and female on Bronze Age rock-carving from Slänge, Sweden. Paul Jenkins, after Glob*

63 *Bronze Age rock-carving of disc-man copulating with female from Finntorp, Sweden. Paul Jenkins, after Briard*

It is during the second and the early first millennium BC that the depictions become more meaningful in terms of religious beliefs: the association between the stag and sun, seen in the Scandinavian repertoire, is very strong here. However, in many respects, the imagery of the two regions is very different: Camonica has no 'disc-men' and the ship was not central to the Camunians' cult. Instead, hunting and fertility are the main themes, and the stag assumes a far greater significance than in northern Europe. Many of the scenes at Camonica display great intimacy between solar and stag-images: the great Zurla rock depicts a being (sometimes interpreted as a god) pushing a solar disc towards an immense stag which is surrounded by smaller animals.[159] Maybe here the union of sun and stag in the art may magically promote a proliferation of beasts which can be hunted or tamed.[160] Visually, the link between antlered stag and sun is extremely close: the animal may be depicted penetrating and merging with the circle of the sun (Fig. 40);[161] the rock-sites at Paspardo and Cemmo have several antler-suns, where an open rayed circle resembles antlers and, when closed, becomes the sun (Fig. 7).[162] There are further similarities between the Scandinavian and Camunian rock-imagery: on the 'sun-rock' at Paspardo,[163] the solar circle is set on a tripod-like stand. Human figures associated with the sun may be ithyphallic, though not disc-bodied. In one scene, a man's erect phallus has a four-spoked wheel-sun attached to its tip (Fig. 66);[164] in the imagery of the Bedolina rock, an armed warrior, surrounded by animals, carries a solar symbol on the top of his spear.[165]

As the Camunian cults evolved, from the Neolithic to the Iron Age, a certain progression may be discerned. The simple scenes gave way to more varied imagery, perhaps evocative of a formalization in solar and other ritual. Many carvings demonstrate that the Camunians had complex ceremonies and festivals, involving processions and dances: one Bronze Age scene displays an enormous radiate sun with many worshipping figures (Fig. 65),[166] perhaps reflective of a real ritual act. In the Celtic Iron Age, the sun could be envisaged as an arbiter or judge: a carving of this date depicts two warriors with, between them, a third individual holding a solar disc high above their heads.[167] This illustrates a trend in Camunian imagery which, in its later phases, tended to depict scenes of everyday life rather than simple acts of worship. But right through the long tradition of rock-art at Camonica Valley, the sun played a part in the religious consciousness of the local community. Fertility, hunting and all aspects of life and death were watched over by the solar powers and, certainly during the Neolithic and Bronze Age, preoccupations of the Camunians included the behaviour of the sun; its morning arrival, its journey through the sky

and its disappearance beneath the earth were central to beliefs, as far as we can judge.[168] We can only speculate as to why the carvings were made; and we are justified in assuming that comparable stimuli affected the remote Camunians in their mountain valley as the lowland Scandinavian rock-carvers and their communities. Making images rendered the acts and concepts they depicted more efficacious and brought these prehistoric peoples as close as possible to their gods.

A prehistoric sun-god?

In Chapter Five we will be introduced to a divinity who takes human form in the Romano-Celtic period and whose attributes proclaim him to be a sun-god. By contrast, for the period of European prehistory considered now, it is the symbols rather than the physical presence of the god himself which give us clues concerning the veneration of the sun. Anthropomorphic imagery is rare in the Bronze and Iron Ages and very rare indeed for the depiction of a solar divinity. Nevertheless, a few pieces of evidence may point to the very occasional manifestation of a prehistoric sun-god perceived in human form.

Our earliest candidate for the representation of an anthropomorphic solar power is perhaps the 'statue-menhir' from the Rocher-des-Doms at Avignon (Fig. 20). The stone takes the form of a domed cylinder on which a carved face is the only human feature. But on the left side of the figure's 'chest' is a deep hole from which radiate seven lines, making a solar or star-sign.[169] The stone belongs to a large group of statue-menhirs, often representing females or men with daggers, which date to the very beginning of the Bronze Age. The rayed motif in the position of the Avignon sculpture's heart is quite deliberate, deeply etched (though perhaps making use of a natural depression in the stone), and presumably has some significance in identifying the figure.

65 Rock-carving showing scene of sun-worship from Camonica Valley. Paul Jenkins, after Anati

Maybe it is not too fanciful to suggest that the depiction is that of a sun-deity, though this interpretation can never be other than extremely tentative.

To somewhat later in the Bronze Age belong the clay figures from Dupljaja in Yugoslavia, a defended site dating from the second millennium BC (Fig. 88). Two pottery statuettes mounted on wheeled vehicles were found here, the more complete one consisting of a tricycle on which stands a beaked male deity, clad in a long robe ornamented with circles and spirals. The carriage is drawn by three waterbirds; and the symbol of the sun is present, not only in the presence of the wheels themselves, which are decorated with concentric circles, but also in the solar motif which is cut into the floor of the vehicle and would have been, to all intents and purposes, invisible.[170] Once again the evidence here is circumstantial, but the association of wheeled carriage, water-birds and clear (albeit hidden) solar symbolism suggests that this being may be a sun-god. His spiral-and circle-patterned robe may serve to endorse his identity, and his beaked face gives him a close affinity with his aquatic birds, perhaps a further suggestion of his divinity.

Hints at an image of such a sun-god recur sporadically in the Iron Age: stylistically of this phase is the radiate-headed figure from Armagh – naked, with his arms by his side and with a huge head encircled by rays.[171] The figure may represent a solar divinity, but it could equally depict a Celtic warrior with lime-stiffened hair, a custom mentioned in respect of the Gauls by the Mediterranean writer Diodorus Siculus:[172] warriors with spiky hair are portrayed on some Celtic coins.[173] Still, the Armagh figure bears no weapon, and the exaggerated head with its nimbus of radiate lines is arguably better-interpreted as a local sun-deity. Certain anthropomorphic heads on Celtic coins may likewise represent a sun-god. It is generally accepted[174] that heads on Celtic coins are to be interpreted as deities rather than as portraits of humans. Certain of these coin-heads, notably from Armorica, bear what may be a sun-symbol attached to the hair,[175] perhaps an emblem to identify the divine head. Other heads bear boar-images, and it is well-known that gods associated with boars were worshipped in the Celtic world before and during the Roman phase.[176]

Finally, a solar wheel-god, whose image is so familiar in the Romano-Celtic world, may be portrayed on the controversial silver cauldron, found dismantled into its component plates in a peat-bog at Gundestrup in Jutland. This cult-vessel is of solid silver, 69 cm (27 in.) in diameter and with a capacity of 130 litres (28 gallons). Once claimed as a Celtic cauldron,[177] and looted by Teutonic raiders, doubt has been cast for some time on its authenticity as a piece of Celtic craftsmanship.[178] But, in terms of iconography, the cauldron's silver plates possess images which are found repeatedly in the repertoire of Celtic religious art and are too idiosyncratic to be interpreted as belonging to other than a Celtic tradition. That said, the style of the art suggests a non-Celtic origin for the vessel. Ruth and Vincent Megaw[179] have pointed out that silver is itself an unusual Celtic medium for anything other than coins but that it was a favoured metal in eastern Europe – Dacia or Thrace. The exotic animal motifs and also the general artistic style indicate a strong oriental influence. It is possible that the combination of Celtic iconography and non-Celtic elements may have occurred because of a link between northern and south-eastern Europe and the Celtic west. The north European Cimbri are known to have raided in eastern Europe before plundering Gaul in the late second century BC. The several different artists who contributed to the cauldron's making[180] could perhaps have been second-century BC Thracians, commissioned to produce a ritual vessel for a Celtic clientèle. Thereafter, perhaps, the vessel was looted from south-eastern Europe by Teutonic tribes who dismantled it and buried it in a Danish bog, either for safe-keeping or as a religious act.

Whatever the circumstances of the cauldron's manufacture and deposition, certain features in the iconography are undeniably Celtic: the ram-horned serpent; the antlered god; the Celtic warriors with their unmistakably La Tène shields, carnyxes (Celtic boar-headed trumpets) and animal-crested helmets. The image which also accords well with Celtic divine imagery is the being depicted on one of the inner plates of the cauldron (Fig. 42). Here is represented the head and shoulders of a male, bearded figure, arms raised and with the fingers clenched: against his right arm is the motif of half a 16-spoked cart-wheel, held by a small kneeling individual in a bull-horned helmet. A convention of the cauldron's imagery is that gods are portrayed larger than human figures. Many scholars[182] are of the view that

66 Rock-carving of man with solar wheel attached to his phallus from Camonica Valley. Paul Jenkins, after Anati

the bearded figure on the Gundestrup vessel is the Celtic solar wheel-god being presented with the emblem of his power, that of the sun, by an acolyte. If this interpretation is correct, the Danish peat-bog has provided us with the clearest surviving evidence for a pre-Roman 'free' Celtic image of a solar divinity.

— 5 —
The Celtic Sun-God: Images and Symbols

When the Romans colonized the Celtic territories of Gaul, Britain and the Rhineland, there grew up a hybrid, Romano-Celtic culture which had a profound effect upon religious expression in western Europe. Before the Roman period, the sun-god was an amorphous entity, very rarely represented except by his inanimate symbols. But now, the stimulus of Graeco-Roman mimetic tradition (whereby the gods were perceived as superior humans) caused Celtic beliefs to be expressed with far greater visuality, and a Celtic or Romano-Celtic sun-god envisaged in anthropomorphic form emerged for the first time.

We saw in Chapter Three that the sun in barbarian Europe could be represented by a number of varied symbols. But in the Romano-Celtic world, the wheel is the dominant solar form, with the swastika occurring in one discrete group of altars in the Pyrenees. In this period, the wheel may occur with an anthropomorphic image, on an altar with or without a dedication, as a talisman worn by a devotee, or it may simply be scratched as a good-luck sign on a pot or tile. The status of the solar sign may be equivocal: if it appears with the image of a god or on an altar, then the religious symbolism is clear. But its occurrence as a model hung on a chain around the neck inevitably presents ambiguity in terms of evidence for sun-veneration. Even here, its solar character is sometimes indicated by its association with a lunar crescent.

Observation of the entire spectrum of Celtic sun-images and symbols raises several points of interest. The variety of forms in which the sun-god himself is presented in human shape is striking. He may appear on public monuments which signify corporate worship,[1] in almost wholly Classical form as the Roman sky-god; sometimes he is actually named as Jupiter (Fig. 67). On such occasions, the deity may be accompanied by his Graeco-Roman panoply of sceptre, eagle and thunderbolt: only his solar wheel is Celtic. But the sun-god may also be presented with more independent, indigenous imagery, as at Churcham in Gloucestershire[2] where he has no Roman element and bears horns. Likewise, non-anthropomorphic solar cult-objects may vary from the Roman military dedications to 'Jupiter Optimus Maximus' ('Jupiter Best and Greatest') accompanied by the wheel-motif in north Britain or Germany (Fig. 73), to the small crudely-made Pyrenean altars,[3] some of which are also

68 Bronze statuette of wheel-god with thunderbolt and lightning-flashes, from Le Châtelet, Haute-Marne. Height: 10.3 cm (4 in.). Miranda Green

67 Bronze statuette of wheel-god, with inscription to Jupiter, from Landouzy-la-Ville, Aisne. Height: 22 cm (8.7 in.). Miranda Green

inscribed with the name of the Roman sky-god.

The role of the solar symbol itself is interesting: the wheel may simply accompany the celestial god, as one of his attributes (Fig. 68);[4] or it may possess a more active role as a protective shield, on the images of the warrior sun-god (Fig. 98).[5] At Netherby in Cumbria[6] the wheel replaces a *patera* or offering-plate and may therefore be seen as a prosperity-symbol (Fig. 69). In the Pyrenees, the wheel and dedication to Jupiter appear to be inter-changeable. Some altars in the Lower Rhône Valley[7] have only a wheel-sign, as if this symbol could represent the god himself. In the Pyrenees, wheel and swastika may be mutually replaceable or may occur together on one and the same stone (Fig. 31): the appearance of a swastika-in-circle on one of these stones[8] may suggest a merging of the two symbols. Where several solar or celestial signs are present on an altar, the wheel often is in

70 Stone altar with wheel and thunderbolt from Nîmes. Height: 80 cm (31.5 in.). Miranda Green

69 Stone relief of wheel-god with cornucopiae *from Netherby, Cumbria. Height: 39 cm (15.4 in.).* By permission of the Tullie House Museum, Carlisle

pride of place: in the Pyrenees, the wheel occupies the frontal position, the swastika the base. In the Lower Rhône, the wheel may be accompanied by a thunderbolt, symbol of Jupiter, but again the sun-sign occupies the central position (Fig. 70): at Vauvert[9] two thunderbolts flank one central wheel; it is arguable that the wheel's central position flanked by thunderbolts gives it precedence.

What emerges from a study of the monuments is the tangle of ethnic elements in the imagery. Celtic and Roman symbols have fused in an inextricable merger of religious expression. The Celtic solar sign may be central to the symbolism, but if a monument is associated with a dedicatory inscription, the god alluded to is invariably Jupiter; no native name for the sun-god emerges. On the larger public monuments, the Graeco-Roman artistic tradition may be dominant; on smaller, more personal objects, like jewellery or pottery, the native element is generally stronger and the Celtic wheel may be the only symbol present. But there is no one-way pattern whereby the public monuments always show more romanization than the smaller votive or cult-objects: the great Jupiter-Giant column at Hausen-an-der-Zaber was erected at the instigation of a Celtic patron (Fig. 71);[10] and the antefixes at Caerleon, (Fig 72) which represent a native-looking human head and solar wheel,[11] were displayed in a Roman military installation. The sky was an important element on the Jupiter-columns (see Chapter Seven), whereby the image of the celestial god was projected as high as possible into his own sphere, but it was equally significant in the native sanctuaries of the Pyrenees, which were in high mountainous positions close to the sky-god's domain.

The distribution of solar imagery indicates that the Celtic sun-god was worshipped over a wide area. The deity was present in virtually every region of Celt-occupied Europe.[12] But there are pockets of territory where the god was especially venerated: the Lower Rhône Valley, the Pyrenees, eastern Gaul and the Rhineland all worshipped the sun-deity. In Britain, the cluster of monuments on Hadrian's Wall may mean that the sun-god in his semi-Roman form may have been imported by the army. Only in Alsace (Chapter Seven) was the funerary cult of the sun prominent and only in the Pyrenees did the swastika rank as a sun-symbol of similar importance to the wheel itself.

In the discussion which follows, I want to focus on some significant aspects of the Celtic sun-god and his devotees. Two major divisions of belief seem to emerge: on the one hand the worship of a sun-god in his rightful domain of the sky, which appears to be linked

71 *Reconstruction of Jupiter-Giant column from Hausen-an-der-Zaber, near Stuttgart. Height: c. 15 m (46 ft). By permission of the Württembergisches Landesmuseum, Stuttgart*

with the more Roman form of the god, associated with Jupiter. But balancing this, the indigenous Celtic element of the cult brings out the other spheres of activity of the sun, namely prosperity and local protection. Finally, the question of worshippers is important, for it may throw a particular light on the character of the sun-god and the hopes and fears of his followers.

72 *Clay antefix with human head and solar symbol from Caerleon, Gwent. Height: c. 17 cm (6.7 in.).* By permission of the National Museum of Wales

The sun-god as Jupiter

In the Celtic world, the Greek Zeus or Roman Jupiter became identified with, or linked to, celestial powers which were already venerated in pre-Roman Celtic lands. The Mediterranean sky-god, whose dual function was as lord of the firmament and the king of the gods, was seen as a suitable entity with which the mainly aniconic Celtic sun-god could identify. So, under Celtic influence the Roman Jupiter may largely keep his Classical visual imagery, but have the native solar symbol added to his panoply of attributes.[13] This merging of identities may be observed in two types of visual presentation. First, the Celtic sun-wheel may be associated with an epigraphic dedication to the Roman sky-god. Second, the god may be presented with the imagery of Jupiter, but with the addition of the native solar symbol. Sometimes both dedication and Jupiter-image are present with the wheel-motif. One important point here is simply that the Roman sky-god and the wheel are so consistently

associated, which indicates that we are dealing with a solar symbol in the wheel, at least in this Romano-Celtic period. The identification of the motif with an undeniable sky-power demonstrates that, whatever other purpose the wheel has in imagery, it is firmly connected with celestial concepts. The evidence of this Romano-Celtic cult gives confidence to the argument for a solar interpretation for the wheel-symbol in prehistory, where the material necessarily lends itself to a less positive interpretation.

The military epigraphy of Britain provides some of the most curious evidence for conflation of Roman and Celtic religious expression. In the area of Hadrian's Wall, soldiers stationed at such forts as Castlesteads and Maryport in Cumbria made the normal annual dedication of an altar to 'Jupiter Optimus Maximus' as a re-affirmation of loyalty to the Empire and to its greatest deity. But this

73 *Stone altar to Jupiter Optimus Maximus, with wheel engraved beneath decoration, from Köln. Height: 86 cm (33.8 in.).* E. R. Aldhouse

blatantly Roman politico-religious act sometimes displays signs that these auxiliary troops
also worshipped the Celtic god of the sun. At
Castlesteads[14] the dedication on the front of the
altar is accompanied by a sun-wheel on one of
the lateral surfaces. The Maryport altar[15] is
even more enigmatic in that, whilst only the
Roman propitiatory inscription is seen from
the front, on the rear surface of the stone is a
wheel-symbol. So the veneration of the Celtic
sun-god was discreet, perhaps not too evident.
One could imagine an army officer giving the
cohort permission for the native solar sign to
be carved as long as it was not too obvious and
provided that it was relegated to an inferior
position. In a Roman military installation,
Jupiter must be seen to reign supreme. At
Köln, the conflation of Roman and native deities was clearer and less hidden: on one altar
was a dedication 'IOM' in good Classical let-
tering; beneath the inscription was carved a
sun-wheel (Fig. 73).[16]

On some of the Jupiter-columns (Chapter
Seven) a dedication to the Roman sky-god is
present: generally the horseman-god image is
as a warrior, brandishing the thunderbolt of
the Roman god. Sometimes he carries a solar
wheel as a shield, as at Butterstadt[17] in the
Rhineland, so here again there is an equation
between Jupiter-dedication and solar symbol.
A bronze figurine at Landouzy-la-Ville
(Aisne)[18] provides a rare chance to link non-
monumental images of the sun-god directly
with the Roman celestial lord. Here, a naked
and bearded male figure balancing a wheel
over a curiously-fashioned altar stands on a
base which bears a dedication to Jupiter Best
and Greatest and to the 'Numen' (spirit) of the
Emperors (Fig. 67).

The Lower Rhône group of solar-decorated
altars contains some examples with invo-
cations to Jupiter: at Collias,[19] Nîmes,[20] Tresques and Lansargues,[21] Jupiter's name is
associated with sun-wheels and on occasions
with Jupiter's thunderbolt as well. One of the

74 *Stone statue of wheel-god as warrior from
Séguret, Vaucluse. Height: 2.05 m (6.7 ft).*
Miranda Green

Pyrenean altars[22] links the swastika with a
Jupiter-dedication, and another swastika-
marked stone invokes Jupiter and Minerva.[23]
At Le Mont Saçon,[24] one of the little altars
from the sanctuary is dedicated to Jupiter, but
the others are without inscription, its place

taken by wheel- or swastika-signs, as if either name or symbol was equally acceptable as a propitiatory presence.[25] One of the most interesting southern Gaulish altars is at Aigues-Mortes near Arles,[26] which bears a dedication to Jupiter and Silvanus, the Roman woodland god, and has a complicated set of relevant accompanying symbols: wheels and thunderbolts for the sky-god; and a billhook, pots and hammers in acknowledgement of the southern Gaulish equation between the Celtic hammer-god Sucellus and the nature-deity of Italy.

Where epigraphic dedications are absent, the imagery of the sky-god provides the identification with Jupiter. Sometimes, an otherwise Classical sky-god appears with the Celtic sun-sign: thus at Séguret near Vaison[27] Jupiter appears as a Roman general; his eagle and thunderbolt mark him as the Graeco-Roman celestial god, but his large ten-spoked wheel gives him a Celtic dimension (Fig. 74). At nearby Vaison itself[28] essentially similar imagery occurs, but here the god is accompanied by his Mediterranean consort Juno, complete with her Classical symbol of the peacock. On one group of monuments, Jupiter appears in typical Roman guise, seated on a throne: at Alzey,[29] a Celtic solar wheel decorating one side of the throne is balanced by the Roman eagle on the other (Fig. 75); but at Alesia[30] the sun-sign is present on both sides. The monument at Tongeren[31] depicts a seated Jupiter and Juno, but here it is the sky-god's consort who is in possession of the solar symbol. Sometimes only the presence of a thunderbolt (the consistent emblem of the Classical sky-god) identifies the sun-god with Jupiter: thus on a quadrangular stone at Niederwürzbach[32] a naked standing deity holds a wheel and a thunderbolt. The bronze figurine from Le Châtelet (Haute-Marne)[33] presents similar imagery, but on this occasion the thunderbolt takes the form of S-shaped strands, and there are further S-shapes hanging from the figure's shoulder, perhaps spare lightning-flashes; the

75 *Stone figure of Romano-Celtic wheel-god from Alzey, Germany. Height: 74 cm (29 in.).* Miranda Green

solar wheel is in the god's left hand (Fig. 68). We may remember the association between spirals or Ss and the sun-cult examined in Chapter Three. Certain clay figures of the wheel-god[34] show him with a thunderbolt, and sometimes the eagle and wheel-motifs are interchangeable, as if some were manufactured to satisfy a more Celtic and others a more Romanized clientèle. On occasions, the god is very unlike Jupiter in terms of physical resemblance to Classical images but does have some identification with him: thus the monuments at Mouhet and Tours[35] belong to the class of Jupiter-Giant representations, but the god has a very Celtic appearance; and on the sceptre-terminal from Willingham Fen, Cambridgeshire,[36] a youthful naked god is shown with his sun-wheel and has little in common with normal representations of Jupiter except for the presence of the Roman eagle (Fig. 76). One final anthropomorphic representation of the sky-god is interesting because of the different relationship between the deity and his solar emblem: at Plessis-Barbuise, Aube[37] (Fig. 77),

77 *Figure of Jupiter within lead wheel-model from Plessis-Barbuise, Aube. Diameter of wheel: 10.2 cm (4 in.).* Paul Jenkins, after Thevenot

76 *Bronze sceptre-terminal with figure of sun-god from Willingham Fen, Cambs. Height: 12.1 cm (4.8 in.).* By permission of the Cambridge University Museum of Archaeology and Anthropology

a lead wheel-model has, in its centre, a figure of Jupiter with his sceptre and thunderbolt.

On altars with neither dedication nor anthropomorphic image, the Jupiter identification may be made by means of the thunderbolt alone. This happens particularly in the Lower Rhône group (Fig. 70).[38] In this region especially, there appears to have been a very genuine blending of Roman and native iconography to produce a hybrid sun-sky deity. In the Celtic world, Jupiter was both a sky- and a sun-god: this latter aspect is not developed in the Classical world, though the equation was not unknown. In Celtic Gaul, the intensity of conflation between Roman and indigenous celestial symbolism is very marked, and it is interesting to speculate as to what degree Roman and native divinities remained at all separate in the minds of believers, or whether conflation was so complete that absolute fusion of ethnic elements had taken place. Were people 'hedging their bets' in propitiating native and intrusive deities together or were they worshipping one divine force whose being was strengthened by the alliance of two originally separate but later fused symbolic traditions? The Celtic sun-god had no name of his own so, when one was required, that of the Roman sky-god was adopted. The Celtic element instead manifested itself entirely visually, by means of symbols which were as potent as any written language.

The sun and thunder

Observation of the identification of the Celtic indigenous sun-god with Jupiter indicates that one of the key factors in this conflation is the presence of the thunderbolt, celestial power-symbol of the Roman god, the means by which he smote his enemies, kept order within the pantheon and displayed his authority. We saw that not only do anthropomorphic images of the sun-sky god wield the thunderbolt and the solar wheel, but also altars simply bearing inanimate motifs frequently present the cosmic power-sources closely associated (Fig. 70), as though to demonstrate the strong affinity between them. At Lansargues in Provence, for instance,[39] a dedication to Jupiter is accompanied by a wheel and two thunderbolts, and there is identical symbolism at Vauvert, without the dedication.[40] On the complicated altar at Aigues-Mortes,[41] among the plethora of other symbols, the two sun-images and thunderbolts are placed together. Thus, in terms of visual association, sun-wheel and thunder-sign are closely linked, as if to display as clearly as possible the affinity between Roman and Celtic sky-symbols. In the Lower Rhône Valley, at any rate, the presence of the

two motifs was crucial to the understanding of the ethnic conflation of the two divine forms. Elsewhere in the Celtic world, the thunderbolt is emphasized above all other attributes of Jupiter, when associated with the sun-god. The rider on the Jupiter-columns often carries a separate metal thunderbolt (Fig. 71), which would glitter in the sun and emit beams of light. The figurine of the sun-god at Le Châtelet[42] (Fig. 68) carries a thunderbolt and wheel, and the lightning-element of his symbolism is enhanced by the S-shaped objects which hang from his shoulder, which each resemble the individual strands of which the god's main thunder emblem is made. Interestingly, on a British pot bearing wheel-decoration, from Silchester,[43] the solar motifs alternate with S-symbols, as if perhaps the lightning-flash is present.

Before we proceed further, we should perhaps draw a distinction between thunder and lightning. They are, of course, closely associated but not identical, though their regular occurrence together during a storm would be clear and understood. But lightning, unlike thunder, involves light and it may not simply be the Jupiter-presence which makes the thunderbolt and lightning-flash such prominent motifs in the Celtic iconographic repertoire. Indeed, the emphasis on the lightning-aspect of storms may reflect the dominance of the solar god, a deity for whom light, in whatever form, was the essential part of his identity and whose believers may have made a link between the sun and lightning. Both were powerful light sources, and it is probable that lightning was envisaged as an emanation of the sun, and thus as capable as the solar sphere of scorching in a hot dry land, but with the capacity also of instant and terrifying destruction. It is also possible that lightning and thunder were seen as the rain-inducing instrument of the sun, reflective of the promotion of life and fertility as well as destruction. To the Romans, ground hit by a thunderbolt was especially sacred,[44] and in this connection it is interesting that a stele at Montmirat (Gard), decorated with two sun-wheels, bears part of an inscription referring to the burial of a thunderbolt.[45]

It is possible that the thunderbolt could, in a Celtic milieu, be sometimes represented by a hammer, reflective of the noise of the thunderclap. Sun-wheels and hammers are juxtaposed at Vernègues (Bouches-du-Rhône)[46] and at Aigues-Mortes (Gard). The situation is more complicated because of the association of the hammer-god, Sucellus, and Jupiter, and it may be that sun and hammer-symbols come together in southern Gaul simply as a result of this link rather than because of an affinity between hammers and thunderbolts. However, where, as discussed below, Sucellus does possess a celestial association, one reason for this could be because, on these occasions, the god's hammer may possess a role as a noisy emblem of the thunderbolt striking the earth in a hammer-blow.

Finally, while looking at sun and thunder, we should remember that the Celts possessed their own thunder-god, Taranis,[47] equated by a later commentator on the Roman poet Lucan with Jupiter.[48] A very small number of Romano-Celtic monuments make the same identification.[49] The name 'Taranis' refers to the element of thunder itself. What we seem to be dealing with is a 'free' Celtic (pre-Roman) thunder-force worshipped long before the Romans arrived, which was subsequently linked with the Mediterranean celestial divinity because one of this god's roles was as a thunderer. There is no clear association between Taranis himself and the Celtic sun-god. Instead, both divine concepts were aligned with the intrusive Jupiter-cult because of similarities seen between his identity and those of pre-existing indigenous gods. The thunder-association was easy since Jupiter possessed a thunder-symbol. The sun-link is more curious: for Jupiter to be associated with a sun-cult meant that he himself had to change and to take on a prominent solar role which he did not possess in his Roman homeland.

The solar warrior

The military, warlike aspect of the Celtic sun-god emerges from both epigraphy and iconography. We have seen that soldiers on Hadrian's Wall and in the Rhineland set up Roman altars to Jupiter Optimus Maximus as an official act of fealty to the Empire but that sometimes they were also acknowledging the power of the Celtic sun-god. The conflated sky-sun divinity may also appear as a soldier himself: he is presented thus on the Jupiter-columns (pp. 133–6), brandishing his thunderbolt and riding down the forces of darkness in the form of a semi-zoomorphic monster. A sun-symbol is carried as a shield to guard him against evil and as a light to shine in the face of his dark enemy (Fig. 98).[50] Some Jupiter-Giant groups occur in strongly military regions, like the Rhineland,[51] but others were erected by civilians, and the imagery thus bears no relation to the way of life of the worshippers. The Celtic Jupiter with his solar emblem appears as a warrior in full Roman military uniform in Provence, which had long been peaceful (Fig. 74) (for example at Séguret and Vaison), where a military presence had no place. The explanation for this imagery may be that either the military costume is simply a power-symbol or the god is here represented, as he is on Jupiter-columns, as a conqueror of evil.[52]

But the Celts may in fact have perceived the sun-god as a genuine deity of war: the wheel-god at Corbridge[53] is depicted with a helmet, a club and long shield; his sun-wheel reposes by his ankle. In addition, Celtic warriors wore solar-wheel models as amulets, to guard them in battle: the stone statue of a Late Iron Age soldier at Fox-Amphoux (Var)[54] portrays him with a pectoral solar pendant; again, on the arch at Orange, probably of early first-century AD date,[55] Celtic helmets and body-armour are ornamented with wheels as solar talismans (Fig. 51). Perhaps oddest of all military associations for the sun-god are those, already referred to above, at Caerleon.[56] Here, in a Roman military fortress, triangular clay antefixes were fastened to the gable-ends of roofs to protect them from the wind and rain. Some of these tiles bear curious images in the form of Celtic-style human heads associated with solar wheels and other celestial symbols (Fig. 72). In the opinion of some scholars,[57] such motifs are merely to be seen as apotropaic or 'good-luck' signs. But I think that here the association of crude native heads with solar symbols makes it likely that the Celtic sun-god is represented on these tiles, in which case we have the apparently bizarre situation whereby members of a Roman garrison – in the potentially hostile Celtic territory of the Silures – adopt the native solar god to guard their fortress against indigenous aggressors. If we can accept Valerius Flaccus' statement, copied in the late first century AD from a third-century BC source, as pertaining to a Celtic tribe,[58] then we have evidence that the solar Jupiter was definitely associated with war:

> *the serried Corallians left their banners; barbaric wheels are their emblem, and the shapes of swine with iron-coated backs, and broken columns, effigies of Jove.*

The war-imagery associated with the sun is supported by the solar associations of the Celtic Mars. The god Mars had peaceful roles in the Romano-Celtic world as a healer and god of prosperity[59] but, in his role as a war-god, he could possess a solar function. Thus, on a tiny stone altar from the villa at Chedworth, Gloucestershire,[60] a spear-carrying warrior is seen accompanied by two stemmed wheel-symbols; Mars might also possess a number of epithets or surnames associated with light, like 'Loucetius' at Bath and Angers in Brittany,[61] although the name more naturally applied to Jupiter.[62] Mars 'Belatucadrus' in north Britain[63] means 'fair shining one' or 'bright one', again a light-epithet. The Celtic Mars could sometimes be envisaged as a god of high places, with mountain shrines, for instance around Lake Antre in the Jura, or as Mars Latobius in Austria;[64] and especially among the tribes of eastern Britain, like the Corieltauvi, the image of the Celtic Mars was as a horseman, here resembling the Celtic Jupiter.

The solar goddesses

Jupiter's Roman consort Juno was adopted into the Celtic pantheon with far less enthusiasm than the sky-god himself. Maybe this was because there was a strong indigenous group of goddesses – like the Three Mothers – who were able to fulfil Juno's role equally well. Indeed, we will see in Chapter Seven that there was a close affinity between the Mothers and the Celtic celestial god. But very occasionally Juno accompanies the Celtic sun-god in the guise of Jupiter: on the stone at Vaison[65] both Jupiter *and* Juno have donned military costume, as if the goddess occupied the role of the solar guardian. The accompanying peacock, symbol of eternity and the bright orb of the sky, serves to identify the goddess as the Roman Juno. The wholeness of the Celtic Juno's absorption into her consort's identity is indicated by two depictions from Gaul, where the female divinity carries a solar wheel: at Autun[66] a worn stone represents a goddess, probably to be identified as Juno, with a thunderbolt and what is probably a wheel; and at Tongeren,[67] though the sky-sun god is present at Juno's side, she is the deity chosen to carry the solar emblem. This total identification of Juno with the solar symbol may have been because the Celts recognized the sun as having a strong fertility element (Chapter Seven) and not, therefore, the sole prerogative of a male divinity.

Another goddess of Classical origin who may have been adopted by the Celts as a sun-deity was Fortuna. In Mediterranean imagery Fortuna or Chance may carry a wheel or a globe representative of movement and the shifting ground of human luck. So Fortuna already possessed a wheel, which could have been associated, in a Romano-Celtic context, with sun-symbolism. On a bronze figure at Autun,[68] Fortuna is depicted with a wheel which is exaggerated in size, and other Gaulish representations of the goddess bear wheel-motifs, like that at Agey in Burgundy.[69] Also present in the same region, around Dijon, were worshippers who dedicated altars to Jupiter and Fortuna together,[70] as if the goddess were purposely chosen here as the consort of the Romano-Celtic sky-god, perhaps because of her wheel-imagery.

In the Celtic world it is possible to detect a hint that a goddess associated particularly with the sun was worshipped. We have already (p. 22) mentioned that the great healer-goddess at Bath has a solar name, Sulis. We should also call to mind the strange category of native goddesses, portrayed in pipe-clay and made in Gaulish manufactories especially in the Allier region of central France and in Brittany, centred around Rennes. These were fertility deities, but some of them were stamped with unmistakable solar designs. This group of votive figurines will be fully examined below in our discussion of the life-giving properties of the sun (Figs. 93 and 94) (Chapter Seven). Finally, the early Irish post-Roman literature may provide us with tentative evidence of a goddess who may be solar. She is Ériu, the eponymous goddess of Ireland: there is a legend in which Ériu, goddess of the land, marries successive mortal kings of Ireland and seals their betrothal by handing to them a golden goblet filled with red wine. Some scholars have seen this goblet as a symbol of the sun and on these grounds would link Ériu with solar divinities.[71]

Sucellus the hammer-god and the solar cult

A devotee at Mainz set up a dedication to 'Jupiter Best and Greatest Sucaelus'.[72] Sucellus was the Gaulish hammer-god: his name means 'the Good Striker' and, in iconography he is represented as a mature bearded god bearing a long-shafted hammer. In support of the Mainz identification between Jupiter and Sucellus, it has been noted that a number of bronze figurines of the hammer-god[73] bear a close physical resemblance to Jupiter. But what is particularly striking is the association between the hammer-god and the symbolism of the sun. This link may be presented in a number of ways: first, the imagery of the hammer- and sun-gods may be juxtaposed – in which instances one could fairly argue that the two divine entities were simply worshipped together, with no close affinity between them in terms of religious conflation; second, Sucellus may be depicted with solar signs on his body; third, there may be a complicated symbolic fusion between sun-wheel and hammer-symbols. Both these two latter occurrences prove beyond reasonable doubt that sun- and hammer-gods could be closely associated, even if total conflation did not take place.

In the first group of iconography, where the hammer-god appears in company with the sun-god, the most important evidence is in the Lower Rhône Valley, where the hammer-god was himself identified with the Roman woodland and nature deity Silvanus.[74] On the altar at Aigues-Mortes is a dedication to Jupiter and Silvanus: so the epigraphy itself presents a Roman cult. But the associated motifs betray the Celtic identity of the divinities: two wheels and two hammers are present, as well as thunderbolts – suggestive of a Roman celestial balance to native solar imagery – and a pot and billhook, the emblems of Sucellus-Silvanus. At Vernègues[75] in the same region, there is no inscribed dedication, but a wheel, a hammer,

78 Sheet-bronze sceptre-binding with repoussé figures, including sun-god, from Farley Heath Romano-Celtic temple, Surrey. Miranda Green

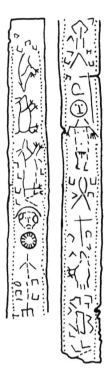

pots and trees convey the same message of an association between sun-god, hammer-god and his Provençal identity as a nature-deity.

The same composite symbolism is repeated on a stone at Courbessac, also in Provence;[76] and far away, at St Quirin in Alsace,[77] a funerary monument again combines a solar symbol and a group of hammers. A very different cult-object in Britain once more displays a liaison between sun- and hammer-gods: a sheet-bronze sceptre-binding from a temple at Farley Heath in Surrey, decorated with simple repoussé figures and designs, associates a matchstick-man figure with a long-handled hammer[78] with a wheel-sun sign, next to which is a human head, maybe that of the sun-god himself (Fig. 78).

There is a group of bronze statuettes of the hammer-god which shows him to have been yet more intimately linked with the cult of the sun. This affinity seems particularly to have commended itself to the tribes of Burgundy, the Aedui and the neighbouring Lingones. Thus, figurines representing Sucellus at, for instance, Prémeaux[79] (Fig. 32) and Santenay[80] bear crosses and circles. Occasionally the hammer-god is linked to the solar cult outside Burgundy: a figure from Lyon[81] bears sun-symbols; and one at Köln has circles and semi-circles stamped on his body and legs.[82] At Viège in Switzerland, a figurine is ornamented with crosses and swastikas.[83] The un-equivocally solar character of swastikas has already been discussed in Chapter Three.

The close connection between the symbolism of Sucellus and the sun-god is demonstrated above all by the merging of the two symbols of hammer and wheel. The bronze image of a god at Vienne (Isère) (Fig. 34) displays this fusion of visual motifs very clearly.[84] Here is depicted a god with a wolfskin over his head and shoulders, and with a very curious implement behind his head; this object consists of a barrel-like hammer-head from which protrude five rays or spokes each of which terminates in a smaller barrel-hammer. The object resembles a wheel with the larger hammer-barrel forming the nave, the smaller ones seemingly representative of a broken rim or felloe. Here we seem to have not only a hybrid hammer-wheel, but a barrel-motif in addition; moreover, the Vienne god's wolfskin allies him with the Sucellus-Silvanus portrayals of the Rhône Valley. In Burgundy, the hammer-god is frequently accompanied by a wine-barrel, signifying his presidency over the wine-harvest; and on a depiction of the hammer-god at Lyon,[85] he is shown with viner's tools. The symbolism of the god at Vienne is virtually replicated on a stone at Dôle (Jura)[86] where the imagery consists of a wheel-like object whose spokes terminate in little barrels.

So, on occasions, wheel, hammer and barrel-motifs may merge to form a composite symbol, which was perhaps evocative of the force of the sun in bringing the harvest to fruition under the mediation of the hammer-god.

To explore further the affinity between the hammer- and sun-deities, we need to look briefly at the role of the hammer itself. First and foremost, it is a striking implement; this is borne out by Sucellus' name. The god also often holds his hammer like a sceptre, a wand of authority or rank, and it may be a power-symbol. But a study of Sucellus[87] reveals that his main function was that of a deity of prosperity and abundance. He was a peasant's god and his hammer may often resemble a mallet used perhaps for driving in fence-posts for field-boundaries. My own view is that with his implement the hammer-god could strike the earth to re-awaken it after the 'sleep' or 'death' of winter and could use it also to guard people against barrenness or disease. Sucellus was often worshipped at therapeutic spring-sanctuaries. Where the image shows the hammer pointing upwards towards the sky, this could reflect its role as a thunder-emblem, bringing rain to the land; inverted, it was in contact with the earth and could fertilize it. So Sucellus' association with the Roman nature-deity Silvanus seems clear. But the sun, too, is a fitting associate in that it also possessed a dual function as a celestial entity and a life/fertility/regeneration source. Both the hammer-god and the lord of the sun could protect against illness, soften the blow of death and cause the earth and its inhabitants to flourish. Where the two cults formed an alliance, the result would have been powerful indeed.

Animals, plants and the sun-god

The iconography of Romano-Celtic Europe presents a visual link between the symbolism of the sun and that of beasts, trees and vegetation, thus enhancing and extending the imagery of the Celtic sun-god. Very frequently, faunal and floral motifs occur together, and it is likely that both bring a cyclical dimension to the solar cult, evoking the idea of life, death and rebirth. Trees played an important role here. Bark- or leaf-decoration in stone on the Jupiter-Giant columns shows that they were probably skeuomorphs (copies) of trees.[88] Oaks are known to have been sacred to the Mediterranean sky-god, and the column at Hausen near Stuttgart is decorated with oak leaves and acorns.[89] Oaks feature again in the imagery of the sky-god at Vaison and Séguret (Fig. 74) nearby,[90] where the Celtic Jupiter stands beside an oak with snake entwining it. The distinctive group of altars of the sun-god from the Pyrenean mountain sanctuaries often combines the motif of wheel or swastika with that of a conifer or palm-branch (Fig. 30);[91] and at Bois-de-la-Neuve-Grange (Bas-Rhin) (Fig. 43)[92] a sun-wheel has tree- or antler-like projections jutting from its rim. The wheel-god from Netherby in Cumbria (Fig. 69)[93] carries a *cornucopiae* brimming with fruit to represent abundance.

In the images of the sun-god as Jupiter, the snake features in the Rhône Valley group, where it is represented twined round an oak tree, perhaps as a symbol of renewal, just as the tree itself presents an evocation of eternity, fertility and a link between upper and lower worlds. Deciduous trees 'die' and are 'reborn', and the serpent sloughs its skin three or four times a year in an allegory of regeneration. Snake and sun-wheel appear together on an altar belonging to the Dobunni, at Lypiatt Park in Gloucestershire (Fig. 92);[94] the reptile here is the Celtic ram-headed variety and it entwines its body round the altar as if encircling a tree. On the Jupiter-Giant sculptures, by contrast, the snake represents darkness, opposed to the sky and solar forces of life and daylight, and we are reminded irresistibly of God's curse in the Garden of Eden.

Other beasts may represent the celestial, fertility and chthonic aspects of the sun-god's mythology and function. The little clay image at Quilly in Brittany is of a cross-legged deity decorated with sun-symbols and with a waterbird at the tips of his fingers (Fig. 95).[95] This is interesting for two reasons: first the bird is a constant associate of the solar wheel in Bronze Age imagery (see Chapter Four) and may reflect the link between sun and water which is so prominent in the Gaulish healing sanctuaries (Chapter Six). The second and important feature is that the Quilly god is in the cross-legged attitude of the antlered god Cernunnos[96] whom we know, from an Iron Age coin at Petersfield in Hampshire (Fig. 79),[97] was

79 *Iron Age silver coin, with head of antlered god and wheel between his antlers, from Petersfield, Hants.* By permission of the National Museum of Wales

occasionally associated with the sun-cult. Bull-horns and solar imagery may also be combined: on a stone at Churcham, Gloucestershire,[98] a horned divinity is accompanied by two solar symbols and, on one of the plates of the Gundestrup Cauldron (Fig. 42),[99] the wheel-god is attended by a small companion wearing a bull-horned helmet and grasping the wheel for the sun-god.

On many images of the Celtic sun-god, where he adopts the formal guise of Jupiter, the Roman deity's eagle is present, perhaps specifically as a sky-symbol, to balance the Celtic solar motif. At Willingham Fen,[100] the sun-god has an eagle and a bull, both companions of the Classical god, and the potent, aggressive bull has been made Celtic by the addition of a third horn.[101] Boars may be linked to the sun-god's imagery, perhaps as warlike symbols of aggression or because they were particularly fond of acorns and were thus associated with Jupiter's oak tree. On one of the carvings of the sun-god at Netherby,[102] where the god holds a wheel instead of an offering-plate, he is accompanied by a boar and a tree. On coins of the Veliocasses and the Aulerci Eburovices, boars are associated with chariot wheels, and this animal is treated sometimes as though it were a substitute for the solar horse. On one coin,[103] a boar with bristles erect has three circles above his back, which may be sun-motifs. The horse itself, an unequivocal solar symbol (Chapter Six) accompanies the Romano-Celtic sun-god in his role as a conquering horseman (Chapter Seven). Here, the horse is present as a prestige animal, king of beasts, and a fitting creature to be the carrier of the sun-god (Fig. 71). The Celtic lord of the sky appears as a cavalryman here and his horse rears to crush the chthonic monster beneath its hooves. Thus, the image of the horse is necessary to provide the precise relationship between god and giant. Finally, there is a plethora of zoomorphic imagery on the decorated bronze strip – perhaps a binding for a sceptre – found at the Farley Heath temple:[104] the repoussé figures include birds, boars and stags, and these may be reflective of fertility and seasonal ritual, associated with the cult of the sun-god who is also present in the iconography (Fig. 78).

Thus trees, plants and animals of different species both widen and support the various aspects of the sun-god. Aggression, fertility, rebirth and prestige are all evoked by the animals, and birds may reflect the sun-god's influence in both celestial and earthly spheres. Trees and vegetation represent the seasons, eternity and abundance; the high oak tree may enhance the solar deity's celestial imagery; the palm may betoken victory; and the *cornucopiae* represents the fruits of the earth ripened by the sun.

Priests and worshippers

Taken as a whole, the images and symbols of the Romano-Celtic sun-god reflect the spectrum of function and of the types of dedicant. We have seen that depictions of the deity or his attributes may vary from the visually Classical to an entirely native Celtic projection of belief. An act of homage to the solar force may take the form of an elaborate public monument set up by a group of people, as some of the Jupiter-Giant columns, or a small, roughly-shaped altar dedicated to the sun-god at a little mountain sanctuary in the Pyrenees. Most stone monuments, large or small, were usually the result of corporate devotion, certainly meant to be dedicated and set up in one place, whether in a large public temple or private shrine. We know that one altar, at Collias in Provence, was dedicated to the sun-god by two clans, the Coriossedenses and Budicenses.[105] But small objects – figurines or amulets – could be personal possessions or parts of ritual regalia. A bronze figurine, like that from Le Châtelet (Fig. 68),[106] could have belonged to an individual, but the presence of two rings

on his back suggests that this image may have been carried in a procession. Little clay statuettes were probably the result of private purchase for dedication in a domestic shrine or a grave; and pots and tiles may have been scratched with the solar sign by individuals, as a 'good-luck' gesture. Bronze model sun-wheels would have been worn for protection by individuals, but the splendid gold and silver wheels and chains were more likely to have been priestly regalia, worn on solemn ceremonial occasions (see below).

Some evidence for organized solar worship is present, but it is difficult to infer the nature of ceremonial. Soldiers and civilians set up statues and altars to the sun-god, but what of the ritual accompanying such dedications? We have some evidence for a priesthood and for liturgical practices: the bronze objects bearing solar signs at Willingham Fen (Fig. 76) and Farley Heath (Fig. 78) may have been items of religious equipment: the latter, found at a temple site, was a sheet-bronze binding from a stave, bearing complicated imagery which includes a depiction of a god whose upper body is in the form of a solar wheel and whose lower limbs and phallus form a trident or thunderbolt image. The Willingham Fen bronze, with its composite imagery of young dancing god, eagle, wheel, triple-horned bull's head and chthonic monster, must have had profound symbolic meaning for the users. Its most likely function was as part of a ceremonial staff or sceptre, perhaps used by priests of the sun-cult; there is some evidence that there was a shrine in the Fens at Willingham. Offerings of wine or oil may have been made by cult officials in pots, such as the ones from Silchester or Littlehampton,[107] which were painted with solar signs and whose decoration could have been especially commissioned for use in solar rituals. Pots with applied sun-wheel designs, like those at Malton and House-steads,[108] may likewise have been used as offering-vessels in cult-ceremonies.

Occasionally, we are shown glimpses of what priests may actually have worn as insignia of the solar cult: jewellery consisting of gold and silver chains with miniature filigree wheels attached was widespread within the Roman Empire,[109] but it may be that the occurrence of such chains in a Celtic context gave them a special significance with reference to the sun-cult. That the wheel here is solar is supported by the addition of little lunar crescents on some of the chains, as at Newstead in southern Scotland, Backworth in Durham and Dolaucothi in Dyfed;[110] moreover the Balèsmes chain was hung with a wheel, crescent and double-axe, perhaps reflective of sun, moon and thunder (Fig. 39). Whatever the empire-wide distribution of these necklaces, the Dolaucothi jewellery, found on the site of

the Roman gold-mines, was certainly made locally; and the Backworth regalia was discovered in a religious context, in a cache of jewellery contained within a *patera* which was dedicated to the mother-goddesses.[111] In my opinion, it is likely that, in a Celtic milieu, such wheels and chains could have been worn by priests of the sun-cult, perhaps as 'badges of office', similar in some respects to mayoral insignia. The precious metal would have shone in the sunlight, and its wearer would have made a very impressive figure in the administration of his ceremonial duties.

A recent discovery at a temple in Surrey throws striking new light on a possible solar priesthood: people worshipped at Wanborough during the free Celtic and subsequent Roman phases. Here were found three chain headdresses, of which two were surmounted by large bronze wheel-models (Fig. 80);[112] it is not too speculative to suggest that these were worn by clergy or officiants on ceremonial occasions, while they performed rites sacred to the sun-god. The wheel-topped headdresses remind us of the Petersfield coin decorated with the head of the antlered god (Fig. 79), who has a wheel-symbol suspended between his horns. Is he too wearing the insignia of the solar-god? Is he indeed a god at all, or could he be wearing a headdress of antlers and the sun-wheel, like a shaman?

In examining items of possible liturgical or ceremonial equipment, a fascinating and very recent discovery from Buckinghamshire should be mentioned. I am grateful to Bob Williams of the Milton Keynes Archaeology Unit for allowing me to include details of this find, which is yet to receive definitive publication. The object, from excavations at Wavendon Gate, was found towards the base of a waterlogged pit of early Romano-British date. It consists of a wooden (probably oak) 'wheel' below which is a tenon pierced by a hole. The overall length of the object is 33 cm (13 in.) (Fig. 81). The wheel originally had

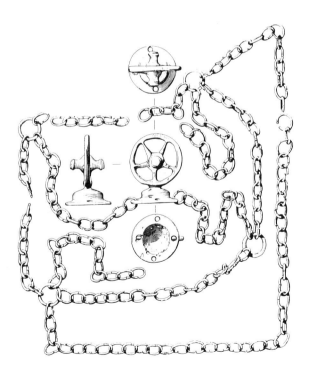

80 Bronze wheel-headdress from Wanborough temple, Surrey. D. W. Williams, by permission of Surrey Archaeological Society

twelve spokes, of which eight survive, an openwork nave and a bevelled felloe. The disposition of the convex 'spokes' is suggestive of a floreate or solar appearance. A possibly significant feature of this discovery is that a tree-trunk was found in association with it.

Further work remains to be done on the context of this find, but it is possible that we have here a discovery of major importance for the Romano-British solar-wheel cult. It appears to be a unique find, owing its survival entirely to the waterlogged conditions in which it was buried. The object is comparatively large, and the presence of the tenon presumably means that it once fitted into a large timber socket. It is possible that the wheel was placed on a wooden post or tree-trunk in a sacred place or temple. We know that the oak was sacred to the Celtic and the Roman Jupiter, and that columns, themselves perhaps stone copies of trees, were linked to the sun-sky cult. It could be that the findspot of Wavendon Gate, among the tribe of the Catuvellauni, was once a sanctuary whose ritual furniture included a solar sign set high on a wooden shaft to honour the local god of the sun.

If we turn now to the worshippers, we have evidence that invocation to the sun-god could be manifested in several ways: people set up images, large and small, to their chosen deity; they offered solar amulets and figurines in shrines, or buried them with their beloved dead in their graves. They scratched solar signs on everyday objects like pots or tiles: swastikas were incised on bricks and vessels in the Pyrenees,[113] precisely the region where swastikas were chosen as solar signs on altars to honour the local version of the sun-god. A lone wheel, incised on a pot,[114] is more likely to have religious significance than if it were part of a decorative pattern encircling the vessel. All these evocations may be little more than apotropaic symbols to bring blessing to a building or to the contents of a container, but, if that is so,

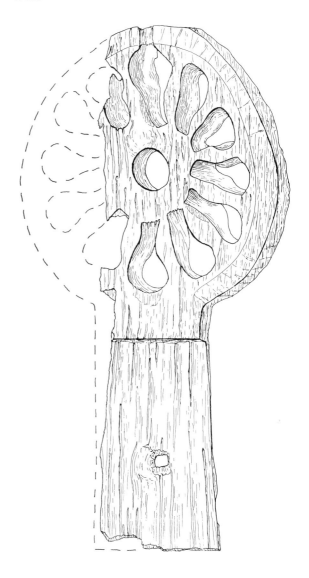

81 Wooden wheel, from base of waterlogged early Roman pit, Wavendon Gate, Bucks. Length: 33 cm (13 in.). June Burbidge, by permission of Bob Williams, Milton Keynes Archaeological Unit

then it is interesting that the sun-sign possessed a function as a general 'good-luck' motif. This means that it penetrated the consciousness of individuals as a beneficent emblem of wide efficacy and potency, even if

awareness of its specifically solar character had
been largely forgotten.

A persistent habit among devotees of the
Celtic sun-god was the wearing of solar talismans, in the form of wheel-shaped pendants
or other jewellery. We may trace this custom
right back into the European Bronze Age
(Chapter Four). We have seen that depictions
of warriors and armour sometimes display
wheel-amulets on cuirass or helmet, and a funerary monument of Roman date at Metz[115]
portrays a man wearing a Celtic torc from
which hangs a four-spoked wheel. Wheel- and
swastika-brooches were worn too, perhaps
with a dual function as decorative and apotropaic signs: a pair of large, superbly-enamelled,
wheel-brooches was dedicated in a temple at
Gusenberg (Fig. 82).[116] Swastika-brooches
may be ornamented with crosses or circles
(Fig. 28),[117] and the arms of a swastika-brooch
at Köln terminate in horse-heads, again
enhancing the solar symbolism.

Wheel-models were frequently dedicated in
shrines or may have other direct religious

82 *Pair of enamelled bronze wheel-brooches
from temple at Gusenberg near Trier. Diameter:
c. 4.2 cm (1.6 in.).* By permission of the Rhei-
nische Landesmuseum, Trier

83 *Bronze wheel-model with part of a votive
inscription: 'Per Beneficiarius V...S...', from
Augst, Switzerland. Diameter: c. 8 cm (3.1 in.).*
Miranda Green

associations: indeed, a model at Augst (Fig. 83)[118] bears a fragmentary inscription attesting its votive nature. But the shrine-offerings are very interesting, partly because they were often dedicated in such numbers: at Ville-neuve-au-Châtelot (Aube), numerous silver, bronze and lead wheels – the last items strung together in cast strips – were offered by late free Celtic and Romano-Celtic devotees of the sun-god in his temple.[119] A number of model wheels was dedicated at a free Celtic wooden shrine at Alesia, along with more than 200 tiny pots (too small to be functional) arranged in groups of nine.[120] This grouping may be significant: we know from vernacular literature that three and multiples of three had religious meaning for the Celts and that nine was a favourite number.[121] Model wheels were offered at the healing sanctuaries of Bolards[122] and Bourbonne-les-Bains,[123] perhaps in acknowledgement of the warmth of the water or the healing action of the sun; and literally hundreds of wheels were cast into such rivers as the Oise, Marne and Seine,[124] attesting to the association between water and the sun (Fig. 84). The offering of precious objects in water was a well-known phenomenon throughout both later prehistory and the Romano-Celtic period, perhaps because water was thought to have a peculiar kind of sanctity and to have bridged the gap between the spirit and the earthly worlds.[125] Finally, ritual deposits of sun-symbols were made, perhaps to the chthonic gods, maybe to light the otherworld: a possible example of this practice is attested at Naix (Meuse) where two vessels were buried after being filled with silver, lead and bronze wheels together with money.[126]

The British wheel-model which is most interesting in terms of its ritual significance is that found at Felmingham Hall in Norfolk (Fig. 85).[127] This belongs to a hoard of religious material, 23 items in all, found in a pot with a coin of AD 260. The group of bronze objects included a figurine of a *Lar* (a Roman

84 Bronze wheel-models from riverine deposits in Gaul. Diameters: 2–4 cm (1–2 in.). Miranda Green

household god), a head of Jupiter, a mask of a deity with solar rays projecting from his head, a pole-tip, and a large, realistic model of a 12-spoked chariot- or cart-wheel. The sacred character of this cache is indicated not only by the religious images but also by the pole-tip, which was probably originally attached to a staff and hung with bells or rattles and used in cult-processions;[128] such regalia is recorded from temples like Brigstock in Northamptonshire.[129] This Norfolk hoard may well have been temple furniture, buried for safety by either priests or looters of the sanctuary, who did not survive or were unable to retrieve their religious treasure.

The other context for miniature sun-wheels which is significant in ritual terms is the grave. We examine the chthonic or underworld aspect of the sun-cult later on (Chapter Seven). But it is worth alluding here briefly to the recurrent sepulchral associations of wheel-amulets. A grave at Colchester[130] produced an urn containing jewellery and a bronze wheel-model. Several of the curious Rhineland burials around Köln and Bonn, which contain numerous, mainly agricultural, model implements, have wheel-shaped sun-symbols accompanying them.[131] These burials are frequently interpreted as indicative of the oriental cult of Sabazius, but the presence of the sun-wheel in a Celto-Germanic context may imply the worship, too, of the local sun-god. The tradition of burial of solar talismans had a long pre-Roman ancestry (Chapter Four). In origin, the idea of placing images of the sun in graves may have been to illuminate the dark world of death and to present hope of resurrection in the otherworld. Alternatively, these images could be seen as gifts to the lords of the dead, to make the new arrival acceptable to the realm of the underworld and its gods.

Finally, we need to pose the question why model wheels were chosen in such numbers to symbolize the sun-god. We discussed earlier the question of the physical resemblance between wheels and the sun, and the bright metal – gold, silver or bronze – flashing like the sun itself. Models could emulate the solar disc still further, by means of spoke-ribbing, which would catch the light, and denticulation of the rim, which would reflect the fiery nature of the sun's orb. But what of miniaturization itself? Was there a sense in which the very act of presenting votive offerings in miniature to the sun-god was significant? One may reasonably argue that cost and convenience were both factors in the custom of offering models rather than full-size objects, but it is equally possible that a miniature object was something whose

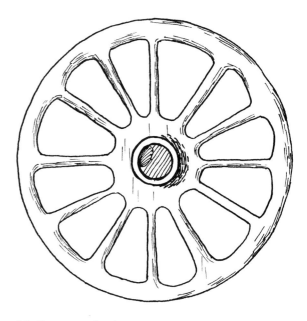

85 Bronze wheel-model from Felmingham Hall, Norfolk. Diameter of wheel: 4.5 cm (1.8 in.).
E. R. Aldhouse

sacral character was made more potent by its removal from the mundane constraints of earthly reality, making it appropriate and suitable as a divine gift.[132] Thus, miniaturization could be seen to have the same function as ritual breakage or twisting out of shape. Neither a model nor a damaged object can be used in the real world; in the case of the model item, this is made especially for the gods. Multiple offerings of sun-models in shrines and rivers meant that repeated homage was paid to the solar god, perhaps by one individual. In its way, this repeated act of veneration was probably as potent as the dedication of an expensive stone altar in a temple to the sun-god.

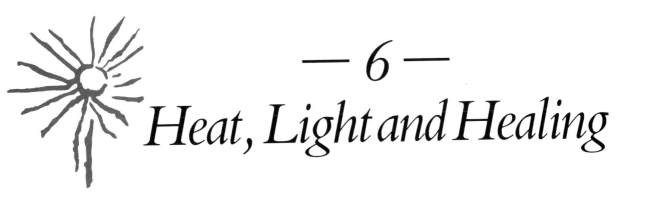

— 6 —
Heat, Light and Healing

The sun is important as a provider of both heat and light. We now explore this role, the imagery it stimulated and the belief-systems it influenced. The immediate and obvious manifestations are in fact complicated and have involved ramifications. We will look at the association between fire and the sun; the link between light and the imagery of the eye, a light-receptor and a gateway to the human soul; the horse and the chariot, which conveyed the sun on its journey through the sky during the day; and the boat, which transported it at night in the regions of the underworld. We will examine the sun's role as a healer, in which both light and heat play a part; and the close association between the sun and water which manifests itself most clearly in the thermal sanctuaries of Celtic Gaul. Both sun and water were seen to possess a regenerative role, where healing, renewal and resurrection after illness or death mirrored the life-giving and destructive properties of both water and the sun.

Heat and fire

In one myth of the origin of fire, the Titan Prometheus – half-god, half-man, the champion of mankind against the tyranny and capriciousness of the new gods – stole the celestial fire for humans from Zeus by rising to the heavens and kindling a torch at the sun's fiery wheel.[1] This story serves to demonstrate the link, commonly made in antiquity, between fire and the sun. Fire was the terrestrial element which corresponds to the sun in the sky: it was seen as a semi-magical thing, able to destroy but also to warm and to make it possible for humankind to illuminate the gloom of the night and to protect himself against the wild beasts who were instinctively afraid of fire. Zeus himself, in the Greek world, could be directly associated with the fire and heat of the sun: he was 'Zeus of the Burning Face', or 'Zeus the Scorcher'.[2] Fire was regarded as a purifier, a cleanser which came straight from the sun.

The worship or veneration of heat and fire is something which we associate especially with the cold, northerly places of the world, though the sun was, of course, revered as the supreme divinity in such warm lands as Egypt, where it was inextricably linked with sovereignty and kingship. But sun-worship is frequently absent in the hot places of the world, where heat and fire are bound up with drought and famine. Thus in East Africa it is the sky-god, the rain-giver, who is propitiated.[3] But after the long cold, dark winter of northern Europe, the heat and light of the sun are welcomed: through them the earth stirs into life and hope is renewed. The fire-festivals of pagan Europe, which spilled over into the Christian period, demonstrate the magical association between the sun and fire. Bonfires were lit at such great pagan Celtic festivals as Beltene on 1 May and

Samhain on 1 November,[4] to mark the turning points of the solar year – perhaps to welcome the sun's heat in May and, in the November ritual, to ensure it returned after the winter. Yule was originally a midwinter sun-festival, when the yule-log was lit to encourage the sun's renewal.[5] The midsummer bonfire-rituals, which were followed at the summer solstice, magically assisted the sun at its critical and high point at the turn of the annual celestial cycle.[6] These pagan midsummer fire-festivals were replaced by celebrations of the birth of John the Baptist. He was born at the time of the summer solstice, and the bonfire was thought to be particularly apposite as tradition has it that the bones of the saint were burnt by the emperor Julian the Apostate, who reigned during the mid-fourth century AD and who briefly reintroduced paganism to the Roman world. So the 'bone-fire' was a fitting festival with which to honour the saint. Christina Hole[7] records that as late as 1800 a Cornish farmer sacrificed his best calf in the flames. The bonfires had both a magical and a practical religious function. They offered reverence to the sun and replicated its heat and light on earth. But the sun's fertility-role was reflected also in the rich ash which was spread on the fields to fertilize the new seed.

Linked to the sun-bonfire ritual is a fire-ceremony which sought to replicate not only the fire/heat properties of the sun but also the image of the sun itself as a fiery wheel. Saint Vincent was a Christian living during the fourth century AD who observed a pagan festival in Aquitaine, in the west of Gaul, which involved rolling a flaming wheel downhill to a river, which was then reassembled in the temple of the sky-god.[8] There is cyclical imagery here: the solar symbol is sent down by the sun-god to fertilize the land, and is then taken back into the sky so that it can warm and light the world.[9] An almost identical ritual was associated with the festival of St John, which was performed until very recently in several parts of temperate Europe. Wheel-rolling for the festival was recorded in some twelfth-century documents, for instance, and in the fifteenth century a British abbot under Henry VI also described the ceremony. The festival traditionally took place at night, when the sight of the great flaming sun-wheel would be at its most dramatic. At the village of Basse-Kontz, on the Moselle, the festival was witnessed as it took place in 1822. A huge wooden wheel was covered in straw and a pole set transversely through it; it was carried to the top of the Stromberg Mountain, set on fire by torches at a signal from the local mayor, and violently rolled down the mountainside towards the River Moselle. It was considered propitious for the coming year, and particularly for the vintage, if the wheel reached the river without hindrance and still on fire: in 1822 it was successful, a rare event, and there was rejoicing at the prospect of a lucky year.[10] The sun had blessed the land and ensured the abundance of the wine crop.

A more sinister fire-ritual, which may have been solar in origin, is recorded by the ancient Greek geographer Strabo and by Julius Caesar, and is remarked on also by a late (probably ninth-century AD) scholiast or commentator on Lucan's poem the *Pharsalia*,[11] in which the poet describes the final battle between Pompey and Caesar. The ritual recorded involved the sacrifice of humans and animals by caging them in huge wicker images of men and setting them alight. It is Lucan's commentator who links the rite with the sky- and thunder-deity Taranis, and thus the power of fire in lightning or the sun may have been invoked. It is interesting that 'straw-men' (without live victims!) are recorded as being burned in the spring-festivals of post-pagan Europe; and in Germany, the images burned at Eastertime were known as 'Judas men'.[12]

Two other features of heat-symbolism should be noted: one is the association of the sun with the birth of metallurgy. When gold was first discovered, its colour must have immediately made it the sun's metal. But new copper and bronze, with their bright reddish hue, can also resemble the sun, and the heat of the smithing furnace, the molten red metal and the awe of the smith's craft probably all contributed to the notion that the metal was the gift of the sun. The smith, the master of fire, was always held in high regard in pagan Europe.[13] The sun's fire purified the ore and made it possible to work. The second feature of heat-symbolism is properly left to our discussion of water and healing. It concerns the association of the sun with some of the great Romano-Celtic spring-sanctuaries of Gaul and Britain. Here it need only be pointed out that one of the reasons for this link may have been that so many of the springs emerged apparently without cause, hot from the ground, and therefore were perhaps envisaged as touched by the sun itself while sojourning underground. At Bath, the hot springs gush out at the rate of a quarter million gallons a day, and it is no surprise that the presiding divinity was, if her name is any indication, a sun-goddess, Sulis. She was equated in the Roman period with Minerva, and it could be that the connection was made because Minerva was a goddess of crafts, and the sun's fire opened up a vast variety of new abilities and skills for humankind, not least the arts of pottery-making and of cooking.

The eye, light and the sun-gods

We saw in Chapter Three that the physical resemblance between the sun and the human eye was noted in European antiquity (Fig. 13) and thus the eye and the sun became associated in terms of religious imagery. But the other, more important reason for the link between the sun and the eye is light: eyes are light-receptors; we see by means of light passing through and acting on the retina. The eye is a reflector of light and of human personality; it was also regarded as the seat of the soul. Eyes close in sleep, mirroring death; blindness emulates death, with the absence of light, and darkness and death have always, naturally, been linked.[14] Eyes were associated with the light and with fire; both the sun and the eye are penetrative and can seek out truth and justice. The sun is an all-seeing eye, and the eye can sometimes represent power, sovereignty and also the divine. This happened in Egyptian imagery; and in Greece, epithets of both Zeus and Helios signify huge visionary power, implying also the possession by these deities of enormous eyes.[15] There are other ways in which the sun, light and eyes could seem associated; plants are observed to respond to light, almost as if they have the power of sight. The reflective qualities of the eye resemble the luminous, mirror-like properties of water which reflects the sun and its light. This may be partly why certain Gaulish healing sanctuaries were associated with the sun, light and eye-afflictions: the spring-shrine to Apollo Vindonnus at Essarois in Burgundy was dedicated to a god whose surname means 'clear light', and here model eyes attest the needs of his devotees. Maybe this deity was a god of clear vision and pure clear water, whose qualities caused human sight to be improved.[16] The god at Essarois was a solar divinity and, therefore, his image on his temple-pediment reveals him as a radiate-headed divinity (Fig. 86).[17] Many other water-shrines like this attest the curing of eye-disease: at the local goddess Sequana's temple at *Fontes Sequanae* near Dijon, eye-models and wooden heads of pilgrims, clearly showing people afflicted with blindness or eye-disease, indicate that devotees came to the pure spring-water in order to enlist the aid of the goddess. There is no connection with this Celtic therapeutic tradition but, for some reason, springs in parts of southern Italy are still sometimes known as 'eyes',[18] as if the reflective properties of spring-water were seen to replicate or imitate the eye. Possibly also, the bathing of eyes in fresh water, sometimes possessing beneficial mineral additives, was shown to have curative effects. In addition, we have the obvious link between water and tears.

Light and the sun have generally been seen as separate entities. This is because the sun may not always be visible in an overcast sky, even in broad daylight. Moreover, in northern latitudes in particular, the sky is filled with light long before the sun's sphere appears over the horizon and long after it sinks beyond vision.[19] So we have always to bear in mind, when examining the imagery of light, that the sun may not always have been envisaged as its direct perpetrator. There are other luminaries, not perhaps seen in antiquity as dependent on the sun. The Celtic healing goddess Sirona has a name which is associated with light, but Sirona is a star-name rather than a solar title.[20] But in the main light and sun were invoked as a single entity. In the Celtic world, brightness could be equated with supremacy, and light-epithets were often applied to the high gods, not only the sky-lords but also the Celtic Mars. We have already seen that an indigenous British war-god was called Belatucadrus ('Fair, Shining One'), and that Mars Loucetius, another light-surname, was invoked in Gaul and in Britain.[21] One interesting Gaulish deity was 'Luxovius', the eponymous and topographical spirit of Luxeuil, whose name has light-associations. He was a healing spring-divinity, of no importance outside the settlement itself, but he was linked with the Celtic sky-sun god in his guise as a conquering horseman and bearing a solar wheel (Fig. 87).[22] In the early Irish tales, which date in extant form to the early Christian period but which frequently refer to pagan myths and deities,[23] a Celtic god was named 'Lugh', 'Luminous One', which may denote his solar associations. His surname or epithet 'of the long arm' and his liking for the sling and the javelin,[24] may link him with the Greek Apollo, whose weapons also struck from a distance and whose arrows imitated the rays of the sun.

In Gaul, the Celtic Apollo, like his Classical counterpart, was concerned both with the sun and with healing. The god presided over therapeutic spring-sanctuaries, and the various surnames of this Celtic healer give him a directly solar association. 'Apollo Belenus' or 'Brilliant Apollo' was widely invoked in Celtic Europe. He had shrines in Gaul, as at Sainte-Sabine in Burgundy, where horse-images were offered to him.[25] The fourth-century AD poet Ausonius from Bordeaux mentions sanctuaries to Belenus in Aquitaine[26] and, significantly, speaks of his priest 'Phoebicius',[27] whose name refers to the Classical solar name of Apollo 'Phoebus'. The Gaulish 'Apollo Grannus' may have been a solar surname related to the Irish 'grían' meaning sun,[28] but it is more likely that the name reflects the topographical name (modern Grand), where the

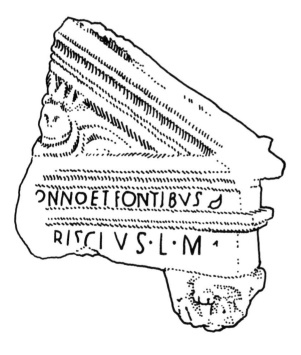

86 Part of temple-pediment from the sanctuary dedicated to Apollo Vindonnus, with radiate sun-god, from Essarois, Burgundy. Paul Jenkins, after Thevenot

87 Stone statue of mounted god with solar wheel and monsters from Luxeuil, Haute-Saône. Height: 1.65 m (5.4 ft). E. R. Aldhouse, after Espérandieu

god had a major spring-sanctuary. But he was a sun-god as well as a healer: at Trier, he is called 'Grannus Phoebus'.[29]

In order that we may comprehend the association of the Celtic Apollo with the sun, it is necessary to look at Apollo's role in the Greek world. He was not, in origin, a sun-god but, as Phoebus Apollo, took over some of the functions belonging to the sun-god Helios, probably sometime in the fifth century BC or maybe earlier.[30] Helios was the physical embodiment of the sun, the sun itself. He did not have a strong cult-following in the Greek world, except for the island of Rhodes, where he was

given anthropomorphic status.[31] There is a charming myth associated with the Rhodian worship of Helios, recorded by Pindar,[32] which relates how Zeus, king of the gods, when parcelling out territory to the other gods, omitted to give any land to the sun-god. By lucky coincidence (as so often employed in myth) it was at this very moment that the island of Rhodes emerged from the sea, and Helios immediately laid claim to it.[33] The Rhodians used to sacrifice a chariot and four-horse team to Helios, by causing it to plunge into the sea, in imitation of the myth of Helios who was perceived as driving a quadriga across the sky by day and plunging into the western sea at sunset.[34] A red-figured *krater* (wine-mixing bowl) shows Helios rising from the sea with his four-horse chariot and boat to carry him, by day and by night.[35] Pausanias records that the Spartans used also to make sacrifice to Helios, in the form not of a chariot but of horses, who were despatched on a peak of the Taygetos mountains,[36] which was sacred to the sun-god. This was because it was perceived that Helios required fresh horses at midday in order to continue his perpetual journey across the sky. The economic loss caused by these sacrifices should not be underestimated: the importance of the sun to such communities must have been very considerable if expensive commodities, like horses or vehicles, were to be destroyed.

The fifth-century BC equation and conflation between Helios and one of the aspects of Apollo is a curious one. Both Helios and Apollo were hunters, archers whose arrows could be perceived as replicating the sun's rays.[37] It is the epithet 'Phoebus', 'bright, shining' which attests Apollo's solar symbolism, first documented by the fifth-century tragedian Aeschylus.[38] Apollo was a son of Zeus; he was associated with purity, clarity and thus may naturally have acquired a solar function. As a hunter, his arrows, like the rays or beams of the sun, could bring pestilence as well as light.[39] The Classical as well as the Celtic Apollo was linked with springs, for example at Delphi[40] and at Claros,[41] though in these circumstances there may have been an oracular association with the bubbling spring-water being understood as the chattering of the oracle. But, as in a Celtic context, water, light, clarity and purity may have been linked in the complex functions and imagery of Apollo. We know that Apollo had other water-associations: swans were sacred to him, perhaps because of their dazzling whiteness, and he was connected in myth with the ability to avert drought.[42] As a master of the sun, he would

clearly have been able to control its power and cause its temporary subjugation to the forces of sky and rain, when it was of necessity obscured by cloud.

The chariot of the sun

The image of the sun as driving in a horse-drawn carriage or chariot is common to many Indo-European peoples. We find it in the Vedic mythology of India; Xenophon[43] observes that the Persians thought of the sun as a charioteer. By the second century BC the Roman sun-god Sol, probably the old Italian Sol Indiges, was represented in a quadriga.[44] In terms of Mediterranean imagery, we know most about Helios/Apollo, who was persistently presented in art and myth as driving a chariot across the sky. There is a story of the son of Helios, the Titanic Phaethon, who mounted the sun's chariot, thus flying in the face of Zeus' authority. The king of the gods struck him with his thunderbolt and he fell into the Eridanus, the ancient river of the sun.[45] We have already mentioned the Rhodian sacrifice of a chariot and horses to Helios; and the sun-god is often portrayed as a shining charioteer, urging his team in a gallop across his celestial territory; this is seen, for example, on a red-figure vessel from Apulia showing the sun-god and his chariot encircled by a solar disc.[46] The association of chariots and horses makes it difficult to comprehend which is the dominant or primary image, whether the horse is linked to the sun because of the chariot or whether the horse is the original solar associate and the chariot naturally followed. Throughout this book, allusion is made to the fact that horse and sun are closely linked in the imagery of Europe (below, and Chapter Seven). There is a further complexity in that it is possible that the chariot came about because of the natural connection between wheels (which look like the sun) and the sun itself.

It is interesting to look for a moment at the

idea of the wheeled vehicle as a means of trans-porting the sun. Wagons or light spoked-wheel carts were regarded as prestigious, as was the animal which pulled them. Light, fast and manoeuvrable, vehicles with spoked wheels were present in the Near East by the seventeenth century BC, and at Mycenae by the sixteenth. In temperate Europe, evidence suggests that chariots were not widely used for secular transport in Bronze Age Europe, but were employed in ceremonial and for burial. Wheeled cult or funerary cars remained characteristic of Bronze Age central Europe for about 800 years: the cremated remains of high-ranking Urnfield people were buried with their vehicles in the thirteenth and twelfth centuries BC; and Hallstatt wagon-burial was practised from about 700 BC.[47] It is appropriate that a mode of conveyance which was regarded as a mark of prestige and respect should be used to transport the sun; the speeding horses would ensure that the sun was able to fulfil his obligation of lighting up the entire sky, travelling across vast distances very fast.[48]

In barbarian Europe during the later Bronze Age, we see not only the use of full-size vehicles for conveying the dead to their burial-places but, in addition, *Kesselwagen* (see Chapter Four), ritual containers carried on wheels and used to carry the cremated remains of corpses (Fig. 47). Christopher Pare[49] would link these *Kesselwagen* to a complex solar and water cult, which appears first at the beginning of the Urnfield period, since sun-wheel and water-bird symbols are frequently associated with this group of material. The ritual involved may well be concerned with the averting of drought by magical means or, indeed, the reverse: vessels full of water might be ritually carried away magically to persuade wet weather to depart and be replaced by warm sunshine. Colin Burgess[50] has recently suggested that the deterioration of the climate in the European Bronze Age could have been caused by volcanic activity, in which case the sun would have been obscured by clouds and particles of dust, perhaps for some time. But there is some independent evidence which

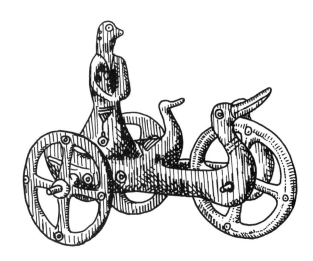

88a Bronze Age clay vehicle with male deity from Dupljaja, Yugoslavia. Length: 24 cm (9.5 in.). Paul Jenkins, after Torbrügge

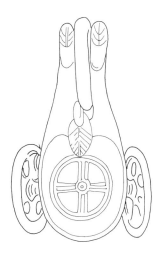

88b Underside of clay vehicle showing solar symbol. Miranda Green, after Sandars

lends credence to the notion of drought-aversion in Greece: the Thessalian town of Crannon had a cult whereby a vessel was drawn on a wagon to induce rain. Coins of the fourth century BC struck by the town show a cart, a vessel and ravens,[51] and in the third century Antigonos Carystos[52] recorded this tradition and the purpose of the ritual.

We actually have an image of what may be a solar deity in anthropomorphic form, himself carried on a cart, at Dupljaja in Yugoslavia (Fig. 88a), perhaps dating to the end of the first millennium BC (see also Chapter Four). The male figure, wearing a spiral- and circle-decorated robe, rides on a three-wheeled cart whose shaft-ends are ornamented with water-birds. The god stands on a solar motif cut into the floor of his carriage (Fig. 88b), and was once covered by a kind of parasol, which may itself be a solar emblem.[53] Once again, we may be witnessing a ritual against drought, the water represented by the bird-figures. But it has been argued (Chapter Four) that, in Bronze Age religious tradition, the water-bird may represent fertility, and the image may be present here to link the sun with florescence and abundance.

For barbarian Europe, the concept of the sun travelling in a cart or chariot is shown conclusively at Trundholm (Fig. 45 and cover illustration). Whilst ploughing in the area of a Danish peat-bog, farmers discovered a bronze figure of a horse, a disc and then parts of a spoked-wheeled cart-model. Complete, the object was found to consist of a wagon with six wheels, drawn by a horse wearing a head-harness or chamfrein with star- or sun-like decoration around the eyes (Fig. 89). On the wagon was carried a large bronze disc, about 25 cm (10 in.) in diameter, one side gilded with a thin sheet of gold, the other left as bronze. The sun-disc itself was made of two discs joined by a bronze ring cast on round them. The entire vehicle measured about 60 cm (24 in.) in length and it was perhaps made in about 1300 BC.[54] The wagon was deliberately broken before burial, a custom which was common throughout ancient European religious tradition[55] when rendering offerings as appropriate to the gods. As John Ferguson puts it, when describing ritual breakage at the sanctuary of Hera on Samos, '. . . they had been used for the service of a divinity and should not be restored to normal human use'.[56] Here at Trundholm, we may envisage the deliberate smashing and burial of a sun-symbol which was 'killed' as a gift to the sun-god, made useless to the profane or secular world, thus separating the spheres of human and divine activity. But before the sun-chariot was committed to the care of its master, we may imagine the kinds of ceremony in which it may have been used. It was built to replicate the light and heat of the sun travelling across the sky: the gilded surface represented the sun in full radiance in the daytime, the bronze side the red sunset and the sun's nocturnal journey to the underworld. So, in the ceremonial, the purpose of the cart was magically to appear to move the sun in the sky. Maybe the priests and the suppliants performed this ritual during a cold wet period or during winter, when the sun required wooing and propitiation in order to entice it back to warm and illuminate the land.

Nancy Sandars[57] has painted a vivid picture of celebrants at Trundholm facing south to the meridian in daytime ceremonies, so that they would see the golden image of the sun moving from east to west in imitation of the sun in the daylight sky. If the carriage were turned round at sunset, the bronze face of the solar disc would replicate the journey back made by the invisible night sun.

Trundholm is a spectacular manifestation of the belief in the sun as a divine entity, able to be summoned, controlled or enticed when needed. But it is not absolutely alone as a symbol in Scandinavian Bronze Age cult-tradition: a similar broken carriage, represented by two small horses and a disc, was found with three

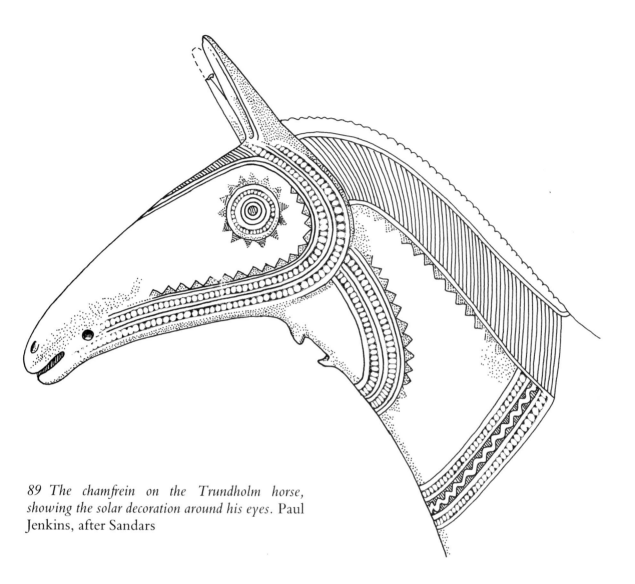

89 The chamfrein on the Trundholm horse, showing the solar decoration around his eyes. Paul Jenkins, after Sandars

bronze oxen and some spears, in a mound at Tågeborg in Scania.[58] The presence of ploughing animals here may connect the cult with a fertility-ritual. In addition, some of the images of Swedish Bronze Age rock-art depict what may be two-wheeled wagons carrying a third wheel-shaped symbol, which may be interpreted as a solar disc.[59]

Before we leave the chariot of the sun, we should briefly consider the other manner in which the sun could travel, namely by boat. It is sometimes suggested that, as believed in Egypt, the sun was transported by boat at night when it visited the underworld. In the imagery of Bronze Age Europe, sun-wheels and boats frequently appear together (see Chapter Four). In Scandinavian rock-art, the horse, sun and ships may occur in association (Fig. 61)[60] as if reflective of the sun's journey by day and night, on land and water. Swedish petroglyphs continually depict suns associated with boats.[61] Ships and suns are repeatedly linked on Bronze Age metalwork;[62] reference has already been made to the frequent motif of the sun carried in a bird-decorated boat, on sheet-bronze vessels.[63] It is interesting to recall that, in Greek mythology, Helios drove in a chariot across the sky and floated back to the east at night in a golden goblet;[64] on pottery, Helios could be portrayed accompanied by both his chariot and a boat.[65]

The solar horse

Discussion of horse-drawn vehicles to carry the solar disc, and the image of the sun in a chariot hurtling across the sky, leads naturally to consideration of the horse as a close and intimate associate of the sun. Horses played a prominent part in Indo-European myth and ritual, and the origins of this may be in the secular value that was placed on the animal. In temperate Europe, the horse was not adopted to any extent for riding-purposes until the eighth century BC,[66] but we have seen that light, horse-drawn vehicles were adopted long before this time. The horse is and was in antiquity an animal of great prestige. It is large, handsome, fast, courageous and invaluable in warfare and hunting. It is also a relatively expensive creature to maintain, requiring quantities of high-quality grain.[67] These two features, relating to war and aggression, on the one hand, and prosperity on the other, may have caused the horse to be adopted as a symbol of both war and peace. The animal is a natural beast to use for parades and display, as a symbol of power and leadership. The long slashing sword of Hallstatt warfare betrays the importance of the horse as a cavalry animal in very late Bronze Age and early Iron Age Europe. During the Iron Age, the charioteer and the knight were regarded as of high status: the burial of chariots with their owners in the Marne region of eastern Gaul and east Yorkshire, sometimes with their horses,[69] from the fifth century BC indicates the value and symbolism of both vehicle and beast. In battle-tactics, the horse made it possible for its rider to develop and display consummate skill and was

revered as a life-saver, able to carry its rider swiftly away from danger.

If the horse was so valued in life, the evidence that exists for horse-sacrifice in the Indo-European world suggests that the divine recipient must have been regarded with great awe. A major horse-sacrifice which took place in Rome was that of the October Horse, a ceremony in which a horse-race was run on the Ides of October and the right-hand horse of the victorious team was killed with a spear and dismembered. The tail of the sacrificed animal was hung up originally in the house of the king

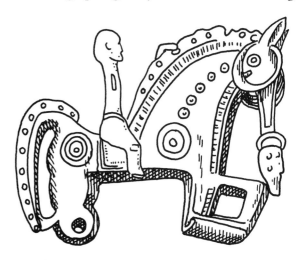

90 Iberian Iron Age brooch in the form of a horse with sun-symbols. Paul Jenkins, after Déchelette

and its blood, mixed with ash from the sacred hearth onto which it was allowed to drip, was collected and used in the agricultural spring-festival of the *Parilia*.[70] We have seen that horses were sacrificed to the sun by the Spartans and Rhodians. Several ancient authors[71] mention that horses were sacred to the Persian sun-god and that they were sacrificed by being burned entire. This type of sacrifice is known as a 'holocaust', an offering where nothing is left for the worshipper, an act generally reserved for the underworld powers or where sacrifice was made for a particularly urgent reason.[72] In the case of a holocaust to the sun-god, the awe and reverence of this high deity is aptly demonstrated, but there may also be the factor of fire, appropriate for the fiery solar divinity and perhaps the idea that the consumed horses would rise in the smoke towards their celestial destination. In a Persian sun-hymn of Zarathustra, the sun is referred to as 'swift-horsed'.[73]

In archaeological evidence, the horse and the sun are closely related as images. We have seen this expressed cogently at Trundholm, and in Scandinavian rock-art, where horses and suns are depicted together (Figs. 59, 61).[74] Far away from north Europe, on the Greek island of Syros near Delos, a Bronze Age silver belt was carved with repetitive images of horses and sun-wheels,[75] representative of either a sun-chariot or a horse and sun-symbols. Horses or horsemen and solar motifs are common on Late Bronze Age and Hallstatt sheet-bronze vessels, like that at Kleinklein in Austria (Fig. 18).[76] The late Hallstatt grave-find of lead images of horsemen, water-birds and solar wheels at Frögg, Carinthia, may have been decoration to be applied to bronze or clay vessels,[77] perhaps to be used in ritual associated with a sun-cult. Also of this Hallstatt phase are small axe-models marked with solar designs and with attached horse-images, which are themselves sometimes stamped with similar solar symbols (Fig. 36).[78]

Horse and sun were still linked images in Iron Age Europe. Iberian *fibulae* were sometimes ornamented with concentric circles (Fig. 90),[79] like those on the Hallstatt axe-model to which allusion has just been made, and which may attest a solar symbolism. An Iron Age stone at Robernier in the south of France bears imagery in the form of a highly abstract horse together with concentric circles and a swastika,[80] both of which I have argued can be seen as solar signs in certain contexts.

It is on Iron Age coinage in western Europe that the horse and sun-images show their persistence as a combined theme (Fig. 91). All the native coins of Celtic Europe began as imitations of Greek and Roman currency, but the models chosen by the Celtic tribes varied according to what appealed to communities in particular areas; imagery which was in some way familiar or appropriate to specific tribes or sub-tribes would generally have been favoured.[81] It is accepted by most scholars that there is probably some kind of religious element in at least some Celtic coin-iconography. There is no doubt that the British and Gaulish Celts' predilection for horses[82] caused them to choose as models for their own coinage those Mediterranean types bearing images of horsemen or chariots. The most common coin-type adopted and then adapted was based on the gold staters of the rule of Philip II of Macedon (359–336 BC) which have on the obverse the beardless head of Apollo as a sun-god and on the reverse a charioteer with a quadriga. Under the influence of the Celtic artistic abstraction, this reverse-type often became a horse by itself with perhaps one wheel beneath it, but in very many instances this creature is accompanied by intense solar symbolism in the form of rosettes, circles, and large, dominant sun-wheels above the horse, in the position proper to the sun. The relationship of wheel to sun-motifs on these coins is complicated. Whilst the wheel beneath the horse may reflect the original chariot depicted *pars pro toto*,[83] this is sometimes replaced by a symbol resembling the sun rather than a true wheel, and the sun in the sky above the horse takes on the genuine wheel-shape (Fig. 91).[84] The triple-phallused horse on a silver coin at Bratislava[85] (Fig. 41) is accompanied by a huge wheel-like sun; and on a British Icenian coin inscribed 'ANTED' – the name of the tribal king – the sun-wheel above the horse has slanting rays or spokes, as if to reflect a fast-spinning wheel with whirling spokes.[86]

The wheel-sign on Celtic coins is probably representative of sun and wheel at one and the same time. The one wheel below the horse represents all that remains of the original chariot, perhaps because horse and sun-wheel were familiar Celtic cult-associates. Sun and wheel are to an extent mutually replaceable; the elements of light, movement and physical resemblance have become inextricably intermingled. It may be that the die-sinkers of the coins persistently included the sun/wheel below or above the horse in their repertoire at least partly because it was such a powerful talisman.

The sun and the horse were tenacious companions. We find that in the Romano-Celtic phase in Gaul the Celtic Apollo, worshipped both as solar deity and healer, was associated with horses. This link was especially prevalent in Burgundy, at such shrines as Bolards (Nuits Saint Georges)[87] and Sainte Sabine, where Belenus was invoked.[88] Interestingly, the Thracians, too, venerated the horse as sacred to the sun-god and the Thracian Horseman at a sanctuary near Lozen in Bulgaria was identified with a solar god, called 'Apollo Gukethienos'.[89] Returning to Celtic Gaul, there are other signs of the solar horse: some of the clay figurines of horses found in a cache at Assche-Kalkoven in Belgium bear solar symbols round their necks, like amulets;[90] and at the Roman military quarry-face at Bad Dürkheim in the Rhineland, Celtic workmen scratched swastikas, horses and also wheel-symbols, some of the last depicted with stands or stems, as if representative of cult-objects carried in processions.[91] We should remember, too, the Celtic version of the cult of the Dioscuri, which was popular in Gaul and Germany:[92] these Classical divinities were represented as horsemen, and were connected with concepts of light and dark, day and night.

Finally, at the risk of anticipating discussions of the solar conqueror in Chapter Seven, we should look briefly here at the solar role of

91a Iron Age silver coin with horse, sun and concentric-circle wheel. British, Midlands

91b Early British uninscribed gold Iron Age coin with horse, sun below, wheel above.

91c Southern British gold quarter stater with triple-tailed horse, sun below, wheel above. By permission of the National Museum of Wales

the horse in the 'Jupiter-Giant' imagery of eastern Gaul and the Rhineland during the Roman period. Here, a mounted sky-god, often with a solar wheel he carries like a shield, rides down a snake-limbed monster of darkness and death (Fig. 87). Here, the horse is an unequivocally solar image: at Weisenhof in Germany, the horse is replaced by a sun-chariot;[93] and on the sculpture at Mouhet (Indre),[94] whilst the chthonic element is present in the form of the giant, the sun-wheel by itself rests on the monster's back as if taking the place of the horse and its celestial rider.

Water and the healing sun

We saw earlier that the sun could be envisaged as travelling by boat as well as by chariot; that the sun and aquatic birds are often associated in Bronze Age imagery; and that vessels carried on wagons are suggested as being part of a ritual against drought or rain.[95] But the religious association between the sun and water was a profound one, with wide-ranging and complex ramifications; it involved light itself, purification and healing.

There is a natural, visual link between water and the sun: water reflects light and may appear to sparkle with its own luminosity; unclouded, translucent water can be seen through, and thus light and purity are associated. A further relationship between the two phenomena is that water and the sun are both life-forces, essential to all living things. But there is a 'dark' side to both, in that the sun may destroy by burning and scorching, and water has the capacity to flood and drown. Both forces, therefore, needed to be controlled by man, by means of ritual, religion and magic. The sun was observed to have regenerative properties, bringing the seed-corn back to life after its 'death' and burial in the soil, in parallel with the cyclical pattern of day and night, summer and winter. Water, too, has the quality of renewal and rebirth: the embryo lies

in life-giving fluid until it is born; cauldrons, among the Celts and their forebears, were symbols of everlasting life and the ability to raise men from the dead. Ever-replenishing springs which gushed up from deep below ground were seen as a further reflection of regeneration. Sun and water were perceived to be associated in the heat of certain springs, and we have already seen how, in European rituals, a symbolic version of the sun's fiery wheel was rolled into water, in replication of the seasonal rhythm of light, warmth and fertility. This ritual could, indeed, account for the Gaulish custom of casting miniature bronze sun-talismans into rivers[96] (Fig. 84) and into such sacred springs as those at Bourbonne-les-Bains and Bolards.[97] The affinity between water and celestial cults is perhaps manifested also in the aquatic context of many images of the Celtic solar warrior (Chapter Seven) in the vicinity of springs and rivers; indeed Apollo Grannus' spring-sanctuary at Grand in the Vosges produced no less than three Jupiter-columns.[98] And interestingly, a connection between the sun and wells persisted in Celtic Britain after the official end of paganism: when visiting holy wells in Wales, the custom was to walk 'sunwise' (or clockwise) around the well three times, to ensure fertility and conception.[99]

In Romano-Celtic Gaul and Britain, there grew up a great number of important therapeutic sanctuaries on the sites of springs, some of which were hot, some with genuine medicinal, mineral properties, others merely a source of clean, clear water. Sometimes, these springs were associated with the worship of the Celtic Apollo who, in Greece, was both a healer and a solar deity, and associated also with sacred springs, such as Delphi and Claros. In many of the Gaulish spring-shrines, there is evidence that light and the sun played a dominant role in the healing process. If we look first at sanctuaries associated with the Celtic Apollo, it is possible to see that worship often emphasized the solar nature of his cult. Thus Apollo Vindonnus at Essarois in Burgundy has the epithet 'clear' or 'white'; his image is that of a radiate sun-god (Fig. 86) and pilgrims brought to him their eye-afflictions, represented by models of eyes, perhaps in the expectation that their sight would become clear and let in the pure light implicit in the god's name. Here, sunlight and the clear translucent water of the spring come together in a single image of purity and light.[101]

It may be that the light-element in water partly accounted for the number of spring-sanctuaries whose presiding deities were invoked in the hope that they would cure the eye diseases of the pilgrims. The great shrine of Sequana at *Fontes Sequanae* near Dijon produced hundreds of immediately pre-Roman wooden votives, mainly of oak heartwood, including models of limbs and internal organs, but also heads of people with obvious eye-problems, including perhaps the bulging eyes of thyroid sufferers; there were also bronze models of eyes.[102] All these offerings were made in the hope that, by reciprocal means, their afflictions would be taken away and that the goddess Sequana would accept models of their sufferings, exchanging these for a whole, cured body. Another such holy place was Chamalières (Puy-de-Dôme), whose water (unlike that of *Fontes Sequanae*) possessed genuine curative properties in its mineral content. Here again, it was eye-disease which was the main scourge afflicting pilgrims to the shrine, perhaps caused by the malnutrition which may have been rife among the rural population.[103]

We have seen that many of Apollo's surnames at these Gaulish spring-sanctuaries were associated with the sun or with light; perhaps most clearly in the case of Apollo Belenus, who was widely revered and had a shrine at the sacred spring at Sainte-Sabine in Burgundy.[104] His solar image there is enhanced by the fact that the horse was sacred

to him and pilgrims visiting his holy temple offered little horse-figurines in hope or in gratitude for a cure.

At Luxeuil, the deity who presided over the sacred spring was not Apollo but Luxovius, his name having associations with light. The relationship between water and the sun is here intensified by the presence of an image of the solar warrior (Fig. 87), with his sun-symbol, his mount trampling the forces of darkness. Sirona, who was another light-deity, was also worshipped here.[105] At another aquatic shrine at Lhuis (Ain), a healing triad of mother-goddesses, themselves personifications of the local stream, shared their sanctuary with the solar god, represented by an altar decorated with a sun-wheel.[106]

In Britain, the link between healing water and the sun is less obvious than is the case in Gaul, but it is nonetheless present. The important Romano-Celtic therapeutic sanctuary to the indigenous Celtic god Nodens was built overlooking the River Severn at Lydney.[107] Oculists' stamps attest to the treatment of eye-diseases, and both sun and water imagery are present at the shrine: the proximity of the great tidal river may be reflected in the depiction of a marine divinity on a mosaic in the *cella* or inner sanctum of the temple. But a bronze diadem, perhaps worn by an officiant of Nodens' cult, displayed the image of a sun-god driving his four-horse chariot-team, in company with tritons and anchors.[108]

Finally, there is important cult-association between the sun and healing spring-water at the great sanctuary of Sulis Minerva at Bath, where steaming hot water pumps out of the ground in abundance and where pilgrims must have visited the holy spot for centuries prior to the arrival of the Romans.[109] They turned this place of ancient Celtic veneration into a massive Graeco-Roman style temple but equated the native goddess Sul or Sulis with their own Minerva. Sul is a Celtic solar name, perhaps the goddess was originally so-named because of the heat of the springs. There is other evidence for a sun-association: Mars 'Loucetius' ('light') was invoked at the shrine; and the great image of the male Gorgon on the temple-pediment[110] has a distinctly sun-like appearance, with his snake-locks and beard forming whirling 'rays' around the fierce moustached face with its hypnotic, staring eyes.

The affinity in the Celtic world between sun, light and water is well-established. The sun could heal and renew by its warmth; water had the ability to cleanse and nourish, and mineral springs could cure and purify. Light dances on moving water, as if it has absorbed the sun; and both elements are powerful forces for life and for death. People threw tiny sun-wheels into water; and pilgrims cherished hopes that the spring-deities of light would restore to them their eyesight.

— 7 —

The Life-Giver and Conqueror of Death

The sun is concerned with life; indeed, it could be perceived as life itself and without its warmth and light no living being could exist. It is, and always has been, seen as one of the two main life-sources, the other being water. But the sun is complicated in terms of its effects: it grants life but it also destroys, scorches, burns and withers. It may be this dualistic element in the concept of the sun which caused the ancient Celts and their ancestors to revere it as not simply a creator of life but also an entity which, because of its destructive properties, could act as a champion against the dark forces of the underworld. This is an idea similar to that of the gorgoneion or Medusa-symbol, worn as an amulet in order to avert the evil eye. If you harness the forces of destruction, it is your enemy rather than you who will suffer. The sun is also fitted for a chthonic or underworld role because of the assumption that its disappearance at night meant that it was visiting the lower regions and giving light to the dead.

This chapter explores the dual role of the sun as a power of fertility and as a fighter against the dark realms of night, darkness and death. We will see that the ramifications of the sun's influence are complex in that, in addition to the solar aspect of both, the two dual concepts of fecundity/florescence and darkness/death are themselves inextricably linked in a cyclical perception of life, death and rebirth.

Life, fertility and the sun-gods

The association between the sun and fertility has already been touched upon in previous chapters. These concepts are natural partners in terms of belief and imagery for many reasons. Crops are observed to flourish only when exposed to sunlight; the seed in the ground germinates in response to the warmth of the sun penetrating the dark ground. In terms of imagery, there is a sexual link in the beams of the sun penetrating the earth like a phallus, its semen or warmth and light fertilizing the ground. The ripe corn is golden yellow like the sun which ripens it, as if the union of father and mother (sun and earth) had produced offspring in the image of their sire. The sky and the sun are closely related and, in antiquity, were both perceived as sources of light. Moreover, the sun – in Mediterranean religions – was sometimes seen as the eye of the sky-god. The Roman imperial Sol Invictus ('the Unconquered Sun') was regarded as the heart of the universe and the source of all life.[1] Sun, sky and fertility are associated on coins of the Hellenistic ruler Ptolemy III, who is portrayed with attributes of Zeus, the sea-god Poseidon and Helios, the sun-god. The reverse of these coins bears the image of a horn of plenty crowned with the rays of Helios and bound with the diadem of the royal Ptolemies. Here is the divine ruler working in company with the sun-god for the fertility and well-being of the land.[2] Sky and fertility are clearly connected in terms of rain which, like the sun's rays, fertilizes the earth in an allegory of semen. Sky-gods were generally also weather-deities, concerned with sun and rain, thunder and lightning. Pausanias[3] speaks of a Greek sanctuary of Zeus Ombrios – Zeus the Rain-God – whose close concern as a weather-divinity was agriculture.[4] Farmers prayed to Zeus Chthonios – Zeus, Lord of the Earth and Underworld, and to Demeter for the crops to grow.[5] The sun possessed powers of regeneration, renewal and rebirth, but it was also envisaged as a hunter whose arrows slew but, by killing, caused the red blood of his victim to fall and fertilize the earth.[6] Apollo was a hunter, but he was capable of healing and destroying, just as the sun itself can grant or deny life.[7] Arrow-shafts and the sun's rays possess similar imagery,[8] and the theme of penetration evoked by both makes the concept of hunting and life-generation comprehensible.

The link in imagery (and presumably in belief) between the solar powers and fertility is amply demonstrated in the Bronze Age rock-art of Camonica and Scandinavia. At Finntorp, Bohuslän, one scene shows two people apparently copulating, the male having a sun-disc body (Fig. 63).[9] In Sweden, ithyphallic beings with human characteristics, but with sun-discs replacing the central portion of their bodies, brandish weapons at each other in a ritual conflict, which may enact a cult-drama where, magically, winter and summer compete for precedence.[10] This notion may be supported by the presence, on one image, of confronting disc-men, one of whom has a

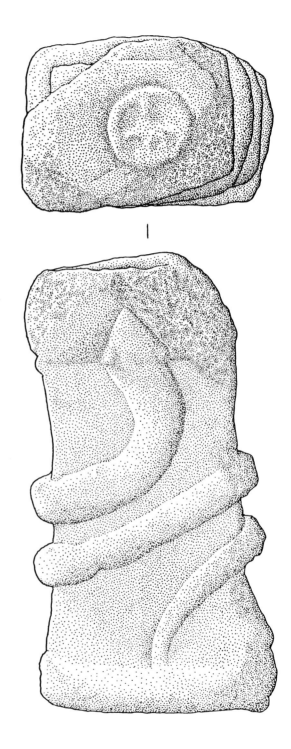

92 *Stone altar with wheel carved on* focus *and ram-horned snake twined round stone from Lypiatt Park, Glos. Height: 15 cm (6 in.). Nick Griffiths*

wheel-body, the other with a torso in the form of a concentric circle. Is it too fanciful to see the 'wheel-man' as the power of midsummer with the sun represented in full, beaming radiance, whilst the 'circle-man' may reflect the cold, red, beamless sphere of the winter months, when the rays of the sun are often invisible? In any event, the erect phalli and sun-bodies of these images reflect a fertility-association. Bertilsson[11] would argue that the depiction of this combat, and of the 'sun-men' in general, must be equated with the valuation and veneration of the concept portrayed and the desire for the association between sun and fertility to be established.

The Celtic festivals were totally bound up with the solar and pastoral year[12] and with fertility in general. Beltene, on 1 May, heralded in the summer and bonfires were lit to encourage the sun's heat.[13] Lughnasad, too, was a sun-festival, celebrating the harvest on 1 August, when the sun-yellow corn would be ripe, a glorious image of the fertility-powers of the sun. The custom of lighting midsummer solstitial fires survived throughout the Christian era, retaining a magical fertility-association (Chapter Six). Fire burns, purifies and makes ready the field for sowing by clearing away the remains of the previous year's harvest; the heat of fire encourages that of the sun and brings prosperity to the cornfields.[14]

The image of the sun as a fertility force is enhanced in both Mediterranean religion and that of temperate, barbarian Europe by its association with the bull. The relationship between sky-sun deities and bulls is very early in origin: in the Minoan period, the bull was associated with the sun probably because of fertility-cults: 'The bull is obviously a power of male fertility'.[15] In the myth of the mating of Pasiphae with the bull, we probably have a legend of the union between the solar bull and the lunar goddess. Pasiphae's name means 'she who shines on all'.[16] The Greek sky-god Zeus was invariably associated with bull-imagery:

the early temple to Cretan Zeus on Mount Ida dates from the time when the god was still the male vegetation-spirit of the Cretans, before he became the high celestial divinity of the Greeks.[17] Here, as early as the Middle-Late Minoan phases, votive or sacrificial offerings of ox-skulls, complete with horns, were dedicated to the resident deity. Bulls were sacrificed to Olympian Zeus, and Harrison[18] suggests that the god's occasional portrayal actually wearing the horns of a bull (as on a depiction of Zeus Olbios in the Musée Impérial Ottoman)[19] could be due to the fusion of the sacrificed animal with the god himself so that they become one. Certainly, myths of Zeus abound in bull-imagery: it was as a bull that he ravished Europa and pursued Io, who was given cow-horns by Zeus' jealous consort Hera, herself referred to in the literature as 'cow-eyed'.[20]

The bull is a virile, potent beast; he is also a roaring creature, simulating the thunder of the sky- and storm-god. Thus the deities of weather, in the East as well as in Mediterranean Europe, like Dolichenus of Syria[21] and Zeus Hadad of Nabataea[22] were traditionally associated with bulls. But in barbarian, proto-Celtic and Celtic Europe, there is further evidence of a specific association between the bull and the sun, again with overtones of a fertility connection. In the southern French Bronze Age rock-art of Mont Bego, more than half the engraved images are of bulls, or horned bulls' heads, or simply horns by themselves; sometimes the horns meet in a circle which may represent the symbolism of the sun.[23] The rock-art contains many circular motifs which may also depict solar images. One of the anthropomorphic carvings has been called 'The Sorcerer' by scholars: he brandishes two objects which resemble daggers, but it has been suggested that he is the weather-god of the mountain, wielding his thunderbolts and accompanied by his celestial bulls.[24]

In pre-Roman Celtic iconography, there

appears to be an unequivocal relationship between bulls and solar symbolism, again perhaps stressing the fertility-aspect of the sun-cult. Bull-horned helmets with wheel-amulets attached to them are depicted on the arch at Orange (Fig. 51), which bears so many carvings of Celtic arms and armour.[25] The devotee or acolyte on the Gundestrup Cauldron who offers the wheel-god his solar attribute, wears knob-ended bull-horns; it is sometimes stated[26] that the knobs which terminate the horns on many Celtic bronze images of bulls may be solar. Romano-Celtic imagery in Britain takes the joint symbolism of fertile bull and solar motif further. At the shrine of Willingham Fen in East Anglia, a sceptre was cast with images of a young god, with solar wheel and sky-eagle, and a triple-horned bull's head. This last is a common Celtic cult-image,[27] and here the normal sky-god/ bull association has the addition of the magical power of three. On a curious stone relief at Churcham, in the territory of the Dobunni, a god with a head of exaggerated size and two wheel-symbols, bears traces of bull-horns.[28]

The other animal whom we have met before as an associate of the sun is the stag. Here again the connection is due, partly at any rate, to the fertility and virility of the beast, coupled with the autumn shedding and spring-growth of the antlers which imitates the cyclical, seasonal imagery of winter and summer, and indeed also the winter and summer loss and regrowth of leaves on deciduous trees and the waxing and waning of the sun's strength according to the season. This is coupled with the visual association of a radiate sun with antlers (Chapter Three). Another allied dimension may involve the hunt, if we may link the killing of an animal with the replenishment of earth by its blood. Stag-hunting is depicted on Scandinavian and Camunian rock-art; it is possible that here is the image of a sacrifice to the sun-god. There is, in addition, a consistent association in imagery between the stag and the sun,

as we have seen.[29] The stag may pull a sun-disc, be driven by men towards the sun, and the motifs of sun and antlers may fuse into one composite solar symbol (Fig. 7). The stag-sun image continues later than the milieu of the rock-art of the Bronze Age: sun, moon and deer appear together on the sixth-century BC gold vessel from Altstetten, Zürich (Fig. 49);[30] it occurs on the late Iron Age silver coin from Petersfield, Hampshire (Fig. 79), which depicts a wheel between the antlers of a fertility-and nature-god.[31] One interesting image dates from the Romano-Celtic phase and was carved on a tombstone at Bois-de-la-Neuve-Grange in eastern Gaul (Fig. 43). Here, a wheel-sign has combined with the motif of antlers or tree-branches, the wheel-spokes extending in a complex formation beyond the felloe.[32] The ambiguity of tree and antlers may be deliberate, in that the stag was a forest creature, its antlers seen as resembling the branches of a tree. Trees themselves were potent fertility-images of the forest's florescence, and, whether the symbolism on this Alsace tombstone reflects the theme of stag or branch, the fertility concept combined with the wheel of the sun is manifestly present. The epitaph was a fitting remembrance that death was transient and renewal and rebirth would transpire beyond the grave.

The imagery of the Celtic sun-god in Britain and Gaul may sometimes make a very overt link between the sun and the concept of fecundity. A sculpture from Netherby, Cumbria, bears the depiction of an individual carrying a *cornucopiae* against his shoulder and a large wheel in the other hand (Fig. 69).[33] What is interesting about this image is that the figure resembles a Roman Genius, evocative of good luck, prosperity and well-being, who usually possesses the attributes of a horn of plenty and a *patera* or offering-plate held over an altar. But here, whilst the fertility-symbol of the *cornucopiae* remains, the small offering-dish is replaced by a huge eight-spoked wheel poised over a diminutive altar, as if this solar symbol is meant to dominate the image to the detriment of all the other motifs. At Naix (Meuse), the Celtic Jupiter is portrayed seated on his throne, with his sun-wheel at his left hand, but associated with the solar motifs are two horns of plenty,[34] curious emblems for the sky god.

The image of the solar fertility-goddess

In the Egyptian myth of Creation, the earth and sky undergo a divine marriage, to reflect and explain the symbiotic relationship between the celestial and earthly aspects of the world. This myth is common to many other cultures of antiquity, not least in the Greek world, where Zeus marries the earth-goddess Hera.[35] In the Romano-Celtic Rhineland, Jupiter was associated with the indigenous mother-goddesses at Trier[36] and at Köln.[37] More important is the stone from Clarensac in Provence, on which was inscribed a dual dedication to Jupiter and Terra Mater, but where the presence of a carved wheel betrays that it is the Celtic sun-god who is here linked with Mother Earth.[38]

Let us look, for a moment, at evidence for a goddess associated with the sun in her own right. In most cultures, the sun-god is male, but there were some female solar divinities. In Greek religion, the sun-god Helios had a daughter, the sorceress Circê, whose name is linked to 'circle' and who may herself be solar.[39] The Celtic British goddess Sulis has a solar name,[40] and whilst she was conflated, during the Roman period, with an aspect of the cult of Minerva, she was in all probability originally the sun-deity of the sacred hot springs. In earlier prehistory, the Early Bronze Age statue-menhir of a goddess at Avignon[41] bears a radiate sun over her breast, which may indicate her solar function (Fig. 20). The mother-goddess depicted between the two

rose-shaped wheels on the Gundestrup Cauldron may be travelling in a cart, as suggested by Olmsted,[42] but the 'rays' which stand out from the felloes could mean that she is associated with the sun-cult.[43] In the early post-pagan Irish literature (see above, p. 97) we learn of the existence of Ériu, the eponymous goddess of Ireland, the deity of the land who blesses her country by marrying the mortal kings and promoting the fertility of the soil. In one legend, she is described as sanctifying her marriages and acknowledging her consorts by handing them a golden goblet of wine. Some scholars interpret this as indicative of Ériu's status as a sun-goddess, the goblet symbolic of the fertile power of the sun. Interestingly, though there can be no direct connection, we saw earlier that in a myth of Helios, the Greek sun-god travels in a golden goblet over the sea.

Certain female divinities in the Celtic world seem, by their imagery, to possess an association with both fertility and the sun. Sometimes this is an occasional implication only: the horse-goddess Epona and Nehalennia, the Dutch sea-farers' deity, both have primary roles in terms of fertility, well-being and renewal after death, but on one or two monuments there is an indication of a solar aspect as well: a funerary 'stèle-maison' or house-shaped stone carved with the image of Epona at Baudoncourt (Haute-Saône) also bears a solar wheel-sign at the apex of the house-gable;[44] and another tombstone, at Agassac (Comminges), depicts a Nereid-like Epona with both sea-monsters and sun-symbols.[45] The situation with Epona is complicated. Classical authors inform us that roses were sacred to her,[46] probably as an image of the spring and yearly renewal of life: we are not far from some of the sun's functions. Nehalennia belonged to two major temples established in the tribal territory of the Morini, close to the North Sea coast of Holland. The goddess was worshipped by sea-faring traders above all, who prayed to her for safe journeys across the ocean and for prosperity in business; in addition, the deity probably possessed a more profound role beyond the grave,[47] perhaps represented particularly by her faithful dog, from whom she is virtually inseparable on her images. One of her shrines, at Domburg on the island of Walcheren, was discovered in the seventeenth century, but, sadly, most of the numerous altars to her were destroyed in a mid-nineteenth-century fire. Two stones dedicated to the goddess at this temple show her to have had some part to play in the Celtic solar cult: on one[48] Nehalennia wears a solar amulet around her neck; at the top of the second altar[49] a radiant sun is present, shining over the goddess.

The Celtic mother-goddesses themselves are sometimes manifestly associated with the solar cult. The veneration of the mother-goddess was well-attested in Romano-Celtic western Europe.[50] The portrayal of a seated or standing female deity with such fertility emblems as babies, children, fruit, fish or bread appears singly or as a double or triple image. The goddess was invoked especially as a triadic group, and dedications to the 'Deae Matres' or a related plural name endorse the multiple character of the cult. Dedicants were often women or people belonging to the lower echelons of the army or civilian life, but in the towns, in the military regions of Roman Britain and in the Rhineland, suppliants could be high officials of the Roman civil administration or army officers of high rank.

In Britain, there is some indication that there was a solar aspect to the mother-goddess cult: a roughly-fashioned stone from the Cotswolds[51] is carved with three seated mother-goddesses in a gabled niche: the sun, in the form of a spoked wheel, shines down on them from the top of the triangle; and at Easton Gray in Wiltshire, a broken figure of a mother-goddess bears a cross or wheel-sign on her forehead.[52] Most interesting, perhaps, is the evidence from a hoard of goldwork found within a silver offering-dish at Backworth in Durham, the handle of which carries an inscribed dedication to the 'Deae Matres'.[53] Inside the vessel were found five gold finger-rings, including one with an inscription to the 'Matres Coccae', the 'Red Mothers', and two gold necklaces and a bracelet all with solar amulets attached, one chain bearing also a moon-crescent.[54] It has to be emphasized that filigree gold wheel-shaped ornaments such as these are found widely distributed within the Roman Empire,[55] being by no means confined to the Celtic world. Nonetheless, in this context it is highly likely that the jewellery possesses some cult-significance and that the imagery of the sun-god and mother-goddess is meaningfully associated.

But there is another, very striking, group of Celtic material which links the sun-cult and domestic goddesses beyond any reasonable doubt. It consists of clay figurines of female divinities which were mass-produced in two-piece moulds in Gaul and the Rhineland.[56] Several different types of pipe-clay statuette were manufactured, mainly during the first two centuries AD. Most widely exported were images of the 'Dea Nutrix', a nursing goddess seated in a high-backed basket chair, suckling or holding either one or two infants. But it is the other major goddess-type which is interesting to us because of the presence of distinct solar imagery. These figurines represent a deity who strongly resembles the Classical Venus, a young naked girl, often with long flowing hair. It may be plausibly argued that this Graeco-Roman form serves only to disguise the identity of the figures as manifestations of a domestic cult reflective of fertility and well-being.[57] Indeed, many scholars believe this 'Venus' to be an image of some kind of mother-goddess.[58] The point is made that the paucity of monumental images of Venus in Gaul argues against this Roman goddess possessing sufficient popularity among the lower classes and poorer purchasers of these figurines for the deity to have been worshipped so widely in her original guise as goddess of love.[59] It is suggested that the art-form of Venus was chosen to represent a Celtic goddess of fertility rather than one specifically or only of sexual love.[60] Indeed, sexuality, fertility and maternity seem to have been combined in these pipe-clay representations, in that the goddess, whilst usually young and attractive, is often shown attended by one or more children. In a Roman context, Venus lent herself to such a Celtic adaptation, since she was originally the 'numen' or spirit of the fertile soil and of gardens and, as Venus Genetrix, was the co-founder of the Roman race, ancestor of Aeneas and of Julius Caesar.[61] Interestingly, the Greek goddess Aphrodite, with whom Venus was later identified, was herself a spring-deity.[62]

The main reason for the indigenous, domestic interpretation of this goddess in Gaul and Britain is her context. She is often found at healing spring-sanctuaries such as Bolards in Burgundy,[63] Vichy[64] and in Britain at Springhead in Kent.[65] She appears also buried in graves, as at Toulvern, Baden.[66] So the picture we have of this deity is that she was part of a domestic cult, favoured by poorer members of society (who could perhaps not afford bronze or stone images), and invoked by women to aid them in conception, to protect them in childbirth and to guard them against disease.[67]

The relevance of this 'Venus' to us is that she is frequently decorated with sun-symbols (Fig. 93): wheels, concentric circles, crosses and elaborate 'sun-bursts'. Many of the solar figurines were made in Breton workshops, only recently discovered in the neighbourhood of Rennes, the ancient town of Condate, capital of the Redones.[68] We need to look at just a few of the most striking sun-ornamented figures. The goddess at Bro-en-Fégréac (Loire Atlantique)[69] was decorated with several solar designs, including two realistic wheels at her calves and her body is flanked by combinations

93 *Pipe-clay statuette of goddess with sun-symbols from Tronoën, Finistère, Brittany. Height: 12.8 cm (5 in.).* Miranda Green

of wheels and circles; the rear surface of the figure is also thus patterned. Some of the wheels have been faithfully rendered, with nave, felloe and even the iron tyre included. The figurine from Caudebec-lès-Elbeuf comes from a grave.[70] Here the solar symbolism attains particular intensity: there are wheels and concentric circles on the breasts, the belly and thighs, beneath her hands and extending down as far as her feet; on her back are sun-wheels and circles; her breasts are in fact formed of complex circles, a pattern of decoration which recurs at La Chapelle des Fougeretz.[71] The goddess from Toulon-sur-Allier,[72] the site of one of the main central Gaulish factories, demonstrates her fertile powers in that she is accompanied by a naked infant, perhaps inspired by the Cupid of Classical iconography. By the child's shoulders are concentric circles and others are grouped in pyramidal formation flanking the lower part of his mother's legs. A similar figure comes from the Morbihan district of Brittany,[73] where the goddess rests her hands on the shoulders of a young person standing in front of her, accompanied by sun-wheels and concentric circles at her side and behind. This imagery is almost precisely repeated on a figure in the Archaeological Museum at Montpellier.[74] Some statuettes possess curious imagery, which recalls some of the Bronze Age solar associations we examined in earlier chapters. A goddess with a child at Moulins (Allier) is decorated with not simply solar wheels but also water-birds,[75] and she has a sun-amulet round her neck. Another 'Venus' is accompanied by concentric circles and a long-beaked wading bird at her feet.[76] Finally, we should glance at the context of some of these solar female images. They were placed in tombs at Caudebec, Toulvern and Lisieux,[77] and they were offered in such sanctuaries as Cracouville, Vieil-Evreux, and at a curious domestic shrine or *lararium* at Rézé[78] where a goddess is clothed in a long garment and is decorated with flowers,

94 Pipe-clay figurine of goddess with sun-motifs from Rézé. Height: c. 20 cm (8 in.). Miranda Green, after Musée de Bretagne

circles and a flamboyant radiant sun on the rear surface (Fig. 94).[79]

A number of features about these images are significant in terms of a solar-fertility association. First, the sheer intensity of the symbolism is very remarkable: the figures are covered with, or are surrounded by, sun-motifs both on their backs, where they would not readily be seen, and on their fronts. Second, we saw on the image at Caudebec that the solar signs are clustered on the most feminine and sexual parts of the body – the breasts, belly and thighs. In addition, a special feature is made of the breasts, which may be formed of a combination of the nipple and the general curve of the breast and solar symbols. This emphasis on sexuality and fertility is enhanced by the presence of children, who are also decorated with sun-signs. The water-birds may reflect a fertility imagery comparable to their association with the sun in prehistoric contexts. Finally, the personal nature of their role is amply demonstrated by their presence in small shrines, homes and tombs. This sepulchral association has further elements of interest in that, here, the solar goddess may be present in order to light the darkness and to guide the dead on their way to the underworld.

The presence of solar symbols associated with these Celtic goddesses whose primary function is that of fertility and prosperity demonstrates very powerfully the relationship between the sun and fecundity, in a visual, unequivocal form. The goddess represented has perhaps married the sun-god and has thus acquired his image or has herself taken over the power of the sun and become an omnipotent divinity of the upper and lower worlds. More

simply, these figures may have been decorated with the sign of the sun just to render them more powerful in their essentially domestic role. But a partnership between sun-god and mother-goddess is an attractive concept. We know that there were many divine couples worshipped in the Celtic world, who share attributes or borrow emblems and functions one from the other,[80] so it would not be so surprising if there existed a divine marriage between the forces representing the most important aspects of life on earth.

The sun, fertility, death and the underworld

The significance of the snake

The thinking behind an association between the sun and fertility is well established and appropriate. A link between fertility and chthonic or earth/underworld forces is equally valid, in that the seed lies dormant, seemingly without life, in the womb of the earth until activated and stimulated by the warmth of the sun. Many Celtic cults, in particular those of the mother-goddesses, have a concern with prosperity and well-being in this life, but also with life beyond the grave, resurrection or rebirth.[81] The intricate relationship between sun, fertility and death may sometimes be manifested in depictions of the sun-god associated with the image of a snake. This creature has a dual role in both Graeco-Roman and Celtic art and belief. It may symbolize the beneficence of fertility and renewal: this is probably due to a number of characteristics which belong to snakes. They slough their skin three or four times a year, in an allegory of resurrection after death; their physical appearance lends itself to phallic imagery, as do their long, involved coupling, the double penis of the male and the multiple offspring which many snakes produce; water-imagery is suggested

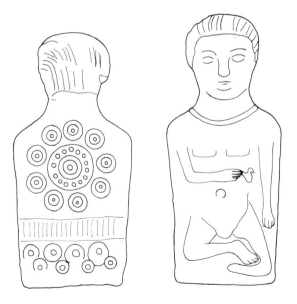

95 Pipe-clay statuette of cross-legged god with water-bird and sun-symbols from Quilly, Loire Atlantique. Height: 13.6 cm (5.4 in.). Miranda Green, after Musée de Bretagne, 1988

by the rippling, sinuous, river-like movement of the creature. But the other side of the snake's image is concerned with earthbound symbolism. It is an awesome, usually ground-based creature, able to insinuate itself into the smallest dark crevice in the rocks; can strike at lightning speed and may be venomous; all snakes are carnivorous. So the reptile is in many ways an appropriate symbol of death and darkness. We will see later in this chapter that snake-imagery may form the embodiment of negative as opposed to positive celestial forces. But, in some iconography, the serpent accompanies the sun-god, as a symbol of life and regeneration, just as the snake may often accompany the mother-goddesses or such healing female divinities as Sirona, herself bound up with fertility, signified by carrying eggs.[82] In addition, it is even possible that the snake-image may have a solar aspect, in that its shape may form an S or spiral, both of which are argued as solar motifs in certain circumstances (Chapter Three). The naked warrior-god on a stone at Bremevaque (Haute-Garonne) holds a pot and has a swastika on the altar-base, and what appears to be a snake ripples down from his arm.[83] Is this deity fighting the forces of evil with his solar symbols and his vessel of wine or honey to bring prosperity to the land? Two representations of the Celtic wheel-bearing god from the neighbourhood of Vaison in Provence, probably both from the Roman town itself, show the god with a serpent: at Séguret,[84] the sun-god is a warrior, in full Roman armour, with the eagle of Jupiter and the Celtic sun-wheel by his side (Fig. 74). Behind the eagle is a snake wound round an oak tree stump. At Vaison itself,[85] the Celtic Jupiter and his consort Juno are accompanied by a solar wheel and a snake. The snake and sun-symbol appear again, in Britain, at Lypiatt Park, the Gloucestershire territory of the Dobunni, on an altar without human representation, but where a sun-wheel has been carved on the *focus* and

around which curls an apparently ram-horned snake (Fig. 92). This ram-headed serpent is a well-known symbol of fertility in the Celtic world, the familiar companion of the great nature-god Cernunnos.[87]

The sun as a comfort to the dead

The Celtic sun-god had power in the realms of the underworld as well as those of the upper air. Time and again, individuals died and were buried with solar talismans to help light their way in the darkness. In the late Iron Age, people were interred at such cemeteries as Wederath-Belginum near Trier and at Basel in Switzerland accompanied by simple wheel-models; sometimes these are the only grave-goods present.[88] An Iron Age Celt was buried at Diarville (Meurthe et Moselle) wearing a torc and with a solar amulet behind his head, as if it had once been attached to a leather helmet.[89] Solar-wheel talismans were buried with children in graves on the Dürrnberg, an important *oppidum* above Hallein in Austria.[90] One burial was that of a small boy who died in about 400 BC: he was interred with jewellery and a realistic bronze wheel-model. We have alluded already to the young girl from the same settlement who was consigned to her tomb in company with ornaments, a model wheel and a miniature axe (Fig. 37). The study of her bones revealed that she was between eight and ten years old but she suffered from a condition which severely stunted her growth. She, perhaps more than most, needed her talismans to light her way in the dark unknown paths to the afterlife. The combination of wheel and axe-models in this grave may lend support to the notion that these symbols were associated in the celestial cults.

Solar-wheel models and chthonicism are occasionally associated with the image of the raven. This happens at Felmingham Hall in Norfolk, where a hoard of bronzes contained the head of the Celtic Jupiter, a radiate god, a wheel-model (Fig. 85) and a pair of raven figurines.[91] Ravens and sun-god recur at Willingham Fen, whose shrine produced the famous sceptre-fitting together with other cult-images including ravens.[92] The raven, as a carrion-bird and one reputedly of great cruelty (note the collective 'an unkindness of ravens'), was a natural chthonic symbol, but it has sharp, bright eyes and is described as 'bright-eyed' in Scandinavian legend.[93] This attribute may explain the presence of the raven as a companion of a Celtic healer-god at Mavilly (Côte d'Or), whose primary function was to cure eye-diseases.[94] One final solar-association for the raven concerns the Irish god Lugh: the vernacular literature informs us that this god, whose name means 'Shining One', was associated with magic ravens who warn him when danger approaches. Lugh was associated with the summer festival of Lughnasad, and he may have been a sun-god.

Sun-symbols accompanied the dead in other ways than as amulets: pots containing their cremated remains might be ornamented with solar motifs, as frequently on Villanovan funerary urns of Early Iron Age Italy.[95] But the most striking manifestation of the sun as companion of the dead is that on some Romano-Celtic tombstones, again associated with cremation-burials, of the first to fourth centuries AD. These tombstones fall into two main distribution groups: one belongs to the Comminges region of south-western Gaul;[96] another – more important – group is found among the tribe of the Mediomatrici of Alsace.[97] The Pyrenean tombs of the first group are decorated with wheels, rosettes, circles or spirals: at Prieuré d'Arnes, a bust of the deceased is represented, accompanied by wheel- and rosette-symbols;[98] and a stone at St Pé de la Moraine[99] is ornamented with spirals and rosette-wheels, recalling one of the solar 'Venus' figurines alluded to earlier, whose body was stamped with a combination of circles, wheels and spirals.[100] The Alsace tombstones form a much more spectacular and

homogeneous collection, in terms of both numbers and imagery. These are in the form of 'stèles-maisons', single- or double-gabled house-shaped stones or rectangular blocks with multiple epitaphs, often with diagonal lines to demonstrate and maintain the symbolic gabled, triangular house-shape.[101] Most of the stones bearing solar designs come from the area of Saverne, quite close to Strasbourg, and may be seen today dramatically displayed in a crypt which forms the Saverne Museum (Figs. 96, 97). The stelai bear geometric decoration in the form of concentric circles, rosettes, crescents and wheels with four or more spokes: one Saverne stone[102] bears wheel and

96 Romano-Celtic gabled tombstone bearing solar ornament from the Saverne area. Height: 83 cm (33 in.). Miranda Green

circle symbols; another has an eight-spoked wheel-sun at its base.[103] A house-stone at Wasserwald, still *in situ*, bears no epitaph but has three well-defined solar wheels.[104] Wheels, rosettes and concentric circles are frequently present on the same monument. There are some curiosities in the group: we have met the stone from Bois-de-la-Neuve-Grange[105] before, with its peculiar combination of wheel/stag/tree imagery (Fig. 43). Another oddity is a tombstone from the Forêt de St Quirin[106] which has a seven-spoked wheel and three hammers beneath. We have noted elsewhere that there is an association between the Celtic sun-god and the hammer-god Sucellus.

The combination and substitution of wheels and rosettes is interesting: we know that the rose or rosette was a Roman funerary motif symbolic of regeneration, and it is possible that the Celtic Mediomatrici may have adopted the rosette and turned it (physically or mentally) into a solar wheel appropriate to their own beliefs. It is interesting to find a tombstone to a four-year-old child decorated with a realistic wheel-motif at Vaison,[107] a town where the cult of the sun-god was so prominent.[108] In the Roman world, there was a genuine belief in both the afterlife and, to an extent, theories of astral apotheosis where, at death, the soul was freed from the body and rejoined the pure element of fire whence it came:[109] emperors were borne to heaven in the chariot of the sun-god.[110] It may be that the people of Alsace and the Comminges had similar beliefs: the symbols of the sun-god on their gravestones may have helped, magically, to transform their souls after death. In any case, the sun-god was there as a comfort and as a light in dark places.

The solar conqueror of death

The peoples of Celtic Gaul worshipped a solar-sky warrior who was envisaged as being in

97 Romano-Celtic tombstone inscribed with Celtic names and decorated with solar signs from the Saverne area. Height: 1.24 m (4 ft). Miranda Green, after Espérandieu

conflict with the forces of evil and darkness.[111] This belief in a conquering celestial power manifested itself in many different kinds of image, of which perhaps the most splendid are the so-called 'Jupiter-Giant columns' (Fig. 71). These are spectacular and complicated monuments, which were mainly distributed in eastern Gaul and the Rhineland.[112] The columns may comprise a quadrangular base with images of Roman or romanizing deities; above this is a circular or octagonal stele bearing images of the Roman planetary divinities and a dedication to the Roman sky-god Jupiter or his consort. But above this last stone the native Celtic element begins to assert itself in the form of a tall pillar; sometimes this is plain, but it frequently bears a scale-pattern in imitation of the bark of a tree. The column at Hausen-an-der-Zaber near Stuttgart is even more explicit in its decoration of oak-leaves and acorns. (Fig. 71). The sculptured group at the summit of the monument is of the greatest interest to us: here a bearded horseman rides down a monster with snakes for legs and a dolorous expression on his human face. The equestrian warrior is a sky-god: he often wields his thunderbolt and – of greatest significance for the sun-cult – he sometimes carries a solar wheel (Figs. 87, 98). His flying cloak betokens his galloping mount. When the god bears a solar emblem, he holds it like a protective shield, sometimes with his hand threaded through the spokes to grasp the reins of his careering horse.[113] This happens at Butterstadt (Hessen);[114] Obernburg (Bayern);[115] Meaux (Seine-et-Marne);[116] and again at Luxeuil (Haute-Saône).[117] The shield-wheel symbolism is demonstrated above all by the sculptures at Eckelsheim (Hessen)[118] and at Quémigny-sur-Seine (Côte d'Or),[119] where the object clasped by the sun-god is mid-way between wheel and shield: the Quémigny example is oval rather than round, but it has the sun's beams radiating out from a central sphere or boss. Most of the wheels are non-realistic but owe substantial influence to the imagery of the sun: thus those at Meaux and Obernburg are rose-shaped, with exaggeratedly concave spokes.[120] So, on these equestrian monuments, the iconography appears to show a solar warrior trampling the forces of earth or underworld, represented by the snake-limbed giant. In the conflict, the horseman protects himself by means of his talismanic wheel-shield, using the force of the sun to repel evil.

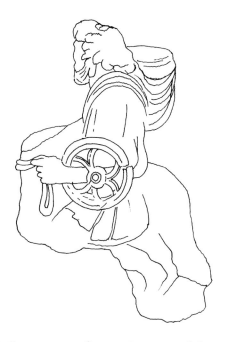

98 Stone statue of equestrian sun-god from Jupiter-Giant column at Obernburg, Bayern. Height: 66 cm (24 in.). E. R. Aldhouse, after Kellner

The imagery of the Jupiter-Giant sculptures presents a complex amalgam of Classical and Celtic themes, concepts and beliefs: the sculptured group may well have been inspired by the Greek gigantomachy, the mythical battle between the Olympian gods and the earth-giants, who were semi-divine. There is another possible prototype of the imagery from the Graeco-Roman world in the form of a later first-century BC or early first-century AD intaglio which carries the image of a rider with a spear and a snake-footed giant.[121] Roman imperial coins of Antoninus Pius and Septimius Severus show a naked charioteer aiming a thunderbolt at a snake-limbed monster.[122] But the underlying thought-processes which deployed these Classical inspirations in the portrayal of a native sun-god appear to be Celtic: the sky-horseman is not a Mediterranean image of Jupiter, who is neither equestrian nor overtly solar. What we may be witnessing is an adaptation of a Classical art-form to represent an indigenous Celtic belief-system.

Before delving further into a search for an interpretation for this iconography, there are other related images which reflect the theme of the sun as a conqueror. On one group of monuments in Gaul, the horse is absent, and sun-god and giant alone represent the conflict.[123] At Champagnat (Creuse)[124] a naked and Celtic-looking deity, very crudely and simply carved, holds his sun-wheel up by his ear and the giant kneels by his leg. The imagery on a stone at Dompierre-les-Eglises (Haute-Vienne)[125] is similar, but here the wheel is suspended above the monster's hapless head. Two other monuments demonstrate the reduction to essentials even further: at Mouhet (Indre) and Tours (Indre et Loire) the concepts of sun and giant are represented, without the presence of the sky-god.[126] The Mouhet giant kneels, hands behind his back, balancing the sun on his back, as if he were Atlas carrying the world.[127] There is a third group of images, where the chthonic forces reflected in the form of the snake-limbed monster are replaced by a diminutive individual whose scroll-limbs depict the same snake-symbolism of the giant and whose size relative to the accompanying sky-god suggests its inferiority. The lost monument at Saint-Georges-de-Montagne (Gironde)[128] showed a massive god, with a sun-wheel by his ear and a small scroll-limbed being by his side; the sculpture from Luxeuil (Fig. 87), commented upon earlier as an equestrian image, doubles the intensity of the chthonic symbolism in that the solar horseman has both giant and small beings as companions. What is interesting about the 'small-being' group is that identical (and far better-preserved) iconography is present on pipe-clay figurines of the sun-god.[129] Here we are able to see that the small individual is crushed and driven into the earth by the weight of the solar

god's hand resting on its head, which is sunk into its shoulders (Fig. 99). The face of the chthonic being reflects sadness and the anguish of its intolerable burden.

It is time to step back and look at the symbolism of all these solar-conqueror images. First, we should examine the column supporting the equestrian god and giant. It seems as though the pillar represents a tree, sometimes an oak, the species sacred to the Classical Jupiter. Trees possessed very profound symbolism in antiquity: they reflected earthly fecundity, but they displayed, above all, the union and relationship between the upper and lower worlds, the underworld and the firmament. The great branches of an oak, reaching towards the heavens, mirror the spreading roots deep underground. Both tree and stone column can represent the antithesis of life and death, light and darkness. But they also both represent the interdependence of the two elements: a tree cannot grow towards the sky without its roots – the deeper the roots, the higher the tree can grow. The solar god and his companion reflect similar symbolism: the horse of the equestrian divinity is itself a solar animal (see Chapter Six). On some images of the celestial conflict, the horse is replaced by a solar chariot which rides down the chthonic giant.[130] The monster on the Mouhet monument holds the sun on his back, as if it alone could represent the solar horseman. Whatever the variations in the imagery of the conquering sun-god, the two elements of sun/sky and underworld are present. By no means all the equestrian column-images of the god bear solar motifs, but the sky-symbolism is invariably present in the deity's thunderbolt and in the dedication to the Roman sky-god by name. Some of the horseman-giant images are quite Classical in style and suggest a marriage between Graeco-Roman and Celtic iconography and belief; there may have been inspiration not only from the gigantomachy, where the gods are not on horseback, and the small gems and coins we mentioned earlier, but also from Roman early imperial cavalry tombstones, where a soldier rides down an enemy, perhaps representative of the triumph of death over life. Nonetheless, a good many of the sculptures are very Celtic in art-form, owing little to the Classical traditional ideals of naturalism and mimesis.

Whatever the details of style in physical expression, the imagery reflects the same system of beliefs. There is conflict between good and evil, light and darkness, life and death, summer and winter, positive and negative. The giant may be crushed by the weight of hooves or the sun, and the small chthonic being may be bowed down by the sun-god's hand. The snake-limbs of the subdued monster represent earthly or underworld forces which are unable to withstand the light of the sun. But there is ambiguity and dualism between the elements of upper and lower worlds, as we observed in the symbolism of the tree. The horse sometimes appears to be uplifted and supported on the giant's shoulders; the giant rarely holds a weapon and the sun-god never actually attacks his dark adversary. So as well as conflict, there is mutual dependence, a recognition that winter is necessary as well as summer, death as well as life, night and darkness as well as day and the sunlight. What is clear from all the iconography is that the sun- or sky-god was the supreme ruler over both life and death, over this world and the afterlife.

99 Pipe-clay statuette of solar wheel-god with small underworld being from Néris, Allier. Height: c. 10 cm (4 in.). Miranda Green

— 8 —
Mythology, Symbolism and Society

This book has sought to investigate the physical manifestations of solar religion in Europe over a span of about 3000 years. Except for the very end of that time, reliance has had to be entirely upon material evidence (there being, of course, no contemporary writing). So we are able only to *infer* that the sun was the object of worship. Nevertheless, imagery and other indications are strongly suggestive of a rich tradition of solar veneration, with its attendant rituals, ceremonials and festivals. Certain cult-objects reflect the perception of divine beings, personifications of the sun itself or symbols of its omnipotence.

We need to enquire in this concluding chapter whether it is possible to construct any kind of mythology or indeed even a theology linked with the sun-cults of ancient Europe. Clearly, the further removed the evidence is from the historical or proto-historical world of the Celts and Romans, the more difficult and problematical this becomes. All we are able to do for much of our period is to point to certain recurring traditions of cult-expression associated with the sun, which imply linked religious themes and a set of belief-systems which was shared by prehistoric communities over a

wide spatial and temporal span. In the Celtic world, issues become clearer in that we are close to the beginning of history, when people wrote about themselves, their fears and their feelings, and the sun-cult is identified with an aspect of the Roman pantheon which underpins it and leads us nearer to an interpretation of solar symbolism and worship.

Study of the images and of other material evidence indicates that there probably existed a complicated series of myths and stories concerning the divine power of the sun, constructed in response to humankind's recognition of this power as of supernatural origin, of magical character and requiring to be propitiated. Persistent associations of solar imagery suggest very strongly that the sun was linked to a seasonal, cyclical mythology concerned with life, death, fertility and regeneration, protection and healing. The prestige associated with solar cults is evidenced by such celestial motifs as the horse, chariot and the aggression of the sun as a hunter and warrior. Fertility is an important aspect of the sun's divine role: thus solar images in human form are often ithyphallic; and there is a Celtic mother-goddess whose solar symbolism may represent the divine marriage between sun and earth in a European myth of Creation.

The persistent link between water and the sun manifests itself first in the Bronze Age where ships and water-birds are important iconographic companions of the solar disc. In Celtic Europe, this association is demonstrated above all in the thermal spring shrines dedicated to the healer-deities. In the Bronze Age, the sun-water connection may be concerned with weather-magic, but the presence of solar-decorated vessels may, in the same way as the later Celtic cult-cauldrons, imply regeneration or renewal. The healing role for the sun is fully developed only in the Celtic Iron Age and Roman period. Death was a concern for the sun from the Neolithic to the Romano-Celtic period: megalithic tombs bore the symbol of the radiate sun, and, interestingly, the same tradition manifests itself in the Celtic tombstones marking the cremation-graves of Mediomatrician tribespeople in Alsace. Solar images were buried with the dead from the Bronze Age to the Roman period. Thus the sun was perceived by ancient European societies as having a dark, nocturnal function with perhaps the ability to shine through the gloom of death and rekindle life in the otherworld.

Is it possible to construct a theology for the sun as a divine entity? The answer must be that it is realistic to attempt this only for the Romano-Celtic world when, for the first time, we possess a multitude of images of a sun-god in human form. Now the multifarious activities, functions and concerns of the divine sun which are hinted at in the prehistoric evidence are fully developed and are overtly displayed in an unequivocally religious milieu. The divine concepts acknowledged in such natural phenomena as the sun, sky, rain and storm-energy are given substance by means of the adoption of an essentially Roman art-form to display the image of the sun-god and by identification between the prehistoric European solar divinity and the formalized cult of the Roman Jupiter. But this conflation of indigenous and Mediterranean religious ideas did not alter the identity or functions of the barbarian sun-god; his concerns were what they had always been: the control of the sky, war and protection, fertility, the underworld and rebirth after death. The evidence clearly shows that the sun's influence penetrated all facets of human activity and that it was revered by all strata of society. The sun-cult appears to have occupied a dominant position within the divine hegemony of Celtic and proto-Celtic religion.

The recognition and acknowledgement of the universal power of the sun caused ancient European communities to react positively in demonstration of that recognition. The physical manifestations of sun-worship differed widely in space and time, but the underlying need to appease and control the sun remained constant. It is fair to say that the same fundamental thought-processes and beliefs may have stimulated communities on Salisbury Plain to build a huge stone monument to the sun at the beginning of the Bronze Age; to enact a complex cult-drama involving a horse-drawn sun-disc in Middle Bronze Age Denmark; and to erect statues of the divine solar horseman high on pillars in Celtic Gaul.

'Wait a minute', the charioteer said, 'until I turn the chariot around to the right, with the sun, to draw down the power of the sign for our safe return'

from the *Táin Bó Cuailgne*

Notes

Abbreviations

C.I.L.   *Corpus Inscriptionum Latinarum*, Berlin, Georgium Reimarum, 1861–1943

Espérandieu   Espérandieu, E., *Recueil Général des Bas-Reliefs de la Gaule Romaine et pré-Romaine*, Paris, Imprimérie Nationale/Ernest Leroux, 1907–66

R.I.B   Collingwood, R. G. & Wright, R. P., *The Roman Inscriptions of Britain: Volume I, Inscriptions on Stone*, Oxford University Press, 1965

Chapter 1 (pp. 11–13)

1 Merrifield 1987, xiii
2 Wheeler 1954, 13
3 Uhde 1981, 5

Chapter 2 (pp. 14–32)

1 Nordbladh 1972, 185–209
2 James 1957, 229–32
3 Pentikaïnen 1972, 555
4 James 1957, 204–28
5 Anati 1965, 229
6 Wood 1978, 57–78
7 Genesis 1: 3, 5, 16
8 Wainwright 1938, 95
9 Herodotus *History* IV, 184
10 Cook 1925, 840ff
11 Cook 1914, 186–95
12 Hole 1950, 14
13 Glob 1969, 311–12
14 Maringer 1956, 179
15 Hawkes 1962, 58
16 Harrison 1912, 184
17 Wood 1978, 79–83
18 Hawkes 1962, 59
19 Burkert 1985, 145–6
20 di Stasi 1981, 83
21 Wainwright 1938, 1; Burl 1981a, 48
22 Anati 1965, 229
23 Frazer 1926, 560
24 Burkert 1985, 200–1
25 Hawkes 1962, 59
26 Herodotus *History* III, 9; Strabo *Geography* XVII, 2, 3
27 Campbell 1969, 297–8
28 Hawkes 1962, 125–6; Frazer 1922, 431
29 Hawkes 1962, 125–43
30 Campbell 1969, 297–8
31 Servius on Virgil *Eclogues* VI, 42; Frazer 1930, 194
32 James 1957, 204–28; Hole 1950, 78; 1940, 63–72
33 Frazer 1922, 614–45; Gaidoz 1884, 23–6; Bertrand 1897, 109–21
34 Ferguson 1970, 44–56
35 Deonna 1965, 251ff
36 Frazer 1926, 529–36
37 Sandars 1968, 292
38 Quoted by Athenaeus XV, 48
39 Frazer 1926, 479
40 Strabo XVI, 4, 26
41 Webster 1973, 247
42 Cook 1914, 186–95
43 Diodorus I, 59; Wainwright 1938, 83, 90
44 Deonna 1965, 14–33, 96ff
45 Lines 88–92
46 Lines 868–70
47 *Antigone*, line 120
48 di Stasi 1981, 112
49 Campbell 1969, 379
50 Frazer 1926, 608–9

51 Briard 1987, 73ff
52 Bertilsson 1987, 188–9
53 Nordbladh 1978, 63–78
54 Lurker 1974, 7ff
55 Nordbladh 1978, 63–78
56 Nordbladh 1972, 185–209
57 Briard 1987, 65–88
58 For example at Granja de Toniñuelo in Spain, where the sun-image appears five times.
59 Maringer 1956, 169, fig. 49
60 Anati 1965, 158–68
61 James 1960, 300–2
62 Frazer 1926, 557–8
63 Butler & Waterbolk 1963, 167
64 Burkert 1985, 175
65 Ferguson 1970, 44–56
66 Harrison 1912, 200, fig. 51
67 Hawkes 1962, 91–2
68 Frazer 1926, 532, 547–8
69 Campbell 1969, 393
70 Déchelette 1987 (re-issue of original 1928 edition), 422
71 Ibid.
72 Sandars 1968, 231
73 *Odyssey* Book 10, 150–80
74 Herodotus *History* IX, 93ff
75 Kerényi 1979, 1
76 Wood 1978, 79–83
77 Campbell 1969, 343
78 Maringer 1956, 169, fig. 49
79 Twohig 1981, 11
80 Megaw & Simpson 1979, 183
81 Twohig 1981, 134, 139–40
82 Burl 1981a, 85
83 For example Twohig 1981
84 Ibid., pp. 23–37, fig. 57
85 Twohig 1981, Class 5, pp. 54, 92, 107, 113
86 O'Kelly 1973, 354–82
87 O'Kelly 1973, fig. 10; Coffey 1977, 70–73, figs. 31, 34, 35–7
88 Burl 1981a, 85; O'Kelly 1989, 110
89 Coffey 1977, 101–2, figs. 72–5; Twohig 1981, figs. 214–35

90 Twohig 1981, fig. 209
91 Forde-Johnston 1957, 20–39
92 Powell & Daniel 1956, 27–9, pls. 24–7
93 Twohig 1981, 136
94 Péquart & Le Rouzic 1927, pls. 45, 44
95 Ibid.
96 Péquart & Le Rouzic 1927, pls. 80, 81; Twohig 1981, figs. 125, 126
97 Twohig 1981, 136
98 Maringer 1956, 171
99 Twohig 1981, fig. 57
100 Ibid., fig. 49
101 Harbison 1976, 28–9
102 Anati 1965, 229
103 Sandars 1968, fig. 217c
104 Ibid., fig. 217a
105 Gutherz 1986, 353–4, fig. 1 on p. 354
106 Crawford 1957, figs. 10c & 10d
107 Ibid., 56ff
108 Sandars 1968, fig. 217b
109 Myron 1964, 82
110 Crawford 1957, fig. 38b, pl. 31a
111 Burl 1981b; Bradley 1989, 251–9
112 Bradley 1989, 251–9
113 O'Brien, Jennings & O'Brien 1987
114 O'Kelly 1978, 5, pls. 3–4; O'Kelly 1989, 106–7, fig. 53; Harbison 1976, 35–7; 1988, 76–7; Burl 1981a, 87
115 Burl 1981a, 124
116 Harbison 1976, 35–7
117 Burgess 1980, 336–43
118 Burl 1987, 81ff
119 Burl 1984, 41–5
120 Burgess 1980, 343
121 Atkinson 1984, 51–6

Chapter 3 (pp. 33–60)

1 Megaw & Megaw 1989, 19
2 Coles & Harding 1979, 370
3 Champion *et al.* 1984, 208
4 Bahn & Vertet 1988, 149–90
5 Pollard 1977, 130
6 Schutz 1983, 151–3

7 Glob 1969, fig. 10

8 Anati 1965, 158–68; de Manteyer 1945

9 Gelling & Davidson 1969, 21–6

10 Asakku is depicted as a human but with a solar head with radiate hair and beard, as on a terracotta from Tell Harmal near Baghdad: Van Dijk, 1982

11 Frazer 1926, 532

12 Déchelette 1909, 316–19, fig. 9

13 Maringer 1956, 169

14 Gagnière 1961, 374–8, figs. 48–50

15 In Ireland, Dowth and Loughcrew are of particular importance: Coffey 1977, fig. 31; Harbison 1976, 28; Twohig 1981, figs. 214, 217; O'Kelly 1973, 354–82. In Brittany, the Dolmen de Mané Lud and the Dolmen de Tachen Paul are decorated with a number of rayed suns with central points: Péquart & Rouzic 1927, pls. 45, 19. Of Iberian passage graves, note particularly Carapito, Espiñaredo and Antelas: Twohig 1981, 23–7

16 Briard 1987, 98–9

17 Déchelette 1987, fig. 175

18 Megaw & Megaw 1989, fig. 30

19 Anon 1980a, 3.58

20 Pittioni 1954, 545, Abb. 380

21 For example in the Bologna Cemetery: Déchelette 1909, 345; 1987, 431, fig. 174

22 Déchelette 1914, 1501–2, fig. 688

23 Briard 1987, 98–9

24 Coles & Harding 1979, 175; Anati 1965, diagram on p. 162; Anati 1976

25 Glob 1969, fig. 167

26 Anati 1965, 162ff

27 Malmer 1981, 66–75

28 Blanchet 1890, 65–224

29 Briard 1987, 36; Gagnière 1961, 337–9

30 Coffey 1977, figs. 73, 74; O'Kelly 1973, 354–82; 1989, 110, 114, fig 58; Twohig 1981, 113, fig. 237

31 For example on the relief of the Celtic solar horseman at Meaux: Espérandieu, no. 3207

32 For example at Maranville in Burgundy: Drioux 1929, 354–8

33 Linckenheld 1927

34 Musée de Bretagne 1988, no. 252

35 Fleischer 1967, no. 119, Taf. 65

36 Toynbee 1971, 63

37 For example on a twelfth-century BC stirrup-jar with one large seven-petalled flower, from Epidaurus Limera, Laconia: Demakopoulou 1988, cat. no. 37. For Cretan flower/sun symbolism, see Ferguson 1989, 6–7

38 Cook 1914, figs. 329–44

39 Deonna 1965, 251ff

40 Cook 1914, 196

41 Cook 1925, 501

42 de Chardin: di Stasi 1981, 61

43 Deonna 1965, 94ff

44 Powell 1966, 108, 113, fig. 109; Jensen 1978, 22; Myron 1964, 82

45 Crawford 1957, 56, fig. 19g

46 Clottes 1977, 550–1

47 Campbell 1969, 379

48 di Stasi 1981, 93–4

49 Harrison 1962, 187–8

50 At Garin and Benqué: Hatt 1945, nos. 69, 70

51 Viz. a huge winged Medusa-head on a bronze shield in the Stoa Museum, Athens

52 Déchelette 1909, 350–1, figs. 25, 26a

53 At Entremont: Benoit 1981

54 As at Fox-Amphoux (Var); Musée Borély, Marseille; Espérandieu no. 8613

55 Cunliffe 1969; 1985

56 Briard 1987, 65–88

57 Wainwright 1938; James 1957, 210

58 Frazer 1926, 604–5

59 Coffey 1977, fig. 36

60 For example Coffey 1977, 93–101, fig. 74

61 Burl 1981a, 86

62 Savory 1980, no. 306, fig. 10, pl. IX; H. S. Green *et al.* 1980, 26–30; H. S. Green 1985, 116–17

63 Déchelette 1987, 423–4, fig. 172

64 Briard 1979, 130, fig. 118; Schutz 1983, fig. 101; Hachmann 1958, pls. 56–61

65 Glob 1974, 124, pl. 37

66 Déchelette 1909, 337

67 Butler & Waterbolk 1963, 167–75

68 Eogan 1964, 304, fig. 15, no. 9

69 Glob 1974, pl. 39

70 Déchelette 1987, 425ff

71 von Merhart 1969, Taf. 44

72 Gimbutas 1965, fig. 229

73 Eluère 1987, 50ff

74 For example those at Vitlycke: Røstholm 1985; Gelling & Davidson 1969, fig. 9

75 At Begby in southern Norway, the convention for wheeled carts and 'suns' is the circle with central dot, which could perhaps represent a spoked wheel travelling at speed. Seen by author May 1988

76 Déchelette 1987, figs. 175, 180

77 Déchelette 1909, 345, fig. 20

78 Bertrand 1897, 153, fig. 13

79 For example at Tongeren, Belgium; Green 1984a, cat. no. A61, p. 310

80 For example Musée de Bretagne 1988, ill. 70–71; Blanchet 1890, fig. 3

81 Musée de Bretagne 1988, no. 167

82 For example Hal Tarxien: Evans 1971

83 For example the eight spirals on the Calderstones, Liverpool: Forde-Johnston 1957, 20–39

84 As on a stone at Seskilgreen; Coffey 1977, fig. 85

85 di Stasi 1981, 101–5; Crawford 1957

86 For example Burl 1981a, 86

87 For example two gold discs from a hoard at Tufălau in Transylvania: Myron 1964, 142, fig. 134; and a large bronze disc from Denmark is decorated with three rings of spirals: Déchelette 1987, 85–6, fig. 27

88 Sandars 1968, figs. 267–8

89 Gelling & Davidson 1969, fig. 10n

90 Sprockhoff 1955, 261, fig. 4,4

91 Gimbutas 1965, pl. 67, 2, 3

92 Reinach 1921, 217; Green 1984a, 24

93 *Natural History* 36, 84

94 I, 61; I, 97

95 Lucian *Saltatores* 49

96 Cook 1914, 476, figs. 337, 340

97 de Lumley 1976, 93

98 Anati 1965, fig. on p. 216

99 Bertrand 1987, 231–4; Grapinat 1970, 54–6

100 Green 1984a, cat. no. C2

101 Déchelette 1909, 345, fig. 20

102 Déchelette 1927, 309, fig. 333

103 Green 1984a, 24–5

104 Déchelette 1927, 377, fig. 378; Drioux 1929, 354–8

105 Green 1984a, cat. no. C54

106 As on a *Viergotterstein* at Niederwürzbach: Green 1984a, cat. no. B90

107 Grapinat 1970, 54–6, fig. 16

108 Pendlebury 1939, fig. 12

109 Bertrand 1897, 140ff; Grapinat 1970, fig. 2

110 For example Mycenaean pots decorated with horses and swastikas in the British Museum (cat. no. 8443) and Geometric pots in the Agora Museum, Athens

111 Cook 1914, figs. 329–44

112 Cook 1914, fig. 269

113 Déchelette 1987, figs. 178, 179, pp. 435–6

114 Higgins 1960–61, nos. 44–7, pl. XVIa, b

115 Bertrand 1897, 167. Lycian coins of fifth–fourth century BC portray wheels or discs with swastika-like lines radiating from them: Cook 1914, figs. 224–33

116 For example at Amarejo in the Province of Albacete, Spain: Déchelette 1914, 1501–2, fig. 688

117 Anon 1980a, 11.2; Bertrand 1897, 144

118 Benoit 1958, 426, fig. 21a

119 Bertrand 1897, 153, fig. 13

120 Green 1984a, pl. 27c

121 Espérandieu no. 10

122 Sprockhoff 1955, 257; 1936, 5, Abb. 8–10

123 Fouet & Soutou 1963, 290, fig. 19; Fouet 1969, pl. XLVIII; Fouet & Soutou 1963, 275–95 (Le Mont Saçon)

124 For example at Geneva and Viège: Deonna 1915, 145–7; 1916, 193–202

125 Courcelle-Seneuil 1910, 70

126 Déchelette 1987, 453ff

127 Déchelette 1927, 309, fig. 33

128 Cook 1914, 304–5, fig. 235

129 Déchelette 1914, 1311ff, fig. 572–3

130 1989

131 Fox 1952, 47–54

132 Savory 1976, 36–7, 60, no. 23.3, pl. IIb

133 Megaw & Megaw 1989, fig. 51

134 Butler & Waterbolk 1963, 167–75

135 For example that from Tednavnet, Co. Monaghan: Harbison 1988, 126, fig. 77; and a pair from Ballina, Co. Mayo: Megaw & Simpson 1979, 188, 200–1

136 Piggott 1938, 78; Taylor 1980, 1–24

137 Briard 1987, 142

138 Pittioni 1954, 615, Abb. 435

139 For example at Köln and at Straubing: Green 1984a, nos. A6, A29

140 Green 1984a, cat. no. B143; Espérandieu no. 4612

141 Green 1984a, 182–3; Linckenheld 1929a, 40–92

142 As at Santenay: Reinach 1894, 171; Geneva: Deonna 1915, 17; Prémeaux: Green 1989, fig. 34

143 Ferguson 1970, 55–6; Potter 1987, 189

144 Glob 1969, 147–62

145 Gelling & Davidson 1969, fig. 25

146 Fredsjo *et al.* 1971, no. 261

147 Ibid. 1981, no. 186a

148 Glob 1969, fig. 94

149 Glob 1969, fig. 74; Görmann 1987, Bild 81

150 For example at Vitlycke: Røstholm 1985

151 Ibid.

152 Maringer 1956, 172

153 Deonna 1923–5, 108–13

154 Drioux 1943–4, 208–9

155 Ibid.

156 Chassaing 1956, 156ff; Boucher 1976, pl. 63, no. 301

157 Espérandieu, no. 5303; Green 1984a, fig. 41

158 Ferguson 1989, 6; Cook 1925, 617

159 Green 1984a, 183

160 Green 1984a, 99; Ferguson 1989, 26

161 Dietrich 1988, 12–25

162 Déchelette 1987, 482

163 For example at Piedmont: Déchelette 1909, 356, fig. 31c, and at Bologna: Déchelette 1987, fig. 205

164 For example at Megyasco, Hungary: Sandars 1968, 276, fig. 255e

165 Déchelette 1987, 482

166 Green 1976, 178; 1979, fig. 20; 1984a, 99, cat. no. AX20. Recently a bronze miniature axe has been found in the vicinity of the Roman temple at Thornborough, Bucks. This is decorated with three circles: information from Mrs Shelagh Lewis, Buckingham

167 Drioux 1929, 354–8; Déchelette 1927, fig. 374

168 Twohig 1981, fig. 49

169 Sandars 1968, 231, fig. 217c

170 Ibid., 231, fig. 217a

171 Briard 1987, 98–9, fig. on p. 98

172 Gelling & Davidson 1969

173 Coles & Harding 1979, 175; Anati 1965, 151–6

174 Fredsjo *et al.* 1971, no. 241

175 Görmann 1987, Bild 29

176 Ibid., Bild 23

177 Fredsjo *et al.* 1981, no. 158

178 Anati 1965, fig. on p. 163

179 Anati 1965, diagram on p. 167

180 Harrison 1912, 148ff; Green 1984a, 188–9

181 de Lumley 1976, 57, figs. 25, 2, 5

182 Sandars 1968, figs. 267–8

183 Green 1990a

184 Hole 1950, 14; Ellis Davidson 1988, 50

185 Spoked wheels first appear in western Asia around the beginning of the second millennium BC, and in Europe from the mid-second millennium: Piggott 1979, 3–17; Childe 1951, 177–95

186 Aristophanes *Daedalos Frag.* 234

187 Lucretius *De Rerum Natura* V, 433

188 Bailey 1932, 260

189 Déchelette 1987, 416–17

190 Harrison 1912, 523–5, fig. 145; 1962, 600–2, figs. 161, 162

191 Green 1984a, 197; Gaidoz 1885, 191–3

192 Green 1984a, 155–8

193 Anati 1960, 63

194 Péquart & Rouzic 1927, pls. 73, 80, 81

195 O'Kelly 1989, 110, 114, fig. 58; Coffey 1977, figs. 34, 39

196 Maringer 1956, 169ff

197 Briard 1987, 65–88

198 Gelling & Davidson 1969; Anati 1965: see Chapter Three

199 For example a coin of the Regni in Sussex: Cunliffe 1981. This question is discussed in Green 1990a

200 Zachar 1987, pl. 201

201 Fol & Marazov 1977, 30; British Museum 1976, no. 509

202 Olmsted 1979; Bergquist & Taylor 1987

203 Green 1984a, 168–9

204 Ibid., *passim*; 1986b; Bauchhenss & Nölke 1981. It is interesting that on an engraved gem depicting the Danubian rider-god, sun and moon deities are depicted as wheel and crescent: Tudor 1976, 182–4

205 Green 1984a, cat. no. B93

206 Hatt 1951, 82–7; Zwicker 1934–36, 302–3

207 Green 1984a, 74–8

208 Ibid., cat. no. A140

209 Gaul, no provenance: Babelon & Blanchet 1895, 631; Green 1984a, cat. no. A82

210 Green 1984a, cat. no. A191

211 Trègnes and Bavay: Green 1984a, 86–8, cat. nos. A155, A166

212 Ibid., B9

213 As at Dompierre and Tongeren respectively: Green 1984a, 266ff, nos. B34 and B150

214 Ibid., B2. This is also the case with the wheels accompanying the Celtic Jupiter at, for example, Obernberg and Vaison: Green 1984a, nos. B102, B144

215 Espérandieu no. 4526; Green 1984a, B15, fig. 28

216 Green 1984a, B62, at Jublains

217 Ibid., 183–4

218 Hatt 1951, 82–7

Chapter 4 (pp. 61–85)

1 Gimbutas 1965, 342

2 Coles & Harding 1979, 369–70; Bouzek 1977, 200; Burgess 1989, 325–9

3 Sprockhoff 1955, 278

4 Atkinson 1978; 1984, 51–6; Burl 1984, 41–5; 1987, 49ff, 81ff, 128ff

5 Atkinson 1978

6 Atkinson 1978; Chippindale 1983, 234ff

7 Chippindale 1983, 216–18

8 Burl 1987, 203

9 As at Corran, Co. Armagh: O'Kelly 1989, 178

10 Butler & Waterbolk 1963, 167–75 (belonging to their Class I sun-discs); Piggott 1938, 78; Taylor 1980, 1–24; Burl 1981a, 136

11 Taylor 1980, 1–24

12 Butler & Waterbolk 1963, 170

13 Ibid., belonging to their Class II sun-discs

14 Glob 1974, 113

15 Torbrügge 1968, 93

16 Eogan 1964, 304, fig. 15, no. 9

17 Briard 1979, 130, fig. 118; Glob 1974, 124, pl. 37; and Krottorf in East Germany: Menghin & Schauer 1983, Abb. 37

18 Menghin & Schauer 1983, Abb. 18

19 Eluère 1987, 50–60

20 Sandars 1957, 114

21 Eluère 1987, 50–60; Menghin & Schauer 1983, Abb. 4, 25; Briard 1987, 65–88, fig. on p. 71

22 Spoked-wheel vehicles were introduced into Greece from Hittite Anatolia in the sixteenth century BC and thence into central and western Europe: Anati 1960, 63; Piggott 1979, 14; 1983, 109

23 Gimbutas 1965, 316

24 Glob 1974, 99–125; Jensen 1978, 36

25 Ashbee 1989, 539–46

26 Piggott 1983, 114–16

27 Glob 1974, 99–125; Briard 1987, 65–88

28 Gelling & Davidson 1969, 9–27

29 Glob 1974, 106, pl. 39

30 Anon 1980a, 11.2

31 Coles & Harding 1979, 335

32 Jensen 1982, 163–5

33 Jensen 1982, 163–5, 176; Gelling & Davidson 1969, 117ff; Champion *et al*. 1984, 285; Déchelette 1909, 338–9

34 Déchelette 1987, fig. 173; Menghin & Schauer 1983, Abb. 18

35 For example at Orvieto: Déchelette 1987, fig. 173

36 I *Kings* 7: 13–51

37 Pare 1989, 80–100

38 Piggott 1983, fig. 72; Pare 1987, 48, fig. 6

39 Piggott 1983, 120–2

40 Gimbutas 1965, 341, pl. 64; Schutz 1983, 151–3

41 Coles & Harding 1979, 369–70; Bouzek 1977, 200

42 Torbrügge 1968, 97; Kromer 1959, 119, pl. 101, no. 3, pl. 225

43 Anon 1980a, 3.58; Pittioni 1954, 615

44 Anon 1980a, 3.57

45 Grave 697: Pittioni 1954, 545, Abb. 380

46 Déchelette 1987, 437, fig. 180

47 Megaw & Megaw 1989, no. 42

48 For example at Queroy à Chazelles, Charente: Briard 1987, 142; and in Bavaria: Déchelette 1927, 309, fig. 333

49 Déchelette 1927, fig. 333

50 Barfield 1971, 104–5; Randall McIver 1927, 18

51 von Merhart 1957, 91–147; Gimbutas 1965, 341, fig. 236

52 As at Ukermark, Germany: Déchelette 1927, 373–80, fig. 355, 1a

53 Megaw & Megaw 1989, fig. 30

54 Duval *et al*., 1962

55 Déchelette 1914, 1566

56 Sprockhoff 1955, 261

57 Espérandieu no. 8613

58 Harding 1978, 95

59 Grave 994: the motif may owe something to Transalpine *situla* art: Megaw & Megaw 1989, pl. VII and fig. 92

60 Déchelette 1914, fig. 572, 2

61 Ibid.

62 Déchelette 1987, fig. 169

63 Sprockhoff 1936, 4–8, Abb. 1

64 Sandars 1968, 299–301

65 Déchelette 1914, 1311ff; fig. 572, 4

66 Sandars 1957, 42–3; Torbrügge & Uenze 1968, 212, 240; Lawson 1979, 82ff

67 A Late Bronze Age example comes from the Lac du Bourget, Savoie: Sandars 1957, 51

68 Pare 1987, 46–61

69 Note also a find from a tumulus at Haguenau, buried with other material: Gaucher 1988, fig. 5; and a Middle Bronze Age pin at Lautenbach, S. Hunsrück: Schindler 1977, pl. 5

70 Association Abbaye de Daoulais 1988, 22–3

71 Gimbutas 1965, 290, fig. 196

72 Behrens 1916, pl. 7, no. 13

73 Audouze 1976, 94, fig. 13

74 Bocquet 1969, 234–6, fig. 48, no. 5

75 Gimbutas 1965, 329, fig. 231

76 Kossack 1954, Taf. 10

77 Gaucher 1988, figs. 8, 9; de Longpérier 1867, pl. 25, fig. 31

78 Gimbutas 1965, 129–31

79 Férrier 1971, 67, fig. 75

80 Déchelette 1914, fig. 560, no. 9

81 Randall-McIver 1927, pl. 32, no. 9

82 Déchelette 1914, 971

83 Stead 1979, 77, fig. 30

84 Déchelette 1914, 1299, fig. 536, 1; Sprockhoff 1955, 259

85 Déchelette 1927, fig. 377

86 Grave 507: Kromer 1959, pl. 98, no. 3

87 Anon 1980b, no. 100

88 Gimbutas 1965, 316

89 Pare 1987, 43–61

90 As at Réallons (Hautes-Alpes): Green 1984a, 22–3

91 Müller-Karpe 1959, Taf. 183

92 As at Lac du Bourget, Savoie: Briard 1988, 108–16; and at Degerndorf, Parsberg: Torbrügge & Uenze 1968, 266, no. 239

93 Břeň 1966, pl. XXV, 7, pp. 116–17

94 Filip 1976, XXXV

95 Filip 1956, pl. CXXVII

96 Primas 1966–76, 98, Abb. 10

97 Déchelette 1914, 971

98 Flemming 1908–9, 391–2

99 Pauli 1975, Abb. 3, no. 27

100 Major 1940

101 Haffner 1971

102 Chenet 1919, 243–51

103 Piette 1981, 367–75

104 Nordbladh 1981, 32

105 Bertilsson 1987, 33, 167, 169–71, 180–1

106 Nordbladh 1972, 185–209; 1986, 142–9; 1978, 63–78

107 Bahn & Vertet 1988, 149–90

108 Røstholm 1985; Glob 1969, 286–302

109 Bahn & Vertet 1988, 149–90

110 Glob 1971, 147–62

111 At Begby in south Norway, all discs are represented by a dotted circle rather than as a spoked wheel

112 Malmer 1981, 66–75

113 Görmann 1987, Bild 46–55

114 Glob 1969, 286–302

115 Glob 1971, pl. 67

116 Glob 1969, fig. 51

117 Glob 1969, 308, fig. 10

118 Seen by author, May 1988

119 Gelling & Davidson 1969, 9–27, figs. 2j, 3c & d

120 Seen by author, May 1988

121 Glob 1969, fig. 8

122 For example in the Bottna area of Bohuslän: Fredsjo *et al.* 1975, nos. 317, 320

123 Ibid., fig. 32

124 As at Rörane: Fredsjo *et al.* 1975, no. 325; and Allestorp: Fredsjo *et al.* 1981, no. 71a. Both Bohuslän

125 As at Egely on Bornholm: Glob 1969, fig. 27; or in Bohuslän: Gelling & Davidson 1969, fig. 4

126 As at Torsbo, Bohuslän: Fredsjo *et al.* 1981, no. 172

127 Seen by author, May 1988

128 Seen by author, May 1988

129 Glob 1969, fig. 187

130 Glob 1971, 147–62

131 Gelling & Davidson 1969, 49–52

132 Glob 1969, fig. 187

133 Glob 1971, 147–62

134 Seen by author, May 1988

135 Görmann 1987, Bild 23

136 Seen by author, May 1988

137 For example at Fossum and Aspeberget, Tanum: seen by author, May 1988

138 Fredsjo *et al.* 1981, no. 158

139 Gelling & Davidson 1969, 21–6

140 At Vitlycke, for instance, there are ten discmen with both wheel and circle bodies: Røstholm 1985, and see Gelling & Davidson 1969, fig. 9

141 As at Bottna: Fredsjo *et al.* 1975, no. 384

142 Gelling & Davidson 1969, fig. 10i

143 Ibid., fig. 101

144 As at Aspeberget: seen by author, May 1988; and Södra Ödsmäl: Fredsjo *et al.* 1981, no. 151

145 As at Fossum, Bohuslän

146 Fredsjo *et al.* 1981, no. 20

147 For example at Svenneby: Fredsjo *et al.* 1975, no. 240; and Torsbo: ibid. 1981, no. 186a

148 Fredsjo *et al.* 1981, no. 158

149 Görmann 1987, Bild 72

150 Coles, pers. comm. 1988

151 Fredsjo *et al.* 1981, no. 168

152 For example at Bakka, Bohuslän: Gelling & Davidson 1969, fig. 10k

153 Gelling & Davidson 1969, 21–6

154 As at Aspeberget and Litsleby: seen by author, May 1988

155 Glob 1969, fig. 74

156 Anati 1965

157 Ibid., 10–12

158 Anati 1976, 46

159 Anati 1965, fig. on p. 160

160 Ibid., fig. on p. 202

161 Ibid., fig. on p. 163

162 Ibid., fig. on p. 167

163 Ibid., 167

164 Ibid., fig. on p. 164

165 Anati 1976, 46

166 Anati 1965, 95

167 Ibid., fig. on p. 185

168 Ibid., 219–29

169 Gagnière 1961, 337–86, fig. 2; Briard 1987, 36

170 Sandars 1968, 268–9, figs. 244A, 250; Piggott 1983, 109, fig. 61; Coles & Harding 1979, 369, 408 – they would date this figure no earlier than 1050 BC

171 Ross 1967, 380, pl. 91b, c; O'Kelly 1989, 290

172 Diodorus Siculus V, 28

173 For example on a coin of the Namnetes: Green 1990a, pl. 1

174 Allen & Nash 1980, 137

175 Ibid., 135, nos. 212, 213

176 Green 1989, 139–41, especially fig. 46

177 Olmsted 1979

178 Bergquist & Taylor 1987, 10–24

179 Megaw & Megaw 1989, 176

180 Recent technological study has shown a number of different hands at work: Megaw & Megaw 1989, 176

181 Olmsted 1979, pl. 2; Green 1984a, cat. no. C1

182 Hatt 1989, 73–8

Chapter 5 (pp. 86–106)

1 Green 1984a, 103–34

2 Ibid., cat. no. BB8; St Clair Baddeley 1923, 91ff

3 For example at Montmaurin: Fouet & Soutou 1963, 290, fig. 19; Fouet 1969, pl. XLVIII; Espérandieu no. 8873; Green 1984a, no. B82; and at Le Mont Saçon: Fouet & Soutou 1963, 275–95, figs. 10, 13, 14; Green 1984a, no. B70

4 As at Séguret: Espérandieu no. 303; Sautel 1926, no. 501, pl. LVIII; Green 1984a, no. B144

5 At Quémigny-sur-Seine: Espérandieu no. 7098; and Eckelsheim (Hessen): Behn 1936, 256–8

6 Green 1983, 41–7; Wright & Phillips 1975, nos. 196, 197

7 For example Collias: Espérandieu no. 7621; and Gilly: Espérandieu no. 430

8 At Montmaurin (see note 3 above)

9 Espérandieu no 6843; Espérandieu 1924, 29, no. 108; Green 1984a, no. B20, pl. LXVIII, fig. 35

10 Bauchhenss 1976, pl. I

11 Green 1984c, 251–8

12 Bauchhenss 1976, 19–20; Lambrechts 1942, map 4

13 Green 1984a, 168–79

14 *R.I.B.* 1981, 1983; Green 1979, nos. 1–2; 1984a, nos. BB4, 5

15 *R.I.B.* 827

16 Espérandieu no. 6380; Ristow 1975, Taf. 37; Green 1984a, no. B29, pl. XVIII, fig. 42

17 Espérandieu no. *Germ.* 76

18 de Villefosse 1881, 1–13; Courcelle-Seneuil 1910, 67, fig. 22

19 Espérandieu no. 2681

20 Espérandieu 1924, 13; Gaidoz 1884, 14

21 Tresques: Green 1984a, no. B152; Lansargues: ibid., no. B66; Espérandieu no. 517

22 Thevenot 1968, 26ff

23 Bertrand 1897, 145ff

24 Fouet & Soutou 1963, 275–95

25 Green 1984a, 125

26 Espérandieu no. 6849

27 Espérandieu no. 303

28 Espérandieu no. 299; Sautel 1926, III, no. 705, pl. LXVIII, 2

29 Espérandieu no. 7749

30 Espérandieu no. 2375; Espérandieu 1906–07, 41, pl. X, 2

31 Espérandieu no. 7217; Vanvinckenroye 1975, 73, Afb. 37

32 Espérandieu no. 5939

33 Courcelle-Seneuil 1910, 66, fig. 21; Musée des Antiquités Nationales, St Germain-en-Laye, acc. no. 32947; Green 1984a, no. C2, frontispiece

34 Blanchet 1890, pl. II, 25, pp. 187–8, no. 1, fig. 25; Gaidoz 1884, nos. 1, 4–5, 7–9; Rouvier-Jeanlin 1972, no. 519

35 Mouhet: Lelong 1970, 123–6, figs. 1, 2; Tours: Picard 1968, 343, fig. 24

36 Alföldi 1949, 19ff; Green 1984a, no. C6, pl. LXXXI, figs. 61, 62

37 Musée d'Epernay; Thevenot 1968, fig. opp. p. 25

38 As at Vauvert: Espérandieu no. 6843

39 Espérandieu no. 517; *C.I.L.* XII, 4179

40 Espérandieu no. 6843

41 Espérandieu no. 6849

42 Green 1984a, no. C2

43 Johnston 1903, 233–4

44 Green 1984a, 184

45 Espérandieu 1924, 28, no. 106; Green 1984a, no. B83

46 Espérandieu no. 1691

47 Green 1982, 37–44

48 Usener 1896, 30; Zwicker 1934–6, 50

49 For example at Chester: Wright & Richmond 1975, 13; *R.I.B.* 452; Thauron (Creuse): Perrier 1960, 195–7; Scardona (Yugoslavia): *C.I.L.* III, 2804

50 For example Butterstadt: Espérandieu *Germ.* no. 76; Luxeuil: Espérandieu 1917, 72ff. But see detailed discussion in Chapter Seven

51 Bauchhenss & Nölke 1981

52 Green 1989, 117–19

53 Forster & Knowles 1910, 224, fig. 6

54 Espérandieu no. 8613; Benoit 1954, 436, fig. 20

55 Gros 1986, 192–201; Rivet 1988, 272–3

56 Green 1984c, 251–8

57 For example Boon 1984

58 *Argonautica* 6, 89

59 Green 1986a, 158–60; 1989, 114–16

60 Goodburn 1972, pl. 10, 3; Green 1984a, no. BB7, pl. LXXVI, figs. 52, 53

61 Cunliffe 1979, 69; *C.I.L.* XIII, 3087

62 Ogilvie 1969, 12; Thevenot 1955

63 Green 1986a, 111

64 Thevenot 1955; Leber 1967, 517–20

65 Sautel 1926, no. 717

66 Drioux 1934, 52

67 Vanvinckenroye 1975, 73

68 Lebel & Boucher 1975, 35, no. 42

69 Espérandieu no. 7526

70 *C.I.L.* XIII, 5474–6; Gaidoz 1885, 194

71 MacCana 1955–56, 76–114

72 *C.I.L.* XIII, 6730

73 Like that at Lillebonne (Seine Maritime) and others: Espérandieu & Rolland 1959, 24

74 Green 1989, 79–83

75 Espérandieu no. 1691

76 Espérandieu no. 6829

77 Espérandieu no. 4528

78 Goodchild 1938, 391ff; 1947, 83ff

79 Green 1989, fig. 34

80 Thevenot 1971, no. 572; and also for example at Maranville: Drioux 1934, 67–72; Aubaine: Thevenot 1971, no. 332; and Saulenay: Linckenheld 1929, 53

81 Green 1986a, fig. 45

82 Green 1984a, fig. 66

83 Musée de Genève: acc. no. M49; Green 1984a, no. C49

84 Chassaing 1956, 156ff; Kent Hill 1953, 205–23; Boucher 1976, no. 301, pl. 63

85 Green 1989; Espérandieu no. 1735

86 Espérandieu no. 5303

87 Green 1989, 76–86

88 Powell 1958, 136

89 Bauchhenss 1976

90 Espérandieu nos. 299, 303

91 For example Goudex: Labrousse 1962, 558–9, fig. 10; Ilheu: Espérandieu no. 8900; Labrousse 1954, 220, fig. 8; Valentine: Fouet & Soutou 1963, 289, fig. 17; Le Mont Saçon: Fouet & Soutou 1963, 275–95, fig. 13, no. 3

92 Espérandieu no. 4526; Musée Archéologique de Metz

93 Green 1983, 41–7

94 Green 1981b, 109–15

95 Musée de Bretagne 1988, no. 164

96 Green 1989, 86–96

97 Boon 1982, 276–82; Green 1986a, fig. 88

98 St Clair Baddeley 1923, 91ff

99 Olmsted 1979, inner plate C

100 Alföldi 1949, 19ff

101 Green 1989, 180–2; 1990b

102 Wright & Phillips 1975, no. 197

103 Nat. Mus. of Wales, no. C512; Green 1990a

104 Goodchild 1938, 391ff

105 Espérandieu no. 2681

106 Green 1984a, frontispiece

107 Johnston 1903, 233–4

108 Malton: Green 1978, 60, pl. 50; Leach 1962; Housesteads: Birley *et al*. 1934, 197, pl. 29c, no. 1; Green 1978, 61, pl. 51

109 Higgins 1961, 186; Galliou 1974, 259–83

110 Newstead: Curle 1911, pl. 87, no. 34; Backworth: *C.I.L.* VII, 1285; Romilly-Allen 1901, 32; Charlesworth 1961, 34; Dolaucothi: Nash-Williams 1950–2, 78–84

111 Green 1981a, 253–69

112 Surrey Archaeological Society 1988, 16; Green 1989, 165

113 A brick-fragment at Toulouse: Labrousse 1959, 430, fig. 27; on a pot in the Pyrenees: Bertrand 1897, 145ff

114 Like Lons-le-Saunier: Lerat 1970, 356, fig. 20; and La Graufesenque: Balson 1952, 8, fig. 7

115 Courcelle-Seneuil 1910, 73; Gaidoz 1885, 199, fig. 13

116 Rheinisches Landesmuseum Trier, acc. no. 20110; Green 1984a, no. A50, pl. LV, fig. 11

117 For example ring-and-dot decoration on the brooch at Tongeren: Tongeren Museum; Green 1984a, no. A61; crosses at Köln: Römisch-Germanisches Museum, Köln; Green 1984a, no. A6, pl. LX, fig. 20

118 Laur-Belart 1942, 20–3, Abb. 2; Green 1984a, no. A140, pl. LVIII, fig. 16

119 Piette 1981, 367–75

120 Le Gall 1963; 1985, 41–4, fig. 17; Green 1989, 164

121 Rees & Rees 1961; Green 1990b

122 Thevenot 1948, 321

123 Chabouillet 1880–1, 15ff

124 Reinach 1894, 34ff; Musée des Antiquités Nationales, St Germain-en-Laye

125 Merrifield 1987, 23–30

126 de Villefosse 1881, 1–13

127 Green 1984a, no. AB5, pl. LXII, fig. 24; British Museum 1964, 60; Gilbert 1978, 159–87

128 Green 1975

129 Greenfield 1963, 228ff; Green 1976, pl. XXVa, b

130 Colchester & Essex Museum; Green 1984a, no. AB17

131 Röttlander 1973–4, 143–52, Abb. 9

132 Green 1986a, 220–2

Chapter 6 (pp. 107–21)

1 Servius on Virgil, *Eclogues*, VI, 42; Frazer 1930, 194

2 At Chios and Thorikos respectively: Cook 1914, 195

3 Frazer 1926, 441–2; Wainwright 1938, 1

4 James 1957, 204–28; Hole 1940, 63–72

5 Hole 1950, 14

6 James 1957, 204–28; Frazer 1922, 624

7 1950, 78

8 Hatt 1951, 82–7; Zwicker 1934–36, 302–3

9 Green 1989, 164

10 Frazer 1922, 643ff; Gaidoz 1884, 23

11 Strabo *Geography* IV, 4; Caesar *de Bello Gallico* VI, 16; Lucan *de Bello Civili (Pharsalia)* I, 444–6; Zwicker 1934–36, 50

12 Frazer 1922, 614–15

13 Briard 1979, 226; 1987, 14–17

14 Deonna 1965, 1–33, 251ff

15 Hawkes 1962, 71–2; Deonna 1965, 96ff

16 Green 1989, 163

17 Espérandieu no. 3414

18 di Stasi 1981, 124

19 Wainwright 1938, 94

20 For example at Hochscheid: Dehn 1941, 104ff; Green 1989, 61–2

21 Green 1989, 113

22 Espérandieu 1917, 72–86; Green 1986a, 152–3

23 MacCana 1983

24 Kruta & Forman 1985, 106

25 Thevenot 1951a, 129–41

26 de Vries 1963, 83

27 Green 1986a, 162; Zwicker 1934–6, 105

28 de Vries 1963, 83

29 Green 1986a, 161; Thevenot 1968, 97ff

30 Ferguson 1970, 44–56; Burkert 1985, 335–6

31 Burkert 1985, 175; Frazer 1926, 484

32 *Olymp.* VII, 54–73

33 Frazer 1926, 481–3

34 Burkert 1985, 175; Frazer 1926, 461–4; Athenaeus XI, 38–9

35 Harrison 1912, 385

36 Pausanias III 20.4

37 Rose 1933

38 *Suppliants*, lines 212–14 & *Eumenides*, Prologue; Burkert 1985, 148–9; Harrison 1912, 385, 388

39 In Book I of the *Iliad* the arrows of Apollo bring plague: Burkert 1985, 145–6

40 Ferguson 1989, 72

41 Ibid., 84

42 Pare 1989, 97–8: the story told by Alkaios *in Himerios Orationes* 14.10 is that Apollo travelled in a chariot drawn by two swans from the land of the Hyperboreans to Delphi, in order to end a drought

43 Xenophon *Cyropaedia* VIII, 3–24; Frazer 1926, 443–5, 460

44 Halsberghe 1972, 26–9

45 Kerényi 1979, 1

46 Cook 1914, 198–253, 333–7

47 Pare 1989, 81–2, 90–3

48 Briard 1987, 51

49 Pare 1989, 80–100

50 Burgess 1989, 325–9

51 Pare 1989, fig. 17

52 *Historiarum Mirabilium*, Chapter 15; Pare 1989, 84, 97–8

53 Sandars 1968, 265, 268–9, figs. 244A, 250; Coles & Harding 1979, 408, pl. 19a

54 Glob 1974, 99–125; Briard 1987, 50; Sandars 1968, 283–5; Ashbee 1989

55 Grinsell 1961, 475–91; Merrifield 1987, 30

56 Ferguson 1989, 138

57 Sandars 1968, 283–5

58 Glob 1974, 99–125; Briard 1987, 65–88

59 For example Gelling & Davidson 1969, 9–27, fig. 6b

60 Glob 1974, pl. 54

61 Gelling & Davidson 1969, figs. 3a, 4

62 Ibid., 117ff

63 For example Kossack 1954, Taf. 8, no. 15

64 Athenaeus XI, 38–9; Frazer 1926, 461–4

65 On a red-figure vase of fifth-century BC date, where the god has both boat and chariot: Harrison 1912, 385

66 Megaw 1970, 13; Powell 1971, 1–15

67 Briard 1987, 5

68 Duval 1976, 17

69 Green 1986a, 124

70 Mallory 1989, 128–42; Ogilvie 1969, 96; de Croon 1981, 260ff

71 Xenophon *Cyropaedia* VIII, 3–24; Pausanias III, 20.4; Ovid *Fasti* I, 385

72 Ferguson 1989, 36

73 Frazer 1926, 460; Hawkes 1962, 174

74 For example at Herrestrup: Glob 1974, pl. 54

75 Déchelette 1987, 416–17

76 Anon, 1980a, no. 3.57

77 Green 1984a, 29–30; Aigner-Foresti 1978–79, 43–7, Taf. 1, fig. 1

78 Anon 1980a, 8.45

79 Deonna 1915, 35

80 Grapinat 1970, fig. 10; Espérandieu no. 10; Déchelette 1987, 407

81 Allen & Nash 1980, 2

82 Ibid., 141–2

83 For example Allen & Nash 1980, no. 575 – on a gold coin of 'EISV', minted by the Dobunni

84 Green 1990a

85 Zachar 1987, pl. 201

86 Allen & Nash 1980, no. 438

87 Planson & Pommert 1986

88 Thevenot 1951a, 129–41

89 Fol & Marazov 1977, 17–37

90 de Laet 1942

91 Spräter 1935, Green 1984a, no. B9

92 Krüger 1940, 8–27, 1941, 1–66

93 Benoit 1950, 15

94 Lelong 1970, 123–6, figs. 1, 2

95 Pare 1989, 84, 97–8

96 Green 1984a, nos. A67, A68, fig. 6

97 Chabouillet 1880–81, 15ff; Gaidoz 1885, 191–2; Thevenot 1948, 289–349

98 And they appear in watery contexts also at, for example, Cussy in Burgundy and at Luxeuil:

Lambrechts 1949, 145–58

99 Gwynn Jones 1929, 28

100 Espérandieu no. 3414

101 Green 1989, 163; Thevenot 1968, 97ff

102 Green 1986a, 150, fig. 68; 1989, fig. 74; Deyts 1983

103 Vatin 1969

104 Thevenot 1951a, 129–41

105 Duval 1976, 58; Espérandieu 1917, 72–86

106 Thevenot 1968, 200–21

107 Wheeler 1932

108 Green 1986a, 160

109 Ibid., 154–5, 158

110 Toynbee 1962, no. 96

Chapter 7 (pp. 122–36)

1 Halsberghe 1972, 36–7

2 Ferguson 1989, 167–8

3 Pausanias I, 32.2

4 Ferguson 1989, 29–30

5 Burkert 1985, 200–1

6 Campbell 1969, 297–8

7 Ferguson 1989, 15

8 Kruta & Forman 1985, 106

9 Briard 1987, 152

10 Gelling & Davidson 1969, 21–6

11 Bertilsson 1987, 188–9

12 Briard 1987, 14–17

13 Ellis-Davidson 1988, 38–9

14 Frazer 1922, 617, 644–5

15 Ferguson 1989, 6

16 Cook 1914, 521ff; Ferguson 1989, 6; Pausanias III, 26.1

17 Dietrich 1973, 81

18 Harrison 1912, 149

19 Bey 1908, pl. V

20 Homer *Iliad, passim*; Cook 1914, 433–64

21 Merlat 1960; Speidel 1978

22 Glück 1965, 203

23 de Lumley 1976, 57

24 Ibid., fig. 49, 4

25 This probably dates to the reign of Tiberius: Rivet 1988, 272–3; Gros 1986; Duval *et al.* 1962

26 Deonna 1917, 124ff; Drioux 1934, 73

27 Green 1986a, 189ff; 1989, 180–2

28 Green 1986a, 59–60

29 Gelling & Davidson 1969, 92, fig. 44a, e; Anati 1965, 151–6, 158–68

30 Déchelette 1927, 281, fig. 312; Green 1986a, 8; 1989, fig. 58

31 Boon 1982, 276–82; Green 1986a, 44, 196, fig. 88

32 Green 1984a, fig. 28

33 Wright & Phillips 1975, 73, no. 196, pl. IVB; Green 1983; 1984a, no. BB18

34 de Villefosse 1881, 1–13; Green 1984a, no. B88

35 Ferguson 1989, 13

36 On a statue of a mother-goddess on which is a dedication to Jupiter Optimus Maximus: Schindler 1977, Abb. 100

37 On a dedication where Jupiter and the mothers are mentioned together: Römisch-Germanisches Museum, Köln; Green 1989, 37–8

38 Espérandieu no. 6825; Green 1984a, no. B25

39 Kerényi 1979, 2–11

40 Mallory 1989, 128–42

41 Torbrügge 1968, 83

42 Olmsted 1979, 129–38, plate B

43 Megaw thinks that the wheels depicted on the Gundestrup Cauldron may be solar: Megaw 1970, 131–2

44 Lerat 1964, 378, fig. 4

45 Hatt 1945, no. 23

46 For example, Minucius Felix, *Octavianus* XXVII, 7; Juvenal, *Satire* VIII

47 Green 1989, 10–16

48 Hondius-Crone 1955, no. 1

49 Ibid., no. 15

50 Haverfield 1892, 314–19; Green 1986a, 72–103; 1989, 10–44

51 Unprovenanced: Green 1976, pl. XVe

52 Ibid., 190; Devizes Museum

53 *C.I.L.* VII, 1285

54 Green 1981a, 253–70

55 Galliou 1974, 259–83

56 Rouvier-Jeanlin 1972; Jenkins 1958; Musée de Bretagne 1988

57 Green 1984b, 25–33

58 Blanchet 1890; Jenkins 1958, 61; Thevenot 1951b, 1ff

59 Lambrechts 1942, 170ff

60 Jenkins 1958, 63

61 Bailey 1932, 119; Altheim 1938, 358; Dumézil 1970, 545–9; Ferguson 1970, 26, 71

62 Ferguson 1989, 19

63 Thevenot 1951b, 1ff

64 Green 1989, 39

65 Green 1976, 228; Penn 1959, 1ff

66 Green 1984a, no. C43; Blanchet 1890, Type 10

67 Jenkins 1958, 70

68 Musée de Bretagne 1988, 46ff

69 Musée Dobrée, Nantes; Musée de Bretagne 1988; Rouvier-Jeanlin 1972, no. 207; Green 1984b, fig. 1b

70 Musée de Bretagne 1988; Green 1984b, fig. 1a; Rouvier-Jeanlin 1972, no. 214

71 Musée de Bretagne 1988, no. 171

72 Rouvier-Jeanlin 1972, no. 303

73 Musée de Bretagne 1988, no. 111

74 Ibid., no. 162

75 Green 1984a, 190; Blanchet 1890, fig. 3; Musée de Rouen

76 Musée de Bretagne 1988, no. 146

77 Musée de Bretagne 1988, 116–28, no. 247

78 Ibid., 129

79 Ibid., no. 252

80 Green 1989, 45–73

81 Ibid., 9–44

82 Ibid.

83 Green 1984a, no. B17

84 Sautel 1926, no. 501, pl. LIII; Courcelle-Seneuil 1910, 68; Espérandieu no. 303

85 Espérandieu no. 299; Green 1984a, no. B158

86 Green 1981b, 109–15

87 Green 1989, 92–3

88 Green 1986a, 41, 46

89 British Museum 1925, 50

90 Pauli 1975, Abb. 3; 1984, 180

91 British Museum 1964, 60; Gilbert 1978

92 Alföldi 1949, 19ff

93 Ellis-Davidson 1988, 86–7

94 Green 1986a, 158; 1989, fig. 25

95 Déchelette 1909, 345, 354, figs. 20, 27

96 Hatt 1945

97 Linckenheld 1927; 1929b, 29–49

98 Green 1984a, no. B104

99 Ibid., no. 126

100 Musée de Bretagne 1988, no. 147

101 Linckenheld 1927; Green 1984a, Type IIa, 119–22

102 Green 1984a, no. B134

103 Ibid., no. B139

104 Ibid., no. B167

105 Ibid., no. B15

106 Ibid., no. B43

107 Sautel 1926, 90, no. 152

108 Green 1984a, nos. B154–8

109 Toynbee 1971, 33–5

110 Cumont 1922, 102

111 Green 1984a, 174–8; 1986b, 65–75

112 Bauchhenss & Nölke 1981

113 Green 1984a, 111–15, Type Ibia

114 Espérandieu *Germ.* no. 76

115 Kellner 1971, pl. 85

116 Espérandieu no. 3207

117 Espérandieu no. 5357

118 Künzl 1975, Taf. 26

119 Espérandieu no. 7098; Drioux 1929, 355, fig. on p. 356

120 Green 1984a, figs. 1, 23

121 Henig 1978, no. 426; Masskant-Kleibrink 1978, no. 401a, b

122 Vian 1951, nos. 537, 539

123 Green 1984a, Type Ibib

124 Blanchet 1923, 156–60, pl. VII

125 Eygun 1965, 381–2, fig. 51

126 Mouhet: Lelong 1970, 123–6, figs. 1, 2; Tours: Picard 1968, 343, fig. 24

127 Green 1986a, 59

128 Espérandieu nos. 1249, 1250

129 As at Néris and St Pourçain, Allier: Green 1984a, nos. C8, C9a

130 As at Besigheim, Stuttgart: Reinach 1917, 157

Bibliography

ABBAYE DE DAOULAIS, *Avant les Celtes: L'Europe à l'âge du Bronze, 2500–800 avant JC*, Musée Départemental Breton, Ministère de la Culture/Association d'Abbaye de Daoulais, 1988.

AIGNER-FORESTI, L., 'Ein Halbplastisches Zierstuck aus dem Gräberfeld von Frög', *Schild von Steier: Beitrage zur Steierischen Vor- und Frühgeschichte und Münzkunde*, vol. 15–16, 1978/9, pp. 43–7.

ALFÖLDI, A., 'The Bronze Mace from Willingham Fen, Cambridgeshire', *Journal of Roman Studies*, vol. 39, 1949, pp. 19ff.

ALLEN, D. F. & NASH, D. (ed.), *The Coins of the Ancient Celts*, Edinburgh University Press, 1980.

ALTHEIM, F., *A History of Roman Religion*, Methuen, 1938.

ANATI, E., 'Bronze Age Chariots from Europe', *Proceedings of the Prehistoric Society*, vol. 26, 1960, pp. 50–63.

ANATI, E., *Camonica Valley*, Jonathan Cape, 1965.

ANATI, E., *Evolution and Style in Camunian Rock-Art*, Brescia, Archivi 6, Centro Camuno di Studi Preistorici, Edizioni del Centro, 1976.

ANON, *Die Hallstatt Kultur*, Internationale Ausstellung des Landes Oberösterreich, 1980a.

ANON, *Die Kelten in Mitteleuropa*, Salzburger Landesausstellung in Keltenmuseum Hallein, 1980b.

ASHBEE, P., 'The Trundholm Horse's Trappings: a Chamfrein?', *Antiquity*, vol. 63, no. 240, 1989, pp. 539–46.

ATKINSON, R. J. C., *Stonehenge and Neighbouring Monuments*, H.M.S.O., 1978.

ATKINSON, R. J. C., 'Stonehenge', in MacSween, A. & Burgess, C. (eds.), *Au Temps de Stonehenge*, Administration Communale de Tournai, 1984, pp. 51–6.

AUDOUZE, F., 'Les Ceintures et Ornaments de Ceinture de l'âge du Bronze en France', *Gallia Préhistoire*, vol. 19, 1976, pp. 69–172.

BABELON, E. & BLANCHET, J. A., *Bronzes Antiques . . . Bibliothèque Nationale*, Leroux, 1895.

BADDELEY, St Clair, 'A Romano-Celtic Sculpture at Churcham', *Transactions of the Bristol & Gloucestershire Archaeological Society*, vol. 45, pp. 91ff.

BAHN, P. & VERTET, J., *Images of the Ice Age*, Windward, 1988.

BAILEY, C., *Phases in the Religion of Ancient Rome*, Oxford University Press, 1932.

BALSON, L., 'Reprise de Fouilles à la Graufesenque (Condatomagus), Campagne 1950', *Gallia*, vol. 8, 1952, pp. 1–15.

BARFIELD, L., *Northern Italy, Before Rome*, Thames & Hudson, 1971.

BAUCHHENSS, G., *Jupitergigantensaülen*, Württembergisches Landesmuseum, Stuttgart, 1976.

BAUCHHENSS, G. & NÖLKE, P., *Die Iupitersaülen in den germanischen Provinzen*, Rheinland-Verlag, 1981.

BEHN, F., 'Neue Funde römischer Skulpturen aus Hessen', *Germania*, vol. 20, 1936, pp. 256–8.

BEHRENS, G., *Bronzezeit Süddeutschlands*, Kataloge des Römisch-Germanisches Zentral Museums, vol. 6, 1916.

BENOIT, F., 'Monstres hippophores Méditerranéens et cavalier à l'anguipède gallo-romain', *Ogam*, vol. 6, 1954.

BENOIT, F., *Les Mythes d'outre-tombe: le cavalier à l'anguipède et l'écuyère Epona*, Latomus, 1950.

BENOIT, F., 'Informations Archéologiques: Aix (Sud), *Gallia*, vol. 16, 1958, pp. 412ff.

BENOIT, F., *Entremont*, Ophrys, 1981.

BERGQUIST, A. & TAYLOR, T., 'The Origin of the Gundestrup Cauldron', *Antiquity*, vol. 61, 1987, pp. 10–14.

BERTILSSON, U., *The Rock Carvings of Northern Bohuslän: Spatial Structures and Social Symbols*,

Stockholm Studies in Archaeology, no. 7, University of Stockholm, 1987.

BERTRAND, A., *La Religion des Gaulois*, Leroux, 1897.

BEY, E., 'Relief votif du Musée Impérial Ottoman', *Bulletin de Correspondance Hellénique*, vol. 32, 1908.

BIRLEY, E. *et al.*, 'Third Report on Excavations at Housesteads', *Archaeologia Aeliana*, 4th series, vol. 11, 1934, pp. 185–206.

BLANCHET, J. A., 'Etude sur les figurines en terre cuite de la Gaule Romaine', *Mémoires de la Société des Antiquaires de France*, 6th series, vol. 51, 1890, pp. 65–224.

BLANCHET, J. A., 'Le Jupiter à la roue trouvé à Champagnat (Creuse)', *Bulletin Archéologique du Comité des travaux historiques et scientifiques*, 1923, pp. 156–60.

BOCQUET, A., 'L'Isère Préhistorique et Protohistorique', *Gallia Préhistoire*, vol. 12, 1969, pp. 121–258.

BOON, G. C., 'A Coin with the head of the Cernunnos', *Seaby Coin & Medal Bulletin*, no. 769, 1982, pp. 276–82.

BOON, G. C., *Laterarum Iscanum: The Antefixes, Bricks and Tile Stamps of the Second Augustan Legion*, National Museum of Wales, 1984.

BOUCHER, S., *Recherches sur les bronzes figurés de Gaule pré-romaine et romaine*, Ecole Française de Rome, 1976.

BOUZEK, J., 'Sonnenwagen und Kesselwagen', *Archéologicke Rozheldy*, vol. 29, 1977, pp. 197–202.

BRADLEY, R., 'Darkness and Light in the Design of Megalithic Tombs', *Oxford Journal of Archaeology*, vol. 8, no. 3, 1989, pp. 251–9.

BŘEŇ, J., *Třísov: A Celtic Oppidum in South Bohemia*, Fontes Archaeologici Pragenses, 1966.

BRIARD, J., *The Bronze Age in Barbarian Europe. From the Megaliths to the Celts*, Routledge & Kegan Paul, 1979.

BRIARD, J., *Mythes et Symboles de l'Europe Pré Celtique: les Religions de l'âge du bronze 2500–800 av. JC*, Errance, 1987.

BRIARD, J., 'Les Religions de l'âge du Bronze', in Abbaye de Daoulais, *Avant les Celtes: L'Europe à l'âge du Bronze, 2500–800 avant JC*, 1988, pp. 108–11.

BRITISH MUSEUM, *Guide to the Early Iron Age Antiquities*, British Museum, 1925.

BRITISH MUSEUM, *Guide to the Antiquities of Roman Britain*, British Museum, 1964.

BRITISH MUSEUM, *Thracian Treasures from Bulgaria*, British Museum, 1976.

BURGESS, C., *The Age of Stonehenge*, Dent, 1980.

BURKERT, W., *Greek Religion*, Blackwell, 1985.

BURL, A., *Rites of the Gods*, Dent, 1981a.

BURL, A., 'By the light of the cinerary moon: chambered tombs and the astronomy of death', in Ruggles, C. & Whittle, A. (eds.), *Astronomy and Society during the period 4000–1500 BC*, British Archaeological Reports, Oxford, British series, no. 88, 1981b, pp. 243–74.

BURL, A., 'Stonehenge et les autres cercles de Pierres Britanniques', in MacSween, A. & Burgess, C. (eds.), *Au Temps de Stonehenge*, Administration Communale de Tournai, 1984, pp. 41–5.

BURL, A., *The Stonehenge People*, Dent, 1987.

BUTLER, J. J. & WATERBOLK, H. T., 'Bronze Age Connections across the North Sea', *Palaeohistoria*, vol. 9, 1963, pp. 167–75.

CAMPBELL, J. *The Masks of God: Primitive Mythology*, Penguin, 1969.

CHABOUILLET, A., 'Notice sur les inscriptions et les antiquités provenant de Bourbonne-les-Bains', *Revue Archéologique*, vol. 39, 1880–1, pp. 18ff.

CHAMPION, T., GAMBLE, C., SHENNAN, S. & WHITTLE, A., *Prehistoric Europe*, Academic Press, 1984.

CHARLESWORTH, D., 'Roman Jewellery found in Northumberland & Durham', *Archaeologia Aeliana*, 4th series, vol. 39, 1961, pp. 1–37.

CHASSAING, M., 'Les Barillets de Dispater', *Revue Archéologique*, vol. 47, 1956, pp. 156ff.

CHENET, G., 'Rouelles de plomb et persistance d'emploi des rouelles gauloises', *Bulletin Archéologique du Comité des travaux historiques et scientifiques*, 1919, pp. 243–51.

CHILDE, V. G., 'The First Waggons and Carts – from

the Tigris to the Severn', *Proceedings of the Prehistoric Society*, vol. 17, 1951, pp. 177–94.

CHIPPINDALE, C., *Stonehenge Complete*, Thames & Hudson, 1983.

CLOTTES, J., 'Informations Archéologiques: Midi-Pyrénées', *Gallia Préhistoire*, vol. 20, 1977, pp. 517–59.

COFFEY, G., *New Grange, and other incised tumuli in Ireland*, Dolphin Press, 1977.

COLES, J. & HARDING, A. F., *The Bronze Age in Europe*, Methuen, 1979.

COLLINGWOOD, R. G. & WRIGHT, R. P., *The Roman Inscriptions of Britain: Volume I. Inscriptions on Stone*, Oxford University Press, 1965.

COOK, A. B., *Zeus: A Study in Ancient Religion*, Cambridge University Press, vol.1, 1914; vol. 2, 1, 1925.

CORPUS INSCRIPTIONUM LATINARUM, Georgium Reimarum, 1861–1943.

COURCELLE-SENEUIL, J-L., *Les Dieux Gaulois d'après les monuments figurés*, Leroux, 1910.

COURTOIS, J-C., 'L'âge du Bronze dans les Hautes-Alpes', *Gallia Préhistoire*, vol. 3, 1960, pp. 47–108.

CRAWFORD, O. G. S., *The Eye Goddess*, Phoenix House, 1957.

CROON, J. de, 'Die Ideologie des Marskultes unter dem Principat und ihre Vorgeschichte', *Aufstieg und Niedergang des römischen Welt*, vol. II, 17.1, 1981, pp. 260ff.

CUMONT, F., *Afterlife in Roman Paganism*, Yale University Press, 1922.

CUNLIFFE, B. W., *Roman Bath*, Society of Antiquaries of London, 1969.

CUNLIFFE, B. W., *The Celtic World*, Bodley Head, 1979.

CUNLIFFE, B. W. (ed.), *Coinage and Society in Britain and Gaul. Some current problems*, Council for British Archaeology Research Report, no. 38, 1981.

CUNLIFFE, B. W. & DAVENPORT, P., *The Temple of Sulis Minerva at Bath: volume I, The Site*, Oxford University Committee for Archaeology Monograph no. 7, 1985.

CURLE, J., *A Roman Frontier Post and its People: The Fort of Newstead in the Parish of Melrose*, Glasgow University Press, 1911.

DÉCHELETTE, J., 'Le culte du soleil aux temps préhistoriques', *Revue Archéologique*, 1909, pp. 305–57.

DÉCHELETTE, J., *Second Age du Fer ou Epoque de la Tène*, Manuel d'Archéologie Préhistorique et Celtique, vol. 4, 1914.

DÉCHELETTE, J., *Premier Age du Fer. Epoque de Hallstatt*, Manuel d'Archéologie Préhistorique et Celtique, vol. 3, Picard, 1927.

DÉCHELETTE, J., *L'Age du Bronze*, Manuel d'Archéologie Préhistorique et Archéologique, vol. 2, 1987 (reprint of original 1928 edition).

DEHN, W., 'Ein Quelheiligtum des Apollo und der Sirona bei Hochscheid', *Germania*, vol. 25, 1941, pp. 104ff.

DEMAKOPOULOU, K. (ed.), *The Mycenaean World. Five Centuries of Early Greek Culture*, National Hellenic Committee, Athens, 1988.

DEONNA, W., 'Le Soleil dans les armoires de la ville de Genève', *Revue de l'Histoire des Religions*, vol. 72, 1915, pp. 1–129.

DEONNA, W., 'Encore le dieu de Viège', *Revue des Études Anciennes*, vol. 18, 1916, pp. 193–202.

DEONNA, W., 'Les cornes bouletées des bovides Celtiques', *Revue Archéologique*, 1917, pp. 124ff.

DEONNA, W., 'Main et rouelle', *Pro Alésia*, 1923–5, pp. 108–13.

DEONNA, W., *Le Symbolisme de l'Oeil*, Boccard, 1965.

DEYTS, S., *Les Bois Sculptés des Sources de la Seine*, XLIIe supplément Gallia, 1983.

DEYTS, S., *Le Sanctuaire des Sources de la Seine*, Musée Archéologique Dijon, 1985.

DIETRICH, B. C., *The Origins of Greek Religion*, de Gruyter, 1973.

DIETRICH, B. C., 'A Minoan Symbol of Renewal', *Journal of Prehistoric Religion*, vol. 2, 1988, pp. 12–25.

DI STASI, L., *Mal Occhio: The Underside of Vision*, North Point Press, 1981.

DRIOUX, G., 'Le Dieu "à la roue" chez les Lingons',

Revue des Études Anciennes, vol. 31, 1929, pp. 354–8.

DRIOUX, G., *Cultes Indigènes des Lingons,* Picard, 1934.

DRIOUX, G., 'Amulette de bronze trouvée à Isômes (Haute-Marne)', *Bulletin de la Société Nationale des Antiquaires de France,* 1943–4, pp. 208–9.

DUMÉZIL, G., *Archaic Roman Religion,* University of Chicago Press, 1970.

DUVAL, P-M., *et al., L'Arc d'Orange,* XVe supplément à *Gallia,* 1962.

DUVAL, P-M., *Les Dieux de la Gaule,* Petite Bibliothèque, Payot, 1976.

ELLIS-DAVIDSON, H., *Myths and Symbols in Pagan Europe,* Manchester University Press, 1988.

ELUÈRE, C., *L'Or des Celtes,* Fribourg, 1987.

EOGAN, C., 'The Later Bronze Age in Ireland in the light of recent research', *Proceedings of the Prehistoric Society,* vol. 30, 1964, pp. 268–352.

ESPÉRANDIEU, E., 'Note sur des images de divinités', *Pro Alésia,* 1906–7, pp. 39ff.

ESPÉRANDIEU, E., *Recueil Général des bas-reliefs de la Gaule Romaine et pré-Romaine,* Leroux, 1907–66.

ESPÉRANDIEU, E., 'Le Dieu Cavalier de Luxeuil', *Revue Archéologique,* 1917, pp. 72–86.

ESPÉRANDIEU, E., *Le Musée Lapidaire de Nîmes. Guide Sommaire,* Imprimérie Générale, Nîmes, 1924.

ESPÉRANDIEU, E. & ROLLAND, H., *Bronzes Antiques de la Seine-Maritime,* XIIIe supplément à *Gallia,* 1959.

EVANS, J. D., *Prehistoric Antiquities of the Maltese Islands,* Athlone, 1971.

EYGUN, F., 'Informations Archéologiques: Poitiers', *Gallia,* vol. 23, 1965, pp. 349–87.

FERGUSON, J., *The Religions of the Roman Empire,* Thames & Hudson, 1970.

FERGUSON, J., *Among the Gods: An Archaeological Exploration of Ancient Greek Religion,* Routledge, 1989.

FERRIER, J., *Pendeloques et Amulettes d'Europe. Anthologie et Réflexions,* Fanlac, 1971.

FILIP, J., *Keltové ve Střední Europé,* Nakladatelstuí Československé Akademie Věd, Praha, 1956.

FILIP, J., *Celtic Civilisation and its Heritage,* Academie, Praha, 1976.

FLEISCHER, R., *Die Römischen Bronzen aus Österreich,* von Zabern, 1967.

FLEMMING, H., 'Les Objets d'Alésia...', *Pro Alesia,* 1908–9, pp. 391–5.

FOL, A. & MARAZOV, I, *Thrace and the Thracians,* Cassell, 1977.

FORDE-JOHNSTON, J. L., 'Megalithic Art in the North-West of Britain: the Calderstones, Liverpool', *Proceedings of the Prehistoric Society,* vol. 23, 1957, pp. 20–39.

FORSTER, R. H. & KNOWLES, W. H., 'Corstopitum: Report on the excavations in 1909', *Archaeologia Aeliana,* third series, vol. 6, 1910, pp. 205–72.

FOUET, G., *La Villa Gallo-Romaine de Montmaurin,* XXe supplément à *Gallia,* 1969.

FOUET, G. & SOUTOU, A., 'Une cime pyrénéenne consacrée à Jupiter: Le Mont Saçon (Hautes-Pyrénées)', *Gallia,* vol. 21, 1963, pp. 75–295.

FOX, C., 'Triskeles, Palmettes and Horse-Brooches' *Proceedings of the Prehistoric Society,* vol. 18, 1952, pp. 47–54.

FRAZER, J. G., *The Golden Bough,* Macmillan, 1922 (abridged version).

FRAZER, J. G., *The Worship of Nature* (Gifford Lectures to the University of Edinburgh), Macmillan, 1926.

FRAZER, J. G., *Myths of the Origin of Fire,* Macmillan, 1930.

FREDSJO, A. *et al., Rock-carvings: Kville Härad, Svenneby,* Studies in North European Archaeology, no. 7, Antiquarian Society, Göteborg/Archaeological Museum Göteborg, 1971.

FREDSJO, A. *et al., Rock-carvings: Kville Härad, Bottna,* Studies in North European Archaeology, no. 13, Antiquarian Society Göteborg/Archaeological Museum Göteborg, 1975.

FREDSJO, A. *et al., Rock-carvings: Kville Härad, Kville,* Studies in North European Archaeology, nos. 14/15, Antiquarian Society Göteborg/Archaeological Museum Göteborg, 1981.

GAGNIÈRE, M. S., 'Informations Archéologiques: circonscription d'Aix-en-Provence', *Gallia Préhistoire,* vol. 4, 1961, pp. 337–86.

GAIDOZ, H., 'Le Dieu Gaulois du soleil et le symbolisme de la roue', *Revue Archéologique*, 1884, pp. 7–37.

GAIDOZ, H., 'Le Dieu Gaulois du soleil', *Revue Archéologique*, 1885, pp. 179–203.

GALLIOU, P., 'À propos de deux pendentifs gallo-romains du Musée Archéologique de Nantes', *Annales de Bretagne*, vol. 81, 1974, pp. 259–83.

GAUCHER, G., *Peuples du Bronze*, Hachette, Poitiers, 1988.

GELLING, P. & DAVIDSON, H. E., *The Chariot of the Sun and other Rites and Symbols of the Northern Bronze Age*, Dent, 1969.

GILBERT, H., 'The Felmingham Hall Hoard, Norfolk', *Bulletin of the Board of Celtic Studies*, vol. 28, part 1, 1978, pp. 159–87.

GIMBUTAS, M., *Bronze Age Cultures of Central and Eastern Europe*, Mouton & Co., Hague, 1965.

GLOB, P. V., *Helleristninger i Danmark*, Jutland Archaeological Society Publications, vol. 7, 1969.

GLOB, P. V., *Danish Prehistoric Monuments*, Faber & Faber, 1971.

GLOB, P. V., *The Mound People*, Faber & Faber, 1974.

GLÜCK, W., *Deities and Dolphins*, Cassell, 1965.

GOODBURN, R., *The Roman Villa, Chedworth*, National Trust, 1972.

GOODCHILD, R. G., 'A Priest's Sceptre from the Romano-Celtic Temple at Farley Heath, Surrey', *Antiquaries Journal*, vol. 18, 1938, pp. 391ff.

GOODCHILD, R. G., 'The Farley Heath Sceptre Binding', *Antiquaries Journal*, vol. 27, 1947, pp. 83ff.

GÖRMANN, M., *Nordiskt och Keltiskt Sydskandinavisk religion under Yngre bronsålder och Keltisk järnålder*, Wallin & Dalholm Boktr. A. B. Lund, 1987.

GRAPINAT, R., 'Les Avatars d'un culte solaire: symbolisme du Swastika', *Forum: Revue du Groupe Archéologie Antique*, no. 1, 1970, pp. 54–6.

GREEN, H. S., 'The Caergwrle Bowl – not Oak but Shale', *Antiquity*, vol. 59, 1985, pp. 116–17.

GREEN, H. S., SMITH, A. H. V., YOUNG, B. R. & HARRISON, R. K., 'The Caergwrle Bowl: its composition, geological source and archaeological significance', *Institute of Geological Sciences. Short Communications*, no. 80/81, 1980, pp. 26–30.

GREEN, M. J., *A Romano-British Ceremonial Bronze Object found near Peterborough*, Peterborough City Museum Monograph no. 1, 1975.

GREEN, M. J., *A Corpus of Religious Material from the Civilian Areas of Roman Britain*, British Archaeological Reports, Oxford, British series, no. 24, 1976.

GREEN, M. J., *Small Cult Objects from the Military Areas of Roman Britain*, British Archaeological Reports, Oxford, British series, no. 52, 1978.

GREEN, M. J., 'The Worship of the Romano-Celtic Wheel-God in Britain seen in relation to Gaulish Evidence', *Collections Latomus*, vol. 38, fascicule 2, 1979, pp. 345–67.

GREEN, M. J., 'Model Objects from Military Areas of Roman Britain', *Britannia*, vol. 12, 1981a, pp. 253–70.

GREEN, M. J., 'Wheel-God and Ram-Horned Snake in Roman Gloucestershire', *Transactions of the Bristol & Gloucestershire Archaeological Society*, vol. 99, 1981b, pp. 109–15.

GREEN, M. J., 'Tanarus, Taranis and the Chester Altar', *Journal of the Chester Archaeological Society*, vol. 65, 1982, pp. 37–44.

GREEN, M. J., 'A Celtic God from Netherby, Cumbria', *Transactions of the Cumberland & Westmorland Antiquarian & Archaeological Society*, vol. 83, 1983, pp. 41–7.

GREEN, M. J., *The Wheel as a Cult Symbol in the Romano-Celtic World*, Latomus, Brussels, 1984a.

GREEN, M. J., 'Mother and Sun in Romano-Celtic Religion', *Antiquaries Journal*, vol. 84, part 1, 1984b, pp. 25–33.

GREEN, M. J., 'Celtic Symbolism at Roman Caerleon', *Bulletin of the Board of Celtic Studies*, vol. 31, pp. 251–8.

GREEN, M. J., *The Gods of the Celts*, Alan Sutton/Barnes & Noble, 1986a.

GREEN, M. J., 'Jupiter, Taranis and the Solar Wheel', in Henig, M. & King, A. (eds.), *Pagan Gods and Shrines of the Roman Empire*, Oxford University Committee for Archaeology Monograph no. 8, pp. 65–75.

GREEN, M. J., *Symbol and Image in Celtic Religious Art*, Routledge, 1989.

GREEN, M. J., 'The Iconography of Celtic Coins', *11th Oxford Symposium on Coinage and Monetary History* (April 1989), 1990a, forthcoming.

GREEN, M. J., 'Triplism and Plurality: Intensity and Symbolism in Celtic Religious Expression', Lecture given at a symposium entitled *Sacred & Profane*, Oxford, October 28–9, 1989, 1990b, forthcoming.

GRINSELL, L. V., 'The Breaking of Objects as a Funerary Rite', *Folklore*, vol. 72, 1961, pp. 475–91.

GROS, P., 'Une hypothèse sur l'Arc d'Orange', *Gallia*, vol. 44, fascicule 2, 1986, pp. 192–201.

GUTHERZ, X., 'Circonscription de Languedoc-Roussillon', *Gallia Préhistoire*, vol. 29, 1986, pp. 353–80.

GREENFIELD, E., 'The Romano-British shrines at Brigstock', *Antiquaries Journal*, vol. 43, 1963, pp. 228ff.

HACHMANN, R., 'Die Goldschalen von "Leer und Swäbisch-Gronünd". Zei Fälschungen aus einer Müncher Goldschmiede-Werkstatt', *Germania*, vol. 36, 1958, pp. 436–46.

HAFFNER, A., *Das Keltisch-Römische Graberfeld von Wederath-Belginum, 1*, von Zabern, 1971.

HALSBERGHE, G. H., *The Cult of Sol Invictus*, Brill, 1972

HARBISON, P., *The Archaeology of Ireland*, Bodley Head, 1976.

HARBISON, P., *Pre-Christian Ireland*, Thames & Hudson, 1988.

HARDING, D. W., *Prehistoric Europe (Making of the Past)*, Elsevier Phaidon, 1978.

HARRISON, J., *Themis. A Study of the Social Origins of Greek Religion*, Cambridge University Press, 1912.

HARRISON, J., *Prolegomena to the Study of Greek Religion*, Merlin Press, 1962.

HATT, J. J., *Les Monuments Funéraires gallo-romains du Comminges et du Couserans*, Annales du Midi, 1945.

HATT, J. J., '"Rota Flammis Circumsepta". . . .',

Revue Archéologique de l'Est et du Centre-Est, vol. 2, 1951, pp. 82–7.

HATT, J. J., *Mythes et Dieux de la Gaule*, Picard, 1989.

HAWKES, J., *Man and the Sun*, Cresset, 1962.

HIGGINS, R. A., 'The Elgin Jewellery', *British Museum Quarterly*, vol. 23, 1960–1, pp. 101–7.

HIGGINS, R. A., *Greek and Roman Jewellery*, British Museum, 1961.

HOLE, C., *English Folklore*, Batsford, 1940.

HOLE, C., *English Custom and Usage*, Batsford, 1950.

HONDIUS-CRONE, A., *The Temple of Nehalennia at Domburg*, Meulenhoff, Amsterdam, 1955.

JAMES, E. O., *Prehistoric Religion*, Thames & Hudson, 1957.

JAMES, E. O., *The Ancient Gods*, Weidenfeld & Nicolson, 1960.

JENKINS, F., 'The Cult of the "Pseudo-Venus" in Kent', *Archaeologia Cantiana*, vol. 72, 1958, pp. 60–76.

JENSEN, E., *Prehistoric Denmark*, Nationalmuseet Copenhagen, 1978.

JENSEN, J., *The Prehistory of Denmark*, Methuen, 1982.

JOHNSON, P. M., 'Roman Vase found at Littlehampton', *Sussex Archaeological Collections*, vol. 46, 1903, pp. 233–4.

JONES, T. GWYNN, *Welsh Folklore and Folk-Custom*, Brewer, 1929.

KELLNER, H. J., *Die Römer in Bayern*, Süddeutscher Verlag, 1971.

KENT HILL, D., 'Le "Dieu au Maillet" de Vienne à la Walters Art Gallery de Baltimore', *Gallia*, vol. 11, 1953, pp. 205–24.

KERÉNYI, K., *Goddesses of Sun and Moon*, Spring Publications Inc., Dallas, 1979.

KOSSACK, G., *Studien zum Symbolgut der Urnenfelder- und Hallstattzeit Mitteleuropas*, de Gruyter, 1954.

KROMER, K., *Das Gräberfeld von Hallstatt*, Association Internationale d'archéologie classique, Firenze, 1959.

KRÜGER, E., 'Die gallischen und die germanischen

Dioskuren...', *Trierer Zeitschrift*, vol. 15, 1940, pp. 8–27.

KRÜGER, E., 'Die gallischen und die germanischen Dioskuren...', *Trierer Zeitschrift*, vol. 16, 1941, pp. 1–66.

KRUTA, W. & FORMAN, W., *The Celts of the West*, Orbis, 1985.

KÜNZL, E., *Corpus Signorum Imperii Romani: Corpus der Skulpturen der Römische Welt: Alzey und Umgebung*, Römisch-Germanische Kommission des Deutschen Archäologischen Instituts, 1975.

LABROUSSE, M., 'Informations Archéologique: Xe Circonscription', *Gallia*, vol. 12, 1954, pp. 211–31.

LABROUSSE, M., 'Informations Archéologiques: Toulouse', *Gallia*, vol. 17, 1959, pp. 409–49.

LABROUSSE, M., 'Informations Archéologiques: Toulouse', *Gallia*, vol. 20, 1962, pp. 547–609.

LAET, S. J. de, 'Figurines en terre cuite de l'époque romaine trouvées à Assche-Kalkoven', *L'Antiquité Classique*, vol. 10, 1942, pp. 41–54.

LAMBRECHTS, P., *Contributions à l'étude des divinités celtiques*, Rijksuniversitaet te Gent, 1942.

LAMBRECHTS, P., 'La Colonne du dieu-cavalier au géant et le culte des sources en Gaule', *Collection Latomus*, vol. 8, 1949, pp. 145–58.

LAUR-BELART, R., 'Eine neue Kleininschrift von Augst', *Urschweiz*, vol. 6, 1942, pp. 20–3.

LAWSON, A. J., 'A Middle Bronze Age Hoard from Hunstanton, Norfolk', in Burgess, C. & Coombs, D. (eds.), *Bronze Age Hoards: some finds old and new*, British Archaeological Reports, Oxford, British series, no. 67, 1979, pp. 42–92.

LEACH, J., 'The Smith-God in Roman Britain', *Archaeologia Aeliana*, 4th series, vol. 40, 1962, pp. 35ff.

LEBEL, P. & BOUCHER, S., *Bronzes Figurés Antiques*, Musée Rolin, Autun, 1975.

LEBER, P., 'Ein Altar des Mars Latobius auf der Koralpe', *Carinthia*, vol. I, 1967, pp. 517–20.

LE GALL, J., *Alésia: Archéologie et Histoire*, Fayard, 1963.

LE GALL, J., *Alésia*, Paris, Ministère de Culture, 1985.

LELONG, C., 'Note sur une sculpture gallo-romaine de Mouhet (Indre)', *Revue Archéologique du Centre*, vol. 9, 1970, pp. 123–6.

LERAT, L., 'Informations Archéologiques: Besançon', *Gallia*, vol. 22, 1964, pp. 375–410.

LERAT, L., 'Informations Archéologiques: Franche-Comté, *Gallia*, vol. 28, 1970, pp. 345–65.

LINCKENHELD, E., *Les stèles funéraires en forme de maison chez les Médiomatriques et en Gaule*, Paris, Société d'Edition 'Les Belles Lettres', 1927.

LINCKENHELD, E., 'Sucellus et Nantosuelta', *Revue de l'histoire des religions*, vol. 99, 1929a, pp. 40–92.

LINCKENHELD, E., 'Le symbolisme astral des stèles funéraires gallo-romaines des Vosges et de l'Illyrie', *Revue Celtique*, 1929b, pp. 29–49.

LONGPÉRIER, H. de, 'Des rouelles et anneaux antiques....', *Revue Archéologique* 1867, pp. 343–62 & 397–405.

LUMLEY, H. de & ABELANET, J., *Vallée des Merveilles*, U.I.S.P.P. IXe Congrès, Paris. Livret-Guide de l'excursion C1, 1976, pp. 47–177.

LURKER, M., *The Gods and Symbols of Ancient Egypt*, Thames & Hudson, 1974.

MACCANA, P., 'Aspects of the theme of King and Goddess in Irish Literature', *Études Celtiques*, vol. 7, 1955–56, pp. 76–114.

MACCANA, P., *Celtic Mythology*, Newnes, 1983.

MACK, R. P., *The Coinage of Ancient Britain*, Spink, Seaby, 1975.

MAJOR, E., *Gallische Ausiedlung mit Gräberfeld bei Basel*, Verlag von Frobenius, Basel, 1940.

MALLORY, J. P., *In search of the Indo-Europeans*, Thames & Hudson, 1989.

MALMER, M. P., *A Chorological Study of North European Rock Art*, Antikvanska serien 32. Kungl. Vitterhets Historie och Antikvitets Akademien, Stockholm, 1981.

MANTEYER, G. de, 'Les dieux des Alpes de Ligurie', *Bulletin de la Société d'études des Hautes-Alpes*, 1945.

MARINGER, J., *The Gods of Prehistoric Man*, Weidenfeld & Nicolson, 1956.

MASSKANT-KLEIBRINK, M., *Catalogue of the Engraved Gems in the Royal Coin Cabinet, The Hague*, Hague, 1978.

MEGAW, J. V. S., *Art of the European Iron Age*, Harper & Row, 1970.

MEGAW, R. & MEGAW, J. V. S., *Celtic Art. From its Beginnings to the Book of Kells*, Thames & Hudson, 1989.

MEGAW, J. V. S. & SIMPSON, D. D. A., *Introduction to British Prehistory*, Leicester University Press, 1979.

MENGHIN, W. & SCHAUER, P., *Der Goldkegel von Ezelsdorf: Kultgerät der späten Bronzezeit*, Germanisches National Museum, Nürnberg, 1983.

MERHART, G. von, *Bericht der Römisch-Germanischen Kommission*, 1956–7, pp. 91–147.

MERHART, G. von, *Hallstatt und Italien*, Verlag des Römisch-Germanischen Zentralmuseums, 1969.

MERLAT, P., *Jupiter Dolichenus*, Institut d'Art et d'Archéologie, Université de Paris, 1960.

MERRIFIELD, R., *The Archaeology of Ritual and Magic*, Batsford, 1987.

MORRIS, R. W. B., 'The Prehistoric rock art of Great Britain, *Proceedings of the Prehistoric Society*, vol. 55, 1989, pp. 45–88.

MÜLLER-KARPE, H., *Beiträge zur Chronologie der Urnenfelderzeit nördlich und südlich der Alpen*, Römisch-Germanisches Forschungen, vol. 22, 7, 1959.

MUSÉE DE BRETAGNE, *Les Mystères de Condate*, Musée de Bretagne, 1988.

MYRON, R., *Prehistoric Art*, Pitman, New York, 1964.

NASH-WILLIAMS, V. E., 'The Roman Gold-Mines at Dolaucothi (Carms)', *Bulletin of the Board of Celtic Studies*, vol. 14, 1950–2, pp. 78–84.

NORDBLADH, J., 'Some problems concerning the relation between rock art, religion and society', *Acts of the International Symposium on Rock Art*, Hånko, 1972, pp. 185–209.

NORDBLADH, J., 'Images as messages in society. Prolegomena to the study of Scandinavian petroglyphs and semiotics', in Kristiansen, K. & Paludan-Müller (eds.), *New Directions in Scandinavian Archaeology*, Studies in Scandinavian Prehistory and Early History, vol. 1, 1978, pp. 63–78.

NORDBLADH, J., 'Knowledge and Information in Swedish Petroglyph Documentation', in Moberg, C. A. (ed.), *Similar Finds: Similar Interpretations*, University of Gothenburg, 1981, pp. G1–79.

NORDBLADH, J., 'Interpretation of south Scandinavian petroglyphs in the history of religion done by archaeologists: analysis and attempt at auto-critique', in Steinsland, G. (ed.), *Words and Objects: towards a Dialogue between Archaeology and the History of Religion*, Norwegian University Press, 1986.

O'BRIEN, T., JENNINGS, T. & O'BRIEN, D., 'The equinox cycle at Cairn T, Loughcrew', *Riocht Na Midhe*, vol. 8, 1987, pp. 3–15.

OGILVIE, R. M., *The Romans and their Gods in the Age of Augustus*, Chatto & Windus, 1969.

O'KELLY, C., 'Passage-grave art in the Boyne Valley', *Proceedings of the Prehistoric Society*, vol. 39, 1973, pp. 354–82.

O'KELLY, C., *Illustrated Guide to Newgrange and the other Boyne Monuments*, C. O'Kelly, Blackrock, Cork, 1978.

O'KELLY, M. J., *Early Ireland: An Introduction to Irish Prehistory*, Cambridge University Press, 1989.

OLMSTED, G., *The Gundestrup Cauldron*, Latomus, Brussels, 1979.

PARE, C., 'Wheels with thickened spokes, and the problem of cultural contact between the Aegean world and Europe in the Late Bronze Age', *Oxford Journal of Archaeology*, vol. 6, no. 1, 1987, pp. 43–61.

PARE, C., 'From Dupljaja to Delphi: the ceremonial use of the wagon in later prehistory', *Antiquity*, vol. 63, 1989, pp. 80–100.

PAULI, L., *Keltischer Volksglaube: Amulette und Sonderbestaltungen am Dürrnberg bei Hallein und im Eisenzeitlichen Mitteleuropa*, C. H. Beck'sche Verlagsbuchhandlung, München, 1975.

PAULI, L., *The Alps: Archaeology and Early History*, Thames & Hudson, 1984.

PENDLEBURY, J. D. S., *The Archaeology of Crete: an Introduction*, Methuen, 1939.

PENN, W. S., 'The Romano-British settlement at Springhead, excavation of Temple I', *Archaeologia Cantiana*, vol. 73, 1959, pp. 1ff.

PENTIKAÏNEN, J., 'The pre-literate stage of religious

tradition', in Anati, E. (ed.), *Valcamonica Symposium '72. Les Religions de la Préhistoire*, Brescia, Centro Camuno di Studi Preistorici, 1972.

PÉQUART, M. & S-J. & LE ROUZIC, Z., *Les Signes Gravés des Monuments Mégalithiques du Morbihan*, Picard, 1927.

PERRIER, J., 'L'Autel de Thauron (Creuse)', *Gallia*, vol. 18, 1960, pp. 195–7.

PICARD, G. Ch., 'Informations Archéologiques: Centre', *Gallia*, vol. 26, 1968, pp. 321–45.

PIETTE, J., 'Le Fanum de la Villeneuve-au-Châtelot (Aube): État des recherches en 1979', *Mémoires de la Société Archéologique Champenoise*, vol. 2, 1981, pp. 367–75.

PIGGOTT, S., 'The Early Bronze Age in Wessex', *Proceedings of the Prehistoric Society*, vol. 4, 1938, pp. 52–106.

PIGGOTT, S., '"The First Wagons and Carts": twenty-five years later', *Proceedings of the Prehistoric Society*, vol. 45, 1979, pp. 3–17.

PIGGOTT, S., *The Earliest Wheeled Transport: From the Atlantic Coast to the Caspian Sea*, Thames & Hudson, 1983.

PITTIONI, R., *Urgeschichte des Österreichischen Raumes*, Wien, Deuticke, 1954.

PLANSON, E. & POMMERET, C., *Les Bolards*, Paris, Ministère de la Culture/Imprimerie Nationale, 1986.

POLLARD, J., *Birds in Greek Life and Myth*, Thames & Hudson, 1977.

POTTER, T. W., *Roman Italy*, British Museum Publications, 1987.

POWELL, T. G. E., *The Celts*, Thames & Hudson, 1958.

POWELL, T. G. E., *Prehistoric Art in Europe*, Thames & Hudson, 1966.

POWELL, T. G. E., 'The Introduction of Horse-Riding to Temperate Europe: A Contributory Note', *Proceedings of the Prehistoric Society*, vol. 37, 1971, pp. 1–15.

POWELL, T. G. E. & DANIEL, G. E., *Barclodiad y Gawres, The Excavation of a Megalithic Chamber Tomb in Anglesey*, Liverpool University Press, 1956.

PRIMAS, M., 'Die Latènezeit im Alpinen Raum', *Archäologie der Schweiz: Band IV, Die Eisenzeit*, 1966–76.

RANDALL McIVER, D., *The Iron Age in Italy (A Study of the Early Civilisations which are neither Villanovan nor Etruscan*, Oxford University Press, 1927.

REES, A. & REES, B., *Celtic Heritage*, Thames & Hudson, 1961.

REINACH, S., *Description raisonnée du Musée de Saint-Germain-en-Laye. Bronzes figurés de la Gaule Romaine*, Musée des Antiquités Nationales, 1894.

REINACH, S., *Catalogue Illustré du Musée des Antiquités Nationales au Château de Saint-Germain-en-Laye, 1*, Musée des Antiquités Nationales, 1917.

REINACH, S., *Catalogue Illustré du Musée des Antiquités Nationales au Château de Saint-Germain-en-Laye, 2*, Musée des Antiquités Nationales, 1921.

RISTOW, G., *Religion und ihre Denkmäler in Köln*, Köln Römisch-Germanisches Museum, 1975.

ROMILLY-ALLEN, J., 'Two Kelto-Roman Finds in Wales', *Archaeologia Cambrensis*, 6th series, vol. 1, 1901, pp. 20–44.

ROSE, H. J. A., *A Handbook of Greek Mythology*, Methuen, 1933.

ROSS, A., *Pagan Celtic Britain*, Routledge & Kegan Paul, 1967.

RØSTHOLM, H., *The Vitlycke Rock Carvings*, The Vitlycke Publishers, Tanum, 1985.

RÖTTLANDER, R. C. A., 'Zur Deutung der Sogennanten Mithrassymbole', *Archäologische Informationen Mittelungen zur Ur- und Frühgeschichtlichte*, vols. 2–3, 1973–74, pp. 143–52.

ROUVIER-JEANLIN, M., *Les Figurines gallo-romaines en terre cuite au Musée des Antiquités Nationales*, XXIVe supplément à *Gallia*, 1972.

SANDARS, N. K., *Bronze Age Cultures in France*, Cambridge University Press, 1957.

SANDARS, N. K., *Prehistoric Art in Europe*, Pelican History of Art Series, Penguin, 1968.

SAUTEL, J., *Vaison dans l'Antiquité*, Aubanel Frères Editeurs, Avignon/Lyon, 1926.

SAVORY, H. N., *Guide Catalogue of the Early Iron Age Collections*, National Museum of Wales, 1976.

SAVORY, H. N., *Guide Catalogue of the Bronze Age Collections*, National Museum of Wales, 1980.

SCHINDLER, R., *Führer durch des Landesmuseum Trier*, Trier, Selbstverlag des Rheinisches Landesmuseums, 1977.

SCHUTZ, H., *The Prehistory of Germanic Europe*, Yale University Press, 1983.

SPEIDEL, M., *The Religion of Jupiter Dolichenus in the Roman Army*, Brill, 1978.

SPRÄTER, F., Der Brunholdistuhl bei Bad Dürkheim', *Mainz Zeitschrift*, vol. 30, 1935, pp. 32–9.

SPROCKHOFF, E., 'Sonnenwagen und Hakenkreuz im nordischen Kreis', *Germania*, vol. 20, 1936, pp. 1–8.

SPROCKHOFF, E., 'Central European Urnfield Culture and Celtic La Tène: an outline', *Proceedings of the Prehistoric Society*, vol. 21, pp. 257–81.

STEAD, I. M., *The Arras Culture*, Yorkshire Philosophical Society, 1979.

SURREY ARCHAEOLOGICAL SOCIETY, *Roman Temple, Wanborough*, Surrey Archaeological Society, 1988.

TAYLOR, J., *Bronze Age Goldwork of the British Isles*, Cambridge University Press, 1980.

THEVENOT, E., 'La station antique des Bolards à Nuits-Saint-Georges (Côte d'Or), *Gallia*, vol. 6, 1948, pp. 289–349.

THEVENOT, E., 'Le Cheval sacré dans la Gaule de l'Est', *Revue Archéologique de l'Est et du Centre-Est*, vol. 2, 1951a, pp. 129–41.

THEVENOT, E., 'Le Culte de déesses-mères à la station gallo-romaine des Bolards', *Revue Archéologique de l'Est et du Centre-Est*, vol. 2, 1951b, pp. 1–26.

THEVENOT, E., *Sur les traces des Mars Celtiques*, Dissertationes Archaeologicae Gandenses, vol. 3, 1955.

THEVENOT, E., *Dieux et sanctuaires de la Gaule*, Fayard, 1968.

THEVENOT, E., *Le Beaunois Gallo-Romain*, Latomus, Brussels, 1971.

TORBRÜGGE, W., *Prehistoric European Art*, Abrams, New York, 1968.

TORBRÜGGE, W. & UENZE, H. P., *Bilder zur Vorgeschichte Bayerns*, Thorbecke, 1968.

TOYNBEE, J. M. C., *Art in Roman Britain*, Phaidon, 1962.

TOYNBEE, J. M. C., *Death and Burial in the Roman World*, Thames & Hudson, 1971.

TUDOR, D., *Corpus Monumentorum Religionis Equitum Danuviorum*, Brill, 1976.

TWOHIG, E. S., *The Megalithic Art of Western Europe*, Clarendon Press, 1981.

UHDE, W., *Van Gogh*, Phaidon, 1981.

USENER, H., *M. Annaei Lucani Commentaria Bernensia*, Leipzig, 1869.

VAN DIJK, J., *Lugal ud Me-lam-bi; Nir-Ĝál*, Brill, 1982.

VANVINCKENROYE, W., *Tongeren Romeinse Stad*, Provinciaal Gallo-Romeins Museum, Tongeren, 1975.

VATIN, C., 'Ex-voto de bois gallo-romain à Chamalières', *Revue Archéologique*, 1969.

VIAN, F., *Répertoire des Gigantomachies figurées dans l'art grèc et romain*, Paris, 1951.

VILLEFOSSE, H. de, 'Note sur un bronze découvert à Landouzy-la-Ville (Aisne)', *Revue Archéologique*, 1881, pp. 1–13.

VRIES, J. de, *La Religion des Celtes*, Payot, 1963.

WAINWRIGHT, G. A., *The Sky-Religion in Egypt*, Greenwood Press, Westport, Connecticut, 1938.

WEBSTER, T. B. L., *Athenian Culture and Society*, Batsford, 1973.

WHEELER, R. E. M., *Report on the Excavations. . . . in Lydney Park, Gloucestershire*, Society of Antiquaries of London, 1932.

WHEELER, R. E. M., *Archaeology from the Earth*, Penguin, 1954.

WOOD, J. E., *Sun, Moon and Standing Stones*, Oxford University Press, 1978.

WRIGHT, R. P. & PHILLIPS, E. J., *Roman Inscribed and Sculptured Stones in Carlisle Museum*, Tullie House Museum, Carlisle, 1975.

WRIGHT, R. P. & RICHMOND, I. A., *The Roman Inscribed and Sculptured Stones in the Grosvenor Museum, Chester*, Chester & North Wales Archaeological Society, 1955.

ZACHAR, L., *Keltische Kunst*, Tatran, Bratislava, 1987.

ZWICKER, J., *Fontes Historiae Religionis Celticae*, de Gruyter, 1934–36.

Index

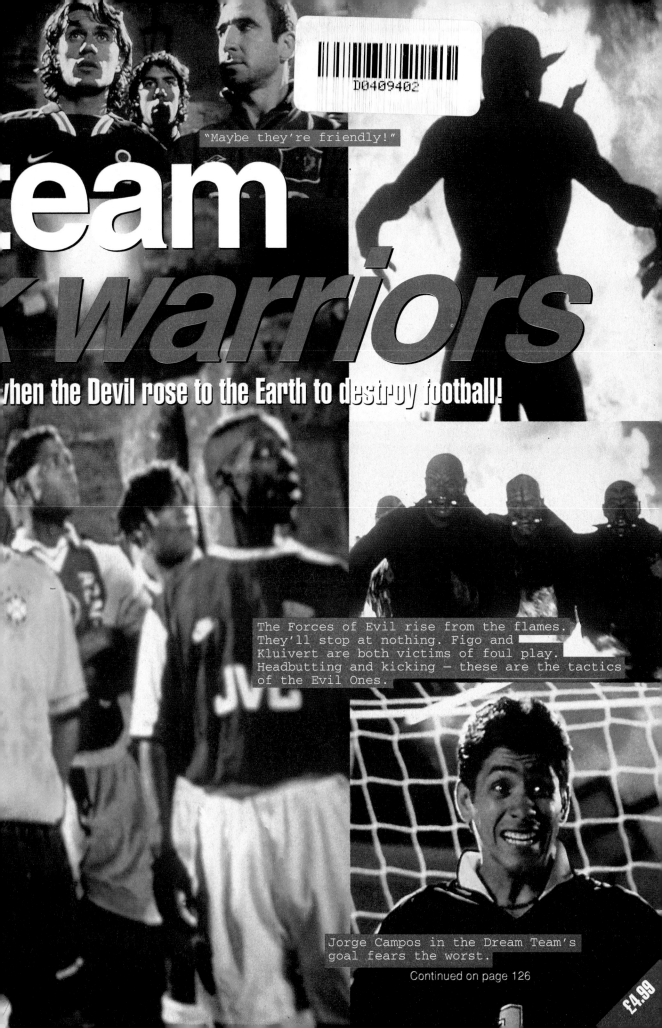

"Maybe they're friendly!"

eam
warriors
hen the Devil rose to the Earth to destroy football!

The Forces of Evil rise from the flames. They'll stop at nothing. Figo and Kluivert are both victims of foul play. Headbutting and kicking — these are the tactics of the Evil Ones.

Jorge Campos in the Dream Team's goal fears the worst.

Continued on page 126

£4.99

D0409402

THE TOPICAL TIMES FOOTBALL BOOK

contents

4

the red ne

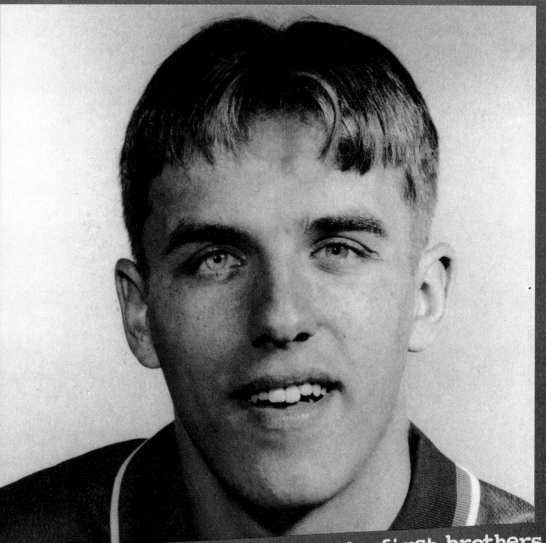

MANCHESTER UNITED'S FAMILY

In May, Gary and Phil became the first brothers since

England team

villes!
DOUBLE WINNERS

MANCHESTER UNITED'S trophy cabinet is the best stocked in football at the moment following last season's League and FA Cup 'double' success.

If United continue to claim the major prizes, Gary and Phil Neville may have to build a trophy room of their own to store their ever-growing collection of medals.

The Bury-born brothers are only just into their twenties, but the Neville household can already boast two Championship medals and two FA Cup winners' gongs, plus several England caps and there is no sign of the success coming to an end.

As youngsters, the pair were both fanatical United supporters and regular visitors to Old Trafford on matchdays. Last season saw them realise the ultimate dream of every United fan by representing the club in a 'double' winning season.

Gary broke into the first team a year earlier than his younger brother, but Phil's emergence last season saw them become the first brothers to play in the same United team since Brian and Jimmy Greenhoff in the late 1970's.

Sharing the experience of United's 'double' meant a lot to Gary and Phil.

Phil admits, "Although Gary and I were the youngest members of the back four last season, we seemed to be the ones who were playing in every game. As far as we are concerned, though, we are just team-mates on the pitch. I think our mum and dad feel the family thing more than we do on matchdays.

Jack and Bobby Charlton to play in the same when they played in a friendly against China in Beijing.

"The only times that impression may have been broken were after the final whistle at Middlesbrough when we clinched the Championship, and after we won the Cup at Wembley.

Continued overleaf

Continued from previous page.

"Gary came straight over to me at the end and gave me a hug. That was a special moment. It was important to us both that he came off the bench in the last five minutes of the Cup Final.

"Gary had been a substitute for a few League games leading up to the final and I think he knew that he wouldn't start the game. After the season he had, he was unlucky, but I was so glad that he came on before the end. He deserved it.

"He was the first man I hugged at the end of the game because he is also my best friend. When he came on with minutes to go, I knew it was going to be a special moment. I was really proud to have him on the pitch with me."

As the older and more experienced sibling, you would expect Gary to be the prime source of help and advice for his younger brother. However, England international Gary dismisses suggestions that Phil needs his help.

He has unshakeable faith in Phil's ability to handle himself. The manner in which Phil quickly established himself in the United side backs up Gary's judgement. On the pitch, Gary sees Phil only in the roles of team-mate and rival.

Gary says, "I don't need to help Phil. He is a good player and I would never dream of assuming that he needs me to look after him. If he does pick up a few tips from me along the way, then fair enough. I would never deliberately set out to influence him, though.

"He did well to break into the team last year, but although we

are brothers and I want him to be successful, I have to treat him just like any other player.

"At home he is my best friend, but at the club we are both vying for the same place. There were times last season when he was keeping me out of the team, so I know how much of a threat he is to my place."

Phil acknowledges the fact the he and Gary are in competition for a place in the team, but he believes it is only a matter of time before he sees Gary off — into the centre of defence.

He goes on, "Gary played a tremendous part in winning the title last season. Having played the majority of the season at right-back, he switched to the centre of defence during an injury crisis and he was unbelievable. In years to come, I believe that will be his best position."

Gary admits that a permanent move into the heart of the back four would suit him.

He reveals, "I'd love to play at centre-half regularly. I played quite a few games there last season and I enjoyed it. It's my favourite position, but when you look at the lads playing there like Gary Pallister and David May, it is going to be extremely difficult for me to make it my regular position."

"Before I broke into the first team, the defence had always been settled. It was a formidable unit and a hard act to follow. I took my chance when Paul Parker was injured and haven't looked back."

With nearly two seasons behind him and several England caps, Gary is certain to be around at Old Trafford for the foreseeable future, whatever position he plays. He has seen enough in his short time in the first team to make him a hardened professional.

Gary continues, "My first season ended with the team missing out on both the League and the Cup. Although it was hard to bear, it was a good experience for me.

"We suffered the agony of missing out on both trophies and I was absolutely gutted. Nobody could console me for about a week afterwards. It had been a brilliant period personally, but from a team point of view it was a nightmare.

"That disappointment hardened me for the campaign last season. Going into the final part of our Championship bid, people were questioning whether we had the mental strength to go all the way because the kids had not been through it before.

"Whoever was saying and writing those things must have had a short memory because we had all gone through it a year earlier and it was not a nice experience."

1995 and 1996 could not have been more different for the Neville brothers. Double disappointment became double joy, but Phil remembers where it all started.

He ends, "I gave my medals to my mum and dad at the end of last season. They have done everything for me and deserve all the credit for what happened to me and Gary last season." ●

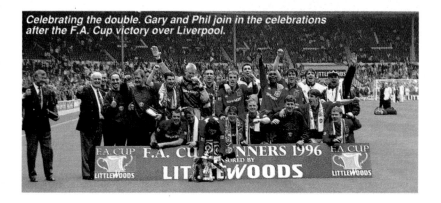

Celebrating the double. Gary and Phil join in the celebrations after the F.A. Cup victory over Liverpool.

● DAVID HIRST   sheffield wednesday

the man

● GOALSCORING COMES EASY TO LIVERPOOL'S ROBBIE FOWLER

I HAD a great season with Liverpool last year, finishing the campaign as the club's leading scorer and forcing my way into England's squad for Euro'96 alongside my Anfield team-mates Jamie Redknapp and Steve McManaman.

Considering how the season started for me, everything turned out better than I could have expected.

The manager, Roy Evans, bought one player before the start of 1995-96 and that was Stan Collymore. The club spent £8.5 million to take Stan from Nottingham Forest and it increased competition for places up front.

I have never taken my place at Liverpool for granted

because I know how quickly you can lose your place. Quite a few players at the club found out last season how hard it is to get back into the side after an injury or suspension. I wasn't happy when I was the one to miss out when the season began.

Stan and Ian Rush started the season together and I was dropped to the substitutes' bench. I hated being out of the team. I was desperate to play and what made it worse was that I didn't think that I deserved to be dropped.

Everybody was saying how good it was for the club to have such strong competition for places. It's great for the manager, but it's a nightmare when you are one of the unlucky ones.

Although I didn't enjoy being out of the team, I knew that the only thing I could do was wait for my chance. Luckily for me, it came in the second game of the season.

We were playing Leeds United at Elland Road and I was on the bench again. Not long after kick-off, though, Stan was tackled by John Pemberton and picked up an ankle injury. He had to go off and I replaced him. I didn't look back after that. It was unlucky for Stan, but that's the only way you can get your place back

"All I want to be known for is scoring goals and it is a gift I have always had."

tural

sometimes.

I might not have been so patient if I had been dropped earlier in my Liverpool career. I had been in the team for two years when Stan arrived and I had grown up a lot in that time. When I first broke into the team under former manager, Graeme Souness, it was easy to take things for granted. As time goes on, though, you accept that you have to set an example.

Being sent off playing for England Under-21's in Austria a couple of years ago wasn't a good example to anybody and it could have damaged my international ambitions. I tried to prove a point after it had happened, though, and show people that it was a one-off and would never happen again.

I didn't agree with the red card, but it cost me a four-match

ban with England and I had to live with it. I wouldn't say I am perfect by any stretch of the imagination, but since that red card in Austria, I have had a pretty good disciplinary record. All I want to be known for is

> **"I have always wanted to score goals and I love to see the net bulging after putting one past the 'keeper."**

scoring goals and it is a gift I have always had. Goalscoring is something that just comes naturally to me.

The one thing I want to put right is my record with England. I have not scored consistently at

Under-21 or full level yet and I really want to sort that out.

My record for Liverpool last year was my best so far. Until last season, my goals came in fits and starts, but I was consistent last term and that helped me to keep Ian Rush out of the team.

People always ask me the secret of scoring goals, but there isn't one. You can't learn it on the training pitch. I just have the instinct of being in the right place at the right time. It's the same with every goalscorer.

When you're a kid, you either want to be an attacker or a defender. I have always wanted to score goals and I love to see the net bulging after putting one past the 'keeper.

When I played as a young lad with my mates, I was always Graeme Sharp or Trevor Steven. They were my idols and even now I look up to them. I was an Everton fan as a kid and one of my favourite memories is of Sharpy scoring a great volley against Liverpool at Anfield.

I don't know why Sharpy was my favourite player. I don't play anything like him! He was more of a target man, but maybe I look up to him because he had qualities that I don't. I admire Mark Hughes as well because I rate him the best around at holding the ball up.

Hopefully, I can do as well for Liverpool as Graeme and Mark did for their clubs. When I came into the team, people said I wouldn't last and the goals would stop. I'm still scoring after three years, though, so I hope I have proved those people wrong. ●

gazza
king or clown?

YOU either love him or you loathe him. You either think he is hilarious or you think he needs locking up. There are no half-measures with Paul Gascoigne, who is without a doubt one of the most colourful characters the game has produced in recent decades. Here are some of the Jekyll & Hyde sides of Gazza . . .

GAME FOR A LAUGH

Gazza's sense of fun has become legendary. Some might find him tiresome but most of those who come into contact with him will tell you that he just likes to have a laugh. It is one of the most important things in life to him.

"I have always liked to have a joke ever since I was a kid," he says. "We are a fun family and, like all Geordies, we see the funny side of things. Whenever I play a joke on someone it is meant to be fun. I never set out to really upset

someone on purpose." What do you think? How would you react if you were on the receiving end of some of these famous Gazza gags? Like . . .

■ Pouring beer over team-mates — whether or not they are wearing an old tracksuit or a smart suit. Gazza will always pick up the cleaning bills after he's had the laugh.

■ Moving his team-mates' cars to make them think they have been stolen. Dangerous one this. "Theft" could could be reported to the police before the truth is realised. Still, Gazza would probably be able to talk his way out of trouble!

■ Cutting the toes out of team-mates' socks. This would really drive you crazy even though Gazza would replace the socks later. The warning sign for most of these gags would be to return to the dressing room and find that Gazza is there before you. If you check your socks you're sure to find something's afoot!

■ Filling the team bath with foam from bottles of shampoo which he then froths so that it is like a massive cloud coming out of the bath. Before you could punish him, you'd have to find him!

■ Changing the drawings on the tactics board — one of Gazza's favourite pranks. Sometimes he will just mess up the tactics plan but at other times all kinds of illustrations appear. If you were Walter Smith, how would you react?

■ Plastering his pals with cream cakes or anything else he can find. David Platt, and everyone else in the England squad with him has been on the receiving end of this one. He usually waits for them to nod off in a chair and then goes to work. Well, would you think it is great fun and try to dream up a trick of your own to play back on Gazza? Or would you take a dim view as did

referee Dougie Smith during Rangers' 7-0 hiding of Hibernian last Christmas. The referee dropped his yellow card without realising it. Gazza picked it up, and showed it to the ref, pretending to book him! Referee Smith did not think it was funny and promptly gave Gazza a REAL yellow-carding for disrespect.

Having a laugh is just one side of Gazza, there are other aspects of his character that are perhaps less well publicised.

GENEROSITY — Gazza has handed over thousands of pounds to people who need it. Very often he gives to people he has never met before in his life. He is a spontaneous giver. If he plays a joke on someone he will always pay for the damage several times over. He has bought houses, cars and even boats for his family and he saved the Spurs Hospital Radio from going out of business a few years ago by stumping up the cash that kept them on the air for the benefit of patients in local hospitals.

SENTIMENTALITY — Gazza is very affectionate, even a romantic at heart. He loves children and for years has made countless visits to hospitals to cheer up sick kids. He does this away from the press cameras and few people know just how much time he gives up for the good of others. As a boy

he used to show his love for his mum by taking her flowers. Admittedly he had picked them from other people's gardens but the thought was a good one!

DEDICATION — When he used to clean Kevin Keegan's boots at Newcastle, Keegan once asked him, "What will you do when the club don't offer you a contract?" Gazza had never even considered such a thing but it made him realise that he would have to work hard to make sure that he was worth a contract. One of his party tricks was juggling with an orange. He could flick it from toe to thigh to head to back of neck to shoulder to chest and back to foot up to 100 times. Now that takes dedication. Gascoigne's whole thesis is work hard — play hard.

Well, have you come to a decision? Could you put up with Gazza's antics?

"If I ever thought I really upset someone, it would upset me," says Paul. "I like to be around people who like to laugh. At Ibrox, they are a great bunch of lads. Ally McCoist had a reputation for jokes long before I signed. He is a great guy. It all helps you to enjoy your job. I don't ever see me being any different. I love football and I shall play for as long as I possibly can and I like to enjoy myself and I intend doing that for the rest of my life."

That's an awful lot of toe-less socks!!!! ●

sea-sig

Gary Stevens and Italy's
Olivero Garlini

Frank
Worthington

soccer

New Brighton beach, Merseyside, was the scene for the first of six European Pro-Beach soccer competitions. Brazil, Italy, England and the USA were the countries competing and with stars such as Junior and Jorginho playing for the Brazilians and an Italian side that contained World Cup winners Alessandro Altobelli, Claudio Gentile and Franco Causio the crowd was guaranteed a feast of football.

Still to lose a game since its inception three years ago, Brazil won the competition in style, trouncing Italy 12-3 in the final. The Americans took third place winning 6-2 against an England team containing Peter Shilton, Frank Worthington, Trevor Francis and Gary Stevens.

Throughout the summer, the event toured Europe culminating in the Tour Championships in Miami Beach.

Gentile, Worthington and Stevens

Peter Shilton and Phil Neal Keep out the Italians

THE LIGHTER SIDE!

A. "I've seen them do this at Twickenham!"

B. "... then you try to hit it past the keeper before he moves!"

C. "I keep on telling you, Faustino! I DON'T carry my wallet in my back pocket!"

D. "Take it easy, Teddy. We'll have that tooth out in no time!"

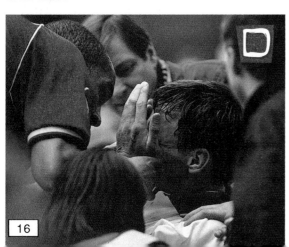

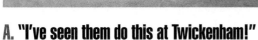

● DANNY WILLIAMSON   west ham united

STAN AND

● **THE STAN COLLYMORE GOAL MACHINE BECOMES GOAL PROVIDER**

YOU have to be a certain kind of person to deal with the hassles of being Britain's most expensive footballer.

The pressure of fans' expectations, the constant demands on your time, and the endless queue of autograph hunters would be enough to deflate the most resilient of people.

Fortunately, £8.5 million man Stan Collymore has the kind of personality that can deal with the baggage of such a fee. No autograph or picture request has been denied, all interviewers obliged with a smile.

The first couple of months of his time at Liverpool were not the most auspicious but he can look back on his first season at Anfield with some considerable pride.

Says Stan, "Life as an £8.5 million player is exactly the same as life as a £0.5 million man — as long as you are doing well. If you aren't, things are different.

"There are obvious benefits. I have a high profile and earn good money because of that, but there are down sides.

"If you struggle, as I did early on, the focus is on you and every little detail is brought up to explain why things have gone wrong.

"For example, when I first arrived from Nottingham Forest I stayed in a hotel in the city, only then to decide to move back to my Cannock home. Because I picked up an injury soon after and was only on the bench on my return to fitness because of the form of Ian Rush, that was interpreted as meaning that I was unhappy at Liverpool and wanted away.

"It was utter rubbish. I moved back to the Midlands because it is only an hour's drive away and there a lot of people there whom I'm close to and who have supported me from the start.

"At the end of the day, if I'm happy personally, I'm more likely to play well. That is what happened when I moved back

DELIVER!

home.

"My game began to improve, but it was never mentioned as a factor in my return to form — it was only mentioned to show why I hadn't settled.

"That is the down side of my fame. Fortunately, I'm a laid-back person by nature and that helped me to deal with the problems I had at the start."

As the British record signing, Collymore expected to be the main man at Liverpool. It was an impression that did not last long. Upstaged by forward partner Robbie Fowler in the goalscoring stakes, Stan had to be the apprentice to Fowler's sorcerer.

It was a role he was more than happy to undertake.

He goes on, " When I arrived, I thought that Liverpool would change their style to suit me. I thought 'why would they pay £8.5 million otherwise?'

"I believed that I would be given the same role as I had at Nottingham Forest. That turned out to be a very naive impression.

"I soon came to realise that Liverpool had played a patient

passing game for years and were not about to change just to accomodate me. I would have to change my game to suit them.

"I didn't understand that and, in my first few games, it led to quite a few problems. Robbie and I were making the same runs into the box and getting under each other's feet.

"It became clear that one of us had to switch and that it had to be me who dropped off.

"Robbie has been at Anfield since he was 14. He knows the system and the club inside out. More importantly, the players knew how he played.

"I was the newcomer and it was unrealistic for me to say that everyone should play around me.

"Robbie is the natural goalscorer and it seemed right that I should work around him.

"I knew that I had to do something other than score goals

" When I arrived, I thought that Liverpool would change their style to suit me."

to catch manager Roy Evans' eye. Then in a game against Arsenal, Robbie scored a hat-trick and I was involved in setting up every one. That set the tone for the season.

"Having to drop deep and not run at defenders was, at times, frustrating. It was something that I just had to get used to.

"My partnership with Bryan Roy at Forest was almost the exact opposite of what I have with Robbie. Bryan was the one who dropped deep and I was the furthest forward.

"However, it was nice to see more of the ball. I find that getting a good cross in for Robbie to score isn't quite as good as scoring myself, but it nearly is.

"Certainly my creative play came on tenfold because of it. I can honestly say that I learned more in my first year at Liverpool than in the rest of my career put together.

"I saw my first season at Liverpool as the apprenticeship I never had. I started out at Walsall, but didn't enjoy it and didn't finish my contract with them. Then I joined Wolves, only to be told that they could not afford to keep me on.

"I'm an individual kind of player because of that background. I had never been taught team skills.

"Liverpool is all about pass-and-move football. It is an evenly spread team effort.

"To fit into that, I had to learn new tricks. That was why I was happy to see Robbie out-score me last year.

"Although I knew that I could do better, I found a role which made the manager happy and, for the first time in my career, my own performance came second to that of the team.

"I carried all the things that I learned last year into this and I hope that I'm now establishing myself as the player Liverpool bought and the one the fans want to see."

The accepted wisdom is that a player who moves from a 'lesser' club to one of the biggest will have a greater chance of international recognition. Last season, Collymore proved the exception to the rule.

Indeed rather than enhance his claims, Stan believes that his move to Merseyside pushed him down the pecking order.

Explains Stan, "Playing in the Umbro Cup a couple of years ago was the highlight of my career — although I disappointed myself against Japan — and it was a source of great regret that I didn't become a fixture in the squads following the competition.

"In the end, my European Championship hopes were ended by a hernia problem, but I doubt I would have figured anyway.

"If I'd stayed at Forest, I believe that I would have been a strong candidate for Euro'96.

"The team pattern was settled there and, despite all the transfer speculation, I was also settled. There was no reason to suggest that I wouldn't have continued scoring goals for them.

"They would have continued to have played to my strengths, I would have scored goals, got the attention and I would have had a strong case for the European Championships.

"I took all that into account when I signed for Liverpool and decided to take a longer term view. I knew that I had to move for the good of my career.

"Playing for England is the icing on the cake but you play football for your club first and foremost. Joining Liverpool gave me a greater chance of winning trophies." ●

howey THE LAD!

NEWCASTLE **UNITED** can look back on a long list of glorious centre-forwards who have delighted the St James' Park crowd with their goalscoring prowess.

From Hughie Gallacher to Malcolm Macdonald, Jackie Milburn to Andy Cole, Newcastle have had many players worthy of a number nine shirt who are revered on Tyneside by the club's followers.

Whoever is lucky is enough to pull on the number nine for Newcastle becomes the focal point of all of the supporters' hopes and ambitions. Last season, Les Ferdinand became the latest player to acquire the famous shirt and he lived up to his predecessors by hitting 29 goals.

As a youngster, Steve Howey was a prolific scorer and was quite happy to occupy the glory role.

However, if it hadn't been for the intervention of former manager Ossie Ardiles — and later current manager Kevin Keegan — Steve might never have given up his striker's role for a spot in the mdidle of the defence.

It was the foresight of Ardiles that persuaded Howey to try his luck in the back four and Steve now admits that the move saved his Newcastle career and put him on the path to international honours.

Steve recalls, 'Moving from centre-forward to centre-half really shaped my career. Most people

think that Kevin Keegan was the man who saw it in me to play at the back, but it was Ossie who first realised I would be a good defender.

"He set the ball rolling but, unfortunately, wasn't here long enough to see the results.

"I have to thank him for making me try a new position because I don't think I would be playing at such a high standard now if I had remained as a striker. I certainly couldn't see myself challenging Les Ferdinand and Faustino Asprilla for a place in the Newcastle team.

"Initially, I wasn't too keen on the idea of playing at the back but I soon realised that it is just as satisfying to stop goals as it is to score them.

"Despite scoring regularly for the reserves, I found the step up into the first team difficult. Although I wasn't the greatest centre-forward in the world, the Newcastle team at that time wasn't the best either.

"I have no complaints about moving back into defence, but I didn't make the best start to my new role!

"Although Ossie didn't use me as a defender in the first team, he often experimented with me in training sessions and he would arrange five-a-side matches specifically for me to

see what I would be like as a defender'.

"I remember the first two challenges I went in for because I totally mis-timed them both and ended up going right through the two players I had tried to tackle! I learned the technique quite quickly, though, and I haven't looked back.

"Finding a settled position is vital if you want to succeed at the top level and I am glad I have found my own niche in the team. It can be useful to have another string to your bow, but it can turn out to be a false friend.

"My brother, Lee, plays for Sunderland and he has operated as a striker and a defender in his time at Roker Park. The problem is that he is often moved about to fill gaps. Steve Watson has found the same problem at Newcastle.

"My days of moving around are over. I don't even think about playing anywhere but centre-half these days. It would be silly to want to play up front again because since I have played in the back four, my career has had a 180 degree turnaround in fortune."

Apart from becoming a key figure

in Kevin Keegan's team, Howey has enjoyed personal success since he made the switch into defence over four years ago.

He has built a reputation as one of the most highly-rated defenders in the country and this was reflected when he was drafted into the England squad. Steve takes pride in the fact that he did it all his way.

He goes on, "I have been a defender for only four years. When you think about players who have spent all of their careers in my position but haven't earned international honours, it is quite an honour to be held in such high esteem.

"I am really pleased by the way things have turned out. I didn't use any role models when I switched positions and, even as a kid, I always went about things my way and played my own game. It's not in my nature to want to be like somebody else.

"I admire players like Colin Hendry because his career has followed a similar path to mine. He

STEVE THE STOPPER - v BULGARIA

started out as a striker, but made his name as a defender at club and international level.

"My time as a striker helped me settle down as a defender. From my own experience, I could read a striker's mind a little bit and anticipate what he was going to do. At times, you rely on experience to get you through.

"As I have grown into the role, I have realised that some strikers can make a fool out of you quite easily. Some of them have earned a living by purposely mis-controlling balls to confuse defenders! That's what you are up against sometimes, but I wouldn't want to swap places with them."

england

THAT agonising defeat in a penalty shoot-out in the semi-final of Euro '96 left Terry Venables' team and their supporters shattered.

But, ironically, that defeat could prove a blessing in disguise to Terry's successor, Glenn Hoddle, in his task of guiding England to the 1998 World Cup Finals in France.

Had England actually won the Championship, the expectation level would have been so high even the most brilliant coach would have found it difficult to live up to the achievement of his predecessor.

As it is, Venables has left Hoddle with a side which has now won global respect and enjoys the full backing of the country.

They are on the verge of greatness and Hoddle will feel that he is the man to take them over that threshold.

The new boss, of course, will make refinements as he goes along. For instance, he will have considered which players have come to the end of their international careers, which of them will carry the flag forward into the World Cup and who is ready to break into the squad.

Fortunately, the legacy bequeathed to him by Venables includes some of the finest young talent in Europe.

Instead of looking to experience, Venables decided to give youth a chance and his successor is set to reap the benefits.

GARY NEVILLE:

The Manchester United defender is already being touted as a future England captain. Still only 21, he has developed into one of the leading defenders in the Premiership and his versatility in being able to play anywhere in the back four will make him an invaluable member of Hoddle's England.

Venables surprised many people by handing Gary his debut against Japan in 1995. He had started just 17 League games for his club, but he immediately settled into international football and made the right-back berth his own.

Although he is among the youngest members of the squad, he is one of the most experienced and nothing seems to faze him. He is a certainty to be involved with England for years to come.

STEVE McMANAMAN:

The Liverpool winger displayed his dazzling club form in Euro'96 and emerged from the tournament as England's number one wide man.

Along with Paul Gascoigne, McManaman was the player who could lift the Wembley crowd with his mazy runs and endless reserves of energy. He noticeably grew in confidence as the tournament progressed and attracted the interest of top Italian and Spanish clubs.

As a player, Glenn Hoddle also had the ability to excite the crowd and he will know just how to get the best out of McManaman. Flair players have often been overlooked by England, but McManaman has proved his worth on the international stage.

JAMIE REDKNAPP:

Another member of the squad whose campaign was dogged by injury last term. But, though inexperienced at international level by comparison with Anderton, it was no surprise when he

GARETH SOUTHGATE:

There were many success stories at Euro'96, but Southgate was one of the most surprising. People will remember his penalty miss against Germany, but the Aston Villa man was an impressive performer on and off the pitch and was one of the finds of the tournament.

Before joining Villa last season from Crystal Palace, Southgate was regarded as a midfielder. However, Villa manager Brian Little converted him into a centre-half and England reaped the benefits last summer.

Late injuries to Mark Wright, Gary Pallister and Steve Howey paved the way for Southgate and he impressed with his clean tackling and reading of the game. He formed a formidable partnership with captain Tony Adams and laid down the foundations for a long international career.

expects...

DARREN ANDERTON:

Although Anderton had a largely disappointing Euro'96, he remains a key figure in England's future.

The Tottenham star made his international debut in Terry Venables' first game in charge — against Denmark — and his early performances encouraged Venables to blood more youngsters. Anderton set the standard for others to follow and he was soon joined by many of his former Under-21 team-mates.

Despite missing most of last season through injury, Anderton battled back in time to play in all of England's matches during Euro'96. Anonymous in the opening match against Switzerland, he gradually improved as the tournament progressed and played his best game against Germany.

Fresh after a summer break and with a full pre-season behind him, Hoddle will expect Anderton to be back at his best during the World Cup qualifying campaign.

forced his way into Venables' final squad of 22.

Having been groomed by his father, Harry, at Bournemouth before his £350,000 move to Liverpool in 1991, he has taken over the important mantle of playmaker at Anfield, further helped by the experienced John Barnes. His ability to drive forward and shoot from long range, allied to his consistently accurate passing have made him a dominant figure in the middle of the field. His half-time introduction in the match against Scotland during Euro'96 turned the match England's way and he will figure prominently in Glenn Hoddle's plans.

PHIL NEVILLE:

Considering the Neville brothers have emulated each other in virtually every field, it seemed only natural that 19-year-old Phil would follow Gary onto the England scene.

Just a year behind his older sibling in establishing himself as a regular Manchester United player, he even kept Gary out of the team which clinched last season's League and FA Cup Double.Comfortable in possession, his willingness to attack down the flank and intelligent use of the ball, together with an ability to play on either side of the field, helped him achieve his international call-up at such a young age.

Having won his first cap during the pre-Euro'96 tour of the Far East, Terry Venables may have felt he was still too inexperienced at this level to throw him into the Finals — particularly when brother Gary was suspended for the semi-final.

But with the retirement of Stuart Pearce from international football, Neville will fight a stern battle with Graeme Le Saux to become England's regular left-back.

ROBBIE FOWLER:

Another young star who had to bide his time before making his England debut. Terry Venables remained cautious while all around him the pundits were screaming for the 21-year-old to be included.

Fowler first came to national attention when he helped the England Under-18 team to win the 1993 European Championship.

Now regarded in many quarters as the most natural goalscorer in the country — even more so than Alan Shearer — Fowler has been Liverpool's most prolific striker since the age of 18.

That was the age at which he first lined up alongside Anfield's scoring legend, Ian Rush. In his first full season as a first-team player, Fowler equalled his idol in the scoring stakes, even though a broken leg forced him to miss part of the campaign.

In only his fourth first-team match, he struck five goals in a Coca-Cola Cup match against Fulham, the first Liverpool player to score so many in a cup match and only the fourth to do so in any competitive match.

After England played out a series of draws last term, Venables finally gave Fowler his first international start against Croatia.

With 36 goals for his club last season, Fowler is a proven goal-getter. Having gradually become acclimatised to international football — he came on twice as a substitute during Euro'96 — it is surely only a matter of time before he takes his scoring form on to the highest stage.

UGO EHIOGU:

A former captain of the England Under-21 side, Ehiogu has gradually flowered at the top level.

Schooled alongside the perfect tutor, Paul McGrath, at the heart of the Aston Villa defence, the 23-year-old is now rated as one of the best central defenders in England.

Commanding in the tackle and in aerial challenges, he uses the ball constructively and fulfils the modern ideal of a defender who can actually play football rather than simply pose a barrier to opponents.

Considered a natural candidate for inclusion in a three-man defensive system when Terry Venables was refining it last term, Ehiogu did not make the final 22 for Euro'96.

However, Glenn Hoddle will probably continue to search for a mobile back-line and Ehiogu should feature in his plans.

In addition to the legacy of youth left by Venables, another wave of young talent has already started to knock on the door. As Hoddle examines the prospects for future international places, watch out for starlets such as David Beckham, Nicky Butt, Garry Flitcroft, Michael Duberry, and Paul Scholes emerging. ●

ONE of the plusses resulting from England's disappointing end to Euro '96 was the return to goalscoring form of striker Alan Shearer. Shearer had gone a staggering 20 months without netting in an England shirt — he had last scored in a friendly against USA in September 1994.

But the critics were silenced with goals in all of England's Group matches in Euro '96 plus one v Germany in the semi-final. Shearer ended up as the tournament's top scorer with five goals, rewarding then coach Terry Venables' faith in the Geordie striker and his refusal to buckle under media pressure.

It is fair to say that, apart from David Seaman's penalty saves, it was Shearer who was most instrumental in England reaching the semi-final — and oh-so-nearly the Final itself.

All England fans will be hoping Alan can continue his scoring run throughout qualification for the World Cup in 1998. ●

On target at

. . . against Scotland . . .

. . . twice

ngic-AL

against Switzerland

SHERINGHAM 10

against Holland . . .

. . . and finally against Germany

25

edited highlights euro '96

Euro '96 — the greatest football spectacle in this country for thirty years. It was a tournament full of action, drama, controversy, agony and ecstasy. Here are a few of its best moments . . .

● A spectacular opening ceremony, showing the Euro '96 special crowd control!

● Goals that were . . . like Germany's Jurgen Klinsmann's against Russia and Karel Poborsky's (Czech Republic) against Portugal. Each had sufficient claim to be Goal of the Tournament . . .

. . . and one that wasn't! Romanian Munteanu's shot crosses the Bulgaria line but the goal isn't given.

● "There! It WAS over the line!"

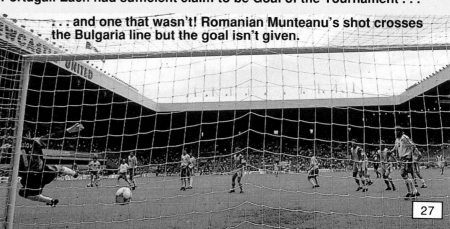

● Crucial penalty misses. . . Scotland's Gary McAllister against England — and Gareth Southgate in England's semi-final against Germany.

● And the Bulgarian Letchkov is looking for a plant into the top pocket!

● An early bath for Paul Gascoigne after his super goal against Scotland.

● Dejection for Italy's Casiraghi as the Italians crash out of the competition.

● We waited anxiously for the first Extra Time Golden Goal — and got one in the Final, courtesy of Germany's Oliver Bierhoff.

● Out of 31 games, only one goal was scored direct from a free kick. Bulgaria's Hristo Stoichkov does the business against France.

● Last but not least — the fans, acknowledged to be the real success of Euro '96. They came in all shapes and colours.

● German captain Jurgen Klinsmann with the European Championship trophy.

1. Back in his native Germany after a spell with Spurs.

2. This Italian is reckoned to be the best defender in the world.

3. Toupee or n̶o̶ from Reading!

whoam

9. Down — and out. Dejection for this goalie after his country's exit from Euro '96.

8. This gentleman has just put Juventus in the lead in last season's European Cup Final.

4. He keeps Croatia bobbin' along!

5. Fair today — dark tomorrow. Who knows with this Geordie midfield ace.

6. French midfielder. Goes to the same hairdresser as Ruud Gullit!

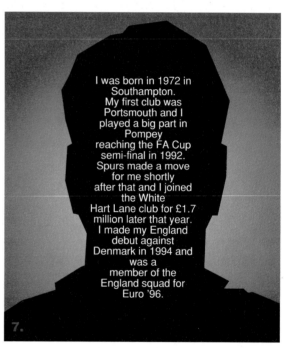

I was born in 1972 in Southampton. My first club was Portsmouth and I played a big part in Pompey reaching the FA Cup semi-final in 1992. Spurs made a move for me shortly after that and I joined the White Hart Lane club for £1.7 million later that year. I made my England debut against Denmark in 1994 and was a member of the England squad for Euro '96.

7.

Bulgar

10. The Man Utd. striker's name sounds like "goal"!

STUART PEARCE | nottingham forest

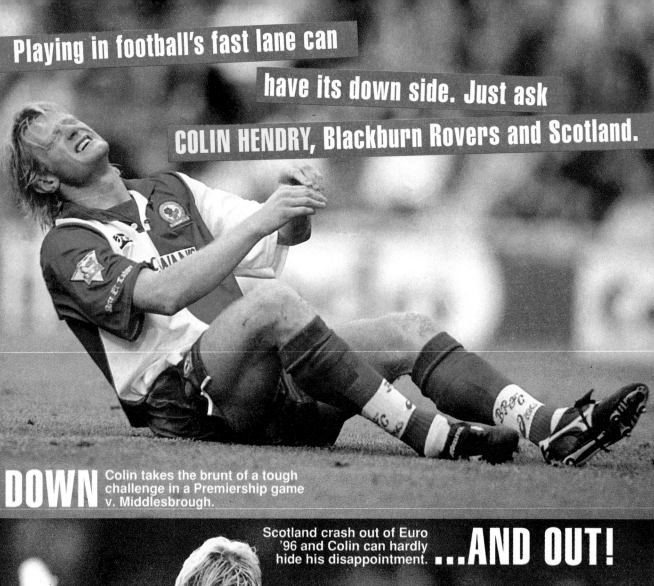

Playing in football's fast lane can have its down side. Just ask COLIN HENDRY, Blackburn Rovers and Scotland.

DOWN

Colin takes the brunt of a tough challenge in a Premiership game v. Middlesbrough.

Scotland crash out of Euro '96 and Colin can hardly hide his disappointment. **...AND OUT!**

"give it to G

34

GGSY!

, MIDFIELD MAESTRO

MANCHESTER **UNITED** midfield maestro Ryan Giggs shed his 'superkid' tag last season and developed a maturity to go alongside his rich abundance of natural talent.

Giggs' greater involvement in the heart of most of United's creative moves is a strong indicator that he is ready to accept more responsibility and reach a high level of performance on a more consistent basis.

Off the pitch, Ryan is also making the transition to becoming a senior professional. He is giving more media interviews and is the subject of various commercial activities, after having that side of his career restricted by his manager, Alex Ferguson, during his formative years.

"I'm enjoying the best form of my career," says Ryan. "Much of that is down to a greater involvement in the play. I have been operating in more central areas of the midfield, as well as down the wing.

"The more involved a player becomes, the better is his form. Sometimes when you are on the wing, you don't receive the ball for up to ten minutes. But that has not been the case recently. I have been getting into positions where I'm more likely to influence play.

"I feel my overall contribution to the team effort has increased. That boosts my confidence. If you are playing wide and lose the ball, then it may be a long time before you can make up for your mistake.

"I didn't become frustrated in the past when I wasn't getting as much of the ball as I would have liked. I have always accepted that being a winger can be a lonely role at times. I didn't ask the boss if I could be more central. It just happened.

"Roy Keane was sent off against Middlesbrough last season and it seemed only natural that I switched to a more central role in his absence. I played well in the next few games and things have progressed since then.

"When you play at United you are encouraged to adapt to various roles. That is the same for most of our players, not just myself.

"It wasn't a position that was new to me, either. I played in central midfield as a schoolboy before I joined United. Of course, the standard required is far higher, but I have been pleased with the way it has gone."

Giggs may still be in his early twenties, but having been a United regular for six seasons, he readily accepts the burden of more responsibility.

"I am still quite young, but I have to accept more responsibility now," he adds. "We have a number of the first-team squad who are younger than me. The onus is on the more senior players, like myself, to help them settle in.

"That doesn't mean that I am talking regularly to the younger players and offering advice. But they know I am available if they wish it."

Ryan has also returned to basics in a successful bid to improve his game. Despite possessing a magical array of skills, he puts the stress on doing the simple things correctly.

Ryan adds, "I have spent a lot of time working on the simple things. In particular, I have worked on my passing. I have also worked on my movement off the ball.

"Some people may have said that passing was a strong point of my game, but you have to work on the strong points as much as the weak ones.

"You cannot afford to neglect parts of your game. If your performance level drops, then you will be out of the team. There is nobody at the club who is guaranteed his place." ●

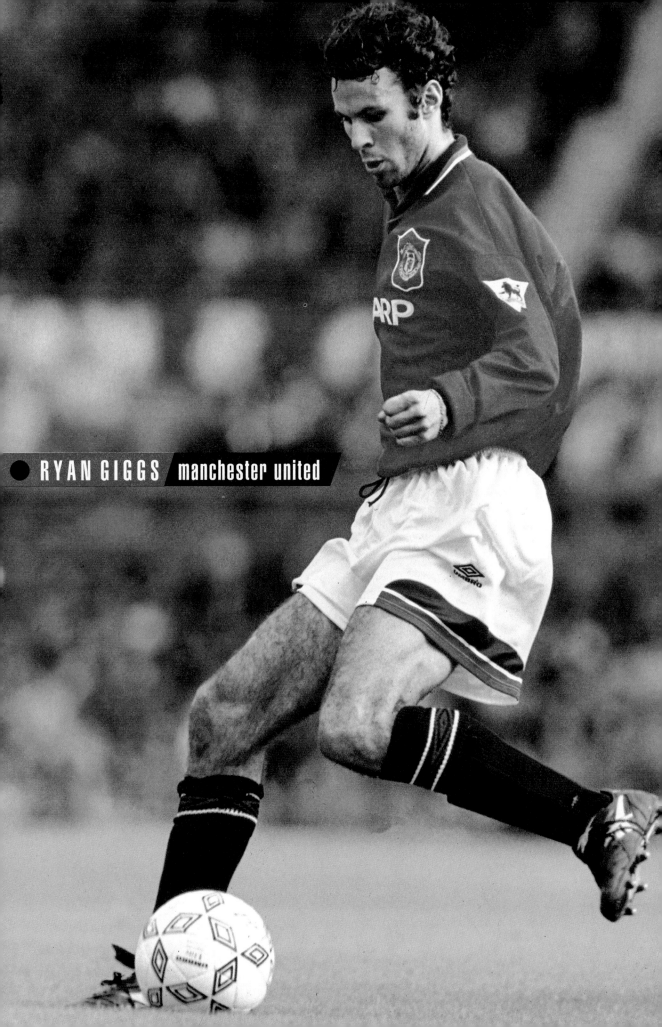

THE LIGHTER SIDE!

LEAPFROG!

A. Steve Bruce, ex-Manchester United, and Dean Holdsworth, Wimbledon.

B. Les Ferdinand, Newcastle United, and Colin Hendry, Blackburn.

C. "No it's not! It's YOUR turn to jump over ME!"

D. Stuart Pearce, Nottingham Forest, and Chris Armstrong, Spurs.

RUUD GULLIT is the most recognisable football star in the Premiership.

His wonderful skills, impressive physique and those trade-mark dreadlocks are a dead give-away.

Yet it wasn't always like that. The Chelsea player-coach must be the only world-class player who made his international debut without anyone in the crowd realising!

The Dutch star was introduced to international football at the age of 18, in a friendly match against Switzerland.

His childhood pal, Frank Rijkaard, was also in the Dutch squad. Rijkaard played the first half of the match as a sweeper.

Gullit took his place for the second period and nobody noticed!

"It was a terrible night, pouring with rain. Frank played the first half, I played the second," recalls Ruud.

"Nobody noticed the switch. Same black guy, same hairstyle ... We lost 1-0. It wasn't a great debut."

But Ruud Gullit has been unmissable almost ever since. Certainly he has been outstanding since joining Chelsea last season.

His role in the development of Chelsea almost earned him the Footballer of the Year award that went ultimately to Manchester United's Eric Cantona.

Gullit, however, is more

dutch ma

interested in team success, than individual prizes.

"The first thing you want is that the team plays well," declares Ruud.

"A football team is like a clock. If you take one part away, it doesn't work.

"It is important that everyone knows his position. Everybody in the team has his job, and knows the team has to keep its shape.

"The team is important to me. One player is not more valuable than another. We win together, and we lose together.

"People think that I have a free role in the side. That's not true. I have a job like everyone else."

Gullit came to Chelsea on a free transfer from Sampdoria, in Italy. He had enjoyed huge success in the past with AC Milan.

The Dutchman picked Chelsea because of his admiration for Glenn Hoddle. But basically he wanted to sample the whole English experience. Premiership football and London culture.

"Football is a game of 90 minutes. When it's over, you return

to real life," he says.

"There are many things in life outside football. I wanted to live in London to enjoy all the other aspects like the theatre, the museums and so on.

"I love the game of football, but only when it's played well. If it is not played well, I would rather do

"I love the game of football, but only when it's played well. If it is not played well, I would rather do something else."

something else.

"I have always thought highly of Glenn Hoddle. He wants football played the way it should be played.

"I love the game in England. It's far more open and exciting than on the continent. People all over the world love to watch it.

"But for a long time, you don't win anything. The records show it. I think the future depends on the coaches. They have to make a choice.

"Coaches and players here have to realise that keeping possession of the ball is important. If you have the ball, you have the power.

"You can make the game as fast or as slow as you like. You can control the game but only if you have possession.

"I think we learned a lot at Chelsea last season. And I think

the fans enjoyed watching us. That is good.

"I'm quite proud of what we achieved last season. But we still have a lot of work to do.

"We have to learn that you can't afford mistakes in the penalty areas, to miss our own goalscoring chances, or give away goals in defence.

"We have to be more cynical in those moments. At the highest level one mistake, one missed chance, can be vital."

34-year-old Gullit developed the class and composure of his own game during spells with Haarlem, Feyenoord and PSV Eindhoven in Holland.

He then moved on to Milan, later to be joined by Dutch colleagues Rijkaard and Marco Van Basten. The three players spearheaded Milan's dominance of European club football.

They also masterminded Holland's 1988 European Championship triumph, sealed with semi-final victory over West Germany and a Final defeat of the Soviet Union.

Gullit was constantly playing alongside outstanding individuals, both for the Dutch side and at Milan.

"I'm quite proud of what we achieved last season. But we still have a lot of work to do."

RUUD CELEBRATES HOLLAND'S EUROPEAN CHAMPIONSHIP IN 1988

"If you play at a high level, you are used to playing with top level players," he says.

"Each one has his own skills, but admires the others for theirs. It's part of the job, to play as a team.

"At Milan, we had a system drilled into us by the coach, Arrigo Sacchi. We worked at it very hard for a year until we could do things without thinking.

"That is the sort of understanding we have to try to achieve at Chelsea."

Ruud Gullit still loves playing football the right way. He will carry on playing while he still enjoys it.

"I'd like to do something with kids in future," he says. "But for the moment I will play on until the kid within me says 'that's enough'."

In May, Glenn Hoddle left Stamford Bridge to take over from Terry Venables as England supremo. Gullit's appointment as Chelsea player-coach was good news for Chelsea fans, who will hope that Ruud's influence, skill and enthusiasm will be a springboard to a serious challenge for the top honours over the next few seasons. ●

GARY McALLISTER leeds united

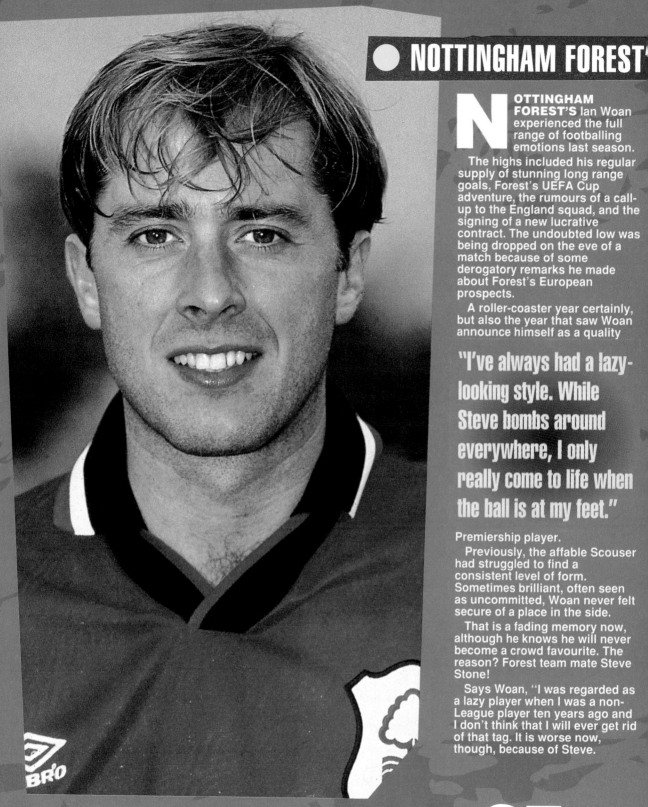

NOTTINGHAM **FOREST'S** Ian Woan experienced the full range of footballing emotions last season.

The highs included his regular supply of stunning long range goals, Forest's UEFA Cup adventure, the rumours of a call-up to the England squad, and the signing of a new lucrative contract. The undoubted low was being dropped on the eve of a match because of some derogatory remarks he made about Forest's European prospects.

A roller-coaster year certainly, but also the year that saw Woan announce himself as a quality

> "I've always had a lazy-looking style. While Steve bombs around everywhere, I only really come to life when the ball is at my feet."

Premiership player.

Previously, the affable Scouser had struggled to find a consistent level of form. Sometimes brilliant, often seen as uncommitted, Woan never felt secure of a place in the side.

That is a fading memory now, although he knows he will never become a crowd favourite. The reason? Forest team mate Steve Stone!

Says Woan, "I was regarded as a lazy player when I was a non-League player ten years ago and I don't think that I will ever get rid of that tag. It is worse now, though, because of Steve.

Woan go

IAN ON ... LAZINESS ... EUROPE ... AND SCORING!

"Goals get you noticed even more so spectacular ones, and I'd love to keep on grabbing the attention."

"Stonie plays wide on the right and I'm a wide left player. People compare the two of us and I come off worse. They see him chasing and harrying then look at me and think, 'Look at that lazy so-and-so.'

"There really isn't a worse player to be compared with effort-wise than Steve. He puts 99 per cent of players to shame.

"I've always had a lazy-looking style. While Steve bombs around everywhere, I only really come to life when the ball is at my feet.

"The problem is that the fans don't take our different styles of play into account. They want me to be like Steve but I can never be like him. I doubt that Frank Clark, Forest Manager, would want me to be either.

"You can't have 11 Steve Stones or 11 Ian Woans in the side. You need to find a happy medium and I think that the boss has done that.

"Despite what people think, I do a lot more running around and defending than I used to. Steve has embarrassed me into it! It has just gone unnoticed because of Steve's work.

"The crowd favourites are always the ones who look lively. The lazy-looking ones are the players the crowd get on to when things aren't going so well.

"At least I'm a lot fitter than I used to be, and the credit for that has to go to Forest's fitness coach Pete Edwards.

"When Pete arrived at the club a couple of years ago, he said that he had never seen such an

unfit bunch of athletes.

"We hardly did any training when Brian Clough was manager and I think that it showed when we were relegated from the top division in 1993."

Woan showed his best form during Forest's UEFA Cup run last season and he can't wait for another taste of European action.

He goes on, "I was an Everton fan as a kid, but I saw plenty of European games at Anfield and I will never forget the St Etienne game in 1977.

"It was the European Cup quarter-final when David Fairclough came off the bench to score the goal that put Liverpool through to the semis.

"European nights always throw up memories, and as it was the only thing that I hadn't experienced at club level, I couldn't wait. Forest missed out on several occasions because of the ban on English clubs in Europe.

"If you walk down a corridor at the City Ground, there are pictures everywhere of the European Cup triumphs of 1979 and 1980. Everyone talks about the good old days when we dominated Europe and it was great to give the fans some more recent memories.

"I found that Continental football suited my game more than the Premiership and I really looked forward to our trips.

"The Premiership can be a bit too hectic at times and ball players like myself don't get the time that they would like. I've adapted to the speed now, but there are still times when I wonder what is going on.

"In Europe, teams like to keep

"I found that Continental football suited my game more than the Premiership."

possession more and build slowly from the back. That is when I can get my foot on the ball and do something with it.

"Our aim has to be to get back into Europe as soon as possible."

Woan's long-range shooting ability has marked him out as a man to watch. Until last season, though, Woan's lack of confidence prevented him from being so adventurous.

Says the former Runcorn player, "When I first got into the Forest side, I looked around at the likes of Stuart Pearce, Des Walker and Nigel Clough and wondered what I was doing there.

"I'd always scored goals in my non-League days and in Forest's reserves, but wasn't quite so confident in the first team. Also, shooting from outside of the box was not encouraged.

"It was my dad, Alan, who suggested that I should be a little bit more selfish and have a few goal attempts myself. I took that advice, backed myself a bit more and got a few rewards.

"Goals get you noticed even more so spectacular ones, and I'd love to keep on grabbing the attention." ●

als!

KAREL POBORSKY *czech republic*

● MATTHIAS SAMMER | borussia dortmund

MIGHTY MOUSE

The story of KEVIN KEEGAN

Kevin Keegan, ex-England star and Liverpool legend, is one of the greatest players England has produced. This story charts his progress from Sunday league soccer to managing Newcastle United, one of the biggest clubs in the country . . .

Born in Armthorpe, near Doncaster, on 16th February 1951, Kevin's football career began at St Francis Xavier's Infants School in goal. Kevin was so small that he needed stilts to touch the crossbar! He became an outfield player at his next school, St Peter's.

Kevin was signed on schoolboy forms by Sheffield United then Coventry City, but nothing came of this. He was then spotted playing in the Doncaster Sunday League by a Scunthorpe United scout and duly signed for manager Ron Ashman as a £7.50-a-week apprentice.

THIS IS LIVERPOOL FOOTBALL CLUB ANFIELD

At the end of the season '70-71, Liverpool manager Bill Shankly paid United £33,000 for Keegan's services. Kevin recalls his arrival at Anfield, "sitting on a dust-bin feeling bemused! No-one would speak to me!"

This was the start of a long and happy association with the Anfield club, with Kevin forging an excellent strike partnership with John Toshack. Three League titles, 1 FA Cup and two UEFA Cups were won but Kevin's greatest triumph with 'Pool was a 3-1 European Cup win over Borussia Munchengladbach in May 1977.

In November 1972, Kevin made his debut for England in a one-nil win over Wales. The Welsh were a particularly lucky side for Kevin because he scored his first goal against them in May 1974 and captained his country for the first time in March 1976 — again against Wales!

Kevin became one of football's top money-earners when he joined S.V. Hamburg in June 1977 for £500,000. With Hamburg, he won the Bundesliga — the German Championship — and was twice voted European Footballer of the Year. His physique and all-action style earned him the nickname "Machtige Maus" — Mighty Mouse.

With a host of top European clubs clamouring for Keegan's signature, Lawrie McMenemy's Southampton achieved an astonishing coup by signing him in July 1980 for £420,000.

Kevin's last club in his illustrious playing career was Arthur Cox's Newcastle United, moving there from The Dell in August 1982 for £100,000. His aim — to help Newcastle out of the Second Division back among the big guns in Division One. That objective achieved, he retired from the game in May 1984.

Kevin spent the next few years on the Costa Del Sol, concentrating on business affairs and relaxing with his wife, Jean, and two daughters. His only contact with football was as an occasional TV pundit.

When Kevin quit, he vowed never to go into management. But that vow was broken in February 1992, when Newcastle Chairman Sir John Hall persuaded Kevin to take over the reins at St James' Park. United were second bottom of the Second Division, the lowest position in the club's history. Never afraid to accept a challenge, Kevin became the 15th manager at United since 1947. Kevin has revitalised United, bringing in a host of talent like David Ginola, Les Ferdinand and Faustino Asprilla.

Last season, Kevin's team were pipped for the Championship by Manchester United. The fanatical Newcastle "Toon Army" will be hoping Kevin can go one better this year and bring the Championship back to Tyneside for the first time since 1927.

Xword

ACROSS

6. Defender Gary of Everton, Rangers and Tranmere (7)
7. In short, a team which was relegated with 8 down (3, 4)
9. Once received for every international appearance (3)
10. Final scores (7)
11. "Double" manager Ferguson (4)
12. Type of foul (4)
15. Danish international John, once of Arsenal (6)

See 25 across

17. Euro '96 began in this city (6)
18. Glasgow-born Robert, twice a Canary (5)
20. You put the ball on this before a penalty (4)
23. English representatives in the Champions' League 1995-96 (9, 6)
25. Welshman Hughes, who moved from Man Utd to Chelsea in 1995 (4)
26. Gazza's club before he went to Rangers (5)
28. Opposite of defence (6)
30. Former Arsenal boss Mr Graham (6)
31. Do the Dutch use this to stem the flood of goals? (4)
33. Chelsea midfielder Dennis (4)
35. Defender Nigel who moved from Sheffield Wednesday to Middlesbrough (7)
36. Turkish internationals play in this colour of shirt (3)
38. Villa's Australian goalkeeper (7)
39. Forward who shoots at goal (7)

DOWN

1. Forward Ripley whose clubs include 23 across (6)
2. Italian side —— Milan (5)
3. A football league, but not a realistic one! (7)
4. Expert (3)
5. Oldham or Charlton (8)
8. Ray Wilkins' side last season (6, 4, 7)
11. Vulnerable joint between foot and leg (5)
13. Describes a resounding victory (7)
14. Annoy a player so that he retaliates (7)
16. Manager of 7 across during the '95-'96 season (4, 4)
19. London-born David who has played for Leeds and Spurs (8)
21. The ref did this to 20 across when he awarded a penalty (7)
22. Surprise champions of Europe in 1992 (7)
24. Standard side from Belgium (5)
27. Coventry manager Ron (8)
29. Romania's Gica who went to Barcelona from Spurs (7)
32. Number of players from one side on the pitch at the start of play (6)
34. German team coach Berti (5)
37. Number of goals England scored in their opening Euro '96 match (3)

IT'S A FUNNY OLD GAME

● **SOCCER is full of tales of the unexpected, yarns you can't believe** and silly stories that seem too crazy to be true. Here are a few that are all of those things but, more importantly, they ARE all true.

■ **NOTTINGHAM FOREST** are steeped in soccer history. First of all, the club was started by members of a hockey team and their first colours were a set of red caps. That wasn't all they wore of course! Later, when Arsenal were formed, it was Forest who gave them their first set of shirts, which is why Arsenal's main colour is red. But that's not all. It was at Nottingham Forest that shinguards were worn for the first time in 1874. Four years later, also at the City Ground, a referee used a whistle for the first time. Previously refs had waved a white handkerchief. Then in 1891 the crossbar and nets made their first appearance — also at Forest's ground.

■ **WHEN** Liverpool and England defender Neil Ruddock was a kid, he once banged his head and had to go to hospital to have stitches in the wound. Then when he was going back to the hospital to have them removed he banged the back of his head and had to have stitches there as well. With so many cuts, it's not wonder they call him Razor!

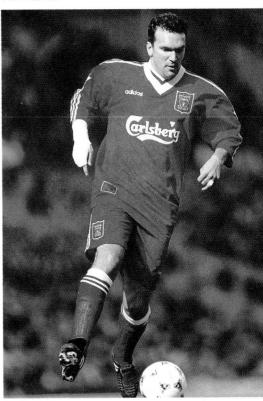

■ **A HULL CITY** goalkeeper once proudly received a magnificent crystal glass trophy as an award for his great performances — and dropped it! And there's more . . . an Irish goalie playing this season caught the ball perfectly, but his hat flew off into the goal. He went back to pick it up — still carrying the ball — crossed the goal-line and the referee awarded the goal!

■ **IN** April 1936, Luton Town had a problem. They were short of a centre-forward and had no alternative but to move Joe Payne, a defender, to the No. 9 shirt. He made his debut in that position on April 13th, 1936, in a Third Division match against Bristol Rovers. When the ref blew his whistle to end the game 90 minutes later, Joe had scored TEN record-breaking goals!

Continued overleaf

Continued from previous page.

IT'S A FUNNY OLD GAME

■ **NEWCASTLE** were playing at home to Swansea in an F.A. Cup-tie everyone had been waiting to see. There were 63,480 fans packed into St. James' Park on January 10th, 1953, for the Third Round tie. The referee blew his whistle and the game got under way. What happened next? A thick fog suddenly enveloped the ground and the match had to be abandoned after just eight minutes! It had been totally clear when the game started. The game was replayed four days later and Newcastle won 3-0.

■ **GORDON STRACHAN** never seems to get tired no matter how hard he works on the pitch. But the Scotland star was totally shattered after one session a couple of years ago. He had not kicked a ball and had not even broken into a trot yet he was completely exhausted. The reason was that he had attended a signing session for his book at a large bookstore and had to autograph 3,000 copies! He got writer's cramp!!

■ **EVERTON** boss Joe Royle will never forget his first day as manager of Oldham. He turned up for work on the back of a coal lorry. His car had broken down on the way to the ground and he didn't want to be late so he accepted the offer of a lift on the back of the truck. It's the first time a manager ever got the sack on the way to his new job!

■ **GRIMSBY** used to be the capital of the fishing world and Grimsby Town until quite recently always gave visiting clubs a gift of a huge box of fish to take home after the match. Imagine the return coach journey if the visiting team was Plymouth or Torquay!

■ **A REFEREE** in charge of the Colombian League match between top clubs Millionarios and Santa Fe had to borrow a notebook from one of his linesman. It wasn't that he had lost his own. It was simply that he ran out of space after booking 12 players and sending one off — all in the first half!

■ **LIAM BRADY** was expelled from school when he was a lad. His crime? He chose to play for the Irish schoolboys in a soccer match against Wales rather than play for his school in a Gaelic football match. It didn't do him any harm, though. Liam went on to become one of the biggest names in soccer.

■ **IF** you think the transfer market has gone crazy how about this? Hutnik Warsaw once signed a player in exchange for a TV set and video recorder. Not long before that, another Polish club had signed two players in exchange for a lorry load of potatoes. Oh well, when the chips are down . . .

■ **HERE'S** another wacky goalie story. In the early days of the Football League, a goalkeeper was threatened with dismissal for pulling faces at opponents. What actually happened was that his dentures had flown out when he dived at an opponent's feet. He picked them up, put them in a bag and then went in for a spot of grotesque grimacing whenever an opponent was trying to shoot.

■ **ONLY 22** fans paid to watch Brazilian side Fluminense beat Volta Redonda 1-0 in a Rio de Janeiro match after the team had conceded eight goals in their two previous matches. Total gate receipts for the game were around £150.

■ **WHETHER** or not pigs may fly, they can certainly play football. York City vice-chairman Bernard Hoggarth introduced pig football to Britain after seeing pigs playing in Denmark. The Danes put a specially made football into the sty to give the pigs something to do. Perhaps a match could be organised against Bolton — the other "Trotters"!

● JURGEN KLINSMANN | bayern munich

● WHY LEEDS UNITED'S RICHARD JOBSON LIKES BEING ON CENTRE STAGE

RICHARD JOBSON wasted little time in establishing himself in the Leeds United team last season following his £800,000 move from First Division Oldham Athletic.

The 33-year-old defender had spent the previous 18 months waiting for his move to Elland Road, but a series of misfortunes delayed Jobson's move across the Pennines to the point where he felt it had passed him by.

During his time at Oldham, Jobson had earned a reputation as one of the leading defenders in the country. However, a last-minute equaliser by Manchester United's Mark Hughes in an FA Cup semi-final at Wembley set

Okay! Where's that Jobson chap?

in motion a nightmare 12 months for Jobson.

Before Hughes broke Oldham's hearts with his vital strike, Jobson was on his way to an FA Cup Final and hopeful of earning a full England cap. However, the Welsh striker ended those hopes and Jobson's career was about to take a nosedive which would last a whole season.

Richard recalls, "Mark Hughes's goal in that semi-final probably killed our season and it was very difficult to get going again afterwards. We lost the replay, had a desperate end to the season and were relegated. It took a lot of getting over.

"The hangover went on into the following season. If we had stayed up I

would have been happy to stay at Oldham, but I was in my thirties and I felt I had to look to the future.

"I thought I would be on my way during that summer because Leeds had made an offer for me and I was very interested in going to Elland Road. I was very disappointed when the manager at the time, Joe Royle, turned down the Leeds bid. That signalled an end to my international ambitions.

"I had been in and around the squads for over two seasons, but once Oldham were relegated I was forgotten about. I felt I was too old to earn my first cap while playing in the Endsleigh League, so I just decided to channel my efforts into returning to the Premiership."

Richard's hopes of a swift return to the top flight were soon dented when he realised the difference between the Premiership and the First Division. He could no longer rely on seeing his name in the newspapers on a Sunday morning.

He goes on, "There is so much publicity surrounding the Premier League that the Endsleigh League hardly merits a mention. Media interest was very small and our games were lucky to get a couple of paragraphs. We always had a good write-up in the Premiership.

"Even television ignored us. The Premiership is on virtually every day, but any action from the Endsleigh League was shown in the early hours of the morning.

"That's why I was so desperate to get back into the Premiership and I would have gladly swapped a successful campaign in the First Division for a struggle in the top flight. It is the only place to be but, unfortunately, I sustained the worst injury of my

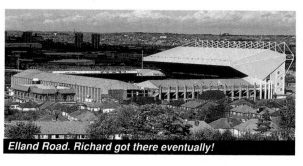
Elland Road. Richard got there eventually!

career halfway through the season and I thought my chance had gone.

"I had dropped quite a few rungs down the ladder already and the ankle injury I had made things worse. It was a novelty for me because it was the first time in my whole career that I had been in plaster.

"I didn't play again all season, but I worked throughout the summer in a bid to get fit. I was

progressing well when Leeds returned with another bid for me. I was shocked because I hadn't played for seven months, but I was willing to make the move.

"I was put through a rigorous medical, but Leeds were not happy with my ankle and they pulled out of the deal. I thought the deal was dead because soon after I failed my medical, Leeds bought another defender, Paul Beesley. I saw no reason for them to come back for me.

"The collapse of the transfer was probably a blessing in disguise. I was disappointed to miss out

again, but after so long out of the game I was just happy to be playing again.

"I was still on the transfer list at Boundary Park, but I put leaving to the back of my mind because I was content to be playing football again. I expected to finish my career with Oldham and was playing with no pressures because I didn't feel as though I was playing to attract

Richard in his Oldham days

somebody's attention.

"It turned out that Leeds had been monitoring me all the time, however, and once I had proved my fitness I was a wanted man again. Several clubs bid for me and I would have joined Coventry City if they had matched Oldham's valuation of me.

"Coventry pulled out, but Leeds came back. It was totally out of the blue to be linked with Leeds yet again, but thankfully the deal went through and I was absolutely delighted to finally make the transfer. It had taken a long time, but it was well worth the wait.

"Once I had made the move I was determined to make the most of it because I was 32 when I signed and that isn't young for a footballer. Manager Howard Wilkinson spent just short of a million pounds to buy me, but I wasn't worried about it being a lot of money for a 32-year-old. I have progressed as I have got older.

"Most players arrive in a blaze of glory in their early twenties and see their career peter out by the time they are 30. However, I was 27 when I left Hull City to join Oldham and didn't win my first England call-up until I was 29.

"It took me 13 years to sign for a big club and I thought the chances of that had passed me by on more than one occasion. I now have what I have always wanted.

"After five years at Oldham you can stagnate. I was becoming part of the furniture there, but I have a new challenge at Leeds and I can now remind people about Richard Jobson.

"You soon become a forgotten man when you drop out of the Premier League and when you are injured as well you become completely anonymous. I'm thankful to have been given the opportunity to play out my career in the spotlight." ●

the**W**

ALAN WRIGHT was ready to shed his inhibitions and confront Aston Villa boss Brian Little if he had been left out of the team during an impressive run of form last season.

You would have to look long and hard to find a player less likely to cause a stir if he was dropped. But the 25-year-old believes that would have been his only option after playing the best football of his career.

Wright joined Villa from Blackburn in January 1995 and replaced Steve Staunton at left-back, freeing the Republic of Ireland player to play in midfield. But the signing of midfielder Mark Draper meant Staunton seemed likely to revert back to left-back.

But Staunton picked up a hamstring injury which sidelined him for several months and Wright took his chance to impress in Staunton's absence. Little had no option but to keep faith with the diminutive defender even when Staunton was fit.

"I am a very quiet lad. Everyone knows I will not shout and bawl and demand a transfer if I am dropped," says Alan. "But I would have asked the boss to explain his reasons for dropping me.

"If I was not playing well and I was dropped, I'd be the first person to hold my hands up and accept the decision. The only confrontations I want are

ight decision

on the pitch!"

Wright's assertive tone has much to do with a new-found confidence in his own ability after a spell on the sidelines at previous club Blackburn Rovers.

Wright struggled to hold down a place at Ewood Park after Rovers signed Graeme Le Saux. He had a spell on the left side of midfield, but joined Villa because he wanted to return to his familiar left-back berth.

"The move to Villa has been a blessing," he goes on. "My form is as consistent as at any time during my career. I've had a new lease of life.

"I played well for Rovers in the club's first season back in the top flight. But Villa are a higher profile club than Blackburn were in those days and that may be a factor in my gaining England recognition when coach Terry Venables picked me for squad

ALAN ON ENGLAND DUTY

"To be honest, if I had stayed and won a Championship medal by playing a few more games, I would not think it really belonged to me."

ALAN JOINS IN THE CELEBRATIONS AS VILLA WIN THE COCA-COLA CUP AT WEMBLEY LAST MARCH.

training last season.

"It was a very tough decision to leave Blackburn, especially with the level of success they were enjoying at the time. But I had to think to the future and reserve-team football was no good to me.

"To be honest, if I had stayed and won a Championship medal by playing a few more games, I would not think it really belonged to me. In my own mind, I didn't play enough matches.

"I've shown that I can hold my own at this level if I get a decent run in the side."

Wright's elevation to receiving a call-up for an England get-together last season was a natural progression for a player capped by his country at schoolboy, Under-17,

Under-18, Under-19 and Under-21 levels.

But despite a welter of good publicity, Wright keeps his feet firmly on the ground.

"I don't spend much time scanning the papers looking for my name. It is my mum who keeps me in touch with all the stories," he says.

"There are too many critics around, but I must admit I have been getting some good press recently.

"I don't grab many headlines at Villa, and that is the way I prefer it. I live near Manchester, quite a distance from Birmingham. Some people know I am a footballer, but I'm never pestered.

"I like the fact that I can go out shopping and not be recognised. Some well-known players admit they can't even go shopping!" ●

THE MYSTERY MILLIONS

Once Bounton Villa had topped the Premiership, now, four years later, they were struggling to avoid the indignity of relegation. Villa's manager, Garry Bannerman, was desperately hoping for three points when Villa played Oldcastle City . . .

IT'S THERE! OLDCASTLE GO ONE UP!

AAAGH!

BERT REYNOLDS IS IN TROUBLE! HE DIDN'T HALF WHACK HIS HEAD AGAINST THE POST!

Villa lost a goal . . . and their keeper!

BERT WON'T BE BACK. HE NEEDS STITCHES! JUST AS WELL JOHNNY RAMSDEN'S ON THE BENCH . . .

RAMSDEN'S NOT IN BERT'S CLASS. WE'VE HAD IT!

Final score, two-nil to Oldcastle —

ALL WE EVER GET IS BAD LUCK. WE HAVEN'T HAD A FULL FIRST ELEVEN OUT FOR MONTHS. INJURIES, SUSPENSIONS . . .

WE'LL GET RELEGATED! WE'RE SECOND FROM BOTTOM NOW . . .

Garry Bannerman had a chat with Villa's Chairman, Ron Daly . . .

VILLA SHOULD BE IN EUROPE WITH A STADIUM LIKE THIS, MR DALY. IT'S ONE OF THE BEST IN THE COUNTRY . . .

WE'LL BE LUCKY IF WE'RE IN THE PREMIERSHIP NEXT SEASON! YOU'VE GOT TO HALT THE SLIDE, GARRY . . . AND SOON!

OUR BIGGEST PROBLEM IS MONEY. WE NEED TO BUY PLAYERS . . .

DON'T TALK ABOUT MONEY, GARRY . . . THERE ISN'T ANY! IF THE LADS WE'VE GOT CAN'T SAVE US . . . THEN WE'VE HAD IT!

Nothing much escaped the ears and eyes of groundsman Phil Stevens —

I HEARD YOU AND MR DALY DISCUSSING MONEY. I DON'T LIKE SEEING THIS CLUB IN TROUBLE. IF I HAD ANY CASH I'D GIVE YOU THE LOT. ANYTHING TO HELP VILLA.

YEAH, I KNOW YOU WOULD, PHIL. IT'S A NICE THOUGHT . . .

WHAT WE NEED IS A BIT OUT OF YOUR LEAGUE, PHIL! WE NEED REALLY *BIG* MONEY . . . *MILLIONS!*

The following Saturday, Villa were away to Lester Town. They started well —

YESSSSS! VILLA HAVE SCORED! CRACKING GOAL!

MAYBE WE'RE GOING TO GET THREE POINTS! IT'S ABOUT TIME . . .

Villa held their lead until three minutes from the end —

THAT'S A GREAT SAVE FROM RAMSDEN!

THE BALL IS STILL LOOSE, THOUGH!

IT'S THERE! OWN-GOAL! LESTER HAVE EQUALISED!

OH . . . NO! I DON'T BELIEVE IT . . .

A few days later, Ron Daly visited Garry Bannerman's office —

WHAT'VE YOU GOT THERE?

THIS ARRIVED ON MY DESK THIS MORNING. NO ONE SEEMS TO KNOW HOW IT GOT HERE . . .

I DON'T BELIEVE THIS! IT SAYS . . . I WON THE LOTTERY LAST WEEK. VILLA NEED THE MONEY MORE THAN ME. £10 MILLION!

ONE OF THOSE CRANK LETTERS! SOMEONE'S ALWAYS MESSING ABOUT. HAVING THEIR LITTLE JOKE!

IT'S REAL! WHO'D DO A THING LIKE THIS?

TEN MILLION QUID! DON'T ASK ME WHO'S RESPONSIBLE . . . BUT VILLA CAN MAKE GOOD USE OF IT. IT COULD SAVE US!

The money was checked out. It was genuine! A board meeting was called!

BUY FAUSTO ADONTINO . . . THE ITALIAN. UNITED ARE AFTER HIM . . . AND THEY'RE OFFERING EIGHT MILLION! WE CAN TOP THAT!

ADONTINO IS REPUTED TO BE THE BEST PLAYER IN THE WORLD!

I SUGGEST WE PLAN FOR THE FUTURE. BUY THREE OR FOUR PLAYERS . . . A BLEND OF YOUTH AND EXPERIENCE!

LEAVE IT TO THE MANAGER, GENTLEMEN. LET HIM DO WHAT HE THINKS BEST.

Garry moved fast. He paid £2.3 million for Under-21 Cap Craig Masters . . .

. . . and played him against Boldingham City.

WHAT A GOAL! THAT WAS MAGIC! CRAIG MASTERS!

Garry made three more buys in the next two weeks —

GORDON FOSTER. 28. TOP GOAL-SCORER IN ENDSLEIGH LEAGUES.

MALKY WILSON. CENTRE-BACK . . . SOLID & TOUGH!

PAUL DRAKE. GOALIE . . . MR DEPENDABLE!

GOT ANYTHING LEFT OF THAT TEN MILLION?

YES! BEST PART OF A MILLION IN RESERVE. IF YOU WANT TO SEE OUR MONEY AT WORK . . . WATCH WEDNESDAY EVENING'S GAME AGAINST SHEFFORD. ALL THE NEW LADS WILL PLAY.

Wednesday evening —

VILLA! VILLA! VILLA!

IF YOU'VE DONE NOTHING ELSE, GARRY, YOU'VE BROUGHT THE CROWDS BACK! WILL WE WIN TONIGHT?

WE'LL WIN! AND THIS TEAM WE'VE GOT NOW . . . WHEN IT SETTLES . . . WILL WIN US THE PREMIERSHIP NEXT SEASON!

Big Malky Wilson soon showed his ability —

MALKY WILSON! THEY'RE BOUNCING OFF HIM!

HE'S A ROCK! HE'S IMPROVING VILLA'S DEFENCE!

Craig Masters was already a favourite!

ONE CRAIG MASTERS . . . THERE'S ONLY ONE CRAIG MASTERS . . .

Masters to Gordon Foster . . .

IT'S THERE! WHAT A GOAL! MADE IT LOOK SIMPLE!

And when Paul Drake was tested —

HE MAKES IT LOOK SO EASY! AS IF HE KNEW WHERE THE BALL WAS GOING!

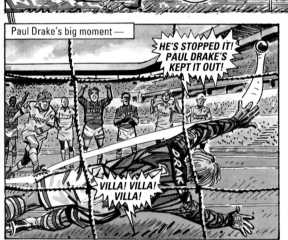

PAUL GASCOIGNE | rangers

EFAN EKOKU wimbledon

LEADER OF TH

IN a game which is increasingly dominated by the cold heart of business and naked ambition, Wolves' prolific striker Steve Bull is a rare breed.

Bull has been a goalscorer very much in demand during most of his career. But, mainly through choice, he has stayed at Wolves in a bid to help the Molineux club regain their status among the Premier elite.

He has scored well over 200 League goals for Wolves in ten years, a remarkable statistic for a player who has played for a club which has struggled for much of that time.

Sadly, almost all of his career has been played in the lower leagues. He played just four times for West Brom in the old First Division before joining a Wolves side that failed to match Bull's own standards.

But Bull's scoring exploits did not go unnoticed at international level. Despite playing in the THIRD Division, he made his international debut for England against Scotland at Hampden Park in 1989 and scored. He went on to play for his country 13 times at senior level.

He would certainly have accumulated more caps if he had been playing in a higher league. But do not rule out Bull adding to his caps total. Bull believes that boss Mark McGhee is just the man to restore the glory days to the famous Black Country club.

The 31-year-old seems to have struck up an instant respect and liking for McGhee, which is obviously reciprocated. He is revelling in working under a fellow-striker, who appreciates what is required to make a player of Bull's calibre click.

Steve says, "You are never too old to learn and whatever advice the gaffer gives me, whether it is in front of goal or defending, I'll take it.

PACK!

"He knows what I have to go through. I am a different type of striker to what he was, but he has an insight into the problems I have to face, which perhaps the previous boss, Graham Taylor, did not have.

"He occasionally pulls me aside in training and asks me 'How about doing it this way or that?' He has made no huge changes to my game, just little things which help.

"Since he arrived, I have contributed a lot more to games. Instead of scoring goals, but playing rubbish, I am getting more involved in games, even when I am not scoring goals.

"We have introduced a passing game which suits everyone, including me. I spent the best part of nine years bustling for the ball. It was very difficult. It is easier to have the ball played to feet.

"People say that Wolves played to my strengths, but I don't necessarily think so. There is more to my game than a physical presence and getting on the end of crosses.

"I have heard that I don't possess a good first touch. That is nonsense. When the ball comes to a striker, instinct takes over. You have to either set up a shooting chance with your first touch or hit the target with the first touch. My record is comparable with anyone's."

There is not a trace of smug satisfaction in Bull's reaction to comments that Wolves were a 'one man band' during most of his career at Molineux. Now that he is surrounded by better quality team-mates, he is relieved that the pressure has been taken off him to provide ALL the fireworks for the long-suffering Wolves support.

He was the club's top scorer for SEVEN consecutive seasons, until he was knocked off the top of the scoring charts by David Kelly a couple of seasons ago. Last term he lagged behind fellow-striker Don Goodman.

"It is about time we had goals coming from other departments," he adds. "I know that it might take the limelight off me, but I'll get the odd goal to keep my name in the papers.

"I was saying for seven years that we need goals coming from other areas, so I am not going to complain."

Bull came very close to leaving

Scotland 0 Bull 1-Hampden, May 1989.

Mark McGhee

his beloved Molineux last season after comments made by previous boss Graham Taylor.

He doubted whether he was wanted at Wolves. At one stage it looked as if he would be on his way to Coventry City, but he did not want to leave. Meanwhile, his confidence dropped and the goals dried up. Bull admits that it was a distressing time.

Confides Steve, "If someone had said to me at the time that I was wanted at Wolves and would be staying here, that would have been a big boost to my confidence.

"Graham Taylor told me that he wanted me to stay a Wolves player. But during that summer he apparently said something else. I didn't know if I was coming or going.

"That is not the case with Mark McGhee. I am sure that he wants me to stay. I know where my future lies and I don't want to leave this club."

That news will come as a relief to those fans who have flocked in their thousands to pay tribute to their local hero in various fund-raising ventures to mark his testimonial year.

"I am proud to have played for Wolves for ten years," he goes on. "Even though there have been some barren spells along the way.

"I could have left this club for money years ago, but money is not everything. If you are happy at a club and the people love you, you stick with them.

"I had opportunities to go to Italy and a host of clubs in the old First Division. I know I could have won more England caps if I had moved on. For instance, I had talks with Aston Villa and Newcastle.

"Of course, there have been times when it has crossed my mind that I may have made the wrong decision, but I have no regrets." ●

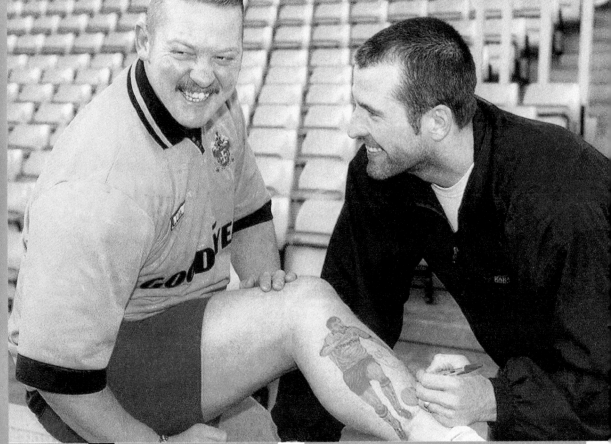

signhere!

● STEVE BULL HAS HAD TO SIGN MANY AUTOGRAPHS IN HIS CAREER, BUT THIS ONE WAS SOMETHING SPECIAL!

A football fanatic now has the present he always wanted — a tattoo of his favourite soccer star drawn on to his right leg.

Keith Nicholls had a 13 inch picture of Wolves ace Steve Bull tattooed on his calf. His wife, Karen, paid £150 to have the player drawn.

Now Keith, of Wombridge near Telford, is considering which other part of his body to dedicate to the striker. But with the club emblem and an English bulldog tattooed on his chest, space is running out for more pictures of his favourite player!

The tattoo took nearly three months to complete, with Keith going to a tattooist once a week to have the picture drawn of Steve Bull with a ball at his feet.

Keith said. "I've wanted this tattoo for years.

"It has only taken this long to have done because I wanted to find the right tattooist to do it.

"After supporting Wolves all my life, it's the best present I could have had."

Anyone thinking of copying the tattoo will need Keith's permission.

He said: "I own the copyright of this tattoo so it cannot be copied by anyone."

Steve Bull signed the tattoo when he met Mr Nicholls at the Wolves ground. He also signed Keith's shirt and photographs he had of the star.

Keith continues, "Steve said he'd never seen anything like this before in his life.

"He said it was a great compliment, but that maybe I was a bit of a nut!"

Karen, who is also a Wolves fan, was quite happy for Keith to have the tattoo.

She said: "I like Steve Bull as well. I paid for the tattoo and wanted Keith to have it done. Our house is covered with Wolves memorabilia. We're both big fans.

"The front room is covered with photographs of different Wolves players. And our loft is packed with stuff to do with Wolves that Keith has picked up over the years."

The couple are both season ticket holders at Wolves, and sit in the Jack Harris stand for all home games. ●

dellboy!

RUUD GULLIT and Dennis Bergkamp brought a touch of Dutch class to Premiership proceedings during their first season in English football.

Gullit delighted Chelsea fans with his silky skills that helped 'The Blues' reach the FA Cup semi-final. He was a universally popular choice to take over as manager when Glenn Hoddle left to become England coach.

Across London at Arsenal, Bergkamp made a slower start in English football. He took a while to find his goal touch but, once he did, he soon got the Highbury faithful on his side.

Gullit and Bergkamp joined many of their fellow countrymen playing in England last season. One of the most experienced is Southampton's popular centre-back Ken Monkou.

Born, like Gullit, in the small South American country of Surinam, Monkou started his career in Holland with Feyenoord. That's where Gullit first came to prominence himself in the early 1980's.

Monkou was a trail-blazer for Gullit because in 1989 he came to England to join Chelsea. He spent three years at Stamford Bridge before moving to Southampton.

When Gullit and Bergkamp arrived in England, nobody was more interested in their progress than Ken Monkou. He was delighted to see his fellow Dutchmen on the Premiership stage.

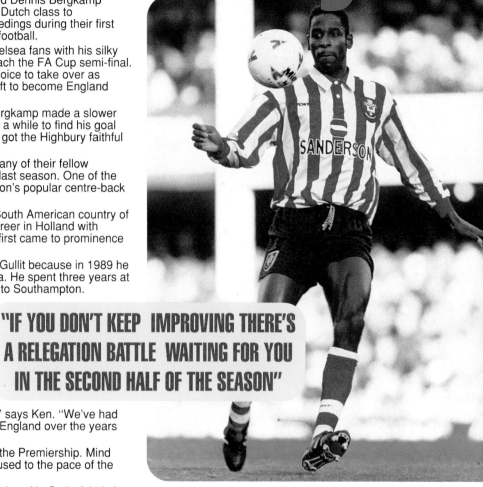

"IF YOU DON'T KEEP IMPROVING THERE'S A RELEGATION BATTLE WAITING FOR YOU IN THE SECOND HALF OF THE SEASON"

"It was great to see Ruud and Dennis playing in England," says Ken. "We've had plenty of good Dutch players in England over the years but those two are the cream.

"I knew they would do well in the Premiership. Mind you, it took them a while to get used to the pace of the English game.

"Dennis and Ruud have both played in Serie A in Italy, which is a high quality league. The Premiership is something else again and I'm sure they found it very different.

"I was very interested to see how they could cope with that change. It does take time for even the greatest players.

"I went to see Dennis playing in one of his first games for Arsenal. He had quite a quiet time but I knew there was still more to come from a great striker.

"Ruud is still a wonderful player, even though he's now become a manager. He's a great passer and an inspiration to everybody around him when he comes forward with the ball."

Ken was quite an inspiration himself last season, a real giant in the Saints defence. Over the last few years, Matthew Le Tissier's goals have got the team out of trouble. Last season it was down to Ken.

Apart from some sterling defensive displays he also scored a vital goal in Southampton's famous 3-1 victory over champions-to-be Manchester United. That was the result which helped keep the South Coast club in the Premiership, although safety was eventually guaranteed by a gruelling nil-nil draw on the last day of the season against Wimbledon.

"It was all too close for comfort," Ken admits. "We don't want to be hanging on like that on the last day again.

"Clubs like Southampton just can't afford to be relegated. We've been in the top flight since 1978 and nobody wants to get relegated like QPR did last season.

"It doesn't get any easier at this level, that's for sure. If you don't keep improving there's a relegation battle waiting for you in the second half of the season.

"Despite that close call last season, I still took a lot of satisfaction from the campaign. It was a job well done as far as I was concerned.

"I was very pleased with my form. In fact, I'm told I came close to selection for the Dutch squad for Euro '96.

"That would have been good but I'm quite happy just to be involved in another Premiership campaign. After all, I still find myself up against some of the world's best players every week, including a couple of very special Dutchmen." ●

THE LIGHTER SIDE!

ANYONE FOR BALLET?

A. Neil Ruddock, Liverpool.
B. Dennis Bergkamp, Arsenal, and Tim Sherwood, Blackburn.
C. Paul Rideout, Everton, and Alan Reeves, Wimbledon.
D. Dion Dublin, Coventry, and David Unsworth, Everton.

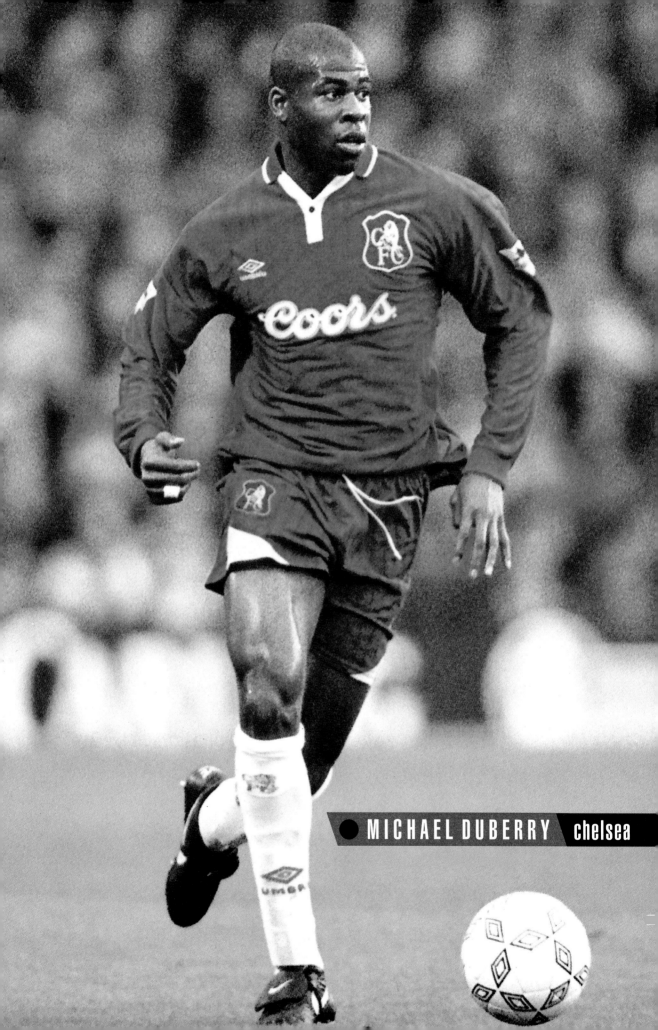

MICHAEL DUBERRY **chelsea**

10 of the best!

● Ally McCoist... Super Ally...Coisty... Rangers' ace striker is one of the most prolific goal-getters Scotland has ever produced. Tap-ins, flying headers, net bursting shots and penalties — they are all in McCoist's repertoire...and here are 10 of his personal favourites —

1 Celtic v. Rangers, League, 1983.
THIS WAS my first Old Firm game, and I managed to score after just 27 SECONDS — the fastest-ever Old Firm goal! To be honest, I don't remember much about it, because I was still getting used to the unique atmosphere!

2 Rangers v. Celtic, League Cup Final, 1984.
IT'S A wonderful feeling to play in the big games, such as Cup Finals. To score in them is even better! But to grab a HAT-TRICK in such a match, against your oldest rivals, is out of this world. But that's what I did here!

3 Scotland v. Hungary, 1987.
THIS WAS my first goal for Scotland, and will always be special for that reason. I've found it harder to score regularly at international level, but I'm always proud to pull on the dark blue jersey.

4 Rangers v. Motherwell, League, 1989.
I LIKE to break records — in fact, I broke a few last se including Bob McPhail's record number of Rangers goals. this strike broke the Premier Division scoring record, and made me very proud.

5 Scotland v. Norway, World Cup qualifier, 1989.
THIS GOAL sent us to the World Cup Finals in Italy, so you can understand why manager Andy Roxburgh was running around celebrating like a madman! It was a nice little lob over the 'keeper, who had rushed out in vain.

6 Rangers v. Celtic, League, 1990.
SORRY, CELTIC, but I seem to keep mentioning goals I scored against you!
This was another of those record-breaking goals. This time, I broke Derek Johnstone's post-war record, with a penalty, under real pressure, and it was all the sweeter because of the opposition!

7 **Rangers v. Celtic, Scottish Cup semi-final, 1992.**
DAVIE ROBERTSON was sent off early in the match, and we had to play with 10 men for over 80 minutes. This was one of my best-ever all-round performances, one I'm very proud of, and it put the icing on the cake when I got the all-important goal.

8 **Leeds v. Rangers, European Cup, November 1992.**
WE'D GONE to Elland Road for our European Cup second leg, knowing the English media had written us off. But Mark Hateley scored with an incredible volley early on and effectively put Leeds out of the Cup. My goal, though, was a bit special! It was Mark who provided the cross, and I flew in with a diving header past Leeds' keeper, John Lukic.

9 **Rangers v. Hibs, League Cup Final, 1993.**
AS I said, grabbing vital goals in big games is especially satisfying — but this one beats them all. I'd had injury troubles and was still coming back from those when I struck in this match, which was played at Celtic Park. It was an incredible overhead kick, and the rush of emotion following it was unbelievable. If you see film of it now, I look as if I'm not sure whether to laugh or cry! But it showed I was back to my best, and of course gave us some more silverware, too!

10 **Scotland v. Greece, 1996.**
I CAME off the substitutes' bench to give us another victory with a glancing header, a goal which almost guaranteed qualification for Euro '96. It's only recently that I've started to get many goals from headers, and this was certainly an enjoyable one, as you could see by the way I did an immediate lap of honour!

GOAL-den e

ASK the current crop of top bosses to name the managers that they admire, and you can bet that Derby County's Jim Smith will be among those mentioned.

In a League management career spanning three decades and eight clubs, 56-year-old Smith has experienced life in all four divisions.

He has built up a wealth of knowledge that his younger counterparts can only dream of.

He has one regret, though. He has never been at the helm of a club with true and sustainable ambition.

Sure, he has managed some of

> **"When I arrived at the Baseball Ground in the summer of 1995, I said that it was one of only a few clubs that I would have considered taking on."**

the biggest clubs in the land. He has enjoyed time at Blackburn Rovers — but before Jack Walker, at Newcastle United — before Sir John Hall and at Birmingham City — before David Sullivan.

He was never given the backing that the current incumbents of those positions now enjoy.

Smith's real success as a manager came at the less glamorous locations of Colchester and Oxford, and it still rankles that he has not had the recognition that his achievements have warranted.

However, having guided the Rams back to the summit after a five-year absence, the man affectionately known as 'Bald Eagle' is hopeful that that is about to change.

Says Jim, "When I arrived at the Baseball Ground in the summer of 1995, I said that it was one of only a few clubs that I would have considered taking on.

agle!

"I knew the club could be built up to earn and maintain top-flight football.

"Even when we started my first season in poor fashion, I was always confident that things would turn out all right in the end. The ingredients of a good side were there.

"In fact, I remember telling a mate of mine to put money on us to go up, even though we were then third from bottom and had taken just nine points from the opening nine games. I wonder how the bookie feels now. He gave odds of 50-1!

"I've had my bit of fortune along the way. I was lucky, for instance, that when I arrived, a lot of highly-prized players wanted to leave the club.

"Don't get me wrong. I would have been more than happy to have worked with Paul Williams, Craig Short and Mark Pembridge, but the fact they departed gave me the cash to do what I wanted with the team. Without that money, the job could have been very different.

"Derby had embarked on a policy of cutting the wage bill and I would have faced similar cash constraints. As it was, I was able to shape the team as I wanted it by bringing in Robin Van der Laan, Darryl Powell, Ron Willems and Igor Stimac.

"That did the trick and, hopefully, we can all look forward to a bright future."

Taking a club into the top division is nothing new to Smith. He took Oxford and Birmingham to the summit — and hardly anyone noticed!

It has been a lot different this time.

He goes on, "I took Colchester up to the old Third Division in 1974 and Birmingham to the First in 1980. At Oxford, we won promotion from the Third to the First in successive years.

"The problem was that Oxford was neither in the Midlands nor London and it missed out on a lot of media coverage. The same thing happened at Portsmouth.

"If they had been nearer to the big cities, I'm sure they, and I, would have gained greater recognition.

"Some of the Press lads were surprised when Derby appointed me. Quite a few weren't aware of what I had achieved in the game.

"It didn't bother me too much because now, at Derby, I have a great chance of making up for some of the things that I have missed out on over the years."

Smith could have been lost to football after losing his job as Portsmouth boss a couple of years ago. Appointed Chairman of the the League Managers' Association soon afterwards, Jim seemed to have found the ideal way of winding down towards retirement.

He explains, "The time I had away from the front line did me a power of good. In all my years as a boss, I'd never had more than a fortnight's break.

"This time I had three months and it more than recharged the batteries.

"I enjoyed the work at the Managers' Association, but I'm a club manager and I desperately wanted to get back and succeed again.

"I'd built a side at Fratton Park that could have competed at the highest level.

"We reached the 1992 FA cup semi-final with a team containing Darren Anderton, Guy Whittingham, John Beresford, Kit Symons and Paul Walsh.

"The next year, we were extremely unlucky to lose out on automatic promotion. We lost in the play-offs to Leicester and things went downhill.

"I had to sell Anderton for financial reasons. £2 million for a 19-year-old was just too good to turn down.

"Losing Whittingham and Beresford was a great deal more frustrating. The side I'd built was dismantled and things just petered out.

"I suppose it was inevitable that my position was questioned and it was one the saddest days of my life when I had to leave.

"I thought that may have been me finished in terms of management, but I didn't want my time in the game to be remembered for the disappointing way things ended at Pompey."

Second only to Coventry City's Ron Atkinson in the Premiership managers' age stakes, Jim has observed the current fashion for young player/managers with great interest.

Says Jim, "I dare say that there were quite a few Derby fans who were disappointed when I was appointed.

"There was speculation that the club was going to go for Manchester United's Steve Bruce.

"In the end, they got a bald-headed bloke like me! I'm delighted to have the chance to show that there is life in the oldies.

"It is great that there are former international players entering the management game. Their experience at the highest level all over the world should not be allowed to drift away from football.

"Having said that, it doesn't necessarily follow that every world class player will turn into a great manager.

"A great number of the men who have been successful managers down the years did not have great playing careers. Ron Atkinson, Howard Wilkinson and Alex Ferguson fall into that category.

"Management does not come naturally. It has to be worked at." ●

IGOR STIMAC

PIERRE VAN HOOIJDONK celtic

GOING FOR GOLD

●ARSENAL'S MARTIN KEOWN IS STILL CHASING THAT ELUSIVE WINNER'S MEDAL

LUCK has not always been on my side during my football career. But things began to change for me last year, and this season I am aiming to win my first major medal.

As a young player, I had just established myself at Highbury when George Graham arrived as manager. I couldn't agree terms and decided it was time to leave.

I joined Aston Villa and was relegated in my first season, while Arsenal went on to win the Littlewoods Cup, and later, the League Championship.

Then, when I returned to Highbury in 1993, Arsenal went on to win the Coca-Cola Cup/FA Cup Double but I

was not eligible for either competition.

A year later, I played in seven of the European Cup Winners' Cup ties on the way to the final. But I was injured the week before the game, and missed the victory over Parma in Copenhagen.

A year later, I did start the Cup Winners' Cup Final in Paris, against Real Zaragoza. But in the first half, I was injured in a clash of heads with a team-mate.

I suffered a badly broken nose and concussion. I tried to carry on but it was impossible.

I had lost over a pint and a half of blood. To have played on would have been dangerous.

By the time I recovered enough to sit on the touchline, the game looked like ending in a draw. I figured I had every chance of earning a winners' medal through

the penalty shoot-out.

But then Nayim's freak 50- yard lob won the match for Zaragoza. I ended up disappointed again.

At that stage I didn't know if I had any future at Arsenal, even though I was still under contract at Highbury.

When Bruce Rioch took over as manager, it seemed I didn't feature in his plans. I did not feature in any of the pre-season games.

But then I was picked for the first Premiership match and never looked back.

Before last season, I never felt my performances were appreciated by the fans. I played a lot of matches for George Graham as a man-marker, and I think the fans don't understand what that role involves.

It's a very restrictive role, just closing down specific players and doing a particular job.

Things were very different under Bruce Rioch. The new manager wanted a complete midfield

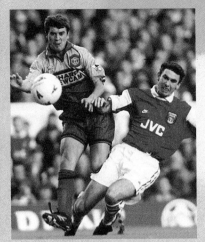

KEOWN v. KEANE. MARTIN TUSSLES WITH MANCHESTER UNITED'S ROY.

performance.

I was encouraged to express myself and be a creator, as well as close down when necessary. The emphasis was on passing the ball.

I wasn't restricted, and that helped me to regain my confidence on the ball.

The result was that my relationship with the fans was much better. The supporters were much more responsive to the way I played.

That helped me tremendously. My form was better than ever before, both in midfield and then in defence when I dropped back.

Supporters probably don't realise what a difference they can make. When you feel appreciated, you grow in stature.

When the fans get behind you, you gain a lot. Once you feel accepted by the crowd, you feel part of the place and part of the team.

For the first time, I think the fans started to take me seriously. That made a huge difference.

At the time, being selected for the first match was a bit of a surprise.

"I'd like to think I could still be considered for the England squad. I'm certainly playing as well as when I was chosen for different roles by Graham Taylor."

But it was a bigger shock to be made skipper after the injury to Tony Adams.

I never expected that. It was a great honour for me and I was really pleased to accept.

I enjoyed playing in midfield and being involved in so much of the play. But when Tony and Steve Bould dropped out, I went back into defence.

I've always considered centre-half to be my best position. What was new to me was the system of using three centre-backs.

Now I believe that style brings out the very best in me, particularly when I play on the right of the three. The position encompasses all my roles rolled into one.

At times you have to be like a right-back, at others like a centre-half. And there is also the chance to push forward into midfield.

The system suits me. But football is about players, not systems. If you are good enough, you can play in any style.

At one time I was pigeon-holed at Highbury as just being a man-marker. Now I've broken out of that mould and I'm really enjoying my football.

I'd like to think I could still be considered for the England squad. I'm certainly playing as well as when I was chosen for different roles by Graham Taylor.

But my first aim is to win honours with Arsenal. I've had more than twelve years in the game and I'm still looking for my first major medal.

I hope it could finally come this season.

● SPURS' CHRIS ARMSTRONG MADE A NAME FOR HIMSELF AT WHITE HART LANE!

jurgen who?

A few eyebrows were raised in disbelief when Gerry Francis spent £4.5 million to take Chris Armstrong from Crystal Palace to Tottenham. Rival fans were licking their lips in anticipation of a rousing chorus of 'what a waste of money'.

After all, Armstrong had just suffered a traumatic season at Selhurst Park when he'd scored just eight League goals, missed numerous chances, failed an FA drugs test and saw Palace get relegated. Why was the Spurs boss spending so much money on such an unreliable player?

Francis took no notice of such comments. He saw something special in the Newcastle-born striker, something that reminded him of Les Ferdinand.

At QPR, Francis had transformed Ferdinand from a rather ungainly young forward into one of the most powerful strikers in the country. Last season, he set about the same task with Chris Armstrong with stunning results.

It was not an easy situation for Armstrong to walk into at White Hart Lane. He was taking the place of Jurgen Klinsmann alongside Teddy Sheringham.

The great German striker had been idolised at Tottenham. Armstrong had a tough act to follow.

It took him seven games to get off the mark but, despite that slow start, the fans were quick to take to their new hero.

"The supporters were great to me right from the start," says Chris. "I think they could see immediately that I was going to give everything for the team.

"They got their reward for that support when I started scoring regularly. I won't forget how they kept me going early on.

"Not scoring in those first few games was a bit worrying but I knew I was playing well. In any case, they tell me it took Gary Lineker a few games to get off the mark when he joined Spurs and we all know how well he did here.

"Other people did write us off

very quickly. I was slaughtered in the press at the time.

"The only opinion that interested me was that of the boss. Gerry remained confident in my ability, even when I wasn't scoring.

"He seemed to know my game better than I did. Watching videos of my games for Palace he was able to point out where I could improve. "Gerry wanted me to follow the example of Les Ferdinand. He made a slow start to his QPR career but became an England player with Gerry's help.

"That's what I thought he could do for me too. International football is a target for any player but it takes a manager like Gerry to bring that potential through.

"The other major influence on my game since I came to Tottenham has been Teddy Sheringham. I learned a lot from playing alongside him last season.

WHO NEEDS JURGEN WHEN YOU'VE GOT CHRIS?

It was not an easy situation for Armstrong to walk into at White Hart Lane. He was taking the place of Jurgen Klinsmann alongside Teddy Sheringham.

The great German striker had been idolised at Tottenham. Armstrong had a tough act to follow.

78

"Right from the start I could tell we would have a good understanding. We worked very hard in training early on to make sure we got everything right.

"Teddy is just the sort of player strikers want to play alongside. He has brought the best out in all his partners.

"Over our first season together I think we did even better than we might have expected. The goals kept coming for both of us, with each of us providing plenty of chances for the other."

It didn't take long for Armstrong and Sheringham to be considered one of the best strike-forces in the Premier League. Only Liverpool's partnership of Robbie Fowler and Stan Collymore could match their consistency in front of goal.

The combination of Sheringham's awareness and Armstrong's pace and power makes them a deadly duo. Few teams manage to keep these two quiet for a whole game.

Armstrong has proved all his doubters wrong. At the start of last season people were calling him a 'waste of money', now he looks a real bargain.

Having started his League career in Wales with Wrexham, moved on to Millwall, then Palace, Armstrong finally joined the Premier League's elite group of strikers at Tottenham. He's now challenging the likes of Fowler, Shearer and Ferdinand to be the Premiership's number one hit-man.

It's not surprising that his old Millwall boss Mick McCarthy was soon checking Armstrong's ancestry to see if he could play for the Republic of Ireland.

Chris is confident that after his impressive first season at White Hart lane there is still much more to come.

"I know I can get better still," says Chris. "You're learning all the time in football.

"This Tottenham team has improved a lot over the last year. Now we're looking to win trophies." ●

● **LARS BOHINEN** | *blackburn rovers*

● WHY A TEAM FROM OLDHAM CAN BOAST OF BEING THE BREEDING GROUND OF MANY OF TODAY'S TOP STARS.

NEW FACES

David Platt—the one that got away.

MANCHESTER UNITED would have a strong case if they argued that their youth policy was the best in the land. No other club in the country could claim to have nurtured such a promising batch of youngsters over such a lengthy period of time.

The club's history-making 'double Double' last season was achieved on the back of manager Alex Ferguson's decision to sell experienced stars like Paul Ince, Mark Hughes and Andrei Kanchelskis to make way for the youngsters he rated so highly.

However, without the help of a small, local junior football team, United could have ended last season empty-handed. No less than FIVE of United's team last season ended up at Old Trafford via an Oldham-based team called Boundary Park.

While rival clubs spent millions on the likes of Stan Collymore, Faustino Asprilla and Dennis Bergkamp, Alex Ferguson built his new team without a cheque-book in sight.

Formed in 1978 by Oldham-based Paul Buckley to allow his son, Matthew, to compete in a competitive junior league, Boundary Park have become an unrivalled academy of footballing talent. Apart from five Old Trafford stars, the club can claim to have nurtured many more professionals and several internationals.

Nicky Butt

Paul recalls the early days of the five United stars and reveals how one professional club missed out on another old boy who would later captain his country.

He tells me, "I formed the club with a couple of other lads in 1978, but within no time, the others pulled out and I was left 'holding the baby.' Fortunately my wife, Joyce, was keen and she helped me along.

"It all started because of my lad, Matthew. He was a good footballer and we decided we wanted to form a team that would do everything properly. We were determined not to run a street team and anybody who wanted to play for the club understood that they wouldn't play if they missed training. Parents also had to get involved with fund-raising.

"Within two or three years, we had grown as a club and were running teams at five different age groups. Initially, we had two lads scouting for players, but as the club grew, players were coming straight to us.

"We have many ex-players currently in the professional game now, most of whom are at Oldham Athletic or Manchester United. However, the likes of Trevor Sinclair, Alan McLoughlin, Mark Robins and Paul Bernard have all played for us.

Continued overleaf.

81

Paul Scholes

Continued from previous page

"Nicky Butt, Paul Scholes and the Neville brothers all played in the same team. They won the Lancashire Youth Cup in 1991.

"I remember representing Nicky Butt on numerous occasions at League Disciplinary hearings. It was usually for bookings or sendings-off and he is no different as a player now. Off the pitch, though, he is a perfect lad.

"Nicky was a real ball-winner. He wasn't malicious, but his game brought him the odd suspension. Whenever he picked up a ban, he was brought into the office to see me and would be chastised. He was told not to do it again, but you knew he probably would!

"I liked his aggression, though, because we wanted to win and Nicky is a winner.

"Paul Scholes was very quiet, even insular to a degree. He was a loner type, but he was terrifically skilful. He has been to watch us play since he left.

"He played in midfield for us with another little lad, whose dad was Eamonn O'Keefe, the former Everton and Republic of Ireland player. They were both very small, but wherever we went, everybody would notice them and comment on their skill because they were both out of this world.

"Nicky and Paul came to us as 11-year-olds, but Gary Neville didn't arrive until he was 14. His dad wanted him to come to us because he could see the effort we were putting in to improve the lads. Phil came a year later, but he ended up in the same team as Gary even though he is two years younger.

"Phil was big enough and good enough and he played at centre-half in the Under-16's Lancashire Cup Final as a 14-year-old. They have both been capped by England and I'm sure that Nicky and Paul will follow them eventually.

"David May also played, albeit a few years earlier and you won't find a nicer lad. David is one of the best lads we ever had and he still keeps in touch. Whenever I want any presentations doing, I know I just have to pick up the phone and ask him. David never lets me down.

"My favourite memory of all the lads who have made it is of Nicky Butt, but it isn't an on-the-field recollection. He bought me a bottle of whisky as a thank you on the presentation night when he left. He knew I had had a lot of trouble to put up with because of him, but he gave me the bottle and thanked me for looking after him."

Had things been different, the five United lads and many others could have ended up at Oldham Athletic. Although the name of the club suggests a close affiliation with Oldham, Boundary Park have always been an independent outfit.

As a small shareholder in Oldham Athletic, Paul was concerned about the number of Boundary Park players slipping through the net of the local club. A meeting with Oldham officials cost the 'Latics' the player that Paul describes as Boundary Park's 'Jewel in the Crown.'

"I was annoyed that some of the lads weren't being picked up by Oldham. The likes of Manchester United were picking them up and if they were good enough for them but not Oldham, something was wrong.

"Oldham chairman Ian Stott asked me to name one lad Oldham could look at. I told them about a boy who had just left us because of his age. He was called David Platt.

"However, it was never followed up, so Oldham lost out.

"Platty went onto great things, of course and I always used him as an example for all of the kids to follow. In his early days with us, he never got a game but he worked hard and finally came good. When I retired three years ago, David sent me the shirt he wore when he captained England for the first time."

Paul adds, "We never tried to link up with professional clubs because we wanted to be self-financing and run our own affairs. We had several offers, but we were determined to be independent.

"Our belief was that if the professional clubs wanted our lads, they would have to make the effort and get them themselves. To their credit they did and we were soon hounded by scouts.

"Brian Kidd, now Manchester United's assistant manager, was one of them and he has picked up half a team off us. Brian was great with the lads and that's why he got them. He was prepared to come and see them play. Apart from a couple of £50 cheques from United when they took Mark Robins and Andy Robinson from us, we have had nothing, but we didn't start the club to make money. It was to help local lads become good footballers.

"When the lads make it, I feel proud to have been associated with them, but it wasn't just me. Other people have suffered cold and wet Sunday mornings to help them on their way, but it has all been worth it." ●

> **"The likes of Manchester United were picking them up and if they were good enough for them but not Oldham, something was wrong."**

in at the deep end!

● **MANCHESTER CITY'S MICHAEL BROWN HAD AN UNFORGETTABLE FIRST SEASON AT MAINE ROAD.**

RELEGATION came as a bitter blow to everyone at Manchester City last season.

Yet the drop to the First Division will not stop City manager Alan Ball from ruthlessly carrying on with his extensive rebuilding programme at Maine Road.

After a painful first season in charge, Ball now clearly believes Manchester City's future lies within the strength of its youth team.

In fact, Ball spent much of his first year in charge clearing his squad of older players, whom he felt were impeding the progress of the most promising set of youngsters City have produced since their FA Youth Cup winning side of 1985/86.

In the midst of the relegation trauma, Ball blooded teenage midfielder Michael Brown, and his impressive displays ultimately led to Ball feeling able to accept a £3.5 million bid from Blackburn for England hopeful, Garry Flitcroft.

Opportunity certainly came knocking for Michael, who made 21 full appearances in a side which spent virtually the whole season fighting and ultimately losing the battle against Premiership relegation.

"To make over 20 appearances in the first year of my professional contract was an unbelievable start," says Michael. "When I came back for pre-season training before the start of last season I thought making myself an aim of gaining regular reserve

team football before the season was finished would be more realistic.

"I'd only been back from the summer break a week when Alan Ball took me to one side and told me I would be going with the first team on a tour of Ireland.

"I followed that up with a couple of appearances in pre-season friendlies, but I was absolutely stunned when the third game of the season came around and Alan told me I would have a place on the bench for the trip to Queens Park Rangers.

"Unfortunately, when I came on in the second half for my first-team debut, I only lasted a short time before I was sent off. As you can imagine, I was really upset at the time.

"However, Alan phoned me the following day, and told me not to worry. Then he added the small matter that I would be making my full debut against Everton at Maine Road three days later!"

Michael adds, "I was a regular in the first-team squad for the rest of the season, and I was even called up to the England Under-21 side for the game against Croatia last April.

"I couldn't believe how fast everything was happening to me at the time. When I made my debut at Loftus Road, I couldn't even have described myself as experienced at reserve team level. That is why the call-up came as so much of a shock.

"The season before Alan took over, we had a lot of older players at the club who were being played in the reserve team until they

could find other clubs. So along with most of the other youngsters, I spent most of my time playing for the youth team.

"That was a great youth squad two years ago, and we achieved more than · any other youth side at Maine Road has done for some time. I skippered the side which won the 'B' team league, reached the Lancashire Youth Cup Final and the semi-finals of the FA Youth Cup. We were all very proud of that record.

"Alan Ball has said that

he feels the future of this club lies within its youth team. Plenty of the lads I played with in that youth side gained a lot of valuable experience in the reserve side last season and it won't be long before they are also given their chance in the first team.

"City have a long and successful history when it comes to bringing through youth team players. I hope in my short time as a professional at Maine Road I have gone some way to carrying on that tradition." ●

IAN WALKER | tottenham hotspur

the topical times football book
QUIZtime!

1) Who did Juventus beat in a penalty shoot-out to win the European Champions' Cup last season?

2) Which tough-tackling Newcastle midfielder, signed by Kevin Keegan towards the end of last season, has enjoyed English Championship success at BOTH his previous clubs.

3) Which country will host the World Cup in 1998?

4) Who scored a hat-trick in Rangers' 5-1 defeat of Hearts in last season's Scottish Cup Final?

5) Who scored the winner in Liverpool's incredible 4-3 victory over Newcastle United last season?

6) Scottish First Division side Stirling Albion used to play their home games at a stadium bearing a similar name to a famous Premiership stadium. What was its name?

7) Which full Scottish internationalist has been on the substitutes' bench for England?

8) Which English Third Division team beat Wales in a friendly match last year?

9) Which country only managed to score one goal in the qualifying rounds for Euro '96?

10) Which two Italians missed penalties in the 1994 World Cup Final ?

11) Which French club does Scottish midfielder, John Collins play for?

12) Which two Blackburn Rovers and England stars used to play for Southampton?

13) Which team put Nottingham Forest out of last season's UEFA Cup?

14) Manchester United imported centre-half William Prunier last season to fill in for injured central defensive pair Steve Bruce and Gary Pallister. Which country was Prunier from?

15) In what year was the first match between Scotland and England contested, and where was it played?

16) Which Greek international striker joined Blackburn Rovers last summer on a free transfer from Panathinaikos?

17) Who scored Manchester United's second goal against Chelsea in the semi-final of last season's FA Cup?

18) Which player scored twice for England in his comeback match against Hungary, after spending most of last season out of action due to serious injury?

19) Which goalkeeper has played Champions' League football with Manchester United and is now plying his trade with Middlesbrough?

20) Which Aston Villa player scored the first goal in last season's Coca-Cola Cup Final

against Leeds?

21) For which country does Manchester City's Georgiou Kinkladze play?

22) Can you name the Dutch star sent home in disgrace from Euro '96?

23) From which club did Newcastle United sign Les Ferdinand?

24) Which nation was the first team ever to have a player sent off in the World Cup Final, and in which year?

25) Who was highest scorer in the 1986 World Cup?

85

REID

ALL ABOUT IT!

● PETER REID IS BACK IN THE BIG-TIME!

PETER REID was always a resilient character during his playing days and his fighting spirit has not diminished since becoming a manager.

The Sunderland boss spent his early playing days with Bolton Wanderers battling back from a series of career-threatening injuries and when he found fame with Everton and England in the mid-1980s, he was always the sort of player who would turn lost causes into winning situations.

Reid is the type of man who seems to relish the opportunity of overcoming the odds, and he succeeded again at Roker Park last season as he guided Sunderland back into the top flight after a five-year absence.

Success on Wearside last season allowed Reid to bury the memory of his remarkable dismissal as Manchester City manager in 1993 and also highlighted his credentials as one of the best managers in the game.

In the space of 12 months, he transformed Sunderland from First Division strugglers into a side which deservedly claimed promotion to the Premiership.

When he arrived at Roker Park, he inherited a sleeping giant that showed no sign of awakening. He admits that was one of the reasons he took the job.

Peter reveals, "When I left Manchester City, I stayed in the game, but I returned to the playing side with Southampton and Notts County instead of taking another management job.

"I did get offers from several clubs to become their manager, but without wanting to sound big-headed, I didn't think they were for me. I was still waiting for something to come up when I returned from a short spell in Spain at the beginning of the 1994-95 season.

"I was struggling to get a club in Britain until Mike Walsh, a mate of mine who was managing Bury, asked me to play for them. Unfortunately, I pulled a hamstring after 20 minutes of the first game of the season against Rochdale and that was the last time I played.

"I knew my playing days were drawing to a close following that injury, but I stayed at Gigg Lane until Sunderland approached me. They had seven games left to avoid relegation to the Second Division and were in a bad position, but I was up for the challenge.

"Initially, the board at Sunderland told me that my job was to keep the club in the First Division. After that, my position would be reviewed. I wanted the job permanently, though, and when we avoided relegation I was delighted to take the job on a permanent basis.

"Working in the lower divisions was something that just didn't turn me on. You have to be enthusiastic to do well in football, and Sunderland was one of those jobs I thought I could really get my teeth into. It's a big club and that was what I wanted. I had waited patiently for a big club to come in for me and Sunderland was just what I was looking for.

"The unfortunate thing about the management circuit is that I had to wait until Mick Buxton lost his job at Roker Park before I could get back in. That's a fact of life and I know it well enough because I lost my job at City."

Reid's dismissal from Maine Road, just four games into the season, was certainly contentious. In his time at the club, City had not finished below halfway in the top flight and were bridging the gap between themselves and neighbours United.

A similar neighbour-catching challenge is part of the task at Sunderland.

As a player at Everton, Reid also helped to end Liverpool's Merseyside monopoly. After taking on Liverpool and Manchester United, Newcastle United don't worry him.

Peter goes on, "I don't mind the

REID CELEBRATES SUNDERLAND'S FIRST DIVISION CHAMPIONSHIP.

comparison with Newcastle. After spending time at Everton and Manchester City, I know all about big and successful neighbours and I think it is great to have such rivalry.

"At City, we finished above United in the table in my first season in charge but unfortunately I didn't guide the club to a trophy. While I was at Everton, we won the League twice, FA Cup and European Cup Winners' Cup.

"I felt I was close to doing something at City. My record at Maine Road is there in black and white. We finished fifth, fifth and ninth and I don't care what people say, that record stands up and there is no case to argue.

"The Sunderland job is a similar challenge, but I don't mind that. I would rather have a challenge in a football region like

the North-East than a job out in the sticks where football isn't as important to the area.

"It's great to be involved in rivalry and I am delighted that we are involved with the likes of Newcastle and Middlesbrough again this season. I missed it last season."

The majority of teams promoted from the First Division in recent years have struggled to make an impact in the top flight and several have been relegated after only one campaign among the big boys.

The expectancy to do well at Sunderland has been increased by the relative success of neighbours Newcastle and Middlesbrough. However, Reid knows only too well that pressure applies at every club and he doesn't believe that Sunderland is a different case.

He adds, "Sunderland has a massive history and tradition and people want success again. There is a pressure attached to that but it is no greater at Sunderland than anywhere else.

"Mike Walsh took Bury to Wembley in the play-offs a couple of seasons ago and a month into the following season they hadn't lost at home in 23 matches. They lost the 24th game 5-0 and he was sacked!

"Graham Taylor lost his job at Wolves last year when a couple of wins would have taken him into the play-off positions. I was sacked by City after winning one point from four matches, yet I had a similar start 12 months earlier and we still finished in the top half of the table.

"Football management is a precarious profession, but I enjoy this side of the game and I know all about the pitfalls." ●

aja
- a

When Patrick Kluivert's goal gave Ajax of Amsterdam victory over AC Milan in the Final of the European Cup in May 1995, a significant shift in the balance of power in European football was sensed by football fans everywhere. It was the triumph of youthful exuberance, skill and flair — the essence of Dutch football — over the efficient, disciplined game that the Milanese masters had perfected and which had given them almost unrivalled domination of the Italian game.

It's not only football that is taught at the academy. Pupils have normal academic subjects to study too.

Lunch-time — and it's beans for everyone!

X chool for soccer

The average age of that cup-winning team was twenty-three and along with Kluivert it contained some of the most exciting talent in world soccer.

Many of the young players could trace their footballing roots to the legendary Ajax training

Continued over leaf

Continued from prevoius page.

school. Run by former Ajax players and coaches, the school takes talented youngsters from around the Netherlands, found through a network of scouts. It seeks to teach them excellence and instil in them the "Ajax way".

However, the end of last season saw the break-up of the 1995 side with several players moving abroad — Edgar Davids, for one, signing for AC Milan. Their reign as European champions came to an end, too, with defeat in the May final by Juventus in a penalty shoot-out.

There are sure to be plenty of eager hopefuls waiting in the wings, graduates of the Ajax academy, ready to continue Ajax's policy of soccer excellence. And with a school that has produced talents over the years like Johan Cruyff, Arie Haan, Johnny Rep, Ruud Krol, Dennis Bergkamp and Marco Van Basten who would bet against it?

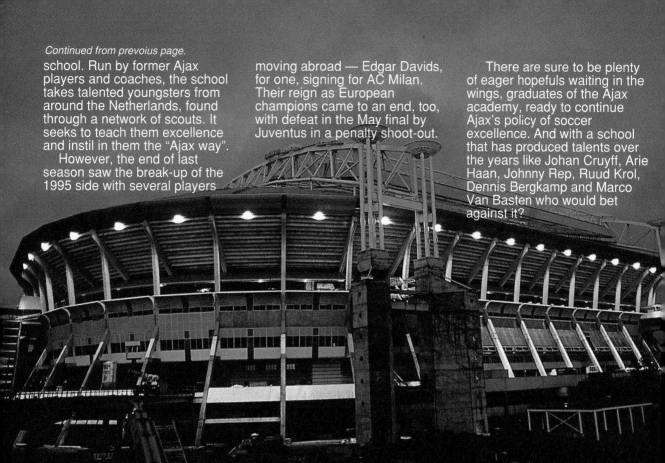

The "school" itself — the Ajax Arena.

What a difference a year can make. Jubilation after beating Milan . . .

Two "old boys" who have reached the top. Marco Van Basten and Dennis Bergkamp.

Every footballer has a spell on the subs bench and these Ajax youngsters are no exception.

. . . and when the ball goes in the river, it gives the subs something to do!

. . . misery after losing to Juventus.

a happy *ENDING!*

● Leicester City striker Steve Claridge scored the final domestic goal of last season when his last-gasp extra-time effort beat Crystal Palace in the First Division play-off Final at Wembley. Claridge admits that goal was the high point of his career, scored in a season in which he endured a succession of severe set backs.

THE 30-year-old had a public fall-out with his manager at Birmingham City, Barry Fry, which ended with Claridge reluctantly being transferred to Leicester City.

During the turbulent last few weeks of his career at the St Andrews club, he was also battling against a rare thyroid complaint which usually affects middle-aged women and has all the symptoms of multiple sclerosis.

Although the former Birmingham man has been relieved to discover that his illness is not MS, he paints a vivid picture of a six-month personal nightmare.

Steve says, "The illness is caused by the thyroid glands in the throat. It affected my metabolism and reduced my energy levels. In effect, I was living my life in slow motion.

"I had been unable to function properly. I suffered from numbness, deafness, cold, unwanted weight gain and had been mentally slower.

"The numbness became so bad that I couldn't even feel the ball when I kicked it!

"My energy level dropped so much that, at times, I couldn't even walk up the stairs. I would be shattered after the first run I made in a match.

"I normally only need five hours of sleep, but I was going to bed at 10pm and getting up at 9am. Even then, I could hardly move. Everything was too much effort. I was tired before I left the house.

"Deafness was another problem. I would have the television on so loud, friends would say that it could be heard next door. Yet I could barely hear it when I was sitting up close to it.

"I didn't know what to do. I rested as much as possible, but because I wasn't training enough, I was getting even more

tired. Then I changed my diet in case I was not eating correctly. But it didn't do the trick.

"Eventually, I went to see a specialist in Leicester and he immediately knew what was wrong with me. I went on a course of vitamin supplements and thyroid tablets and gradually got my fitness back, although I had occasional numbness in my left leg.

"We are not quite sure what caused the illness, but it may have something to do with a heart condition I have had since I was a boy.

"I have an irregular heartbeat and I'm required to take a tablet before a match. If the thyroid condition had anything to do with my heartbeat it's too bad,

because I can't stop taking the tablets."

The bustling front man's £1.2m move was not without controversy. He was shown the door at St Andrews after a reported bust-up with ex-Blues boss, Barry Fry.

Now, with his illness behind him, Claridge is confident he has a bright future.

Steve goes on, "When you move to a new club it's hard enough to make the transition. Leicester were not exactly buzzing when I signed, and my illness didn't help matters.

"I didn't want to leave St Andrews. I've moved enough in my career. I was settled at the club and had a good rapport with the fans. It was an honour to play for those supporters.

"The club had come back from the dead and I wanted to be a part of moving it on to even greater things. But it wasn't to be.

"The Leicester staff and fans must have wondered

what they had signed. It was just after I moved that my condition became noticeably worse. I couldn't understand what was wrong and had a couple of chats with the boss, Martin O'Neill.

"I thought it may have been caused by the stress of leaving Birmingham, but I have been told that it was purely a physical complaint.

"I played against Millwall and my legs were so heavy, I asked to come off. It was the first time in my career I have ever wanted to be substituted. In the end, I played through it, but it was a terrible experience.

"Now I have an opportunity to put all those setbacks behind me in the Premiership and I'll give it my best shot." ●

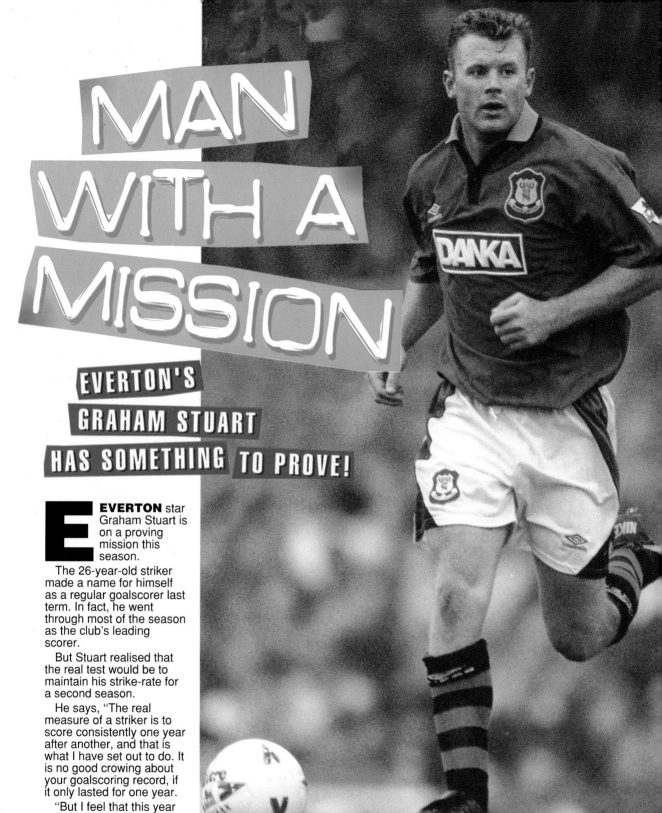

MAN WITH A MISSION

EVERTON'S GRAHAM STUART HAS SOMETHING TO PROVE!

EVERTON star Graham Stuart is on a proving mission this season.

The 26-year-old striker made a name for himself as a regular goalscorer last term. In fact, he went through most of the season as the club's leading scorer.

But Stuart realised that the real test would be to maintain his strike-rate for a second season.

He says, "The real measure of a striker is to score consistently one year after another, and that is what I have set out to do. It is no good crowing about your goalscoring record, if it only lasted for one year.

"But I feel that this year was always going to provide the real measure of my ability in front of goal.

"I may have taken a few defences by surprise last term. Until then, I had never really been known as a regular goalscorer.

"Last season, was the first occasion on which I had been given the chance to put together a lengthy run as an out-and-out striker.

"Although I regard that as my best position, and had always managed to score goals on the odd occasion when played up front, I was more often used as a winger at Chelsea.

"It was only when I had scored a few goals during a brief spell as a striker in the Everton reserves that manager Joe Royle decided to give me a run in that berth for the first team.

"It was very pleasing to hit a rich vein of scoring form and prove a few people wrong. I was able to reach the end of the season and say, 'The boss moved me up front and I have done the business.'

"However, I was also aware that I may have caught a few teams on the

hop. When playing alongside somebody like Duncan Ferguson, the main concern of our opponents was to stop him. Perhaps I benefitted from that.

"But having made people sit up and take notice of me, I knew they would be out to make it harder for me this season. That is why I went into this campaign regarding it as the real test of my scoring ability."

Before proving himself as a goalscorer, however, Stuart had to prove to manager Joe Royle that he was even worth a place in the Everton first team. Doing so has been something of a triumph for the player who, early in Royle's reign, was so much out in the cold that he believed his Everton career was over.

not even being in contention," says Stuart.

"When Joe took over, we were already battling against relegation. As I was one of the players who had put us in that position, I wanted to be one of those who got us out of it.

"But week after week I was completely out of the picture and eventually the boss told me, 'Although I don't want you to go, if the right offer comes along, I will listen to it.'

"That was a jolt, but I took it on the chin and knuckled down even harder to work myself back into favour. There was no way I was going to sit around feeling sorry for myself.

"On the other hand, I couldn't go around knocking the boss or claiming that it was unbelievable that he wasn't picking me.

"IT'S STUART. CAN HE BEAT SEAMAN?" GRAHAM DID AT HIGHBURY LAST SEASON

"In the end, I think I proved Joe WAS wrong!"

"When Joe took over in November 1994, one of his first decisions was to leave me out of the side," Graham recalls.

"After a couple of months when I had not been given a look-in, I believed my days at Goodison Park were numbered and would have to look elsewhere in order to gain first-team football.

"That would have disappointed me, but I was determined not to let it happen. You need nothing more than the knowledge that somebody does not fancy you as a player to inspire you to prove him wrong. In the end, I think I proved Joe WAS wrong."

Stuart had been bought for £850,000 from Chelsea by former Everton manager Howard Kendall, and remained in favour when the latter was replaced in the manager's hot-seat by Mike Walker.

But Walker remained at the club for just 10 months before being sacked and Stuart's problems began.

"It hurt my pride that I quickly went from being a regular in the first team to

"Despite being left out, I couldn't question his team selections, because gradually he was turning things around, the team was getting the results which would eventually secure Premiership survival and of course go on to win the FA Cup.

"But I refused to lie down and accept that my Everton career was almost over. I took a long, hard look at myself and wondered what more I should be doing to regain my place in the team.

"I couldn't be working any harder, and decided to concentrate on some of the aspects of our play which Joe had been emphasising.

"For example, he had

JOE ROYLE

called for the forwards and midfield players to improve on pressurising opponents by closing them down more quickly. So I worked very hard at my tackling back and shutting people down, hoping that he would notice.

"Gradually, I began to make the odd appearance. In some ways, that was worse because I sometimes found myself being dropped again even after I had played well.

"In one FA Cup match, we beat Norwich City 5-0. I scored once and was involved in two of the other goals, yet I was relegated to the substitutes' bench for our next match.

"I was distraught and couldn't help asking myself, 'Am I banging my head against a brick wall?' After all, we had given one of our best performances of the season and I had played a big part.

"However, I made the breakthrough when we beat Tottenham Hotspur 4-1 in the semi-final.

"After the match, Joe was interviewed on television and made a point of saying that he had not been 100 per cent fair with me in the past, but I had been as good as gold that afternoon.

"I took that to mean that he had been unfair to leave me out of previous matches, such as that Norwich City game. I also saw it as an acknowledgement that he had been wrong about me and not given me the credit I deserved from the start.

"He did not have to make that admission publicly and I respected him for being big enough to say it on

national television.

"Following that episode, I saw a bit of light at the end of the tunnel and finished the season on a high note by playing my part in beating Manchester United at Wembley to lift the FA Cup.

"I completed my personal recovery by being a regular starter last season."

In addition to proving his manager wrong, however, Stuart is just as pleased that his own reversal of fortune has gone hand-in-hand with the process of stabilising the club.

"Having won the cup and escaped the threat of relegation, it was very important that we put Everton back on an even keel," he goes on.

"During my first two years at the club, I had played under three different managers and a caretaker manager.

"Each one had different ideas about the game and for most of that period there was no consistency or stability at the club. That uncertainty is bound to affect the performances of the players.

"I suffered personally as a result of those changes when, following the sacking of one manager who had me in his team every week, the new manager didn't fancy me. But, just as I like to think I won him over and put the problems of the past behind me, so Joe has also guided the club through that period of imbalance.

"I believe he has achieved the stability that we needed and that will help us to maintain a place among the Premiership's top clubs." ●

CRAIG RUSSELL sunderland

THE LIGHTER SIDE!

LOOK, REF...!

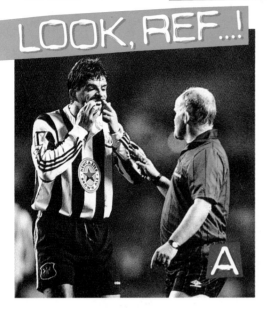

A. "Don't you think this makes me look like Bugs Bunny?"
"Only if you shave your moustache off, son!"

B. "Mr Willard . . . Mr Cantona . . .! Mr Cantona . . .! Mr . . ."
"Keep it short, Gareth. Five seconds to kick-off!"

C. "Look, it's W.R.I.G.H.T.! Right?"
"Right, Wright! I'll write Wright — RIGHT?"

D. "Sorry, son. You lose. You get to keep today's mascot!"

beat the drop

● SHEFFIELD UNITED'S MICHAEL VONK ADDED SOME STEEL TO THE BLADES' DEFENCE

RELEGATION seemed more than likely at Sheffield United last Christmas. But after the resignation of long-serving manager Dave Bassett and a boardroom takeover, the new owner of the club, Mike MacDonald, appointed former Everton boss Howard Kendall as manager.

The Blades have not looked back since!

One of the many contributing factors in United's remarkable revival during the second half of last season was the inspirational form of their Dutch defender, Michael Vonk.

Kendall made Vonk his first signing when he took over last December, and the former Manchester City centre-back certainly proved his worth.

In fact, Michael influenced the United defence to such an extent that a previously leaky rearguard only conceded four goals in the final two months of the season.

"We had to stop conceding goals," says Michael. "I think that was one of the main team problems before Howard took over. If Howard had not managed to stop the team leaking goals quickly, there is no question that we would have been relegated to the Second Division.

"It took some time for the results to come good, we'll admit that. But when we all started out together the club was in a very difficult position.

"The turnover of players was unbelievable. With so many moving either into or out of the club, at one stage it seemed as if there were two or three lads making their debuts each time we played.

"Having all the new faces around the club meant that, for the first couple of months, we really did have to put in a lot of hard work.

"When the crunch came in March and April, we showed just how much we had improved with all the changes. We felt that all the hard work had paid off because we only lost one game during that crucial stage of the season.

"At the end of the term we were not in any danger of relegation. The fact that we finished in ninth position really was a remarkable achievement when you consider how low the club had sunk before Howard took over.

"Hopefully we can move on now, and we should all be looking forward to a bright future at Sheffield United. The players and manager believe we are among the top teams in the First Division, and the board has big plans for the next two years."

For Vonk, the new dawn at Bramall Lane also heralds a new chapter in his English career. His five-year spell at Manchester City ended on a disappointing note with a lengthy period in the reserves.

"When I arrived here, I felt that I would have to prove myself all over again at a new club in a new division," he says. "I want to show everyone that I still have the ability to play at the highest level.

"The first two and a half years of my spell at City were great and I have some fantastic memories of my time there. But I was frozen out by the now-defunct 'three foreigner' rule.

"While that was in place, I was considered the fourth foreigner behind Eike Immel, Uwe Rosler and Georgi Kinkladze. They were among the best players at the club, so I had no alternative but to play in the reserves.

"The end was in sight for me last November when City manager Alan Ball gave goalkeeper Immel an extended contract after originally only signing him on just a three-month deal. I knew then that I would have to leave the club in order to find first-team football.

"I certainly made the right move, though. Sheffield United are a go-ahead club and after settling in I feel that I am appreciated here. The local newspapers have even vaunted me as the best centre-back at the club since the 1970s. That really is very flattering!

"Sheffield United's bad spell is now over. You can almost feel the optimism running around the veins of the club. With everybody at Bramall Lane on such a high, we must take advantage of the situation out on the pitch.

"Promotion to the Premiership HAS to be our aim." ●

ea

SOMETIME soon I aim to be going for an Olympic Gold medal.

Not at football. And not in the Olympic Games itself.

The medal I want to win belongs to Daley Thompson — as he keeps reminding me!

Daley is one of my best pals and my partner in soccer coaching schools. He looks after the fitness side, while I concentrate on the football skills.

We've been friendly ever since Daley turned up to train with the Wimbledon squad. He fancied having a go at playing professionally.

It started out as a television documentary, but Daley began to get serious about football. After training we would go on to a local tennis complex to work out.

We played a few games of tennis, and exercised in the gym. While I was recovering from a foot injury, Daley helped me get back into condition.

rle's court!

I picked his brains on fitness training. He picked my brains on football.

In conjunction with Wimbledon physio Steve Allen and athletics coach Jenny Archer, I worked with Daley to build up my fitness.

They would sort out a programme, and we'd go off and work at it for two or three days.

DALEY THOMPSON – MANY HAPPY RETURNS!

Daley had me jumping over hurdles and doing aerobic exercises in the swimming pool. I learned a lot about fitness methods.

I could take him on in some types of exercise, but mostly Daley would set targets I couldn't match. Trying to beat him was a good incentive to push myself.

Daley is so competitive there were times we were almost fighting to beat each other. It was a great experience for me, and from it we got the idea to do some coaching courses.

Football at top level is getting quicker and quicker. Kids can't survive these days in the professional game without being really fit.

So Daley takes them for athletic-type drills, while I work on the football side. It's important to get the balance right.

He is a great role model for the kids. People thought it was a gimmick when Daley turned up to train with

THE WIMBLEDON DALEY – "... A USEFUL FOOTBALLER, WITH GOOD SKILLS."

> The way football is developing, tennis might be my best chance of winning a medal.

Wimbledon, but he's a useful footballer, with good skills.

But all the time I have to put up with a lot of gold medal chat from Daley. 'How many medals have you got ?' or 'Show us your medals.'

I'd really love to win a major medal with Wimbledon just to help keep him quiet. In the meantime, I'm waiting to challenge him at tennis.

Daley, naturally, is pretty good at tennis. But I've been having regular coaching sessions.

If I can get him to play me in a match, maybe I can win one of his gold medals that way!

The way football is developing, it might be my best chance of winning a medal. It's getting harder and harder for a club like Wimbledon to survive.

Our income is a fraction of what the big clubs can generate

through the gate and off the field with their marketing methods.

Wimbledon have done tremendously well to survive over the years. I think other clubs could learn a lot from us.

People are quick to knock us. But maybe they should take a step back and look at what we have achieved.

However, I don't think it's possible for any club these days to establish themselves in the Premier League on our sort of resources.

Nobody now could 'do a Wimbledon'. The gap is too big between the Premier League and the First Division.

Promoted clubs have to be able to spend millions on building up the squad to stand a chance of surviving at the top level.

Obviously it all reduces my chances of winning medals with the Dons. But I will keep battling.

I love it at Wimbledon. The spirit is great. On our day we are capable of beating anyone.

The problem for a club like us is coping with injuries over a long season. We can't just go out and spend big money on replacing players.

Last season I was really pleased with my form. After recovering from another injury, I scored 13 goals from midfield, which was close to my best.

It was nice to get back to that level after all my injury problems. I hope I can repeat that kind of form this season.

Wimbledon won the FA Cup in 1988 and one of the cup competitions is still our best chance of winning honours.

I just hope some of Daley Thompson's gold-winning touch has rubbed off on me. ●

die-hard!

NOEL WHELAN'S career with Leeds United came to an abrupt end when he was sold to Coventry City for £2.1 million last season.

But the 26-year-old striker, who was born in Leeds, has not given up hope of playing for them again.

His transfer came at a time when Whelan felt he was being edged out of the first-team picture at Elland Road, so he welcomed the chance to further his career with a new club.

However, he dreams that one day he will return and pull on a white jersey again.

So he has set out to prove to his old club that they were wrong to close him out and entice them to buy him back eventually.

"Don't get me wrong. I am nothing less than fully committed to Coventry City. This is an excellent club and I am very pleased that my transfer brought me to such a superb set-up," says Noel.

"But, hopefully, I have many years of football ahead of me and it would be tremendous to think that I might finish my career at Leeds. If that cannot happen, perhaps I might play the last match of my career at Elland Road.

"Leeds were my club as a boy, so it was great that I joined them as a youngster. Even since moving to Coventry, I have found it hard to stay away from Elland Road. On days when Leeds are playing and Coventry do not have a match, I go to watch them."

...HAT COVENTRY CITY'S NOEL WHELAN CAN'T SHAKE OFF!

"I was very disappointed when, after progressing through the ranks at Leeds, I realised that I would have to leave in order to advance my career because I had become surplus to the club's requirements.

"Maybe it is natural that, since then, I have wanted to prove them wrong and I hope that in the brief period I have been at Highfield Road, I have started to do that.

"I would like to think that they are now thinking twice about the wisdom of selling me and whether they really needed to spend £4.5 million on buying the Swedish striker, Tomas Brolin, when they had a young player already at the club who was desperate to play for them."

For Whelan, it was a sad end to an Elland Road career which had begun very promisingly.

"I had come up through the ranks and made my first-team debut when I was still a YTS trainee," Noel recalls. "At the start of season 1994-95, I scored seven goals in my first 14 outings. I also made my debut for the England Under-21 side and scored the winner against the Republic of Ireland.

"I felt that at that point I had established myself in the team and I was there for the rest of the season. I had the other players thinking of me as part of the side and my confidence was high."

Things began to go wrong for Whelan, however, when he suffered a bout of tonsilitis — a recurrence of a problem which had dogged him ever since signing for the club as a youngster.

He goes on, "It used to flare up three or four times a season and it had kept me out of action on a number of occasions.

"This time, however, I tried to play through it. Though I could have had my tonsils removed, I think manager Howard Wilkinson wanted me to wait until the end of the season. We had a heavy schedule of matches and he wanted me available.

"At least by waiting until the summer, I would have more time to recover from the operation. So I took antibiotics and carried on playing.

"But the more I persevered, the weaker I became. Once I was on the field, I tried to forget about it but couldn't. Before long, I would be struggling to regain my breath and tiring rapidly during the second half.

"As soon as a match was finished, all I wanted to do was go home to bed. I felt under par for the rest of the week, and hardly trained at all.

"I desperately wanted to carry on, but the boss finally realised that I could not go on playing, so decided to rest me.

"He was also in the process of signing Tony Yeboah, who replaced me in the team.

"The situation depressed me. I could have accepted my absence more easily if I had been sidelined by a leg injury sustained during a match. But I found it soul-destroying to be kept out by something trivial like tonsilitis.

"In the end, I had my tonsils removed during the summer and by the start of last season, I felt I was back to the form and fitness of a year earlier.

"I was full of ambition. I felt as though I had to make up for a lost season, so I had a point to prove and I was just in the mood to do it.

"Although Tony had established himself in the team by then, I believed I had a good chance of winning back a regular place, either alongside him, just behind the front two or playing in a wide position. My confidence was so high, I was sure I could make a mark in any of those roles.

"Though I started the campaign on the substitutes' bench, I was back in the team for Leeds' first

UEFA Cup match against Monaco in September.

"We won that match 3-0 and, after the game, the gaffer told me, 'The shirt is yours for as long as you want it.' But in my next outing, I dislocated a shoulder!

"It seemed that whenever I appeared to be getting somewhere, something happened to stop me in my tracks.

"The injury kept me out for two months. When I was fit again, I couldn't win back my place, despite what the boss had said. I didn't blame him at that point, because he was trying to keep a settled team.

THOMAS BROLIN - THE LAST STRAW

"But when the club signed Tomas Brolin, that was the last straw. I felt there was no need to buy new players for the forward positions. I kept reading in the papers that Leeds were linked with various strikers, and I wanted to cry out, 'What about me?'

"When Brolin arrived, I decided it was time to find a new club and put my career back on track.

"It was nice to say that I played for Leeds United, especially as I had supported the club. But there is no point in being with a big club if you are playing in the reserves. If you want to earn your money, you must play for the first team on a Saturday.

"Coventry have given me the chance to do that, and I quickly realised that I had joined a club as good as Leeds.

"Although I signed at the time when City were in the middle of their relegation battle last season, I looked at the squad and the management and realised there was very little wrong at the club.

"I knew it was the right move. This is a club with ambition, which they proved by subsequently signing Eoin Jess and Liam Daish.

"Fortunately, things started going well for me quickly, and I soon began to chalk up a decent tally of goals for the club.

"That is what manager Ron Atkinson bought me for, and I intend to go on scoring goals for the club."

NOEL IN HIS UNITED DAYS

ALESSANDRO DEL PIERO *juventus*

STEVE McMANAMAN liverpool

fromsinn

N February 1995, after his infamous kung-fu kick over the perimeter wall at Crystal Palace, the career of Manchester United's Eric Cantona in English football looked to be at an end.

Public condemnation, a record ban and a huge fine saw Cantona head back to his native France asking for a transfer from the Old Trafford club.

Manchester United manager Alex Ferguson flew after him and persuaded him to return. Cantona rewarded the persistence of Ferguson by not only orchestrating his side's dramatic League and Cup Double, but also by proving he was a reformed character. Just one booking since his comeback

reinforced that point.

Cantona also became the rescuer in times of crisis. When his team-mates ran out of goals, he fired in 13 in 18

> ## "He stepped in during our hour of need until the rest of the players began to score again."

appearances, almost single-handedly keeping his team on the Double trail.

Says Ferguson, "During January, we enjoyed a spell when the players were

spreading the goals around, but suddenly they dried up.

"However, Eric took over and chipped in with a series of really crucial goals. He scored in five matches running. One of those helped us reach the FA Cup semi-final, one was a vital late equaliser against Queens Park Rangers and the others were all match-winners which earned precious League points.

"He stepped in during our hour of need until the rest of the players began to score again.

"But it is not just his goals which were important. He played some magnificent football for us, too."

Cantona's reformation even swayed many of his fiercest critics as he was named

Here are just **SOME** of the highlights of **Eric'**

Eric makes his comeback against Liverpool in October, 1995 . . .

. . . and celebrates by scoring United's equaliser from the penalty spot in the 2-2 draw.

Eric scoring against Arsenal.

Eric 1 — Liverpool 0. The goal that clinched the F.A. Cup — and the Double.

Posing happily with Alex Ferguson and this season's haul — F.A. Cup, Carling Premiership trophy . . . and Footballer of the Year award.

ertosaint

Footballer of the Year at the end of last season.

"He is such a big influence on the young players because they look up to him," adds the United boss.

"He trains brilliantly, then practises after training and is the last to leave the car park, signing autographs.

"The young players see that and it is important to them. He has become a father figure on the field. They look up to him and take their cue from him.

"I don't think Eric's nature changed. We all know he is an emotional person. But he kept the volatile side of his nature in check. I think he was very conscious of the need to do that." ●

season . . .

...and against Newcastle.

WHEN a footballer realises his days are numbered at Manchester United, you would expect him to be downhearted at the prospect of moving to a new club.

Few players can say they have benefited by leaving a club like United, but since leaving Old Trafford before the 1995-96 season, Middlesbrough goalkeeper Gary Walsh has gone from strength to strength.

Walsh ended a 12-year association with United when he quit the club in the summer of 1995. At 27, he felt he could no longer face life as understudy to one of the world's best goalkeepers, Peter Schmeichel.

In his time at Old Trafford, he had played less than 50 League games and had become desperate for first-team football. While the sales of Paul Ince, Mark Hughes and Andrei Kanchelskis caused uproar among United supporters, Walsh quietly slipped out of the club to join 'Boro.

After a season at the Riverside Stadium, Walsh now wishes he had left United earlier.

Says Gary, "I should have left a bit sooner than I did and I regret not doing something about it. However, I am still only 28 so I have plenty of years ahead of me.

"I am still young for a 'keeper, though everybody thinks I am in my thirties because I had been at Old Trafford for such a long time! People are often surprised when they realise how young I am.

"I had to leave. I was on a week-to-week deal after my contract expired and although I was offered an extension, I told manager Alex Ferguson that I wanted first-team football. He wanted to keep me, but he understood my feelings and was good about it.

"I knew I wasn't guaranteed regular football with Middlesbrough, but I felt I had a better chance of getting it at any other club than United because Peter Schmeichel is such a good 'keeper.

"They say you can only down when you leave a club like United. I can understand that, but in my case that hasn't been true.

"I am United through and through and have supported them all my life, but I was playing reserve-team football at Gigg Lane, Bury, in front of 500 people.

"I knew I would have to overcome competition

out of the shadows

for a place wherever I went but, with respect to my 'Boro rival Alan Miller, battling for a place with him is a more even a battle than with Peter.

"No matter how well I played while covering for him, I always knew that Peter would displace me when he was fit. That was the worst thing about United and I'm sure young Kevin Pilkington feels the same way that I did.

"I played in the Champions League in front of 120,000 against Barcelona at the Nou Camp knowing that I would soon be back playing for the reserves in the Pontins League at Gigg Lane. It is very difficult to raise yourself for big games when you have spent so long in the reserves.

"That's why I would never regard leaving United as a step down. Instead of reserve matches, I am now playing to nearly 30,000 at the Riverside Stadium every other week.

"I am now in charge of my own destiny for the first time in eight or nine years. I made myself number one at United in 1987 but I picked up an injury and ended up understudying the likes of Jim Leighton, Les Sealey and Peter.

"I don't regard myself as Boro's number one yet. I still have a long way to go before I can genuinely call myself the club's first-choice 'keeper. Tottenham's Ian Walker said that it took him two years to feel like the number one at White Hart Lane and I don't see myself being any different.

"I signed a three-year contract when I came here and I wouldn't mind if it took that long for me to establish myself. If I am playing regularly, I will settle for that." ●

THE LIGHTER SIDE!

FOUR-LEGGED FOOTBALLERS

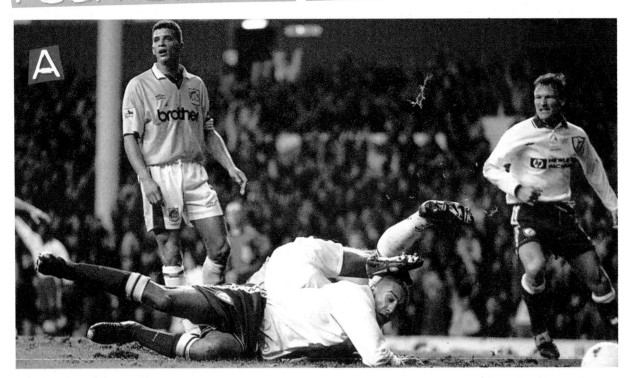

A. Chris Armstrong, Spurs.

B. Ryan Giggs, Manchester United.

C. Ray Parlour, Arsenal.

D. ...and two four-feet footballers!

LAST year was my most enjoyable in the professional game — and it's all down to joining the Foreign Legion!

That's West Ham's foreign legion. The largest contingent of overseas players to be found at any English club.

When I was a kid, I was a West Ham supporter. It was a club famous for producing young players through the ranks. All I wanted was to be one of those youngsters. But I wasn't considered good enough by ANY club. I left school and found a job with British Aerospace, before being spotted by Luton, while playing in non-League football.

In the last couple of years, West Ham have had to cast the net a lot wider to be able to compete with the big-money clubs.

Last season, there were over a dozen overseas players on the books at Upton Park — but I was delighted to be asked to join them.

Our five-a-side matches in training are always based on teams of foreign players against teams of English. The games are always hard fought.

We play for £5 a head each game to add a little spice. As I'm an Irish internationalist, I play for the foreign lads.

Just for fun, if we lose, we pay up in foreign currency! It's a real Thomas Cook job, with Czech, Danish, Romanian, Croatian and Portuguese money floating around!

It's all a sign that the dressing room is a happy place. The atmosphere is very light-

THE CONTINENT

MARC RIEPER

hearted.

They are all smashing lads, the foreign players. Some of them speak better English than I do! They all get a certain amount of stick, but it's just part of the team spirit.

I play my part in it. I enjoy a laugh and a joke, and I think that's one of the reasons why manager Harry Redknapp signed me from Crystal Palace last season.

West Ham were struggling a bit at the time. The side was a bit

naive and lightweight. There was rather a soft centre.

I'm quite a strong character. I think Harry felt I could do a good job, on and off the field. I'm not afraid to speak my mind. I can be quite pointed in what I say.

It's vital in any team to have players who can lift the others when things are not going well. When I was at Southampton, we had Dave Beasant and Jim Magilton to keep the banter going. You need three or four players who can do that.

At Upton Park, we've Julian Dicks, Ian Bishop and one or two others who are great in the dressing room. The club is very lively these days.

When I was signed, there were people who said I was not a West

Our five-a-side matches in training are always based on teams of foreign players against teams of English. The games are always hard fought.

Ham type of player. But I believe their style suits me down to the ground.

When you are 6ft 1 inch tall, and used as a target man up front, people don't expect you to be able to play a bit as well. But I work hard on ball skills and passing.

It's great for me to be used as the focal point of the team. I get a great service from players like Michael Hughes and Julian Dicks.

Sure, I use my size to make life hard for defenders. But I feel my all-round play has

improved a lot in the last couple of years.

I've spent a lot of time in training, trying to add other strings to my bow. I feel I can pass the ball as well as most players, and my control has developed.

I've gained in my appreciation of the play. My whole understanding of the game is better. I've learned how to play to my strengths, and make the most of what I have.

I've got the confidence to try different things. Things have come together for me.

This is my second spell at West Ham. My first stay lasted only six months before I was sold to Southampton, because of the club's financial position.

I have come back a much better player. But it's not true that I wasn't well received when I first joined the club from Luton.

I scored five goals in twelve appearances, helping West Ham win promotion. But the club needed the money and accepted the offer from Southampton.

It's great to be back. I'd like to think I can finish my career at Upton Park.

At international level, as well, the last year has been great. In one spell of eight matches for Northern Ireland, I managed to score six goals.

That has to be one of the highlights of my career, but I hope to improve on it in the future. I think we have the makings of a good young side.

My ambition is to help Northern Ireland qualify for the 1998 World Cup Finals in France.

That would really help me hold my head up among the foreign stars at Upton Park. ●

TOUCH

SLAVEN BILIC

HOW A DREAM MOVE TO BLACKBURN ROVERS COULD HAVE SPELLED DISASTER FOR BILLY McKINLAY

IT was every Scotsman's dream to be part of last summer's European Championships in England, grouped with the home nation in the opening group stages.

Billy McKinlay, though, put all that on the line when deciding to move south from Dundee United to Blackburn Rovers with just eight months left to the start of the tournament.

After just two starts in his first eight weeks at the Lancashire club, it began to look as though the gamble was not going to pay off.

McKinlay could see his European Championships hopes fading as Rovers boss Ray Harford decided to introduce him slowly to the demands of English football.

Things were so bad that he could not even claim to be the forgotten man at Rovers —he had not done

living on the e

anything to be remembered by in the first place!

He admits that it was a worrying period when he began to have second thoughts about his £1.75 million move.

Fortunately, the 27-year-old stuck it out — and has reaped the rewards.

Says Billy, "In the long term, I didn't see my move to Blackburn as any sort of gamble. My only real concern was about my immediate Scotland prospects.

"Dundee United were in the First Division at the time. Swopping that for the Premiership was the right move without question.

"It was also the right stage of my career for a change. It took me seconds to decide on the move.

"The Premiership has it all —the big clubs, the Media focus and the world class players. There was no other option but to make my way to Lancashire.

"On top of that, I was moving to one of the biggest clubs in the League. Financially, Rovers can compete with anyone.

"On the other hand, with the European Championships so close, it was a risk. I didn't want to miss out on that.

"If I'd stayed on with United, I'm pretty sure that there would not have been a problem with the Scotland squad.

"Staying with United would have been the easiest option to take.

"Even though United had been relegated from the Scottish Premier League, I was still being selected by Craig Brown. There is no reason to suggest that things would have changed.

"I felt that I needed to stretch myself, though, and experience something different. I knew that it wasn't going to be easy,

"If I'd stayed on with United, I'm pretty sure that there would not have been a problem with the Scotland squad."

but I just had to join Blackburn.

"I had hoped that I would go straight into the Rovers team. A few decent performances in the Premiership could have strengthened my Scotland cause.

"In contrast to that, I could have found, as many before me have, that the upheaval of a move to a new club in a different league had an adverse effect on my game. With Euro'96 so close, a few poor games would have been very costly.

"I didn't experience that, but I wasn't getting a game. Ray Harford wanted to ease me into things.

"Looking back, it wasn't a bad thing to do. By the time I had a run in the team, I was settled into the club and the area. I didn't have any outside worries.

"At the time, though, I didn't agree with Ray's plan. I'm the kind of player who needs to have a good

run of games before I can show a consistently good level of form. Denied that, I struggled.

"After being a first-team regular at Tannadice for a number of years, I found it hard to accept a diet of an odd appearance here and there. I wasn't happy.

"During that time, I began to wonder if I'd made the right decision. I cost a lot of money and wanted to play to prove I was worth it.

"It certainly wasn't helping my Scotland cause. I needed to be playing regular first-team football to be considered and, although Craig Brown kept faith with me during my time out of the side, I knew that I had to break into the first team.

"Fortunately, just as I was feeling at my lowest, I was given my chance and, after a few games, began to show the form I knew that I was capable of. All of a sudden everything seemed to fall into place.

"I felt the benefits of playing in the Premiership almost straight away.

"Playing with and against quality players each week has taken my game on that bit further. The experience was certainly an advantage when the European Championships started. I felt well prepared.

"In the end, moving to England was a gamble that more than paid off.

"It increased my anticipation of Euro'96 as well. I couldn't wait for it to happen.

"With few English players in Scottish football, there were few opportunities to wind people up about it. That wasn't the case at Blackburn!

"Towards the end of last season especially, there was plenty of crack between the English and the Scots. It added something to the whole event." ●

● DAVID BECKHAM manchester united

strange...
but true!

HAS YOUR CLUB'S GROUND GOT A SPECIAL CLAIM TO FAME? THESE DO!

SOME managers have been on thin ice when results were going against them. Some players have been frozen out when their form has dropped. But you wouldn't expect to see people skating on a soccer pitch, would you? Yet, it has happened.

One of the worst seasons for bad weather was 1962-63. All previous records for postponements were broken with more than 400 League and Cup games being hit by the

weather during the first six weeks of 1963. Most clubs just shivered and waited for it to pass but enterprising Halifax Town, who were then in Division Three of the Football League, decided to take advantage of their frozen pitch.

Halifax charged 2s 6d (13p) to

■ Villa Park is well used to having visitors. It was an amusement park long before it was a soccer ground, a sort of 19th century Alton Towers. Visitors could enjoy the magnificent gardens, fountains and walkways as well as seeing exhibitions, animals and entertainers.

skate on the pitch and to help things along they played pop music over their public address system. Hundreds of locals who had never been to the ground for football turned up to have some fun on the ice.

The Halifax ground was also unusual because it had a speedway track around the pitch and was used throughout the summer for racing. Today Halifax are a non-League side but the spirit of enterprise is still there. If all goes according to plan, they will be moving to a new super stadium which they will share with the local Rugby League side.

■ The San Siro Stadium, home of Milan and Inter, has also shown a flair for earning a few extra lire during the close season. Bungee-jumping and abseiling from the top tier of the huge stands are regular activities throughout the summer and some of the players have even been known to pay to have a go.

Continued overleaf

Continued from previous page.

■ There is the well at Leeds United. It is in a corner of the West Stand. The ground used to be just a pile of rubble. When Elland Road was built it was decided to keep the well in case there was ever a water shortage. It is still there to this day although there is no truth in the rumour that many Leeds managers have gone to it before a game to make a wish!

■ Most of the big grounds in Britain now have museums and tours. Manchester United were among the first to go for such a venture. Now they have hundreds of thousands of visitors every year passing through their doors to take a look behind the scenes and see the wonderful exhibits of the legendary club.

■ Another ground which had a fair share of visitors before it became a soccer stadium was Bramall Lane, home of Sheffield United. It was the headquarters of Yorkshire Cricket Club long before there was any football involvement and cricket was still played there until 1973.

■ During World War Two, a number of grounds were commissioned for use in the war effort. The army took over Preston's Deepdale ground while Rugby Park, Kilmarnock, was used as an oil and coal store. It had its compensations, though, when Italian prisoners of war were put to the task of building the terracing.

■ Raith Rovers found the perfect solution to hooliganism when they were playing a Cup-tie in 1887. Rival supporters fought their way onto the pitch but landlord Robert Stark knew how to stop it. He brought his bull from an adjoining field and let it loose. That's the first time fans have been charged to get out!

■ But if you want some really bizarre stories, how about Highbury, where Arsenal have played since 1913? When the terracing was being built, a delivery cart fell down a hole in the famous North Bank, now a super new stand. The horse attached to the cart died and was left there. So the North Bank at Highbury is, in fact, the grave of a horse.

■ Many football grounds are close to rivers, but they don't get any closer than Shrewsbury's Gay Meadow. It is so close that the ball regularly flies out of the ground and into the River Severn. The club has a boatman standing by to retrieve the balls before they float away down the river.

■ Wimbledon do not talk too much about their ground — no, not Selhurst Park which they share with Crystal Palace on a rental arrangement — their REAL ground, Plough Lane, which they still own. Originally, the ground was a swamp and then it became a rubbish dump before being bought by the football club.

■ Every ground has a tale to tell, even the mighty national stadiums like Hampden and Wembley. Hampden Park has been home to Queen's Park since 1873. The oldest club in Scotland and the only amateur club in the League plays in front of virtually empty stands every week in but would anyone volunteer to tell them to move?

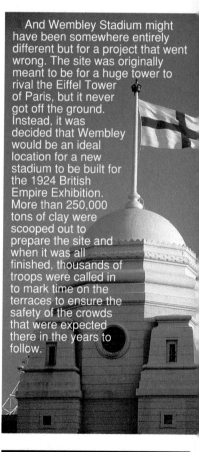

And Wembley Stadium might have been somewhere entirely different but for a project that went wrong. The site was originally meant to be for a huge tower to rival the Eiffel Tower of Paris, but it never got off the ground. Instead, it was decided that Wembley would be an ideal location for a new stadium to be built for the 1924 British Empire Exhibition. More than 250,000 tons of clay were scooped out to prepare the site and when it was all finished, thousands of troops were called in to mark time on the terraces to ensure the safety of the crowds that were expected there in the years to follow.

■ From skating on the pitch at Halifax to marking time in the stands at Wembley, soccer grounds have many historic stories. None more so than Blackpool's Bloomfield Road, which is rumoured to be haunted by the ghost of Nelson! Perhaps that could be put down to good, old-fashioned team spirit!

DAVID BATTY   newcastle united

fastfor

DANISH STRIKER

Erik Bo Andersen is delighted with the way his career in Scotland has taken off since Rangers signed him for £1.4 million from Denmark's top side, Aalborg.

The 24-year-old came to Ibrox with a well-earned reputation for being a prolific goalscorer, having netted 24 goals in 32 appearances last season — the highest in the Danish League for 14 years.

And, although he has yet to firmly establish himself as a first-team regular for the star-studded Scottish Champions, he did manage six goals in only five starts.

Furthermore, he earned the rare distinction of making a valuable contribution to his club's acquisition of the double, having been in the country a mere two months.

"I haven't encountered any problems since coming to Rangers, even though I was warned about the club's awesome reputation and the quality of the players who were already there," says Erik.

"Because the side has been settled for so long, I haven't become one of the regulars yet, but I expect that to change soon and I hope to really make my mark.

"However, to be part of a double-winning side, especially within such a short time, is a real thrill, and something I have never experienced before."

The Great Dane, who picked up his first-ever Cup winners' medal when Rangers hammered Hearts 5-1, expresses how proud he is at following a great tradition of foreign imports at Ibrox.

"Some of the biggest names in Europe have turned out for Rangers over the last few

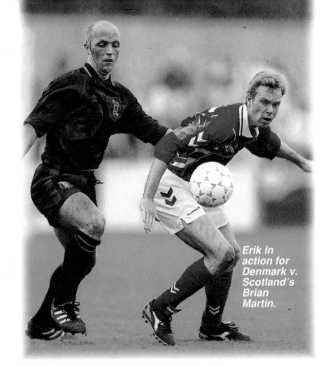

Erik in action for Denmark v. Scotland's Brian Martin.

years and, at the moment, we have players of the calibre of Paul Gascoigne, Ally McCoist and Brian Laudrup at the club."

Cup Final hero Laudrup is, of course, an international team-mate of Andersen's, and the striker admits to being delighted to have the opportunity to play alongside his fellow-Dane at club level.

"Everyone knows that Brian is an excellent midfielder for both Rangers and Denmark and, with him providing me with passes, I am going to have plenty of opportunities to bang in the goals in season 1996/97," predicts Erik.

"To be honest with you, I'm really looking forward to developing our partnership at both international and club level.

"And if we are successful at linking up together in Denmark games, we should be deadly in Scotland, especially since so many other players at Ibrox have a great understanding of one another's game."

It's perhaps significant to note that Erik Bo Andersen has fitted

in really quickly at Ibrox, where other recent imports have failed to blend in at all.

For instance, French international defender Basile Boli left after one miserable season, Russian five-goal World Cup record-holder Oleg Salenko lasted only a matter of months and HIS replacement Peter Van Vossen has yet to demonstrate why he once was the Dutch £2.8 million-record signing.

Van Vossen, who was the top goalscorer and one of the best players for 1995 European Cup winners Ajax, only netted once between being snapped up by 'Gers boss Walter Smith in February and the end of last season, while Andersen managed six, including a hat-trick against Partick Thistle.

"I'm happy with the goals I've scored for Rangers and the fact that I could be playing in the Champions League again," confesses the man who won a 1994/95 Danish Championship medal with Aalborg.

Out of all the current first team squad at Ibrox, Erik was the highest goalscorer in last season's Champions League, and he's hoping to better that this term as the Scottish Champions bid to extend their domestic domination.

"I'm very optimistic at the moment, and I feel I have a very bright future with Rangers," he concludes. ●

BOZ-nich

ASTON VILLA goalkeeper Mark Bosnich has chosen to play his international football for his native Australia, but the 24-year-old reveals that he should have bided his time for an England call-up.

Bosnich is generally regarded as the most promising of the crop of young 'keepers learning their trade in the Premiership. His ambition is to be the best in his position in England. He certainly has the potential.

But when Bosnich accepted Australia's offer to appear for them, he was just another struggling and impressionable footballer who saw the opportunity of playing for his country as another step up the ladder.

Bosnich could have trod a similar path to that of Leeds United full-back and fellow Australian Tony Dorigo.

Dorigo decided that he wanted

"People might call me disloyal to my home country, but playing for Australia is hard."

to play for England and activated residency rights which enabled him to qualify to play for his adopted country.

But any chance Bosnich had of qualifying to play for England disappeared when he played for Australia in the qualifying matches for the World Cup Finals in the United States in 1994. He has now committed his future to Australia.

Mark explains, "It is a touchy subject but, if I am brutally honest, I have to say that I might have made the wrong decision".

"People might call me disloyal to my home country, but playing for Australia is hard.

"It takes me a day to travel

and a day to return — and that is just for home games. On top of that, there are the economic considerations.

"My efforts are not as appreciated as, say, those of a Rugby League player. Football in Australia is not the number one sport.

"On reflection, perhaps I should have waited and chosen to play for England. But I played for Australia in the Under-16 World Cup and also at Under-20 level. Before I knew it, I had played at senior level in the World Cup qualifiers.

"Another consideration at the time was that I didn't know how things would work out in England and I reckoned David Seaman and Tim Flowers might be around for the next ten years.

"If I had waited, I might never have played international football. People would have said, 'You could have played for Australia in the World Cup!' It was a Catch-22 situation."

Mark has sought advice from his best friend and Villa team-mate Dwight Yorke. Both players were born in countries which are unlikely to make the World Cup Finals during their careers.

Mark adds, "I must admit that it now plays on my mind quite a bit.

"But I have been able to talk it over with Dwight who represents Trinidad and Tobago. He is in the same boat.

"We have made our choices and have to live with them. It is not the worst thing in the world and we can take comfort from playing for a big club side." ●

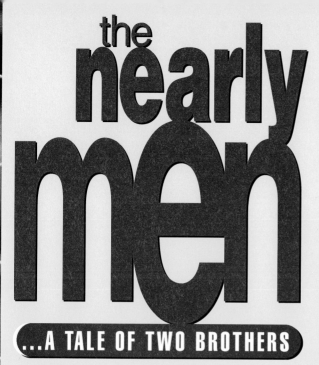

the nearly men

...A TALE OF TWO BROTHERS

AT the end of last season, two brothers suffered the disappointment of missing out on championship-winning medals — but for two totally different reasons.

27-year-old Shaka Hislop's Newcastle were pipped at the post by eventual Double-winners Manchester United. Younger brother Kona actually played in Scottish Third Division Livingston's championship-clinching game, and scored a goal. But he appeared in only a handful of matches during the season — not enough to justify a winner's medal.

London-born Shaka studied mechanical engineering at Howard University in the USA before coming back to Britain in 1992, signing for Reading. Brilliant displays for the Elm Park club made him the target for several Premiership clubs, but it was Newcastle United who swooped for the giant 'keeper following Reading's First Division play-off defeat by Bolton in May 1995.

Shaka started last season as number one choice ahead of Pavel Srnicek, but injury and the form of Srnicek saw him struggle to regain his first team place.

However, he figured prominently in manager Kevin Keegan's plans as the season drew to its close, suffering heart-break defeats by Liverpool and Blackburn — defeats which severely dented Newcastle's title hopes.

Kona has been to watch his brother play many times.

"He is one of the best in England and that is why Newcastle spent a lot of money on him and one of the reasons they did so well in finishing runners-up in the championship. I know he was upset that they were pipped in the end but Newcastle did really well and I'm sure that is not the end of the story.

"He is willing, a worker and a very good young player."

"I am proud of my brother and delighted with the way his career has gone. If I can do even half as well as him I will be well pleased. Coming to Livingston was a great move for me. Winning the Third Division Championship was great and all credit is due to the manager, Jim Leishman, for the way he took us through it. Everyone is confident that Livingston can have a really good season in the Second Division and perhaps win that title as well!"

Shaka Hislop is no stranger to Livingston either. When Newcastle don't have a fixture, he often travels up to see his brother in action.

"I have become quite a fan",he says. "I like the way Livingston play. I think that Kona can do very well in Scotland and he seems to fit in well with Livingston. The other players look very useful too and I think that Livingston have a great future. They are definitely a team to watch and I would not be at all surprised to see them in the Premier Division in a few seasons, hopefully with Kona banging in lots of goals."

Jim Leishman has a similar view.

"Kona Hislop played his part in our season and I am sure he has a healthy future in Scottish football," says Jim. "He is willing, a worker and a very good young player."

Both brothers have put the disappointments of last season behind them, and hope that 1996-97 will see some silverware in the Hislop household. ●

KONA HISLOP.

●SHAKA HISLOP - 1995 —
DISAPPOINTMENT WITH READING.
1996 — DISAPPOINTMENT WITH
NEWCASTLE.
1997...?

5th time

'M BEGINNING to suspect that I'm Scottish football's very own 'nearly man'!

After THREE seasons of heartbreak at my previous club, Dunfermline, where we had to endure final-day agony by missing out on promotion, I landed a dream move at the start of last season to my boyhood heroes Celtic — and still ended up just missing out on trophy success!

I'd spent years cheering on the Bhoys from the terraces, so it was incredible to walk through the main door at Parkhead, in the shadow of the imposing new North Stand, and past the portraits of all the legendary Celtic players, knowing that I had joined their ranks.

It was an emotional moment for me, especially since I thought I'd blown the opportunity of a lifetime!

I'd first been informed of Tommy Burns' interest on the eve of a League clash with Morton.

The story had surfaced in the press that morning and gaffer Bert Paton admitted to me that Celtic had made an offer.

I was stunned, to say the least!

Although pundits had been praising my recent

performances, I was still amazed that Celtic were willing to shell out for a relatively unproven lower division player.

Especially since big-money foreign imports like Pierre van Hooijdonk and Andreas Thom had been the order of the day since Tommy Burns took charge.

Unfortunately, I let the prospect of my dream move affect my game that day and I had an absolute NIGHTMARE.

I trudged off the park a dejected figure after that 2-0 defeat, convinced that my prospects of a dream move had bitten the dust.

So you can imagine my delight, and surprise, when Celtic still forked out the £600,000 to take me to Celtic Park.

At first I was a little intimidated by all the big names here, with a team full of internationals and big-money stars.

But the lads all helped me settle in straight away and that made a huge difference to me.

I was also helped by the fact that my father had been a Celtic player during the mid-Seventies and was able give me useful advice on how to cope with the pressures that go with being an Old Firm player.

Fortunately, we won in my first game, a 1-0 win over Falkirk at Brockville and that gave me a real confidence boost.

Even so, I was still awestruck when I stepped out of the tunnel for my home debut against Partick Thistle the following Saturday.

The sound of 35,000 Celtic fans roaring us on was a real change from what I was used to in the First Division, where

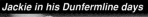

Jackie in his Dunfermline days

● A CHAMPIONS' MEDAL WILL BE WORTH THE WAIT FOR CELTIC'S JACKIE McNAMARA!

3,500 was a much more typical figure!

I'd joined the club at an exciting time, with us having secured a glamour Cup Winners' Cup-tie with French aces Paris St Germain and hot in pursuit of Rangers at the top of the table.

Off the field, too, there were visible signs that the club was moving in the right direction once again.

The huge new stand, seating 32,000, was a towering symbol of the staggering potential at the club.

All that was needed was for us to halt Rangers' march to the title.

While every game for my new club was like a cup final to me, I was DESPERATE to get my first taste of the unique

I was distraught and just headed straight up the tunnel with the jeers of the Rangers fans ringing in my ears.

atmosphere of an Old Firm clash.

And what a baptism of fire it proved to be!

We fought out a breathtaking 3-3 draw at Ibrox, in a game described as 'one of the finest Old Firm clashes in history'!

Unfortunately, that titanic tussle was to prove to be the highlight of the season's Celtic-Rangers meetings for me and I was destined to have decidedly mixed fortunes against Walter Smith's side.

I achieved a lifelong ambition just a few weeks after the match at Ibrox when I grabbed my first-ever goal for Celtic, the first in a 4-0 win against Hibs at Easter Road.

Simon Donnelly knocked in a superb cross and I just caught it perfectly on the volley to send it past Scotland 'keeper Jim Leighton.

To have scored my first goal so soon after signing was beyond my wildest dreams.

While that strike was undoubtedly the highlight of the season, there's no question what was my worst moment.

The Celtic-Rangers

lucky?

meeting at Ibrox on St Patrick's Day was being billed by the media as a title decider and everyone at Celtic Park knew that defeat was an unthinkable prospect.

With just over twenty minutes remaining, and with us already 1-0 down to an Alan McLaren header, I launched into a reckless challenge on Charlie Miller and picked up my second yellow card, followed by the inevitable red version.

I was distraught and just headed straight up the tunnel with the jeers of the Rangers fans ringing in my ears.

I didn't even realise that big John Hughes had saved my bacon with a last gasp equaliser until the lads trooped up the tunnel!

In the end, it still wasn't enough to prevent Rangers clinching their eighth Championship in succession and moving a step closer to our record nine-in-a-row mark.

To make matters worse, Dunfermline finally clinched the First Division title that had always eluded them in my time at East End Park!

But I'm delighted for Bert Paton and the boys, now I just need to emulate my old mates and collect a Championship medal this term! ●

ANDREI KANCHELSKIS everton

picturelist
ACTION! PIN-UPS! FEATURES!

ISBN 0-85116-630-X Printed and Published in Great Britain by **D. C. THOMSON & CO., LTD.,** 185 Fleet Street, London EC4A 2HS. © **D. C. THOMSON & CO., LTD., 1996**

dream team
v. *dark warriors*

But then, out of the shadows of darkness comes the power of good. Skill will win in the end, and the tide turns.
The Dream Team turn on the style. Evil play is overpowered by scintillating soccer. Ronaldo and Maldini torment the Evil Forces . . . . Brolin and Kluivert set up Cantona. He shoots — and the Nightmare ends.

"Au Revoir!"